England Under The Tudors

by

Arthur D. Innes

Double 9 BOOKS

England Under The Tudors
by Arthur D. Innes

ISBN: 978-93-59325-71-2

Published by

DOUBLE 9 BOOKS
2/13-B, Ansari Road
Daryaganj, New Delhi – 110002
info@double9books.com
www.double9books.com
Tel. 011-40042856

ABOUT THE AUTHOR

Arthur D. Innes was born on September 15, 1863, in Shimla. He passed away in 1938 in Uplyme, United Kingdom. Innes had a partner named Helen Pittis with whom he shared a relationship starting from 1901. He was survived by his children, including Neil McLeod Innes, and his grandchildren: Catherine McLeod Innes, Fiona McLeod Innes, and Roderick Temple McLeod Innes. His parents were Lucy Jane Macpherson and James John McLeod Innes.

CONTENTS

INTRODUCTION

[Sidenote: An era of Revolutions]

The historian of the future will, perhaps, affirm that the nineteenth century, with the last years of the eighteenth, has been a period more fraught with momentous events in the development of the nations than any equal period since the Christian era commenced. Yet striking as are the developments witnessed by the last four generations, the years when England was ruled by Princes of the House of Tudor have a history hardly if at all less momentous. For though what we call the Tudor period, from 1485 to 1603, is determined by a merely dynastic title affecting England alone, the reign of that dynasty happens to coincide in point of time with the greatest territorial revolution on record, a religious revolution unparalleled since the rise of Mohammed, and an intellectual activity to match which we must go back to the great days of Hellas, or forward to the nineteenth century: revolutions all of them not specifically English, but affecting immediately every nation in Europe; while one of them extended itself to every continent on the globe. Moreover, the accompanying social revolution, though comparatively superficial, was only a little less marked than the others. Nor was there any country in Europe more influenced by the general Revolution in any one of its aspects than England.

Nihil per saltum is no doubt as true of historical movements as of physical evolution. Before Columbus sighted Hispaniola, Portuguese sailors had told tales of some vast island seen by them far in the west. Botticelli had passed out of Filippo Lippi's school, and Leonardo was thirty, before Raphael was born; the printing press had reached England, and Greek had been re-discovered, in the last years of the previous "period"; the Byzantine Empire had fallen; the power of the old Baronage in England and France had been broken before Richard fell on Bosworth field. There were Lollards at home and Hussites abroad before Luther came into the world. The changes did not begin in 1485, or in any particular year. In Italy the intellectual movement had already long been active, and had indeed produced its best work; outside of Italy, its appearances had been quite sporadic. At that date, the Ocean movement was in its initial stages. There had been foreshadowings of the Reformation; and, to speak metaphorically, the castles which had maintained the power of the nobility, overshadowing the gentry and the burghers, were already in ruins. But the fame of every one of the great English names which are landmarks in every one of these great movements belongs essentially to the years after 1485. And every one of those movements had definitely and decisively set its mark on the world before Elizabeth was laid in her grave.

[Sidenote: The Intellectual Movement]

The intellectual movement to which we apply the name Renaissance in its narrower sense [Footnote: In the more inclusive sense the Renaissance of course began in the time of Cimabue and Dante, but it was not till the latter half of the fifteenth century that it became a pervading force outside of Italy.] has many aspects. Whatever views we may happen to hold as to schools of painting and architecture, it is indisputable that a revolution was wrought by the work of Raphael and Leonardo, Michael Angelo and Titian, and the crowd of lesser great men who learned from them. The limitations imposed on Art by ecclesiastical conventions were deprived of their old rigour, and it was no longer sought to confine the painter to producing altar pieces and glorified or magnified missal-margins. The immediate tangible and visible results were however hardly to be found outside of Italy and the Low Countries; and if English domestic architecture took on a new face, it was the outcome rather of the social than the artistic change: since men wanted comfortable houses instead of fortresses to dwell in. The Renaissance in its creative artistic phase touched England directly hardly at all.

On its literary side, the movement was not creative but scholarly and critical, though a great creative movement was its outcome. In the earlier period the name of Ariosto is an exception; but otherwise the greatest of the men of Letters are perhaps, in their several ways, Erasmus and Macchiavelli abroad and Thomas More in England. Scholars and students were doing an admirable work of which the world was much in need; displacing the schoolmen, overturning mediaeval authorities and conventions, reviving the knowledge of the mighty Greek Literature which for centuries had been buried in oblivion, introducing fresh standards of culture, spreading education, creating an entirely new intellectual atmosphere. An enormous impulse was given to the new influences by the very active encouragement which the princes of Europe, lay and ecclesiastical, extended to them, the nobility following in the wake of the princes. The best literary brains of the day however were largely absorbed by the religious movement. The great imaginative writers, unless we except Rabelais, appear in the latter half of the sixteenth century—Tasso and Camoens and Cervantes, [Footnote: *Don Quixote* did not appear till 1605; but Cervantes was then nearly sixty.] Spenser and Marlowe and Shakespeare, as well as Montaigne. But even in the first half of the century, Copernicus enunciated the new theory that the Sun, not the Earth, is the centre of the astronomical system; and before the end of our period, the new methods had established themselves in the field of science, to be first formulated early in the new century by one who had already mastered and applied them, Francis Bacon. Essentially, the modern Scientific Method was the product of the Tudor Age.

[Sidenote: The Reformation and the Counter-Reformation]

For many centuries, Christendom had in effect been undivided. There had indeed been a time when it was uncertain whether the Arian heresy might not prevail over orthodoxy, but that was a thousand years ago. The Byzantine Church later had separated from the Roman on a subtle point of Theology; but in spite of various dissensions, and efforts on the part of kings and of Churches which may be called national to assert a degree of independence, all Western Europe had acknowledged the supremacy of the papacy; and though reformers had arisen, the movements they initiated had either been absorbed by orthodoxy or crushed almost out of sight. The Tudor period witnessed that vast schism which divided Europe into the two religious camps, labelled—with the usual inaccuracy of party labels— Catholic and Protestant: the latter, as time went on, failing into infinite divisions, still however remaining agreed in their resistance to the common foe. Roughly—very roughly—in place of the united Christendom of the Middle Ages, the end of the period found the Northern, Scandinavian, and Teutonic races ranged on one side, the Southern Latin races on the other; and in both camps a very much more intelligent conception of religion, a much more lively appreciation of its relation to morals. The intellectual revolution had engendered a keen and independent spirit of inquiry, a disregard of traditional authority, an iconoclastic zeal, a passion for ascertaining Truth, which, applied to religion, crashed against received systems and dogmas with a tremendous shock rending Christendom in twain. But the Reformers were not all on one side; and those who held by the old faiths and acknowledged still the old mysteries included many of the most essentially religious spirits of the time. If the Protestants won a new freedom, the Catholics acquired a new fervour and on the whole a new spirituality. For both Catholic and Protestant, religion meant something which had been lacking to latter-day mediaevalism: something for which it was worth while to fight and to die, and—a much harder matter than dying —to sever the bonds of friendship and kinship. That these things should have needed to be done was an evil; that men should have become ready to do them was altogether good. The Reformation brought not peace but a sword; Religion was but one of the motives which made men partisans of either side; yet that it became a motive at all meant that they had realised it as an essential necessity in their lives.

[Sidenote: The New World]

It is hardly necessary to dwell at length on the magnitude of the maritime expansion; the Map [Footnote: See Map 1] is more eloquent than words. In 1485 the coasts that were known to Europeans were those of Europe, the Levant, and North Africa. Only such rare adventurers as Marco Polo had penetrated Asia outside the ancient limits of the Roman Empire. In 1603, the globe had been twice circumnavigated by Englishmen. Portuguese fleets dominated the Indian waters; there were Portuguese stations both on the West Coast of India and in the Bay of Bengal; Portuguese and Spaniards were established in the Spice Islands whence there was an annual trade round the Cape with the Spanish Peninsula: the English East India Company was already incorporated, and its first fleet, commanded by Captain Lancaster, had opened up the same waters for English trade. Mexico and Peru and the West Indies were Spanish posses-*

** Two pages missing from original book here

[Sidenote: Nobility, clergy and gentry]

In the business of managing the Estates, the problem was further simplified to the Tudors because circumstances enabled them arbitrarily to replenish their treasuries largely from sources which did not wound the susceptibilities of the Commons. Henry VII. could victimise the nobles by fines or benevolences, and Henry VIII. could rob the Church, without arousing the animosity of the classes which were untouched; while neither the nobility nor the clergy were strong enough for active resentment. In each case the King made his profit out of privileged classes which got no sympathy from the rest—who did not grudge the King money so long at least as they were not asked to provide it themselves, and in fact felt that the process diminished the necessity for making demands on their own pockets.

The disappearance of the old almost princely power of the greater barons, completed by the repressive policy of Henry VII., with the redistribution of the vast monastic estates effected by his son, were the leading factors which changed the social and political centre of gravity. The old nobility were almost wiped out by the civil wars; generation after generation, their representatives had either fallen on the battlefield, or lost their heads on the scaffold and their lands by attainder. The new nobility were the creations of the Tudor Kings, lacking the prestige of renowned ancestry and the means of converting retainers into small armies. With the exception of the Howards, scarce one of the prominent statesmen of the period belonged to any of the old powerful families. For more than forty years the chief ministers were ecclesiastics; after Wolsey's fall, the Cromwells, Seymours, Dudleys, and Pagets, the Cecils and Walsinghams, and Bacons, the Russels, Sidneys, Raleighs, and Careys, were of stocks that had hardly been heard of in Plantagenet times, outside their own localities. It was the Tudor policy to foster and encourage this class of their subjects, who from the Tudor times onward provided the country with most of her statesmen and her captains, and in the aggregate mainly swayed her fortunes. At the same time the political influence of the Church was reduced to comparative insignificance by the treatment of the whole hierarchy almost as if it were a branch, and a rather subordinate branch, of the civil administration; by the appropriation of its wealth to secular purposes, to the enrichment of individuals and of the royal treasury; and by the suppression of the monastic orders. The effect of this last measure, limiting the clerical ranks to the successors of the secular clergy, was to restrict them much more generally to their pastoral functions; and at any rate after the death of Gardiner and Pole, no ecclesiastic appears as indubitably first minister of the Crown, and few as politicians of the front rank. England had no Richelieu, and no Mazarin. Lastly while the diminution in the importance of the ecclesiastical courts increased the influence of the lay lawyers, the great development in the prosperity of the mercantile classes, due in part at least to the deliberate policy of the Tudor monarchs, led in turn to their wealthy burgesses acquiring a new weight in the national counsels which, however, did not take full effect till a later day.

[Sidenote: International relations]

Finally we have to observe that in this period the whole system of international relations underwent a complete transformation. At its commencement, there was no Spanish kingdom; there was no Dutch Republic; the unification even of France was not completed; England had a chronically hostile nation on her northern borders; the Moors still held Granada; the Turk had only very recently established himself in Europe, and his advance constituted a threat to all Christendom, which still very definitely recognised one ecclesiastical head in the Pope, and—very much less definitely—one lay head in the Emperor. Elizabeth's death united England and Scotland at least for international purposes; France and Spain had each become a homogeneous state; Holland was on the verge of entering the lists as a first-class power. The theoretical status of the Emperor in Europe had vanished, but on the other hand, the co-ordination of the Empire itself as a Teutonic power had considerably advanced. The Turk was held in check, and the Moor was crushed: but one half of Christendom was disposed to regard the other half as little if at all superior to the Turk in point of Theology. The nations of Western Europe had approximately settled into the boundaries with which we are familiar; the position of the great Powers had been, at least comparatively speaking, formulated; and the idea had come into being which was to dominate international relations for centuries to come—the political conception of the Balance of Power.

CHAPTER I
HENRY VII (i), 1485-92—THE NEW DYNASTY

[Sidenote: 1485 Henry's title to the Crown]

On August 22nd, 1485, Henry Earl of Richmond overcame and slew King Richard III., and was hailed as King on the field of victory. But the destruction of Richard, an indubitable usurper and tyrant, was only the first step in establishing a title to the throne as disputable as ever a monarch put forward. To establish that title, however, was the primary necessity not merely for Henry himself, but in the general interest; which demanded a secure government after half a century of turmoil.

Henry's hereditary title amounted to nothing more than this, that through his mother he was the recognised representative of the House of Lancaster in virtue of his Beaufort descent from John of Gaunt, [Footnote: See *Front.* and Appendix B. The prior hereditary claims of the royal Houses of Portugal and Castile and of the Earl of Westmorland were ignored.] father of Henry IV.; whereas the House of York was descended in the female line from Lionel of Clarence, John of Gaunt's elder brother, and in unbroken male line from the younger brother Edmund of York. On the simple ground of descent therefore, any and every member of the House of York had a prior title to Henry's; the most complete title lying in Elizabeth, eldest daughter of Edward IV.; while the young Earl of Warwick, son of George of Clarence, was the first male representative, and John de la Pole, Earl of Lincoln, son of Edward's sister, had been named by Richard as heir presumptive.

But Henry could support his hereditary title, such as it was, by the actual fact that it was he and not a Yorkist who had challenged and overthrown the usurper Richard.

[Sidenote 1: Measures to strengthen the title]
[Sidenote 2: 1486 Marriage]

Now the idea that the rivalry of the Houses of York and Lancaster should be terminated and their union be effected by the marriage of the two recognised representatives had been mooted long before. But in Henry's position, it was imperative that he should assert his own personal right to the throne, not admitting that he occupied it as his wife's consort. His strongest line was to claim the Crown as his own of right and procure the endorsement of that claim from Parliament, [Footnote: The intricacies of descent, and the position of the crowd of hypothetical claimants, are set forth in detail in Appendix B, and the complete genealogical chart (*Front.*).] as Henry IV. had done on the deposition of Richard II. He could then without prejudice to his own title effectively bar other rivals by taking as his consort Elizabeth of York; since the Yorkists, as a group, would at any rate hesitate to assert priority of title to hers for either Warwick or De la Pole (who in fact never himself posed as a claimant for the throne). In accordance with this plan of operations, the contemplated marriage with Elizabeth of York was in the first instance postponed as a matter for later consideration. Henry proceeded forthwith to London, entering the City *laetanter*, amidst public rejoicings; [Footnote: Gairdner, *Memorials of Henry VII.*, p. xxvi, where a curious misapprehension is explained for which Bacon is mainly responsible.] writs for a new Parliament being issued a few days later. The coronation took place on October 30th; a week afterwards Parliament met, and an Act was promptly passed, declaring—without giving any reasons, which might have been disputed—that the "inheritance of the Crowns of England and France be, rest, remain and abide, in the person of our now Sovereign Lord, King Harry the Seventh, and in the heirs of his body". This was sufficiently decisive; but the endorsement of Henry's title in the abstract was confirmed by further enactments which assumed that he had been King of right, before the battle of Bosworth (thus repudiating title by conquest), since they attainted of treason those who had joined Richard in levying war against him. Thus Henry had affirmed his own inherent right to the throne; and had hedged that round with an unqualified parliamentary title. In the meantime he had also disqualified one possible figure-head for the Yorkists by lodging the young Earl of Warwick in the Tower. It remained for him to convert the other and principal rival into a prop of his own dignities by marrying Elizabeth of York. Accordingly he was formally petitioned by Parliament in December to take the princess to wife, to which petition he graciously assented, and the union of the red and white roses was accomplished in January. Any son born of this marriage would in his own person unite the claims of the House of Lancaster with those of the senior branch of the House of York.

[Sidenote: The King and his advisers]

It is difficult to think of the first Tudor monarch as a young man; for his policy and conduct bore at all times the signs of a cautious and experienced statesmanship. Nevertheless, he was but eight and twenty when he wrested the kingdom from Richard. His life, however, had been passed in the midst of perpetual plots and schemes, and in his day men developed early—

whereof an even more striking example was his son's contemporary, the great Emperor Charles V. Young as Henry was, there was no youthful hotheadedness in his policy, which was moreover his own. But he selected his advisers with a skill inherited by his son; and the most notable members of the new King's Council were Reginald Bray; Morton, Bishop of Ely, who soon after became Archbishop of Canterbury and was later raised to the Cardinalate; and Fox, afterwards Bishop of Durham and then of Winchester, whose services were continued through the early years of the next reign. Warham, afterwards Archbishop, was another of the great ecclesiastics whom he promoted, and before his death he had discovered the abilities of his son's great minister Thomas Wolsey. For two thirds of his reign, however, Bray and Morton were the men on whom he placed chief reliance.

[Sidenote: Henry's enemies]

Difficult as it was after Henry's union with Elizabeth to name any pretender to the throne with even a plausible claim, Bosworth had been in effect a victory for the Lancastrian party, and many of the Yorkists were still prepared to seize any pretext for attempting to overthrow the new dynasty. Not long after the marriage, Henry started on a progress through his dominions; and while he was in the north, Lord Lovel and other adherents of the late king attempted a rising which was however suppressed with little difficulty. A considerable body of troops was sent against the rebels, while a pardon was proclaimed for all who forthwith surrendered. Many of the insurgents came in; the promise to them was kept. Of the rest, one of the leaders was executed, Lovel escaping; but the affair, though abortive, illustrated the general atmosphere of insecurity which was to be more seriously demonstrated by the insurrection in favour of Lambert Simnel in the following year—some months after the Queen had given birth to a son, Prince Arthur.

Outside Henry's own dominions, the Dowager Margaret of Burgundy, widow of Duke Charles the Bold and sister of Edward IV., was implacably hostile to Henry, and her court was the gathering place of dissatisfied Yorkist intriguers. Within his realms, Ireland, where the House of York had always been popular, offered a perpetual field in which to raise the standard of rebellion, any excuse for getting up a fight being generally welcomed. In that country the power of the King's government, such as it was, was practically confined to the limits of the Pale—and within those limits depended mainly on the attitude of the powerful Irish noble, Fitzgerald, Earl of Kildare, who held the office of Deputy.

[Sidenote: 1487 Lambert Simnel]

At the close of the fifteenth century accurate information did not travel rapidly, but vague rumours were readily spread abroad. Rumours were now rife that one of the princes murdered by Richard III. had really escaped and was still living; and on the other hand that the boy Warwick was dead in the Tower. Some one devised the idea of producing a fictitious Richard of York, or Warwick. A boy of humble birth named Lambert Simnel was taught to play the part, carried over to Ireland, and produced after some hesitation as the Earl of Warwick. Presumably the leaders of the Yorkists intended to use the supposititious earl only until the real one could be got into their hands; but Lincoln, who certainly knew the facts, espoused the cause of the pretender, in complicity with Lovel and Margaret of Burgundy. In Ireland, Simnel was cheerfully and with practical unanimity accepted as the king, and a band of German mercenaries, under the command of Martin Swart, was landed in that country to support him; though in London the genuine Warwick was paraded through the streets to show that he was really there alive. Lincoln, who had first escaped to Flanders, joined the pretender; they landed in Lancashire in June. Within a fortnight, however, the opposing forces met at Stoke, and after a brief but fierce conflict the rebel army, mainly composed of Irish and of German mercenaries, was crushed, Lincoln and several leaders were slain, and their puppet was taken captive. Henry's action was the reverse of vindictive, for Simnel was merely relegated to a position, appropriate to his origin, in the royal kitchen, and was subsequently promoted to be one of the King's falconers. Kildare, [Footnote: The narrative in the *Book of Howth* gives the impression that Kildare was at Stoke, and was made prisoner; but this is probably a misinterpretation arising from a lack of dates.] in spite of his undoubted complicity in the rebellion and the actual participation therein of his kinsmen, was even retained in the office of Deputy. Twenty-eight of the rebels, however, were attainted in the new Parliament which was summoned in November, the Queen's long-deferred coronation taking place at the same time.

The same Parliament is noteworthy as having given a definitely legal status to the judicial authority of the Council by the establishment of the Court thereafter known as the Star Chamber, of which we shall hear later. Besides this, however, it had the duty of voting supplies for embroilments threatening on the Continent.

The complexities of foreign affairs form so important a feature in the history of the next forty years that it is important to open the study of the period with a clear idea of the position of the Continental powers.

[Sidenote: The state of Europe]

Lewis XI., the craftiest of kings, had died in 1482, leaving a tolerably organised kingdom to his young son Charles VIII., under the regency of Anne of Beaujeu. With the exception of the Dukedom of Brittany, which still claimed a degree of independence, and of Flanders and Artois which, though fiefs of France, were still ruled by the House of Burgundy, the whole country was under the royal dominion; which had also absorbed the Duchy of Burgundy proper. The daughter of Charles the Bold, wife of Maximilian of Austria, inherited as a diminished domain the Low Countries and the County of Burgundy or Franche Comté.

East of the Rhine, the kingdoms, principalities, and dukedoms of Germany owned the somewhat vague authority of the Habsburg Emperor Frederick, but the idea of German Unity had not yet come into being. On the south-east the Turks who had captured Constantinople some thirty years before (1453) were a militant and aggressive danger to the Empire and to Christendom; while the stoutest opponent of their fleets was Venice. Switzerland was an independent confederacy of republican States: Italy a collection of separate States—dukedoms such as Milan, kingdoms such as Naples, Republics such as Venice and Florence, with the Papal dominions in their midst. In the Spanish peninsula were the five kingdoms of Navarre, Portugal, the Moorish Granada, Aragon, and Castile. The last two, however, were already united, though not yet merged into one, by the marriage of their respective sovereigns Ferdinand and Isabella. Sardinia and Sicily were attached to Aragon.

Finally we have to note that Maximilian, son of the Emperor, had married Mary of Burgundy; but on Mary's death the Netherlanders recognised as their Duke not Maximilian but his young son Philip—the father exercising only a very precarious authority as the boy's guardian; while the Dowager Margaret, the second wife of Charles the Bold, the lady whose hostility to the House of Lancaster has been already noted, possessed some dower-towns, and considerable influence. In 1486 Maximilian was elected "King of the Romans," in other words his father's presumed successor as Emperor.

[Sidenote: France and Brittany]

For the time, then, the consolidation of France was more advanced than that of any other Power; her desire was to complete the process by the absorption of Brittany. Spain, i.e., Castile and Aragon, had made considerable progress in the same direction, but for her the conquest of Granada was still the prime necessity.

The absorption of Brittany, however, was opposed alike to the interests of Maximilian, of the Spanish monarchs, and of England. To the former two, any further acquisition of power by France was a possible menace. To the last, France was traditionally the enemy, and if Breton ports became French ports, the strength of France in the Channel would be almost doubled. Henry personally was under great obligations both to France and to Brittany, especially to France; but political exigencies evidently compelled him to favour the maintenance of Breton independence.

During 1487 France had been carrying on active hostilities in Brittany, but the results had been small and a treaty had been signed. Lewis, Duke of Orleans, and others of the French nobility who were hostile to the regency of Anne of Beaujeu, were actively promoting the Breton cause within the dukedom; there was no longer an active French party there; and now that Henry in England had suppressed the Simnel rising France became anxious to secure English neutrality. But, if Henry could not keep clear of the complication altogether; if once the parties in the contest began appealing to him; he was liable to find himself forced to take part with one side or the other. Hence the necessity for calling upon Parliament to vote money for armaments.

[Sidenote: 1488 Henry intervenes cautiously]

Thus in the opening months of 1488 we find Henry on the one hand fitting out ships, and on the other offering friendly mediation both to France and to Brittany: while his policy was not simplified by the unauthorised interposition of his queen's uncle Edward Woodville, who secretly sailed with a band of adventurers to support the Bretons. Henry repudiated Woodville's action, and extended the existing treaty of peace with France to January, 1490. In the same month (July, 1488) the Bretons suffered a complete defeat, and the Duke was obliged to sign a treaty on ignominious terms. Within a fortnight, however, the Duke was dead, and his daughter Anne, a girl of twelve, succeeded him.

The result was the renewal of war; since Anne of Beaujeu and the Breton Marshal de Rieux both claimed the wardship of the young Duchess, for whose hand the widower Maximilian was already a prominent suitor. Now up to this point Henry had refused to adopt a hostile attitude towards France, and had treated overtures from Maximilian with frigidity. But in six months' time he was concluding alliances both with Brittany and with Maximilian.

[Sidenote: England and Spain]

The determining factor in this change of attitude, practically involving a French war, is probably to be found in Henry's relations with Spain. It was of vital importance to him to get his dynasty recognised in an emphatic form by foreign Powers. In Spain under its very able rulers he saw the most valuable of allies, and during the first half of 1488 he had made it his primary concern to procure the betrothal of his own infant son Arthur to their infant daughter Katharine. And virtually his hostility to France was the price they demanded. The preliminaries were settled in July, 1488; the treaty was not definitively signed till March of the next year; and as the essential nature of the Spanish requirements became more apparent, Henry found himself compelled to accept active antagonism to France as part of the bargain. With his subjects, a French war was always secure of a certain popularity, though the provision of funds for it would entail a degree of opposition. Moreover, though foreign wars might give extreme malcontents their opportunity, it is a commonplace of politics that they distract attention from domestic grievances. Thus it is easy to perceive how the benefits of the Spanish alliance would very definitely turn the scale. And we shall still find that Henry had no intention of expending an ounce of either blood or treasure which might be saved consistently with the ostensible fulfilment of the Spanish Compact.

[Sidenote 1: 1489 Preparations for war with France]
[Sidenote 2: Spanish treaty of Medina del Campo]

So in December, 1488, Henry was sending friendly embassies to all the Powers, but while that to France was merely offering mediation, the envoy to Brittany was offering military assistance—on terms. In January a new Parliament was asked for, and after considerable debate granted, £100,000. In February the embassy to Maximilian concluded an alliance for mutual defence; while that to Brittany pledged Henry to defend the young Duchess, but exacted in return the occupation by the English of sundry military positions in the duchy, and the right to forbid any marriage or alliance except with Maximilian or Spain. Then in March the Spanish treaty was completed: whereof the terms were very significant. The children were to be betrothed. If Spain declared war on France, England was to support her. Spain might retire independently if she recovered the small districts of Roussillon and Cerdagne, which had been surrendered (though only in pledge) to Lewis XI.; England might similarly withdraw if she got back Guienne—a very much more visionary prospect. Otherwise, one was not to retire without the other being equally satisfied. If England attacked France, Spain was to help; but occupied as she was with Granada the amount of aid likely to be forthcoming was problematical. In brief, Henry was prepared to pay for the marriage, and Spain could exact a high price.

France then was occupied in the west with the contest in Brittany, and in the north she was supporting the Flemings in their normal resistance to Maximilian. The English could use Calais as a base for operations on this side, and also began to throw troops into Brittany. Incidentally there was a rising in the north of England headed by Sir John Egremont, of which the pretext was resistance to the levying of taxes; this, however, did not take very long to suppress, nor was any one of importance involved in it. Still the hostilities with France were carried on in a very half-hearted fashion; being confined to defensive operations in Brittany which were supposed to be no violation of the peace recently prolonged to January, 1490.

[Sidenote: The allies inert]

Henry was satisfied to make a show of fighting, and Spain made no haste to help him, England not being formally at war. As early as July, Maximilian, shiftiest and most impecunious of princes, concluded at Frankfort an independent treaty with France; who agreed to give up the places she occupied in Brittany if Henry were compelled to withdraw his garrisons; while there were signs that she might cede Roussillon and thus deprive Henry of his claim to Spanish support. Within the duchy itself, the Marshal de Rieux and his ward were in a state of antagonism; since he wished her to marry the Sieur D'Albret, a powerful Gascon noble who was not too submissive to the French monarchy; while the Duchess declared she would rather enter a convent. Anne at last announced her adhesion to the treaty of Frankfort; but as Henry had no intention of evacuating his forts, nothing particular resulted. The English King could not afford simply to drop the contest, and when the New Year came in, he demanded and obtained from Parliament fresh supplies for carrying on the war.

[Sidenote: 1490 Object of Henry's foreign policy]

The game Henry had to play in 1490 was a sufficiently difficult one: and he played it with consummate skill. He meant to hold his position in Brittany until he received adequate indemnities; he had to satisfy his own subjects that he was not going to draw back before the power of France; and he had to carry out the letter of his obligations to Spain under the treaty of the previous March, On the other hand, he had in fact no ambitious military projects, and while Spain abstained from sending active assistance in force, she could not complain if he merely stood on the defensive. The Duchess, finding herself no better off for accepting the Frankfort treaty, adopted the alternative policy of throwing herself on his protection. So he welcomed a mediatorial embassy from the Pope and showed no unwillingness to negotiate, but continued to strengthen his own position; while he could exhibit a sound reason for abstaining from aggressive action and still accumulate war-funds.

By Midsummer France had enlarged her demands since the treaty of Frankfort, requiring the withdrawal of the English from Brittany as a preliminary not to her own withdrawal but to arbitration on her claims. In September the shifty King of the Romans reverted to an alliance with Henry for mutual defence; and the scheme of his marriage with the Duchess Anne was pressed on. Marshal de Rieux had by this time become reconciled to the Duchess, thrown over D'Albret, and come into agreement with Henry. At this time, moreover, Henry ratified publicly the Spanish treaty which had been accepted by Ferdinand and Isabella eighteen months before; but he also submitted an alternative treaty [Footnote: Busch, *England under the Tudors*. pp. 59, 330; and Gairdner's note, p. 438.] (which Spain rejected) modifying the portions which placed the contracting Powers on an unequal footing. By this step he forced the Spanish monarchs to resign any pretence of having treated him generously or having placed him under an obligation; and the step itself was significant of the increased confidence he had acquired in the stability of his own position. In December Maximilian was married by proxy to Anne—whom he had never seen—and not long afterwards she assumed the style of Queen of the Romans.

[Sidenote: Apparent defeat of Henry's policy]

Ostensibly, the object of Henry's diplomacy had failed. Spain had rejected his proposals: and the direct results of Anne's marriage were that the activity of France was renewed; Spain, with the pretext of the Moorish war to plead, was less inclined than ever to render assistance; Maximilian as a matter of course proved a broken reed; D'Albret, his pretensions being finally shattered, surrendered Nantes to the French by arrangement. England was apparently to bear the entire brunt of the war. Henry was justified in appealing to his subjects for every penny that could be raised, and resorted to "benevolences"—an insidious method of extortion which had been declared illegal in the previous reign, but under the existing abnormal conditions could hardly be resisted. A great demonstration of warlike ardour was made, on the strength of which Spain was urged to pledge herself to throw herself into the war next year with more energy and on more reasonable terms than the existing treaty of Medina del Campo provided for. But in the meantime the French were reducing Brittany, and held the Duchess besieged in Rennes. The French King, Charles VIII., proposed that the marriage with a husband whom she had never seen should be annulled, and the dispute be terminated by his wedding her himself. Resistance seemed hopeless; Anne assented; the necessary dispensations were secured from Rome, and Anne of Brittany became Queen of France.

[Sidenote: 1492 Henry's bellicose attitude]

Now the defence of Brittany had been the primary ground of England's quarrel with the French; with Henry himself, however, this object had been secondary to the matrimonial alliance with Spain, from which the latter was now not likely to withdraw. Henry, moreover, had made use of the whole affair to acquire a full money-chest; and since it was of vital importance that this should be done without turning his subjects against him, it had been necessary to lend the war as popular a colour as possible. Hence it was part of his policy to emphasise at home as his ultimate end the recovery of the English rights in the French Crown, so successfully utilised by his predecessor Henry V. in the first quarter of the century. It would have been manifestly dangerous for him in establishing his dynasty to recede from a claim which both Yorkists and Lancastrians had maintained. Incidentally also, there was the matter of indemnities owing to him by Anne of Brittany for which Maximilian had been made responsible.

[Sidenote 1: France makes peace]
[Sidenote 2: Treaty of Etaples (Dec.)]

Since then it was impracticable simply to retire, the alternative course was to demonstrate; and Henry spent the greater part of 1492 in making the greatest possible display of preparation for war on a great scale—with a view to obtaining satisfying terms of peace. The one real piece of military work taken in hand was the siege and capture of Sluys in Flanders (in conjunction with Albert of Saxony, on behalf of Maximilian); from which port much injury of a piratical order had been wrought upon English merchants. Meantime negotiations had been carried on, but with no appearance of success. At last in October the King actually crossed the Channel to take command of the army of invasion; and sat down before Boulogne. Then on a sudden the air cleared. Charles in fact did not want a serious English war, out of which he could make nothing. But he had developed a very keen ambition to enter Italy and win the Crown of Naples. Henry by himself, or even in conjunction with the much offended Maximilian, was hardly likely to penetrate very far into France, if the forces of that kingdom were arrayed against him; but while he threatened, Charles could not move on Italy; moreover, his presence was an encouragement to those of the nobility whose allegiance was doubtful. So the French King resolved to buy off the English King at his own price. Lewis XI., threatened by Edward IV., had agreed to pay what Edward called a tribute, in return for which he held his claim to the French throne in abeyance. Henry need have no qualms about following his Yorkist predecessor's example. Beyond that, Charles was prepared to pay off the Brittany indemnities. Thus Henry secured Peace with Honour and a solid cash equivalent for his expenditure; besides being able to silence the complaints of the warlike by emphasising the gravity of embarking on a great campaign with winter coming on. He threw over Maximilian, but the faithlessness of the King of the Romans was so palpable and notorious that at the worst Henry was only paying him back in his own coin. As to

Spain, Henry knew that the monarchs had been endeavouring to negotiate a separate peace, and they had never carried out their part of the contract. So far as he was breaking engagements with his allies, their own conduct had given him ample warrant. The event had justified Henry's management of a very difficult situation. The Peace of Etaples was ratified in December; and Henry emerged from the war with England's continental prestige restored to a respectable position, a full treasury, and his throne in England infinitely more secure than it had been three years before. He was never again driven to enter upon a foreign war; and now the appearance of Perkin Warbeck on the scene, though it kept England in a state of uneasiness for some years, was incomparably less dangerous than it would have proved at an earlier stage.

CHAPTER II
HENRY VII (ii), 1492-99—PERKIN WARBECK

[Sidenote: Ireland, 1485]

Before entering upon the career of Perkin Warbeck, we must give somewhat closer attention to the affairs of the sister island, to which reference has already been made in connexion with the Simnel revolt. Ireland had never been really brought under English dominion. Within the district known as the English Pale, there was some sort of control, extending even less effectively over the province of Leinster, and beyond that practically ceasing altogether, except in a few coast towns; the Norman barons who had settled there having so to speak turned Irish, and even in some cases having translated their names into Celtic forms. The most powerful of the nobles at this time were the Geraldines, at whose head were the Earls of Kildare and of Desmond, and the Butlers whose chief was the Earl of Ormonde. But the primacy belonged to Kildare, who moreover had stood high in favour with the House of York. It had been the practice for the English kings to appoint a nominal absentee governor, whose functions were discharged by a Deputy; and Kildare was Deputy under both Edward IV. and Richard.

[Sidenote: 1487-92 The Earl of Kildare]

Henry, on his accession, had seen that the one chance of keeping the country in any degree quiet lay in securing Kildare's allegiance and support; and proposals for his continuation in the office of Deputy had been under discussion when Lambert Simnel was hailed as King and crowned, with the open support not only of Kildare but of nearly all the barons and bishops. It did not suit Henry's policy to attempt punishment under these conditions; he preferred conciliation; and after Stoke, Kildare was retained as Deputy, when he and Simuel's principal adherents had sworn loyalty. In 1490 Henry had found it necessary to reprimand Kildare for sundry breaches of the law, commanding his presence in England within ten months. Kildare made no move, but at the end of the ten months wrote to say that he could not possibly come over, as the state of the country made his presence there imperative. The letter was written in the name of the Council, and signed by fifteen of its members. This was backed by another letter from Desmond and other nobles in the south-west, declaring that they had persuaded the Deputy that the peace of Ireland quite forbade his departure.

Probably it was much about this period—that is, some time in 1491—that a new claimant to Henry's throne (Perkin Warbeck) appeared in the south-west of Ireland, declaring himself to be that Richard Duke of York who was reported to have been murdered in the Tower along with his brother Edward V. Desmond espoused his cause, while Kildare and others coquetted with him. Agents from Desmond and the pretender visited the court of the young King of Scots James IV., in March, 1492, and in the summer Charles VIII., whose territories Henry was then ostentatiously preparing to invade, invited the young man over to France where he was received as the rightful King of England. The conclusion of peace, however, at the end of the year, made it necessary for the French King to withdraw his countenance from Henry's enemies; and the pretender retired to the congenial atmosphere of the court of Margaret of Burgundy. In the meantime Kildare, whose complicity with Desmond it had become impossible entirely to ignore, had been deprived of his office, and a new Deputy appointed.

[Sidenote 1: 1491 Perkin Warbeck's appearance]
[Sidenote 2: Riddle of his imposture]

The self-styled Richard of York is known to history as Perkin Warbeck. The account of his early career subsequently given to the world in his own confession is generally accepted as genuine. The son of a Tournai boatman, he served during his boyhood under half a dozen different masters in three or four Netherland cities and in Lisbon. At the age of seventeen he took service with one Prégent Meno, a Breton merchant, and incidentally appeared at Cork where he paraded in costly array. Such was the effect of his appearance and bearing that the citizens of Cork declared he must be a Plantagenet. Taxed with being in reality either the Earl of Warwick or an illegitimate son of Richard III., he swore he was nothing of the kind; but his admirers declared that in that case he could only be Richard of York, who had somehow been saved from sharing his brother's fate in the Tower. Perkin found himself unable to resist such importunity, accepted the dignity thrust upon him, and set himself to learn his part. The partisans of the White Rose had shown in the case of Lambert Simnel their preference for even a palpable impostor bearing their badge, as compared with the objectionable Tudor; and a genuine Duke of York would have the advantage of a claim stronger even than that of his sister Elizabeth, Henry's queen. Perkin, however, must have acted up to his part with no little skill to have maintained himself as a plausible impostor up to the time when Margaret of Burgundy received him—even though he met no one in whose interest it was to pose him with inconvenient questions. So apt a pupil would then have had little difficulty in assimilating the instructions of Margaret; and, after a couple of years' training with her, in at least supporting his role with plausibility. That Perkin himself told this story is not very conclusive, since the confession was produced under circumstances quite compatible with the whole thing having been dictated to him; yet difficult as it is to believe, it is less incredible than the alternative—that he was the real duke, who had been smuggled out of the Tower eight years before he was produced, and kept in concealment all through the interval, even while the Yorkist leaders had been reduced to setting up a supposititious Earl of Warwick for a figurehead.

[Sidenote: 1492-95 Perkin and Margaret of Burgundy]

It certainly does not seem that on Perkin's appearance in Ireland he had any active supporters outside that country, or that he caused any perturbation in Henry's mind. Foreign princes, whether they regarded him as genuine or as an impostor, would certainly not espouse his cause unless they were at enmity with Henry. Even Charles VIII. made no haste to lend him countenance until it seemed almost certain that there was to be a war with England on a great scale; and he had no hesitation in dismissing the pretender when peace was concluded; while the Spanish sovereigns, though quite ready to intrigue against their Tudor ally, had no intention of committing themselves to an open breach with him. The peace, however, which dismissed Perkin from France, gave him a zealous adherent in the person of Maximilian, who was now filled with a righteous animosity to Henry; and the young lord of the Netherlands, his son Philip, Duke of Burgundy, declared that he had no power to control the Dowager Margaret, dwelling on her own estates. So Perkin made her court his head-quarters—a useful tool for the weaving of Yorkist intrigues. Henry might, if he would, have legitimately founded a *casus belli* on this attitude, but he preferred to institute a commercial war; from which, however, the English merchants suffered little less than the Flemings.

In 1493 the Emperor died, and was in effect succeeded by the King of the Romans, though his election to the Imperial throne did not take place for some years. Maximilian, however, remained impecunious and inefficient; Charles VIII. was giving his entire attention to his Italian projects; the whole affair of Perkin Warbeck was carried on mainly below the surface on both sides, by a process of mining and counter-mining. Henry was well served by Sir Robert Clifford and others, who wormed themselves into the confidence of the Yorkist plotters, revealing what they learnt to the King. When the time was ripe (January, 1495), Henry's hand fell suddenly on the unsuspecting conspirators in England; whose chiefs, including Sir William Stanley, who was supposed to be one of the King's most trusted supporters, were sent to the block. It was this same Sir William Stanley who, striking in at Bosworth on the side of Henry, had been mainly instrumental in deciding the fortunes of the day; and he had been rewarded with the office of Chamberlain.

[Sidenote: Diplomatic intrigues]

During the two years following the Treaty of Etaples Charles VIII. had early made his peace also with Spain by the treaty of Barcelona'and with Maximilian by that of Senlis. The desired provinces, Roussillon and Cerdagne, were restored to Ferdinand and Isabella, who adopted a distant attitude to Henry. The French King, free to follow his own devices, entered Italy towards the close of 1494, marched south without opposition, and was crowned at Naples in February, 1495, the reigning family fleeing before him. So early and important an accession of strength to the French Crown had hardly been anticipated, and the European sovereigns made haste to form a League against France. Spain was desirous of bringing England into the league; but the wayward Maximilian was still determined to support Perkin Warbeck, apparently thinking that by substituting a Yorkist prince for Henry he would secure a more amenable ally.

[Sidenote: 1492-95 Ireland]

Meanwhile, Ireland also had been undergoing judicious treatment. Kildare, removed from the Deputy-ship in 1492, came over to England to give an account of himself in the following year. Here he was detained until, in the autumn of 1494, the King appointed a new three-year-old Governor in the person of his second son Henry, whom he also created Duke of York, making Sir Edward Poynings Deputy. Poynings was an experienced and capable soldier, who had been in command before Sluys in the recent campaign; and on his departure for Ireland Kildare went with him. Both the ex-Deputy and the Earl of Ormonde promised to render loyal service; but it was no very long time before Kildare was sent back to England under accusations of treason. We may here anticipate matters by observing that this was the last case of misbehaviour on his part. He won his way once more into the royal favour, and when Poynings left Ireland in 1496 Kildare yet again went back as Deputy, which office he retained for the remainder of Henry's reign, and a portion of his son's also.

It is curious to observe in the turbulent Deputy traits of that audacious humour which we are wont to regard as peculiarly Irish: a characteristic fully appreciated by the English King. When taken to task for burning the Cathedral at Cashel, he is reported to have said that he would not have done so, only the bishop was inside. His casual announcement on a previous occasion that he could not obey the royal summons to England because the country could not get on without him was paralleled either in 1493 or

1495 —it is uncertain which—by his defence against the Bishop of Meath's charges. He said he must be represented by Counsel; the King replied that he might have whom he would. "Give me your hand," quoth the Earl. "Here it is," said the King. "Well," said Kildare, "I can see no better man than you, and by St. Bride I will choose none other." Said the Bishop, "You see what manner of man he is. All Ireland cannot rule him." "Then," said the King, "he must be the man to rule all Ireland."

[Sidenote: Poynings in Ireland 1494-96]

The government of Poynings was not prolonged, but it was very much to the point. "Poynings' Law," passed by the Parliament assembled at Drogheda in December, 1494, fixed Constitutional procedure for a very long time. Irish Parliaments were to be summoned only with the approval of the King's Council in England, and only after it had also approved the measures which were to be submitted to them by the Irish Deputy and Council. In effect, however, these legislative functions at this time were hardly more limited than those of English Parliaments, which were summoned at the King's pleasure, and only had what might be called "Government Bills" submitted to them. The royal Council was practically in the position of a Cabinet holding office as representing not the parliamentary majority but the King's personal views. The Parliament might discuss and accept or reject, but had not as yet acquired a practical initiative itself. At the same time that this law was passed, a declaratory Act abolished the theory which had grown up at an early stage of the conflict between the White and Red Roses, of regarding Ireland as a country where a rebel in England was a free man: a notion which had greatly facilitated the intrigues of both Lambert Simnel and Perkin Warbeck on Irish soil. Further, besides some enactments for checking feudal customs which tended to disorder, it was ordained that the principal castles should always be under the command of Englishmen. Poynings also endeavoured, by bestowing pensions (on terms) on some of the principal chiefs outside the Pale—such as O'Neill in Ulster and O'Brien in the west—to convert their position into one of semi-official responsibility to the official Government. A basis for the maintenance of law and order having thus been provided, the Irish difficulty was solved for the time when "the man to rule all Ireland," benevolently disposed to a King who had shown that he knew the right way to take him, was restored to the office of Deputy.

[Sidenote: 1495 Survey of the situation]

In the early spring, then, of 1495, this was the position of affairs. Perkin Warbeck lay at the court of Margaret of Burgundy; but his plans had been upset by Clifford's information and the punishment of the ringleaders in

England. Poynings was in Ireland, and the prospect of keeping that country in reasonable order was unusually promising. Charles VIII. had just made himself master of Naples; and the Spanish sovereigns (who had completed the destruction of the Moorish dominion in Granada some three years earlier) were now occupied in forming with the Pope, Venice, Milan, and Maximilian the Holy League against French aggression; into which they were anxious to draw Henry, whose weight if thrown into the other scale would be of considerable value to France. For the last two years, since the treaty of Barcelona, they had evaded the recognition or reconstruction of any compact with England; but under the changed conditions, while they would not admit that the old engagements were binding, they offered to frame new treaties for Henry's inclusion in the League, at the same time confirming the project of the marriage between their daughter Katharine and the Prince of Wales. Henry, however, was now in a much stronger position at home; and though he desired the Spanish alliance, he had no intention of allowing that bait to seduce him into making himself a cat's-paw. France was offering a counter-inducement in the shape of a marriage with the daughter of the Duke of Bourbon; Henry indicated that while Maximilian was fostering the pretensions of the impostor Warbeck, it was not serious politics to talk of being associated with him in the League. Spain might make promises on Maximilian's behalf, but could not ensure that he would keep them.

[Sidenote: 1495 Warbeck attempts invasion]

Time was working in Henry's favour. In July (1495) an expedition sailed from Flanders to place Perkin on the English throne. Maximilian's hopes were high: he bragged to the Venetians that the "Duke of York" would immediately unseat the Tudor, and when he was on the throne, England would be at the beck of the League. The Emperor's impracticability was sufficiently shown by his having procured from Perkin his own recognition as heir, if the pretender should die without issue. The expedition attempted to land at Deal, but the men of Kent assembled in arms, and drove it off with ignominious ease. For once Henry was severe, and put to death no fewer than 150 of Warbeck's followers, who had been taken prisoners. Warbeck himself did not even set foot on the realm he claimed, but made for Ireland where he had first been so warmly welcomed. Here his old supporter Desmond took up his cause again, and Waterford was attacked by sea and land; but there was no general rising, and Poynings had no difficulty in raising the siege. Foiled both in England and Ireland, Perkin now betook himself to Scotland to obtain the help of the young King, James IV.

[Sidenote: Success of Henry's diplomacy]

The affair showed conclusively how small was the danger in England of a Yorkist rising in favour of the pretender—a fact very fully recognised by Ferdinand and Isabella, though Maximilian clung pertinaciously to his protégé. Moreover, the position of the League was somewhat precarious, since both Ludovico Sforza, Duke of Milan, and the Venetians, were suspected with justice of readiness to make their own terms with France. It was more than ever necessary to bring Henry into the combination; and Henry, still diplomatically suave, was less than ever prepared to accept conditions which would fetter him inconveniently. He would not commit himself to make war on France except at his own time; and Maximilian must definitely and conclusively repudiate Warbeck. At last in July, 1496, the new League was concluded. Henry's diplomacy achieved a distinct triumph. His alliance had been won, but only on his own terms; all he wished to secure had been secured. The Spanish sovereigns were so far from feeling that they could make a tool of him that they were in considerable trepidation lest he should still throw them over if a tolerably legitimate excuse offered, and were anxious to do all they could to conciliate him without betraying the full extent of their fears. Henry had already, in February, terminated the commercial war with the Flemings by the treaty with Philip known as the *Intercursus Magnus*, which included a proviso against the admission into Philip's territories of rebels against the English King.

[Sidenote: 1496 Warbeck and the King of Scots]

When Perkin Warbeck made his way to Scotland the young King of that country was already fully informed as to the nature of his claims. James, when a boy of sixteen, had taken part in the rebellion headed by Douglas Earl of Angus, in which his father the late King had been overthrown at Sauchie Burn and murdered after the battle. He was now twenty-four years of age, of brilliant parts, no mean scholar, an admirable athlete, and ambitious to raise the name of Scotland among the nations. His weakness lay mainly in a boyish impulsiveness, which often caused him to mar well-laid plans on the spur of the moment, and in an exaggerated fondness for chivalric ideas more appropriate to a knight-errant than to a king or a leader of armies. Perkin appealed to him as early as 1492; and before the pretender's expedition sailed, Tyrconnel, chief of the O'Donnells of the north-west of Ireland, presented himself in Scotland to renew the appeal. The antagonism of Scottish feeling to the ruling powers in England was chronic. There was a treaty of peace between England and Scotland, but the unfailing turbulence of the borders kept each country constantly provided with a tolerable excuse for accusing the other of having broken its engagements. James was well within his rights in receiving the claimant; of the justice of whose title he evidently persuaded himself, since he bestowed a kinswoman of his own upon him in marriage, Lady Katharine Gordon. In the summer of 1496 he was making active preparations for an incursion into England on Warbeck's behalf; largely influenced no doubt by the promise that, should it prove successful, Berwick, which had been finally ceded to England fourteen years before, was to be once more surrendered to the Scots. The astute Henry turned all this to account, by impressing on the Spanish and Venetian agents the urgent necessity laid on him to abstain from military operations against France while Scotland was so threatening.

[Sidenote 1: A Scottish incursion (Sept.)]
[Sidenote 2: 1497]

James did in fact raid the North of England in September; but the incursion was a raid and nothing more. Perkin, to the surprise and even contempt both of Scots and English, protested against the sanguinary methods of border warfare, on behalf of the people whom he aspired to rule over. But the people themselves would have none of him. The expedition withdrew without having produced even the semblance of a Yorkist rising. After that, James no longer felt eager to plunge into a war on behalf of the pretender: but was inclined to retain him as a political asset. When, in the following year (1497), Charles VIII.—with a precisely similar object in view— offered him a considerable sum if he would send his guest over to France, the Scots King declined. In July, however, Perkin sailed from Scotland, apparently with intent to try Ireland again, where Kildare was once more Deputy. Henry had utilised the raid to obtain the recommendation of a large grant and loans from the Great Council forthwith; Parliament, which was called for January (1497), ratifying the grant as a subsidy. The raising of the loans had, however, been proceeded with, without waiting.

[Sidenote: The Cornish rising]

The defence of England against invading Scots was a matter of much importance to the northern counties, but lacked personal interest in Cornwall. Year after year the King had been receiving subsidies to arm for impending wars, borrowing, and levying benevolences. When a hostile France was the excuse, the population might murmur but was quite as willing to pay as could reasonably be expected. But the Scots had never invaded Cornwall, and the Cornishmen felt that it was time to protest. They would march to London—peaceably, of course—to demand according to custom the removal of the King's evil counsellors; Morton and Bray, to wit, who probably used their influence in reality to mitigate rather than intensify the royal demands. The insurgent leaders were a blacksmith, Joseph, and a lawyer, Flamock—appropriate chiefs for working men trying honestly enough to formulate what they had been led to regard as a grievance of what we should now call an unconstitutional character. With bills and bows, some thousands of them started on their march; preserving their peaceable character, till at Taunton the appearance of a commissioner for collecting the tax proved too much for their self-restraint, and the man was killed. A little later they were joined by Lord Audley, who became their leader. They expected the men of Kent, who of old had risen under Wat Tyler and again under Jack Cade, to take up the cause: but Kent did not recognise the similarity of the present conditions and gave them no welcome.

[Sidenote: The suppression (June)]

Meantime, Henry had not been idle; but he saw that the insurgents were not rousing the country as they progressed, and therefore he judged that the further they were drawn away from their own country the better. Except for a slight skirmish at Guildford, the Cornishmen were not actively interfered with till they encamped on Blackheath. Then, on June 17th, the royal forces proceeded to envelop them. Some two thousand were slain on the field. Audley, the lawyer, and the blacksmith, were put to death as traitors; the rest were pardoned, as having been not so much rebels as victims of demagogic arts.

[Sidenote: Warbeck's final failure (Sept.)]

The policy of leniency was not entirely successful, for the Cornishmen imagined it merely meant that the King recognised the impossibility of dealing sternly with every one who thought as they did. Warbeck, now in Ireland, where he was not finding the sympathy for which he had hoped, received messages to the effect that if he came to Cornwall he would find plenty of supporters. He came promptly, with a scanty following enough; but only a few thousand men joined him. He marched on Exeter, but that loyal town stoutly refused to admit him, and his attempts to carry gates and walls failed completely. Royal troops were on the march: the gentlemen of Devon, headed by the Earl, were up for the King. Perkin marched to Taunton, and then fled by night to take sanctuary at Beaulieu in Hampshire, where he was surrounded, and very soon submitted himself to the King's clemency.

[Sidenote: The Scottish truce]

In the meantime the Scottish King, though his sentiments towards Perkin had sensibly cooled, had no intention of leaving him in the lurch, and had advanced on Norham Castle very shortly after his protégé had sailed for Ireland. The Earl of Surrey, however, who commanded in the north, was well prepared, and very soon took the field with twenty thousand men. James was obliged to withdraw, and though he challenged the Earl to single combat with Berwick as the stake, Surrey replied that Berwick was not his property but his master's, and he must regretfully decline the proposed method of arbitrament. He advanced over the border, making some captures and doing considerable damage; but after a week, commissariat difficulties made him retire in turn. In September Perkin's Cornish rising collapsed, and a seven years' treaty was entered upon between the two countries.

[Sidenote: The end of Perkin Warbeck 1497-99]

Towards the pretender and his followers, the King behaved with his usual leniency. A few leaders only were put to death; other penalties were reserved. Warbeck was compelled publicly to read at Exeter and later in London a confession of the true story of his own origin and that of the conspiracy; and was then relegated to not very strict confinement under surveillance. His supporters were allowed to purchase their pardon by heavy fines, which satisfactorily aided in the replenishment of the royal treasury.

The end of the pretender's story may be told in anticipation. It was ignominious and less creditable in its accompanying circumstances to Henry. In the summer of the next year, 1498, Perkin tried to escape, was promptly recaptured, set in the stocks, and required to read his confession publicly both in Westminster and London. He was then placed in strict confinement in the Tower, where the luckless Warwick had been kept a prisoner for thirteen years. The son of Clarence, still little more than a boy, was the only figure-head left for Yorkist malcontents. Another attempt to impersonate him by a youth named Ralph Wilford was nipped in the bud at the beginning of 1499; but Henry's nerve seems to have been seriously shaken by it, and probably he now began to make up his mind to get rid of his kinsman. Then some kind of conspiracy was concocted, in which both Warbeck and Warwick were involved; on 23rd November, 1499, Perkin was hanged, and five days later Warwick was beheaded, dying as he had lived a victim to his name; suffering for no treason or wrong-doing of his own, but simply because he was the nephew of Edward IV.

[Sidenote: 1498 The situation]

When the year 1497 closed, the preliminaries of a Scottish peace had been agreed upon; Perkin Warbeck was a prisoner: and the French King had already found his position in Italy untenable, and agreed to evacuate Naples and surrender the crown. His death and the accession of the Duke of Orleans as Lewis XII. in April of the next year further altered the face of international politics, already changing with the final collapse of Warbeck and his disappearance as a pawn in the game.

CHAPTER III
HENRY VII (iii), 1498-1509-
THE DYNASTY ASSURED

[Sidenote: Scotland and England]

From time immemorial almost, it might be said that Scotland had been a perpetual menace to her southern neighbour. Since the days of Bruce she had, it is true, been torn by ceaseless dissensions; a succession of long royal minorities with intrigues over the regency, family feuds between the great barons, strong kings who found themselves warring on a turbulent nobility, weak ones who could exercise no control, had not given the country much chance of consolidation; but the one binding sentiment that could be relied on in a crisis was antagonism to England. To settle the question by conquest had been proved impossible. Scotland might be over-run, but she could not be held in subjection. If England's eyes were bent on France, she must still manage to keep a watch on the north: but so long as dissensions were raging, there was not much fear of anything more serious than raiding expeditions.

[Sidenote: Henry's Scottish policy]

To keep Scotland innocuous was a primary object with the Tudor King. At the time when he grasped the sceptre of England, the King of Scots, James III., was a feeble ruler surrounded by unpopular favourites, with a baronage preparing to rise against him, and there was little danger to be apprehended. He was over-thrown and murdered in 1488. But James IV, who succeeded to the throne was of a different type. He was only a boy, however, and Henry was not long in initiating a policy, more fully developed by his descendants, of purchasing the support of leading nobles, notably at this time and for forty years to come, the Earls of Angus-with whom there was a compact as early as 1491. James, however, soon proved himself a popular and vigorous monarch, of a type which attracted the loyalty of his subjects, with a strong disposition to make his country a serious factor in the politics of the time, and by no means devoid of political sagacity despite his unfortunate impulsiveness and want of balance. To block Scotland out of the field by the simple process of keeping her thoroughly occupied with internal factions was not practicable under these conditions, and the attitude of James in the affair of Perkin Warbeck showed that he must be taken into serious account. Henry's political acuteness recognised in alliance with Scotland a more hopeful solution of the national problem than in eternal strife. The idea of a matrimonial connexion had indeed once before, since the days of Edward I., taken shape in the union of James I. to Jane Beaufort; but with little practical effect. This idea Henry revived in a form destined ultimately to revolutionise the relations of the two kingdoms. His own eldest daughter Margaret was but eighteen years younger than the King of Scots—quite near enough for compatibility. From the time of the peace entered upon after Warbeck's capture, Henry began to work with this marriage as one of his objects. His foresight and sagacity is marked by the fact that he recognised—and did not shrink from the possibility—that a Scottish monarch might thus one day find himself heir to the throne of England.

[Sidenote 1: France and England]
[Sidenote 2: 1498]

The peace-policy towards Scotland was facilitated by the development of friendly relations with France, especially after the accession of Lewis XII.: for the traditional "auld alliance," between France and Scotland, had proved times out of mind too strong to be over-ridden by English treaties. If France wanted Scottish help, or Scotland wanted French help, there was always some excuse for rendering it; the plain truth being that no treaties could restrain the forays and counter-forays of the border clans on both sides of the Tweed, whether the Wardens of the Marches winked at them or not; so that there was, in either country, a standing pretext for declaring that the other had broken truce. An instance of these border difficulties occurred within a few months of the truce of December, 1497. A small party of Scots crossed the border, and appeared in the neighbourhood of Norham. They were challenged, and replied—with insolence or with proper spirit, according to the point of view. Thereupon they were attacked by superior numbers; some were slain; in the pursuit, damage was done on the north side of the border. The Scots King felt that he had been outraged, and was on the verge of breaking off all negotiations with his brother of England. It required all the diplomatic skill of Fox (at this time Bishop of Durham), and the mediatorial efforts of the Spaniard Ayala to prevent a serious breach from resulting.

[Sidenote: Marriage negotiations, 1498-1503]

The opportunity, however, was seized by Fox to emphasise his master's pacific intentions by bringing forward the proposal for the marriage of James with Margaret. Nevertheless, for the next twelve months, Henry displayed no eagerness in the matter. Margaret was only in her eighth year, so that in any case the marriage could not be completed for some time; but apart from that, there was already existing a project of marriage between James and one of the Spanish princesses—which Spain had no real wish to carry out, while James was disposed to push it. It would appear, therefore, that Henry meant to give effect to his own scheme, but did not intend Spain to feel free of the complication while it could be used as a means of pressure.

[Sidenote: Marriage of James IV, and Margaret 1503]

At last, however, in July, 1499, a fresh treaty of peace was concluded with Scotland, but it was not till January, 1502, that the marriage treaty was finally ratified; the marriage to take place in September, 1503 (when Margaret would be nearly thirteen), and the two Kings to render each other mutual aid in case either of them was attacked. James, however, declined to bind himself permanently to refuse renewal of the French alliance. There was much characteristic haggling over dower and jointure, matters in which the Tudors always drove the hardest bargain they could. The ceremony was performed by proxy, after the fashion of the times, the day after the treaty was ratified; and the actual marriage took place at the time fixed, in the autumn of 1503—a momentous event, since it brought the Stuarts into the direct line of succession, next to descendants of Henry in the male line; and—inasmuch as one of Henry's sons had no children, and the other no grandchildren—ultimately united on one head the Crowns of England and Scotland, exactly one hundred years after the marriage.

[Sidenote: Spain and England: marriage negotiations, 1488-99]

In the meantime the other and much older project for the union between the Prince of Wales and a daughter of Spain had been carried out. Originally, Henry's prime motive in this matter had been to secure a decisive recognition of his dynasty by the sovereigns, whom he regarded as the greatest political force in Europe. By this time, however, (1498), the stability of his throne and of the succession was no longer in peril; but Spain was still the Power whose alliance would give the best guarantees against hostile combinations. Neither Spain nor England wished to be involved in war with France; but neither country could view her aggrandisement with complete equanimity. At the same time, while her ambitions were chiefly directed to Italy both could afford for the most part to abstain from active hostilities. On the other hand, times had changed since Henry had been ready to go almost cap-in-hand to Ferdinand and Isabella for their support. The Spanish sovereigns were now quite as much afraid of his joining France as he was of any step that they could take. So the marriage treaty was ratified in 1497 on terms satisfactory enough to Henry; and both in 1498 and 1499 proxy ceremonies took place. In the latter year, clauses left somewhat vague in the earlier treaties were given a clearer definition in a sense favourable to Henry.

[Sidenote: 1499 Lewis XII]

The accession of Lewis XII. in 1497 affected French policy. Lewis required in the first place, to gain the friendship of the Pope Alexander VI., in order to obtain a divorce from his wife and a dispensation to marry Charles's widow, Anne of Brittany, so as to retain the duchy. In the second place, he claimed Milan as his own in right of his descent from Valentina Visconti (not as an appanage of the French Crown). He was anxious then to conciliate both Spain and England, and ready to make concessions to both in order to hold them neutral. His first steps, therefore, aimed at satisfying them, and at detaching the Archduke Philip from his father Maximilian; all of which objects were rapidly accomplished, England obtaining the renewal of the treaty of Etaples, with additional undertakings in the matter of harbouring rebels. Lewis made separate treaties with Spain and with Philip; but the former remained none the less anxious on the score of a possible further *rapprochement* between France and England.

[Sidenote: The Spanish marriage negotiation, 1499-1501]

So long as Perkin Warbeck had been able to pose as Richard of York, he was necessarily, to all who believed in him, the legitimate King of England. Setting him aside, it was still possible to argue for the Earl of Warwick as against his cousin Elizabeth, Henry's queen. But when Perkin and Warwick were both put to death at the end of 1499, there was no arguable case for any one outside Henry's own domestic circle. Even if it were held that Henry's title was invalid, and that a woman could not herself reign in her own right, Elizabeth's son had indisputably a title prior to any other possible claimant. It was stated, though the truth of the statement is doubtful, that the Spanish sovereigns had never felt at ease as to the stability of the Tudor dynasty till November, 1499; but, at any rate, after that date they could not even for diplomatic purposes pretend to feel any serious apprehensions. The year 1500 presents the somewhat curious spectacle of Henry on one side and Ferdinand and Isabella on the other, each quite determined to carry through the marriage of Arthur and Katharine, but each also determined to make a favour of it. In this diplomatic contest, Henry proved the more skilful bargainer, though the Spaniards were adepts. He frightened them not a little by crossing the Channel and holding a conference with the Archduke Philip, which was suspected of having for its object the negotiation of another marriage for the Prince of Wales with Philip's sister (Maximilian's daughter) Margaret, who was already a widow. [Footnote: Margaret had been married to Don John, son of Ferdinand and Isabella; while Philip married their second daughter Joanna. Their eldest daughter married the Portuguese Infant.] In fact, there was no such intention; but an agreement was actually made that Prince Henry should many Philip's daughter, while the youngest Tudor princess, Mary, should be betrothed to Philip's infant son Charles, then a babe of four months, in after years the great Emperor Charles V.

[Sidenote: Marriage of Prince Arthur and Katharine 1501]

So the marriage treaty was once more ratified. But it was not till the summer of the next year (1501) that Katharine sailed from Spain; and in November the actual marriage took place with no little display. It is probable, however, that Arthur and Katharine were still husband and wife in name only when, six months later, the Prince of Wales was stricken with mortal illness and died; leaving his brother Henry heir to the throne, and a fresh crop of matrimonial schemes to be matured.

[Sidenote 1: 1502 New marriage schemes]
[Sidenote 2: 1504 Dispensation granted]

The truth was that Ferdinand of Aragon and Henry of England were men of very much the same type. Both were crafty diplomatists, cautious and long-headed, not to be inveigled into rash schemes, keenly suspicious, masters of the art of committing themselves irrevocably to nothing; both had a keen appreciation of the value of money, and were experts at striking a bargain; while each wanted the political support of the other. Each had been working up to the matrimonial alliance which was now nullified by Arthur's death. Ferdinand had already paid over half his daughter's dower; he now declared that the Princess and her dower ought to be returned to Spain. Henry argued on the other side that the balance of the dower should be paid over. The Spaniards then proposed that the young widow should be betrothed to the still younger prince, Henry; but at a comparatively early stage in the negotiations over the new project, Henry's own queen died (February, 1503), and it was no long time before the English King began to contemplate a new marriage for himself. He is even said [Footnote: Gairdner, *Henry VII.* (*Twelve English Statesmen*), p. 190. The rumour was current, but it is doubtful whether it was more than a rumour; *cf.* Busch, p. 378.] to have thought of proposing that he should take his own son's widow to wife. Logically, of course, as a mere question of affinity, the idea was not more inadmissible than that of Katharine's marriage with Henry Prince of Wales; but it was infinitely more repellent, and Isabella was horrified at the suggestion. At any rate, nothing came of it, and an agreement for the marriage of Katharine with the younger Henry was ratified in the course of the year [Footnote: It was in the August of this same year (1503) that the other marriage, between James of Scotland and Henry's elder daughter Margaret, was finally concluded.]—subject, of course, to a papal dispensation. This was obtained, during 1504, from the successor of Alexander VI., Pope Julius II., and Isabella had the satisfaction of seeing it before her death. Political exigencies had only recently been accepted by Pope Alexander as justifying a dispensation for the divorce of Lewis XII. from his wife, to enable him to marry Anne of Brittany; but this dispensation of Pope Julius was destined to an immense importance in history—to be the hinge whereon swung open the gates of the English Reformation.

[Sidenote: 1499-1506 Affairs on the Continent]

The years from 1498 to 1503 had not been without importance in Franco- Spanish relations, more particularly with reference to the position of the two Powers in Italy. Lewis had made himself master of Milan in 1499; but the kingdom of Naples presented a more difficult problem; since, after disposing of the reigning family, the French King would still find a rival claimant in Ferdinand of Spain. In 1500 these two monarchs agreed to a partition; but French and Spaniards quarrelled, war broke out, the Spanish captain Gonsalvo de Cordova expelled the French; and in 1508 Naples was annexed to Aragon. A renewed attempt of France upon Naples in the following year proved a complete failure.

In 1503 died the Borgia Pope, Alexander VI.—poisoned, as it was believed, by the cup he had intended for another. The personal wickedness of Alexander and his relatives was the climax of papal iniquity, the *reductio ad absurdum* of the claim of the Roman Pontiff to be the representative of Christ on earth. His immediate successor hardly survived election to the Holy See; and was followed by Julius II., an energetic and militant Pope, who was bent on forming the Papal States into an effective temporal principality.

In the next year Isabella of Castile died, and by her death the European situation was again materially affected. While she lived she worked in complete accord with her husband, Ferdinand of Aragon; her name stands high among the ablest of European sovereigns. But with her death the Crowns of Castile and Aragon were no longer united. Ferdinand was not King of Castile; the sceptre descended to the dead Queen's daughter Joanna, [Footnote: The elder sister was already dead, as well as the one brother.] and in effect to her husband, the Archduke Philip, Maximilian's son, and after her to their son Charles. At the most, Ferdinand could hope only to exercise a dominant influence (converted after Philip's death in 1506 into practical sovereignty as Regent), with a perpetual risk of Maximilian turning his flighty ambitions towards asserting himself as a rival.

[Sidenote: The Earl of Suffolk 1499-1505]

Although both Warbeck and Warwick had been removed in 1499, Henry had not been altogether free from Yorkist troubles in the succeeding years. Edmund de la Pole, Earl of Suffolk, was brother of that Earl of Lincoln who had fallen at the battle of Stoke, and son of a sister of Edward IV. The Earl had not hitherto come forward as a claimant to the throne; but in 1499 he developed a personal grievance against the King, and betook himself to the Continent, where a certain Sir Robert Curzon espoused his cause with Maximilian. At the time, nothing came of the matter; Henry was not afraid of Suffolk, whom he induced to return to England with a pardon. In 1501, however, the Earl again betook himself to the Continent and made a direct appeal to Maximilian for assistance. But Henry was now on particularly good terms with the Archduke Philip, and Maximilian was inclining to revert to friendly relations with England. He was in his normal condition of impecuniosity, and Henry was prepared to provide a loan to help him in a Turkish war if his own rebellious subjects were handed over. The issue of these negotiations, towards the end of 1502, was a loan from Henry of fifty thousands crowns, and a promise from Maximilian to eject Suffolk and his supporters. In the meantime several of Suffolk's accomplices were executed in England, including James Tyrrel who had abetted Richard III. in the murder of the Princes in the Tower; and [Footnote: See genealogical table (*Front*.).] William de la Pole and William Courtenay (son of the Earl of Devonshire) were imprisoned on suspicion of complicity. Suffolk, however, remained at Aix la Chapelle, Maximilian making him many promises and providing inadequate supplies, while with equal lightness of heart— having got his loan—he left his pledges to Henry unfulfilled by anything more substantial than professions that he was doing his best to carry them out. In 1504 the migratory Earl had the misfortune to fall into the hands of the Duke of Gueldres, who detained him for use as circumstances might dictate—to the annoyance of the Kings of France and Scotland, both of whom wished him to be handed over to the King of England.

[Sidenote: 1505 Henry's position]

In 1505 then Henry's relations with all foreign Powers were satisfactory: that is, none of them were hostile and most of them were anxious for his friendship. In these later years, however, of Henry's reign he appears consistently in a more definitely unamiable light than before. The two counsellors who, however thoroughly they endorsed his policy, had probably exercised a moderating and refining influence—Cardinal Morton and Reginald Bray—were now both dead, and there is no doubt that Elizabeth of York, popular herself, had been a very judicious helpmeet to her husband. Moreover, though he was still by no means an old man, Henry was becoming worn out; yet he could never escape from dynastic anxieties, the younger Henry being now his only son. Marriage schemes had always been prominent features in his policy, and the marriage schemes for himself which he evolved one after the other in the closing years of his reign show him in a singularly unattractive light, at the same time that his financial methods were growing increasingly mean, and his evasions of honourable obligations increasingly unscrupulous.

Now the Duke of Gueldres was in conflict with the Archduke Philip—at this time not only lord of the Burgundian domains, but also in right of his wife King of Castile and not on the best of terms with his father-in-law of Aragon. In 1505 Philip got possession in his turn of the person of Suffolk, by capturing the town where the Duke of Gueldres held him. Therefore during this year Henry became particularly anxious to make friends with Philip, and lent him money; having got which, Philip preferred placing his hostage again in the hands of the Duke of Gueldres, who had submitted to him.

[Sidenote: Schemes for his marriage]

Out of these conditions rose another futile suggestion of a marriage for Henry: who had already considered and dismissed the idea of marrying the younger of the two living ex-Queens of Naples—both named Joanna—a niece of Ferdinand of Aragon. The wife now proposed was Philip's sister, Margaret, who on her first widowhood had been spoken of as a possible alternative to Katharine for Arthur of Wales. Since then, she had become Margaret of Savoy, the name by which she is generally known; but had been widowed a second time. This proposal probably came from Philip, but was resolutely resisted by Margaret herself.

[Sidenote: 1506 Philip in England]

In 1506 fortune favoured Henry. Philip sailed from the Netherlands in January to take possession of the throne of Castile: but was driven on to the English shores by stress of weather. The English King received him royally, but while the utmost show of friendliness prevailed, Philip found that he had no alternative to acceptance of Henry's suggestions. Before the King of Castile departed, he had not only entered on a treaty for mutual defence against any aggressor, but had actually delivered over the person of the unhappy Suffolk [Footnote: So Busch. Gairdner is doubtful.] to his sovereign, though under promise that he should not be put to death. The prisoner, however, was committed to the Tower, and though Henry kept his word, he is reported to have advised his son that the promise would not be binding on him. At any rate Suffolk was executed, apparently without further trial, early in the next reign. His brother Richard, known as the "White Rose," who had abetted him, remained abroad, and was ultimately killed in the service of Francis I. at the battle of Pavia in 1525, leaving no children.

Philip had hardly departed from England when a new commercial treaty which he had authorised was signed with the Netherlands, terminating the war of tariffs which had again become active in recent years. This treaty, it is not surprising to remark, was so favourable to England that in contradistinction to the older *Intercursus Magnus* the Flemings entitled it the *Intercursus Malus*.

[Sidenote: Death of Philip]

The few remaining months of Philip's life were troubled. The position in Castile was difficult enough, and in his absence the Duke of Gueldres again revolted, with some assistance from France. Henry interfered, as he was bound to do by the recent treaty, not without some effect. But Philip's death in September left his wife Joanna Queen of Castile, with her father Ferdinand as Regent, and her young son Charles Lord of the Netherlands, with Margaret of Savoy at the head of the Council of Regency. Under these new conditions Henry agreed to modifications in the new commercial treaty, which indeed, as it stood, was almost impossible of fulfilment; probably in the hope that his project of marriage with Margaret of Savoy might still be carried out, the dowry she would bring being very much more satisfactory than that of Joanna of Naples.

[Sidenote: 1507-8 Matrimonial projects]

In a very short time, however, Margaret had another rival, at least for the purposes of diplomacy. This was Joanna of Castile, Philip's widow, whom Henry had seen in the spring of 1506. That her sanity was already very much in question seems to have made very little difference. Throughout the greater part of 1507 and 1508 the English King was making overtures to Margaret herself, and for Joanna to Ferdinand, blowing hot and cold in the matter of his son Henry and Katharine, and pushing on the betrothal of his younger daughter Mary with the boy Charles—a proposal brought forward, when the latter was but four months old, in 1500, but not at that time sedulously pressed. In part, at least, the explanation of all this diplomatic play lies in Henry's relations with Ferdinand. The King of Aragon, having lost his wife Isabella, wished to retain control of Castile; at the same time he was in difficulties about paying up the balance of Katharine's dowry, without which Henry would not allow her marriage with his son to go forward, while the luckless princess was kept scandalously short of supplies. Henry certainly wished to put all the pressure possible on Ferdinand to get the dowry; perhaps he seriously contemplated marriage with Joanna as a means of himself depriving Ferdinand of control in Castile; the marriage of Charles to his daughter Mary would have a similar advantage. On the other hand, if he married Margaret of Savoy he would get control of the Netherlands, and still grasp at the control of Castile through Charles, while playing off the boy's two grandfathers, Maximilian and Ferdinand, against each other. Henry was in fact paying Ferdinand back in his own coin; but the picture is an unedifying one, of craft against craft, working by sordid methods for ends which had very little to do with patriotism and no connexion with justice.

[Sidenote: 1508 The League of Cambrai]

If, however, it was now Henry's primary object to isolate Ferdinand so that he could impose his own terms on him, the object was not attained. Maximilian had just taken up a new idea—the dismemberment of Venice; an object which appealed both to Lewis of France and to Pope Julius. Ferdinand could generally reckon that if he joined a league he would manage to get more than his share of the spoils for less than his share of the work. The League of Cambrai—a simple combination for robbery without excuse—was formed at the end of 1508. Henry was left out, for which, indeed, he cared little, knowing that the process of spoliation would inevitably result in quarrels among the leaguers. But though he advanced the arrangements for the marriage of Charles and Mary so far as to have a proxy ceremony performed, the marriage project with Joanna was withdrawn, and his overtures were also finally declined by Margaret of Savoy.

[Sidenote: Wolsey]

In the last year of his life, however, his diplomatic successor—destined to outshine him in his own field—came into employment as a negotiator. It was Thomas Wolsey who probably carried through the arrangement for the union with Charles; Wolsey also who re-established friendly relations with Scotland, which had been becoming seriously strained. In 1505 James had more definitely promised not to renew the French alliance; but had considered himself absolved from this and other obligations, on the usual ground of border raids, in which Wolsey himself admitted that the English had been very much more guilty than the Scots.

[Sidenote: 1509 Death of Henry VII.]

But Henry's own days were numbered. As a boy and as a young man he had lived a hard life; throughout the four-and-twenty years of his reign he had never been free from the strain of anxiety, never relaxed his labours, never allowed himself to cast his cares upon other shoulders. In 1508 he had a serious illness, from which he never fully recovered; in the early spring of 1509 his health finally and fatally broke down. On April 21st the founder of the Tudor dynasty and of the Tudor system left the throne, which he had won by the sword, to a son, whose right by inheritance was beyond dispute.

CHAPTER IV
HENRY VII (iv), 1485-1509—
ASPECTS OF THE REIGN

[Sidenote: 1485 Henry's position]

The task before Henry when he ascended the throne was a difficult one. He had to establish a new dynasty with a very questionable title, under conditions which could not have allowed any conceivable title to pass without risk of being challenged. It was therefore necessary for him not merely to buttress his hereditary claim by marrying the rival whose title was technically the strongest, and securing the pronouncement of Parliament in his favour, together with such adventitious sanction as a Papal Bull afforded; but further to make his subjects contented with his rule.

Two things were definitely in his favour. The old nobility who between the spirit of faction and the love of fighting had kept the country in a state of turmoil for half a century were exhausted—not merely decimated but almost wiped out; while the mass of the population was weary of war and ready to welcome almost any one who could and would provide orderly government. The country was craving to have done with anarchy.

[Sidenote: Studied legality]

A firm hand and a resolute will were thus the primary necessities; but tired as the nation was, it was still ready to resent a flagrant tyranny. The Yorkist Kings had seen that absolutism was the condition of stability; Henry perceived that, applied as they had applied it, the stability would still be wanting. He had to find a mean between the wantonly arbitrary absolutism which had been attempted a century before by Richard II. and recently by Edward IV. and Richard III. on the one hand, and on the other hand the premature application of constitutional ideas under the House of Lancaster. The actual method evolved was the concentration of all control in the hands of the King, accompanied by an ostentatious deference to the forms of procedure which were liable to be put forward as popular rights, and a very keen attention to the limits of popular endurance.

Thus Henry's first step was to summon Parliament and follow the Lancastrian precedent of obtaining its ratification of his own title to the throne. The next step, necessitated by his position, was to cut the claws of the Yorkists as a faction by striking at Richard's principal supporters. This could only be done effectively by treating them as traitors—a proceeding which could not but savour of tyranny, since they had at any rate been supporting the *de facto* King: so again Henry took the only means of minimising the arbitrary character of his action, by obtaining parliamentary sanction. Some ten years later, at the time of Perkin Warbeck's attempted landing at Deal, he procured the remarkable enactment that support of a *de facto* King should not in the future be accounted as treason to the successor who dethroned him—a measure characterised by Bacon, writing a hundred years later, as too magnanimous to be politic. In 1485 it would have been so; but at the actual time Henry was himself the *de facto* monarch; he had no wish to punish his predecessor's supporters further; and he was really providing an inducement to his subjects to be loyal to the ruling dynasty. At the same time he could pose as advocating abstract justice in preference to the prevailing practice by which he had himself profited; strengthening his own hands in fact, while in theory he was introducing into politics the recognition of an ethical principle which—as it happened—no longer conflicted with his own advantage.

[Sidenote: Policy of lenity]

In fact Henry had an unusual perception of the political uses of a judicious leniency: but the leniency was deliberate and considered. He could also strike hard, on occasion. The rebels who were taken in the fighting near Deal met with scant mercy; and a very few months earlier, the execution of the apparently trusted and powerful William Stanley had been a sharp reminder that the royal clemency could not be taken for granted. Three years later he carried severity altogether beyond the limits of justice in executing Warwick. But as a rule he was lenient to a degree which had even its dangers. Simnel was treated as of too small account to be worth punishing. Warbeck from his capture till his attempt to escape was maintained in comfort and almost in freedom. Suffolk's earlier escapades were pardoned. Kildare was repeatedly forgiven, and really converted into a loyal subject. The Cornish insurgents of the Blackheath episode were dealt with so tenderly that they took clemency for weakness. Warbeck's Cornish rising was turned conveniently to account for the replenishment of the royal treasury by the infliction of fines, but no one who had supported it could complain of harsh treatment; rather they must have felt in every case that they had been let off very easily according to all precedents.

Even when Lovel's and Simnel's risings were in actual progress, pardons were offered to such of the rebels as would make haste to repent; and there was no withdrawal of those pardons afterwards on more or less plausible pretexts, in the manner of preceding Kings and of Henry's successor after the Pilgrimage of Grace. Broadly speaking it was the King's policy to emphasise the fact that he had no intention of attempting to play the tyrant, or to vary a rash generosity by capricious blood-thirstiness, like Richard III. The sole victim of tyrannous treatment in this sense throughout the reign was the unhappy Warwick.

[Sidenote: Repression of the nobles]

But the attitude of strict conformity to law was entirely compatible with that steady concentration of all real control in the King's hands, which was the leading object of Henry's policy. For this purpose the primary condition was that none of his subjects should be sufficiently powerful to challenge his authority and raise the standard of revolt, as the King-Maker and others had done in the past. The old nobility were practically wiped out. Insignificant husbands were chosen for the daughters of York. The blood of the Plantagenets ran in the veins of the house of Buckingham; but it was only in the last generation that the De la Poles had mated with the royal house, and their estates were much diminished; the Howards had suffered as supporters of Richard. Surrey indeed was deservedly restored to grace; but no amount of personal loyalty or of royal favour exempted the nobles from the severe restriction of the old practice of maintaining retainers in such numbers as to form a working nucleus for a fighting force; nor were they allowed to accumulate wealth dangerously. Henry was well pleased that his subjects should gather sufficient riches to feel a strong interest in the maintenance of order, but not enough to use it to create disorder.

Beyond this, however, he was careful to employ the nobles as ministers no more than he could help. He laid the burdens of statesmanship as much as possible on the clergy—on Morton and Fox and Warham. Fox, as Bishop of Durham, played a part in the relations of England and Scotland at least as influential as that of Surrey. After Morton's death Warham became Chancellor. Yet each of these three bishops felt happier in the conduct of his ecclesiastical functions than as a minister of the Crown. All three did worthy and conscientious service, but would willingly have withdrawn from affairs of State. They were counsellors, not rulers; the one real ruler was the King himself.

While the King restrained the power of the nobility as military factors in the situation, he developed his own control of military force by the revival of the militia system, always theoretically in force, but practically of late displaced by the baronial levies; and his hands were further strengthened by the possession of the only train of artillery in the realm, the value of which was markedly exemplified in the suppression of the Cornish insurgents.

[Sidenote: The Star Chamber]

Another instrument in the King's hands, invaluable for the purpose of holding barons and officials in check, was the institution which came to be known as the Star Chamber. [Footnote: *Cf.* Maitland in *Social England*, vol. ii., p. 655, ed. 1902; Busch, p. 267.] Beside the development of the House of Peers as the highest court of judicature in the realm, the development of the Great Council on similar lines had long been going on. The two bodies differed somewhat in this way—that the peers had the right of summons to the former, when the judges might be called in to their assistance; whereas there were *ex officio* members of the Council who were not peers, and considerable uncertainty prevailed as to the right of peers as peers to attend the Council. The customary powers of the Council arose from the need of a court too powerful and independent to be in danger of being intimidated or bribed by influence or wealth, able to penalise gross miscarriage of justice fraudulently procured, and to take in hand cases with which the ordinary courts would have had grave difficulty in dealing. In exercising this function the Council practically came to resolve itself into a judicial committee, meeting in a room known as the Star Chamber, and its authority was regularised by Act of Parliament in 1487. Absorbing into its hands offences in the matter of "maintenance" and "livery,"—*i.e.*, broadly speaking, practices which the nobility had indulged in for the magnification of their households, and the provision of a military following—and being peculiarly subject to the royal influence, it was exceedingly useful to the King in keeping the baronage within bounds. Following, on the other hand, a procedure analogous to that of the ecclesiastical courts, unchecked by juries, and having authority to punish officers of the law whom it found guilty of illegal or corrupt practices, its influence was gradually extended, so that the fear of it guided the judgments of inferior courts. Under Henry VII., however, its functions were exercised at least mainly in the cause of justice—they were used, not abused—to the public satisfaction, as well as to the strengthening of the King's own hands. The moderation with which Henry used the powers he was accumulating concealed the latent possibility of the misuse of those same powers by a capricious or arbitrary monarch.

[Sidenote: Henry's use of Parliament]

Not less conspicuous is Henry's application of the same principles in his dealings with Parliament. He was careful, as we have seen, to secure for his own claims the sanction of the National Assembly, and to give due recognition to the authority of the estates of the realm. But he gave it no opportunity of acquiring powers of initiative, and he directed his financial policy to placing himself in such a position that he could escape that extension of its controlling powers, which naturally followed whenever a King found himself dependent on it for supplies. Throughout the first half of his reign he summoned frequent Parliaments, obtaining considerable grants on the pretext of foreign wars which were in themselves popular; but he turned the wars themselves to account by evading extensive military operations, and securing cash indemnities when peace was made. He even resorted, when a serious emergency arose, to benevolences, which were illegal; but he first secured the approval of the Council, which could still act to some degree as a substitute for Parliament when the Legislature was not in session, and he afterwards obtained the ratification of Parliament itself. By this means he obtained more than sufficient for the actual expenditure; in the meantime accumulating additional treasure by forfeitures from rebels and fines for transgression of the law. We have already observed his method of consistently resorting to pecuniary penalties as an apparently lenient form of punishment, which conveniently replenished his treasury. Thus, during the latter part of his reign, he was able to do without Parliaments almost entirely; supplementing his revenues through his agents Empson and Dudley, who made it their business to discover pretexts for enforcing fines under colour of law, and often with the flimsiest pretence of real justice.

[Sidenote: Financial exactions]

It was in this field that Henry overstepped his normal policy of not only working through the law but avoiding misuse of it. For the filling of Henry's treasury, the law was abused. The exactions of Empson and Dudley were made possible by the statute of 1495, empowering judges, upon information received, to initiate in their own courts trials of offenders who were supposed to have escaped prosecution through the corruption or intimidation of juries. Empson and Dudley being appointed judges found it an easy task to provide informers, who laid before them charges on which a case could be made out for fining the accused. In theory, of course, the King was not responsible, and the guilty judges paid the penalty with their lives early in the following reign. But the King did in fact get his full share of the discredit attaching; and perhaps his methods in this particular have been emphasised out of proportion to other traits in his character and policy by popular writers. There is some reason to doubt if Henry was ever quite fully aware of the extent to which these extortions were distortions of law; and there is no doubt at all that Empson and Dudley did not conduct their operations with a single eye to their master's benefit, but contrived to intercept ample perquisites on their own account. The statute was soon repealed under Henry VIII.

[Sidenote: Trade theories]

Modern economic theories depend for their validity on the postulates of the transferability of capital and of labour. In proportion to the limitation of the industries possible to a community, their laws apply, or fail to apply, within that community. The development of a new industry may be impossible, in the competition with established rivals, without artificial assistance—assistance given to that industry at the expense of the community at large; the preservation of an existing industry may demand like assistance. When the labour and capital employed can be transferred productively to another industry, it is obviously better that the transfer should take place, and the failing industry lapse, than that the community should be charged with maintaining an industry which cannot support itself —whether or no the competitors driving it out of the market are enabled to do so only by like extraneous assistance. When the capital and the labour cannot be transferred, but the industry can be maintained by assistance, the question becomes one of weighing the cost of maintenance to the community against the injury to the community from the collapse of the industry. Thus in any state with its commerce in the making, when the transferability of capital and labour is at best in dispute, the theory of buying in the cheapest market, wherever it is to be found, is not in favour. It is held better to raise the prices to the point at which the native product pays its native producers. In mediaeval times the foreigner was *prima facie* a person who came not to bring trade but to appropriate it. Hence he was subjected to regulations, limitations and charges for permission to carry on his operations. The next stage is reached when reciprocal free trade is recognised as an advantage and mutual concessions are made, restrictions and duties becoming, so to speak, implements of war, often enough proving two-edged.

[Sidenote: Henry's commercial policy]

Henry VII. was not an economist far in advance of the theories of his age; but economic considerations, as they were then understood, carried much more weight, and generally played a much larger part in his policy than was customary with the king-craft of the times, or with state-craft outside the commercial republic of Venice, the commercial association of German Free cities known as the Hansa or Hanseatic League, and the Netherlands. Accordingly we find him using every available means to obtain a footing in fresh foreign markets for the main English products of his day—wool and woollen goods; to secure for English merchants the rights and privileges which would enable them to compete on equal terms with the foreigner, and to curtail those privileges of the foreigner in England. In the matter of wool, the primacy of the English article was so thoroughly established that little extraneous aid was required. But with manufactured woollen goods the case was different, since the Flemings held the lead; and shipping also demanded artificial encouragement—first, because it was necessary to enterprise in the development of the export trade, at present largely carried on in foreign bottoms; second, because the King was, at least to some extent, alive to the strategic uses of a fleet which could be requisitioned for war purposes.

[Sidenote: The Netherlands trade]

The great mart for English wool was the Netherlands, whose manufacturing business required the raw product: the Netherlanders were more dependent on England than the English were on them. Hence this trade was used by Henry throughout his reign as a political lever—a means to political ends rather than an end in itself. If his own subjects suffered from a customs war, Philip's suffered more. So long as Burgundy made trouble on behalf of Perkin Warbeck the battle went on. In 1496 Philip gave up the contest, and the *Intercursus Magnus* followed. Soon after the beginning of the new century the fight was renewed, to be terminated by what the Flemings called the *Intercursus Malus*, an arrangement so one-sided and pressing so hard on them that its terms were practically impossible of fulfilment; and Henry assented to their modification before his death, partly with a view to overcoming the reluctance of Margaret of Savoy to accept his matrimonial overtures.

[Sidenote: The Hansa]

When Henry came to the throne, he found the export trade mainly in the hands of two foreign groups—the Hansa, who had acquired privileges in England which they did not reciprocate, and the Venetians, who held their own without privileges by superior commercial acuteness—and of two English groups, the Merchants of the Staple, who controlled the wool markets, and the Merchant Adventurers, who were mainly interested in the manufactured goods. The King therefore followed a consistent policy of straining, in a restrictive sense, the interpretation of the concessions made to the Hansa, of emphasising grievances against them and of pressing for counter- privileges; and he successfully negotiated with Denmark in 1489 a commercial treaty, which interfered with the Hansa monopoly of the Scandinavian trade, by placing English merchants on a competitive footing with them. In a similar manner, he brought pressure to bear on the Venetians by opening direct relations with the Florentines at their port of Pisa. It is curious to note incidentally that the export dues on raw wool were enormously heavier than those on the manufactured goods; the difference being made in order to encourage the home sale of the wool and to stimulate the home manufacture by this means, as well as by encouraging the foreign sale of the manufactured goods. It is also observable that when an attempt was made by the London merchants to capture the worsted trade, Henry nipped it in the bud. It was no part of his policy to allow corporations—any more than individuals—to become powerful enough to demand terms for their political support.

[Sidenote: The Navigation Acts]

Recognising, as we saw, the commercial advantage to England of doing her own carrying trade and of multiplying ships and seamen, Henry—tentatively at first, but with increasing confidence—adopted artificial methods of encouraging this branch of industry, at the expense of free competition. Very early in the reign a Navigation Act required that goods shipped for England from certain foreign ports should be embarked on English vessels, during a specified period. Then the Act was renewed for a longer period, and finally without a time limit, and with more extended application. A great impetus was given to English shipping, with momentous results which can hardly have entered into Henry's calculations. He could not have anticipated the vast extensions of empire which were to be the prize of the nations with ocean-going navies, with the ocean itself for the great battlefield; or even the extent to which commerce and naval preponderance were destined to go hand in hand. The monopoly of the States with a Mediterranean sea-board was coming to an end.

[Sidenote: Voyages of discovery]

Yet it was in his reign that the vast change was initiated. In 1492 Christopher Columbus made his great voyage: in 1497 Vasco da Gama sailed for India, not westwards but southwards and eastwards round the Cape of Good Hope. Ten years later, Albuquerque was founding a Portuguese Empire in the Indian seas. Spain and Portugal, pioneers of the great movement, led the way, one in the new world of the West, the other in the fabled world of the East; where for many a year to come they were to divide a monopoly authorised by the Papal Bull of Alexander VI. Before another century closed, their dominion was to be challenged by England grown mighty and by Holland emancipated. As yet, however, men dreamed only formless if gorgeous dreams of what the unknown realms might bring forth. England played no very large part in these early voyages. Christopher Columbus, craving to discover a westerly route to the Indies, and failing of Portuguese support, sent his brother Bartholomew to petition the English King for aid; but Bartholomew was captured by pirates. Ultimately he reached England, but before he could achieve his purpose, Christopher had found other helpers; the prize fell to Ferdinand and Isabella. The first historic expedition which sailed from English ports was captained not by an Englishman but by another Italian, John Cabot, and his son Sebastian, in 1497. The Cabots were Venetians who had for some time been established at Bristol. They aimed for a north-west passage, and found Labrador and Newfoundland, cold, inhospitable, producing no wealth: the explorers who sailed under Spanish auspices struck the wealthy and entrancing regions of the south. There was little enough material inducement beyond the simple spirit of enterprise to attract capital to expend itself in aid of the Bristol men who followed in the wake of Cabot. Henry deserves full credit for the encouragement and actual pecuniary help which he rendered at first, and no blame for its discontinuation. The daring of the adventurers was but ill repaid for the time; yet a mighty harvest was to be reaped by England in the days to come.

[Sidenote: The rural revolution]

If England, however, did not for more than half a century turn the new discoveries to material account, wealth and prosperity did increase greatly in the towns, and the country recovered her lost position among the commercial nations—partly from Henry's policy directed to that end, partly from the comparatively settled conditions of life which gradually prevailed. In the agricultural districts, however, this was hardly the case, owing to the increasing tendency to substitute pasture for cultivation. The country had no difficulty in producing sufficient for its own consumption; and the development of the woollen manufacture made sheep-farming in particular much more lucrative. But sheep-farming called for the employment of many fewer hands; proprietors dispossessed small tenants to make large sheep-runs; migration from the rural districts to the nascent manufacturing centres was not a simple matter; and thus there was no little distress, and a great multiplication of beggars and vagabonds. The monasteries, which in the past had been progressive farmers, had degenerated into landlords easy-going indeed but without enterprise. The wealth of the gentry increased, but unemployment increased also, and labour at the same time became cheaper. The evil was to a great extent realised; in the Isle of Wight, which was rapidly becoming depopulated, an attempt was made to improve matters by limiting the size of farms; the heavy export duties on raw wool were doubtless intended actually to restrict the output as well as to divert it to English rather than foreign manufacturers; but since this did not effectively check the growing demand at home, the production of wool remained so lucrative that it continued to be more attractive than cultivation. Attempts were made to transfer labour from agriculture to manufacture by interfering with, the restrictions imposed by the trade-guilds (which always aimed at making themselves close bodies), the object of such legislation being quite as much to prevent idleness as to relieve distress. Nevertheless, the evil grew. Sir Thomas More in his introduction to the *Utopia*, written early in the next reign, gives a vigorous sketch of the prevalent vagabondage just before the death of Cardinal Morton, adding to the causes above mentioned the number of lackeys employed by the wealthy who when dismissed became a useless burden on the community. He also charges the land-owners, expressly including many abbots and others of the clergy, with causing depopulation and misery by forcing up rents. From him too as well as from other sources we learn of the frequency of crimes of violence, attributed by him to the reckless employment of the death penalty for minor offences, encouraging the fugitive criminal—already doomed if caught—to take life without hesitation.

[Sidenote: The Church]

To a certain extent, then, we have to note among the causes of change in rural districts the failure of the monasteries to discharge their old function of agricultural leadership. In other respects, also, these communities had fallen from the high standards of earlier days. Discipline was lax. Visitations instituted by Cardinal Morton revealed the presence of gross immorality, not only among the very small houses, but in so great an institution as the Abbey of St. Albans, where the highest officials were guilty of the gravest misbehaviour; and the correspondence seems to imply that the disapprobation was by no means in proportion to the offences, from which it is fair to infer that no high standard was normally expected. The most to be looked for was an absence of flagrant misconduct. The clergy were much more particular about ceremonial observances and ecclesiastical privileges than about the morals either of themselves or of their flocks. But as yet there was no sign of a coming Reformation. Lollardry, it is true, had never been killed; its anti-clerical propaganda was by no means inactive. But it worked beneath the surface, and could not be taken to indicate an approaching convulsion. The greatest Churchmen of the day, Morton, Warham and Fox, were absorbed—albeit reluctantly—in affairs of State. Blameless, even austere in their own lives, patrons of learning, sincerely pious, they lacked the Reformer's passion, without which it was vain to combat the *vis inertiae*; generated by long years of clerical sloth, and of the formalism by which the highest Mysteries were vulgarly distorted into superstitions and Faith into ceremonial observances.

[Sidenote: Henry and Rome]

The first Tudor himself was a pious man, as piety was reckoned: punctual in observances, commended and complimented by Popes. His chapel in Westminster Abbey is evidence of his zeal in one direction; he gave alms with a business-like regard to their post-mortem efficacy. Throughout his reign the Popes made much talk of a new crusade, and Henry seems to have been the one European monarch who took the idea seriously. It is true that when Alexander VI. appealed in 1500 for funds to that end, the English King preferred to be excused; but the polite irony of his refusal was more than justified by his confidence that if the Pope got the money it would not be expended for the benefit of Christendom; moreover, he did actually hand over four thousand pounds. In fact, he took the Church as he found it. There was but one almost infinitesimal curtailment of ecclesiastical privileges in his reign, necessitated by political considerations and accepted by the Pope, whereby the right of Sanctuary was withdrawn in cases of treason.

[Sidenote: Learning and letters]

Practically it is only in the beginnings of an educational revival that we find promise of the dawn of a new order. It was in Henry's reign that the study of Greek, and with it the new criticism, began to establish itself. Grocyn and Linacre led the way. In the last decade of the century John Colet was lecturing at Oxford, the apostle of the new learning on its religious side; calling his pupils to the study of the Scriptures themselves, rather than of the schoolmen or doctors of the Church; treating them as organic treatises, not as collections of texts. There he won the friendship of young Thomas More; thither on flying visits came Erasmus twice. Colet, made Dean of St. Paul's about 1505, continued to carry on his educational work as the founder of the famous St. Paul's School; winning renown also as a great preacher and a fearless moralist; a man of rich learning, of a reverent enthusiasm, of a splendid sincerity, of a noble simplicity; the prophet of much that was best, and of nothing that was not best, in the coming Reformation.

But during Henry's reign Colet's figure is almost the only one—apart from such representatives of erudition and scholarship as Grocyn and Linacre— which stands forth holding out a promise of intellectual and moral progress. In effect there was no literature; in this respect Scotland was in advance of England with the verse of William Dunbar. More's *Utopia* was still unwritten. When Henry died the Universities had not yet, or had only just, received within their portals the men who were to fight the theological battle of the Reformation. More than half a century was to pass before the splendid sunrise of the Shakespearian era.

It has hardly, perhaps, been the custom to render full justice to the founder of the Tudor dynasty. His reign is stamped with a character sordid and unattractive. There is no romance in it, no clashing of arms, no valiant deeds, no suggestion of the heroic. The King's enemies are, for the most part, contemptible persons; the King himself is a cold-blooded, long-headed ruler, merciful indeed, but from policy, not from generosity, and of a meanness in money matters very far from royal. Yet he was not without virtues. He was not unjust; he was a statesman more loyal to his pledges than most of his contemporaries or their successors. He gave something like order and rest to a distracted land, and raised her again to a position at least respectable among the nations, securing himself on a most unstable throne without resorting to the usual methods of the tyrant. Had he died when Morton died, the baser aspects of his reign would never have achieved so unlovely a prominence as they have done.

The truth is, indeed, that judged by the first half of his reign alone Henry might have been numbered among the princes with a title to be regarded almost with affection. It is only in the light of the later years that even his financial policy really assumes a mean aspect, though occasionally it came perilously near what may be called sharp practice—and the excuse was great, seeing that a full treasury was an absolutely necessary condition of establishing the new rule. The imprisonment of Warwick was an act of palpable injustice, yet the risk of letting him go free would have been enormous. In another ruler than Henry, the leniency which we attribute to astute policy would have been freely described as surprising magnanimity. He never betrayed a loyal servant. His genuine appreciation of the true spirit of chivalry was shown when he took Surrey [Footnote: Surrey, the son of "Jockey of Norfolk," Richard's supporter, was imprisoned in the Tower. At the time of Simnel's insurrection his gaoler offered to let him escape, but he refused, saying that the King had sent him to confinement, and only from the King would he accept release.] from the Tower to entrust him with high command in the North. The luckless Lady Katharine Gordon, the wife of Perkin Warbeck, was treated with remarkable courtesy and liberality. There was even a genial humour in the King's behaviour to Kildare. His own marriage he doubtless looked upon as a purely political affair; but while his wife lived his loyalty to his marriage vow is in strong contrast to the general licentiousness of the princes of his day; and the picture of Henry and Elizabeth striving in turn to comfort each other on Prince Arthur's death, as recorded by a contemporary, [Footnote: Gairdner, *Chron.*, i., p. 36; Leland's *Collectanea*, v., p, 373.] can hardly be fitted on to the conception of Henry as a man almost without the more tender feelings of humanity.

[Sidenote: Deterioration after 1499]

Yet all this is forgotten or discoloured by reason of the ugly picture of those later days when Morton and Prince Arthur and Elizabeth were gone. It seems, indeed, as though a certain moral deterioration had set in from the time when Henry made up his mind to do violence to his conscience by making away with Warwick in 1499. Morton, his wisest counsellor, of whom More gives a most attractive portrait in the *Utopia*, died the next year; Arthur, whom he loved, in the spring of 1502; Elizabeth, always a refining and softening influence, within a twelvemonth of Arthur. To these latter years belong almost entirely the extortions of Empson and Dudley; the harsh treatment of Katharine of Aragon, a helpless hostage in his hands; the revolting proposal for a union with the crazy Joanna of Castile. This view is further borne out when we observe that in these years also his political foresight degenerates into craftiness, personal animosities playing a larger part. The intellectual falling off is hardly less marked than the moral. For the personal repute of a King who was almost, if not quite, one of the great, it is to be regretted that his last years have cast a permanent cloud over a reign which emphatically made for the good of the nation over which he ruled.

CHAPTER V
HENRY VIII (i), 1509-27—EGO ET REX MEUS

[Sidenote: Europe in 1509]

Roughly speaking, the forty years preceding the accession of Henry VIII. had witnessed the birth of modern Europe. The old feudal conception of Christendom had passed away: the modern conception of organic States had taken its place. The English Kings had for some time ceased to hold sway in France, whether as claimants to the throne or as great feudatories. France herself had become a united and aggressive nation; the fusion of the Spanish monarchies was almost completed: the Emperor was no longer regarded as the titular secular head of Christendom, but was virtually the chief of a loose Germanic confederation. The Turk, finally established in Eastern Europe, was shortly to find himself regarded as a possible ally of Christian Powers; Christendom still reckoned the Pope as its spiritual head, but the cataclysm was already preparing; and the enterprise of daring seamen had but just rent the veils that had hidden from the nations of Europe the boundless possibilities of a new world in the West and an ancient world in the East, converting the pathless ocean into the great Highway.

[Sidenote: England's position in Europe]

Since the death of the conqueror Henry V., England herself had been rent and torn by internal broils. For many a long year she had taken but little share in the affairs of Europe. But it had been the part of the first Tudor King to win for her breathing time; to secure a period for rest and internal recuperation, which should fit her to hold her own in the counsels of Europe should her interests demand it. The civil broils were ended; trade had revived; wealth had been accumulating. Henry had not sought military glory, but he had played the game of diplomacy with acuteness and finesse. When he ascended the throne, the princes of Europe had regarded England as a Power that might safely be neglected unless she could be used as a cat's-paw; but before he died they had learned that they could no longer negotiate with him except on equal terms. In a sense, perhaps, it is true that England was still reckoned as no more than a third-rate [Footnote: *Cf.* Brewer, *Reign of Henry VIII.*, i., p.3; Creighton, *Wolsey*, p. 11. The estimate, however, seems to be rather the outcome of an inclination to magnify Wolsey's achievement.] power, since her military prestige had fallen and the chances of its restoration were untested, while her interests would not naturally lead her into active participation in European complications; but she had at least achieved sufficient importance for the Powers to desire her favour rather than her ill-will, and for herself to be able to put a price on her support when it was asked.

[Sidenote: The new King]

So far, however, it was rather respect for the personal ability of Henry VII. than a high estimate of the English nation that had secured the English position; and when the astute old monarch was succeeded on the throne by a frank, high-spirited lad of eighteen, the Princes of Europe flattered themselves that England would revert to the position of a cat's-paw. From this point of view the first beginnings of the reign were promising. Europe, however, was soon to be undeceived; to discover that the young King had an unfailing eye for a capable minister, a sincere devotion to his own interests, and an unparalleled power of reconciling the dictates of desire and conscience.

At home, circumstances combined to render Henry extraordinarily popular. Handsome, endowed with a magnificent physique, a first-rate performer in all manly exercises, gifted with many accomplishments, scholar enough to be proud of his scholarship, open of hand, frank and genial of manner, with a boyish delight in his endowments and a boyish enthusiasm for chivalric ideals, all English hearts rejoiced in his accession. The scholars looked forward to a Saturnian age; his martial ardour fired the hopes of the fighting men; the populace hailed with joy a King who began his rule by striking down the agents of extortion to whom he owed the wealth inherited from his economical sire. Henry in fact was blessed with the most valuable of all possessions for a ruler of men, a magnetic personality, which made his servants ready to go through fire and water, to stifle conscience, to forgo their own convictions at his bidding.

When he ascended the throne, however, none had the glimmering of a suspicion whither that imperious will was to direct the destinies of the nation: his earliest acts gave little indication of the later developments of his character and policy.

[Sidenote: 1509 Marriage]

His first step was to complete the marriage with Katharine of Aragon, to whom he had been betrothed, under the papal dispensation, on the death of his elder brother, her husband. It is not without interest to note, in view of a plea put forward against the "divorce" in later years, that the bride was arrayed for the wedding as one who was not a widow but a maiden. Shortly afterwards Empson and Dudley, his father's unpopular agents, were brought to the block after attainder on a not very credible charge of treason, [Footnote: Brewer, i., p. 44; *L. & P.*, i., 1212.] since the misdeeds of which they had been guilty could hardly be construed into capital offences.

Now, however, events on the Continent were to offer a field for Henry's ambitions, and incidentally to disillusion, at least in part, his young enthusiasms.

[Sidenote: The Powers: 1509-12]

The three great Powers—France, Spain, and the Empire—which had been evolved out of the mediaeval European system, were united in the desire of preventing Italy from following their example and consolidating into a nation. Venice, as the one Italian State strong enough to have some chance of combining the rest under her leadership, was the object not only of their jealousy but also of the Pope's. A few months before the death of Henry VII., these four combined in the League of Cambrai, for the dismemberment of Venice. The allies, however, were not guided in their actions by any altruistic motives—any excessive regard for the interests of their associates. The French King, Lewis XII., by prompt and skilful action, made himself master of the north of Italy before the rest were ready to move. This was by no means to the taste of Ferdinand or of Pope Julius; but as yet Maximilian had seen no reason to be displeased. Ferdinand would not risk a quarrel with Maximilian, which might have led to that monarch's interference in Castile on behalf of the boy Charles—his grandson as well as Ferdinand's— the nominal King of that portion of what Ferdinand looked on as his own dominions. So the crafty old King bided his time, dropping a quiet hint to young Henry in England that a moment might be approaching favourable to an English attack on France, in revival of the ancient claim to the crown, or at any rate to Guienne.

Henry, as yet unskilled in the tortuous diplomacy of his father-in-law, was well content to be guided by his advice. Ferdinand intrigued to unite Julius and Maximilian against France, and to shift the burden of battle, when it should come, off his own shoulders on to Henry's. Meantime, the outward professions to France remained of the most amicable character.

[Sidenote: 1512 Dorset's expedition]

Then Lewis made a blunder which gave his enemies their opening. He called a General Council at Pisa which was in effect an attack on the spiritual authority of Rome. By the end of 1510, Julius was at open war with the French King; Ferdinand was in alliance with the Pope; in the course of the next year, the Holy League was formed; a combined attack was concerted; and in June, 1512, an English expedition, under the command of Lord Dorset, landed in Spain, on the theory that it was to be assisted by Ferdinand in the conquest of Guienne.

The expedition was a melancholy failure. The English troops and their commander were alike inexperienced in war; Ferdinand would not move against Guienne, urging with some plausibility that the securing of Navarre was a needful preliminary; the soldiers wanted beer and had to put up with Spanish wines; finally they insisted on returning to England, and Dorset had to put the best face he could on a very awkward situation. Officially it was announced that the withdrawal was made with Ferdinand's approval.

So far, the European anticipations of England's incapacity had been duly fulfilled. A military fiasco had accompanied an innocence of diplomatic guile which looked promising to the Continental rulers. But the promise was to be disappointed.

[Sidenote: Rise of Wolsey]

Henry VII. had avoided war and had been his own foreign minister; when he died, he left to form his son's Council some capable subordinates like Fox the Bishop of Winchester, but no one experienced in the responsibilities of control. Among the noble houses, the Howards were shortly to display at least a fair share of military capacity. But it was to a minister of at best middle-class origin, a rising ecclesiastic who had, however, hitherto held no office of the first rank, that England was to owe a surprisingly rapid promotion to European equality with the first-class Powers.

With that skill in selecting; invaluable servants which distinguished his entire career, Henry VIII. by the time he was one-and-twenty had already discovered in Thomas Wolsey the man on whose native genius and unlimited power of application he could place complete reliance.

Wolsey had been employed on diplomatic missions by the old King; whose methods he had gauged and whose policy he had assimilated, but only as a basis for far-reaching developments. He was brought into the Royal Council by Fox, partly no doubt in the hope that he would counteract the influence of Thomas Howard, Earl of Surrey, and others of the nobles who were martially inclined and imbued with a time-honoured hostility to France. It was no long time before he outshone his patron, who, however, had rightly judged his tendencies. Wolsey was no friend to war, and had no hostility to France, for the plain reason that he preferred diplomatic to military methods, and was quite as well pleased to advance English interests by alliance with France as by alliances against her if he saw his way to profit thereby. It is probable enough that he would have avoided the war with

France if he had had the power; since he had not, he devoted his energies to making the war itself as successful as possible.

[Sidenote: 1513 The French war]

The arrangements for the Guienne expedition had not unnaturally been singularly defective. Wolsey devoted himself with untiring zeal to the organisation of a new expedition in the following spring. Nothing was left to chance over which it was possible for one man's energy to exercise supervision. The first outcome was a naval engagement off Brest on 25th April, wherein the English admiral, Sir Edward Howard, restored at least the English reputation for valour, falling—overwhelmed by numbers—on the deck of the French flag-ship which he had boarded almost single-handed. The French fleet was much larger than that of the English, and the attack on it which he led was a desperate enterprise in which his ships were beaten off; but those who had jeered at the failure in Guienne were silenced, and Henry was enabled to land his troops undisturbed at Calais at the end of June. Both the King and Wolsey were with the army, and proceeded to lay siege, on 1st August, to Terouenne, which was partially re-victualled by the bold dash of a relief party of horsemen through the besieger's lines. Here the besiegers were shortly joined by a contingent under Maximilian (who professed himself a mere volunteer under the English King). The advancing French array was put to complete rout in the "battle of the Spurs"—the consequence of a sudden panic—and on August 22nd Terouenne surrendered. Tournai followed suit a month later.

In the meantime, events of moment had been taking place on the Scottish border.

[Sidenote: Scotland 1499-1513]

James IV., as we have seen, had by no means been on continuously good terms with Henry VII., and had lent a good deal more than merely moral support to the pretensions of Perkin Warbeck. At the close of the adventurer's active career in the end of 1497, a treaty was made between England and Scotland which was to remain in force till a year after the death of either monarch; and there were further treaties when James married Margaret Tudor in 1503. On the other hand, James had always maintained the traditional alliance with France, and in 1507 had declined the papal invitation to enter the league then formed to resist French aggression. Since the accession of Henry VIII., the relations between the two countries had been exceedingly strained. There were personal quarrels about jewels retained in England which James claimed for his wife. Scottish sea-captains had been treated as pirates by the English authorities. Henry, having joined the league against France, wished to patch up the quarrel with James; James, incited by the French, would not make friends with the active enemy of France; the French Queen sent him a message bidding him strike a blow on English ground as her knight. West, [Footnote: Brewer, *Henry VIII.*, p.29. *L & P.*, i., 1926, 3128, 3129, 3811, 3838, 3882.] the English ambassador, gives a highly uncomplimentary account of James's bearing at this time, but his evidence may be coloured. At any rate, there can have been little doubt in James's mind that a successful war with France would leave Henry ready to make himself extremely unpleasant to Scotland, even though he might not patently set the treaty aside; and for himself there was a degree of obligation to help France when she came to open hostilities with England; while Henry's instructions to West are hardly consistent with a character for stainless and unassailable honour. [Footnote: *Cf.* Lang, *Hist. Scot.*, i., p.375; commenting on Brewer, *Henry VIII.*, pp.28, 29 *q.v.*]

[Sidenote: 1513 James invades England (Aug.)]

At any rate, the conclusion of the matter was that when Henry sailed for Calais, James soon made up his mind, with the support of most of the nobility, to declare war, and sent Henry his defiance—as he had promised West to do before opening hostilities. On 22nd August he was in England at the head of a great army; by the end of the month, Norham Castle, Ford, and other strongholds were in his hands. [Footnote: *Cf.* Lang, *Hist. Scot.*, i., p. 377.] Thereafter, he entrenched himself on Flodden Ridge, and awaited the approach of the English army.

Queen Katharine and the Earl of Surrey had been left in charge at home when the King with Wolsey and Fox also crossed the channel. To the Queen's energy the successful results were in no small degree due, as well as to the military skill and audacity of the Howards, and to James's reckless disregard of strategical and tactical principles.

Had the Scottish monarch held to his plans, his campaign could hardly have failed to be successful. His army was large, and well victualled; his position on Flodden Edge was exceedingly strong; he had secured the fortresses which might otherwise have threatened him on flank or rear. His object was to entice the English commander, Surrey, away from his base, and force him to fight at a disadvantage, or to see his levies melt away, for lack of provisions. Surrey, advancing from Alnwick to Wooler, tried to inveigle him into descending from the Ridge to the open plain, but James was not to be tempted.

[Sidenote: Flodden (Sept.)]

Eastward of Flodden the Till flows north to join the Tweed. Surrey put the Till between himself and the Scottish army, and marched north, his movement masked by hills on his left, with the intention of reaching

Berwick, or of threatening the Scottish communications. Arrived at Barmoor Wood, the Admiral, Thomas Howard, Surrey's son, proposed to march west, cross the Till, and move south again, threatening the rear of James's position. The operation, involving a very hard march, was carried out. The main army crossed at Twizel Mill, the rearguard fording the stream as high up as Sandyford; the junction being effected behind Branxton Marsh. The passage of the troops might easily have been prevented; but James, very inefficiently served in scouting, knew nothing of what was going on. When the approach of the English became known, he suddenly resolved to descend and give battle [Footnote: The traditions concerning the King and the old Earl of Angus on this occasion have been very untenderly handled by Mr. Andrew Lang, *Hist. Scot.*, 1., p. 390.] on the plain, instead of remaining in his almost impregnable position. So on the afternoon of September 9th was fought the bloody and decisive battle of Flodden. Of the two armies, the Scottish was probably the larger; but the English captains had their troops better in hand than the border lords on the Scottish left, or the highland chiefs on their right. After fierce fighting, the Scottish wings were broken, and the Scottish centre was completely enveloped. There, headed by the King, fought the pick of the Scottish chivalry. The stand made was magnificent, the slaughter appalling. The English victory this time was one not of the bow—as so often before—but of the bill or axe against the spears in which the northern nation trusted. By hewing away the spearheads, the English disabled their opponents; yet they fought on, till man by man they fell around their monarch. The King himself, brave as any man on the field, was slain; in the ring of his dead companions in arms were found the bodies of thirteen earls, three bishops, and many valiant lords. There were few families in Scotland which did not contribute to that hecatomb, whereof the memory is enshrined in the national song of lamentation, "The Flowers of the Forest".

[Effects of Flodden]

For many a long year the military power of Scotland was broken on the black day of Flodden. From that quarter Henry was to have no more serious fears. Great and decisive, however, as Surrey's [Footnote: Surrey was rewarded with the Dukedom of Norfolk, held by his father. Accordingly, after this he becomes "Norfolk," and his son Thomas becomes "Surrey". In 1524 the son succeeded to the Dukedom, and is the "Norfolk" of the latter half of the reign, the "Surrey" of its last years being his son Henry.] triumph was, the English also had paid a heavy price, and were unable to follow up victory by invasion. But Scotland had not only lost the best and bravest of her sons; the King's death left the Crown to a babe not eighteen months old, and the government of the country to the babe's mother, Margaret, the sister of Henry VIII., and to a group of nobles, to whose personal feuds and rivalries, constantly fomented by English diplomacy, the interests of the Scottish nation were completely subordinated.

[Sidenote: Recovery of English prestige]

The year 1513 had completely restored the reputation of the English arms. The sea-fight off Brest, the successes at Terouenne and Tournai, and, finally, the great victory of Flodden, proved beyond dispute that Englishmen only needed to be well led to show themselves as indomitable as ever they had been in the past. The march of 8th and 9th September immediately before Flodden was a feat which not many commanders would have cared to attempt, and few troops could have carried out. And it had become evident that generalship was not, after all, a lost art. It was now time for Europe to discover that England, habitually inferior to other nations in the arts of diplomacy, possessed in Wolsey a diplomatist of the highest order. The old King had indeed been as little susceptible to the beguilement of fair promises, as shrewd in detecting his neighbours' designs, little less capable of concealing his own, little less tenacious in pursuing them; but his designs themselves had not the amplitude of Wolsey's, who shewed all Henry's skill combined with a far greater audacity in execution, commensurate with the greater audacity and scope of his conceptions. Wolsey was one of those statesmen, rare in England, who for half a generation aimed, with a large measure of success, at dominating the combinations of the European Powers without involving the country in any tremendous war.

[Sidenote: 1514 Foreign intrigues]

Before the winter of 1513 Henry VIII. returned to England, with every intention of following up his successes in the French war in the ensuing year. The campaign, however, had not been at all to the liking of Ferdinand, who gained nothing by the English victories in the north-west. These tended to strengthen his grandson Charles in the Netherlands, where Maximilian's influence over him was stronger; while Ferdinand was bent above all things on maintaining his own control over the boy, and by consequence over Castile. So Ferdinand set about making his own peace privily with France, and trying to draw off Maximilian so as to isolate Henry. In April, 1514, he accomplished his object, and a truce was declared between Ferdinand, the Emperor, and France.

In mid-winter Henry had been struck down by small-pox; he recovered to find these intrigues in active progress, and was highly indignant. His martial projects were, of course, thrown entirely out of gear. Ferdinand, however, had found his match. The English King, when the dictates of his personal interests, translated into terms of conscience, did not obscure the issues at stake, had an acute perception of political expediency, untrammelled by the traditional sentiment which biased the judgment of advisers of the type of Surrey (now raised to the Dukedom of Norfolk). It was Wolsey who swayed his counsels, and Wolsey perceived in an alliance with France an effective alternative to the collapsed alliance against her.

[Sidenote: Policy of French alliance]

No sooner had he detected the intrigues of Ferdinand than he set his counterplot on foot through the medium of the Duc de Longueville, who had been taken prisoner at the battle of the Spurs and sent over to England. The death of the French Queen, Anne of Brittany, gave him a convenient opening as early as January.

Throughout this century, as in the reign of Henry VII., royal betrothals and royal marriages play an immense part in international negotiations: princesses are the shuttlecocks of statesmen. This particular form of diplomatic recreation now springs again into sudden prominence.

[Sidenote 1: The French marriage]
[Sidenote 2: 1515 Francis I]

Henry's younger sister Mary was plighted to the young Charles of Castile and the Netherlands, who was to marry her in the ensuing summer; he being now fourteen, and she about seventeen. The boy's two grandfathers, now both disposed to leave England detached and isolated, began finding excuses for deferring the match. Wolsey pressed them, while secretly negotiating for Mary's marriage with Lewis of France. Thus when his plans were ripe, and not before, he found himself able to declare that the breach was entirely the fault of the other side, whose objects were frustrated by the new alliance, which had not entered into their reckoning. There was no further prospect of keeping France and England embroiled while they appropriated the spoils. Mary was married to the French King in October, and Henry was certainly projecting, in conjunction with him, an aggressive movement against his former allies, on the plea that his wife Katharine shared with her sister the succession to Castile, when the tangible results of the marriage were nullified by the death on January 1st of Lewis, and the succession to the French throne of his cousin Francis I., a prince who was some years younger than Henry himself, and quite as much athirst for military glory.

Again diplomacy intrigued about the person of Lewis's widow. Charles Brandon, [Footnote: Edmund de la Pole, Earl of Suffolk in the last reign, and Yorkist intriguer, was executed, apparently without further trial, in 1513. The Dukedom of Suffolk was bestowed on Brandon whom Mr. Froude's imagination has somehow developed into "the ablest soldier of the age," but he never did anything to justify a high estimate of his abilities.] Duke of Suffolk, an intimate personal friend of Henry's and a stout man-at-arms, who was also personally devoted to the Princess Mary, was selected by Wolsey as a better negotiator than one of the anti-French party. Henry and Francis were both keen hands at a bargain, and there was serious trouble as to Mary's dower and the financial arrangements connected with her return. Francis gained his purposes by alarming Mary and at the same time encouraging Suffolk to marry her out of hand; which he did, secretly. After that, there could be no more talk of Mary's dowry being repaid; and Henry had to content himself with making heavy demands on Suffolk's purse. The event is of further significance, because Henry at present had no offspring, and the young King of Scotland, son of his sister Margaret, was heir presumptive to the throne; whereas if his younger sister Mary should have children, it was certain that there would be a party to support their claim in preference to that of the Scottish monarch. In fact, ultimately, Mary's grandchild Lady Jane Grey was actually put up as a claimant to the throne.

[Sidenote: Marignano (Sept.)]

The general effect however was, that Francis drew away from the English alliance, and associated himself more closely with Ferdinand; having Italian conquests and more particularly Milan in view. In the summer he set out, crossed the Alps with unexpected success, and in September won the great victory of Marignano, routing the Swiss troops which had hitherto been reputed invincible. Such triumphant progress however was more than the other monarchs or the Pope, Leo X., had reckoned for, and there was a rapid and general reaction in favour of checking the French King's career. The inflation of the power of France was satisfactory to no one else; but incidentally the effect was not disadvantageous to Wolsey, since it forced Pope Leo into an attitude of compliance with English demands in order to secure English support, with the result that Wolsey was raised to the Cardinalate, having recently been made Archbishop of York. "The Cardinal of York" is the title by which he is named in official references from this time (Nov., 1515).

Here it may be noted that a daughter, afterwards Queen Mary, was born to the King early in 1516. Before this time, two sons at least—according to some authorities no fewer than four—had been born, but had died either at birth or shortly after.

[Sidenote: 1516-17 European changes]

During the winter, Wolsey—having no wish to plunge England into war— persuaded Maximilian (by means of a very able diplomatic agent, Richard Pace) to take up arms against Francis in Italy. As a rule, Maximilian took sides with any one whose gold he expected to divert into his own pocket; but Pace managed to keep the English subsidies, which were to pay the Swiss Mercenaries, out of the Emperor's hands; so the Emperor retired from the war in the spring. Early in this year, too, Ferdinand died, leaving Charles lord of all Spain as well as of the Netherlands. This left the young King to the guidance of advisers whose interests were mainly Flemish, and who were consequently anxious in the first place for the friendship of France. Hence in August the treaty of Noyon was contracted between Francis and Charles; in which the Emperor shortly afterwards joined when he found that England would not provide him with funds unless he earned them. Wolsey's real strength lay in the fact that neither Maximilian nor Charles could afford any serious expenditure without his financial support; Francis was waking up to the fact that as allies they were both broken reeds, though in active combination with Wolsey against him they would be dangerous; and as the year 1517 passed, the inclination for France and England to revert to amicable relations revived; becoming more marked in the following year when the birth of a dauphin suggested his betrothal to the little Princess Mary.

[Sidenote: 1518-19 Wolsey's success]

During these two years, the reality of Wolsey's control of the situation was further demonstrated by his management of the Pope, who refused him the office of legate after having reluctantly made him Cardinal. Leo however, like other Princes, was in want of cash, and sent legates to the European Courts to raise funds under colour of a crusade: whereupon Henry declined to admit Cardinal Campeggio to England, on the ground that to receive a legate *a latere* was against the rule of the realm. Wolsey seized the opportunity to suggest that if he himself, being an English prelate, were placed on the same official footing as Campeggio, the objection might be withdrawn; and Leo had to agree.

In the result, an alliance was concluded with France under which the infants were betrothed, Tournai was restored to France. France was to pay 60,000 crowns and promise not to interfere in Scottish affairs to the detriment of England, and Wolsey was enabled to pose as the pacificator of Europe; the other Powers with more or less reluctance all finding themselves constrained to give their adherence to the new treaty of Universal Peace.

Thus when the year 1519 opened, Wolsey's policy was triumphant. France was bound to England; the young King of Spain wanted her friendship; Maximilian was still looking to her for money; and the Pope was obliged to applaud her for having usurped his official function as peacemaker. But in the days when war and peace and the movements of armies turned habitually on the personal predilections, quarrels, and amours of monarchs, the political atmosphere was liable to violent disturbances without warning. In January, 1519, Maximilian died suddenly; and his death in fact involved a complete rearrangement of ideas as to the positions of the Powers.

[Sidenote 1: 1519 Charles V.]
[Sidenote 2: The Imperial election]

Ten years before, when Henry came to the throne, he was the only young man among the European sovereigns. The Emperor and the King of France were both more than middle-aged: so was the King of Aragon who was virtually King of Spain and the Sicilies. Before six years were out there was a youthful King of France; not much later, all Spain was under the dominion of a boy. These three Kings were now twenty-eight, twenty-four, and nineteen respectively, while the succession to the Empire lay with the Electoral Princes. Charles was an obvious candidate, since the Habsburgs had actually retained the office among themselves for three generations; yet the Electors were in no way bound to maintain the tradition. In ability and in character, one of their number was fit for the purple—Frederick of Saxony; but Saxony was only one among a number of German States, and Frederick himself had no mind to undertake the office. Thereupon ensued the somewhat curious spectacle of the French King entering the lists, he being the one possible rival of Charles. Of all the Continental Princes, these two alone were powerful enough to sustain the burden of the Empire: yet either of them, achieving it, would have his power dangerously expanded, and would become a serious menace to the Pope.

So Charles and Francis both intrigued and bribed the Electors; the Pope tried to avoid helping either; Wolsey promised support to both; and the Electors themselves watched for opportunities of raising the price of their suffrages. And presently Henry himself conceived the idea of getting himself put forward as a third candidate, through whom a way of escape might be found for those who regarded Francis and Charles as Scylla and Charybdis. The combination however of the Crown of England with the Imperial diadem was no improvement in their eyes. Leo did not wish to find himself in Wolsey's grip. The scheme must almost inevitably have been fraught with disaster both to England and the Empire. Wolsey of necessity made himself the instrument of his master's desires; but while he selected as his agent Pace, the most astute of his subordinates, Pace's own correspondence is a good deal concerned with hints that an over-zealous pursuit of the policy would be a bartering of the substance for the shadow of power, and with explanations of the impracticability of an effective electoral campaign. Pace, in fact, went very little beyond sounding the Electors and declaring the results to be extremely unpromising; a state of things to which we may infer that neither he nor Wolsey had any objection. In the end, the influence of England was employed in favour of Charles, who was chosen Emperor in the middle of summer. The three sovereigns, Charles V., Francis I., and Henry VIII., dominated Europe for nearly thirty years to come—an unusually long period for three princes to reign side by side.

It was now Wolsey's difficult business to keep both Francis and Charles as suitors for the favour of England; and, having placated the latter in the contest for the Empire, to turn his attention to the former.

[1520 Wolsey's triumph]

Francis was at this time ready to meet Wolsey more than half way. He was particularly desirous of holding a formal interview and a personal interchange of courtesies with the King of England; and to this end he actually appointed Henry's minister his own plenipotentiary, a position without precedent or parallel for an English subject. Wolsey prepared to make the meeting an occasion for such a display of magnificence as has rarely been witnessed. At the same time he emphasised the independent position of England by arranging for a separate preliminary interview between Henry and the Emperor, and making it clear that herein it was not the Emperor who was doing the King a favour, but the contrary. If Charles wished to meet Henry, he must come to England for the purpose. Meantime both monarchs sought to obtain the great minister's goodwill by promises of support when the Papacy should become vacant—promises which Wolsey would not permit to influence his plans; whether because he rated them at their true value, or because he had no great anxiety to barter the position he had already secured for one which, however magnificent, however dominant in theory, might convey actual power of a much less substantial kind.

[Sidenote: Rival policies]

The French alliance, it must be observed, was never popular in England. Tradition was against it; the nobles of the old families were against it; the Queen was also naturally against it and very anxious for close and friendly relations with Spain. A degree of antagonism was thus generated between Katharine and the Cardinal, who held resolutely to his policy of maintaining the balance and never so committing himself to one party as to preclude a *rapprochement* with the other.

There was much intriguing on the part of Francis to bring on the meeting of the Kings before Charles could visit England. The state of the French Queen's health on one side and of the English Queen's wardrobe on the other figured largely as conclusive reasons for haste or delay. Wolsey however gained the day. The meeting was fixed to take place early in June between Guisnes and Ardres. In the last week of May (1520), Charles came to England, remaining three days; a week later, Henry sailed for Calais.

[Sidenote: Field of the Cloth of Gold]

It might almost be said that the entire courts of England and France, nobles and knights and ladies, met on the famous "field of the Cloth of Gold". Jousts and feastings were the order of the day. Wolsey understood how to impress the popular imagination; and he had a magnificent scorn or a cynical contempt for the enmities and jealousies aroused, of which he himself, as responsible for all the arrangements, became the centre. It may be doubted, however, whether any great goodwill between the two nations was born of all the display of amity; nor were there any very marked diplomatic results. If it was Wolsey's particular object to evolve a triple league, he was disappointed. The two Kings met and parted, Henry proceeding to a fresh conference with his nephew of Spain, from which Francis, in his turn, was excluded. Neither Charles nor Francis knew in the end which of them stood in the more favourable position with England; but the little Princess Mary, betrothed to the Dauphin, was half-pledged to Charles himself; while Charles was still formally betrothed to the French Princess Charlotte, and was inclining to substitute for both the well-dowered Infanta Isabella [Footnote: Otherwise called Elizabeth. The names are interchangeable.] of Portugal. Among all the surprising matrimonial complications of this half-century, one particular feature appears to be tolerably constant—that when Charles was not actually married, he was rarely without at least one fiancée actual, and another prospective.

At any rate, the total result in 1520 was that Henry was in separate alliance with Francis on one side and with Charles on the other; alliances which neither could afford to break, but on which neither could rely.

[Sidenote: Wolsey's aims]

The main interest of Wolsey's career, from the national point of view, attaches to his conduct of foreign policy: and in the confusion of alliances and counter-alliances it is not always easy to recognise the objects of that policy or its fundamental consistency. The aim always in view was to prevent any Power or combination of Powers from dominating Europe; to substitute diplomacy for the actual arbitrament of arms; to secure for England recognition as the true arbiter without involving her in war. The three first-class Powers of the earlier years were reduced to two by the combination under one head, Charles V., of Spain and the Empire, with France as the sole Continental rival.

But behind Wolsey's own policy was the traditional one of hostility to France, popular in the country, supported by the nobility, and offering attractions to an ambitious and martial-minded monarch who was not yet thirty years of age: whose Queen moreover was by birth and sympathy a strong partisan of Spain. Hence the Cardinal was liable to be forced out of his mediatorial position into one of hostility to France.

[Sidenote: Charles and Francis]

On the other hand, Francis and Charles each desired to strengthen his own position at the expense of the other. Each therefore desired an alliance with England close enough to secure her aid in an aggressive programme. But while Charles required active assistance and subsidies, seeking to throw on England the real burden of accomplishing his designs, Francis was comparatively satisfied with English neutrality. Again, while an aggressive alliance with Charles offered some uncertain prospects of the acquisition of French territory, circumstances were once more tending to enable Francis to utilise the ancient Scottish alliance as a means of holding England in check.

[Sidenote: Scotland 1513-20]

Since the decisive battle of Flodden, Scotland had not to any marked degree influenced Wolsey's European diplomacy. The blow dealt to her had been too serious: and the nobles, always turbulent, had never been more so than during the years which followed the great defeat. Queen Margaret, sister of the English King, a woman of only five and twenty when James was killed, made haste to marry the young Earl of Angus within a year of the event. The Douglases had frequently headed the Anglicising factions of the Scottish nobility, whereas the country at large constantly favoured the traditional alliance with France and hostility to the Southron. At present, the Douglases of whom Angus was the chief headed one faction: the Hamiltons, whose chief was Arran, headed the other. The marriage put an end to the arrangement under which Margaret had been Regent; there was intriguing and fighting to obtain possession of the person of the infant King; the Duke of Albany, [Footnote: Albany's father had been brother of James III.; their sister was Arran's mother.] of the royal house, who had been bred in France, was sent for, in the hope that as Regent he would compose discords. In the summer of 1515 he arrived. In the meantime, Dacre, in charge of the English border, had been fomenting quarrels [Footnote: *Lang, Hist. of Scotland*, i., 395. L. & P., ii., 779, 795.] and suborning outlaws to raid and devastate in the border counties, and plotting unsuccessfully to have James carried off into England to the tender care of his uncle. Albany, for his part, demanded the custody of the child, which was refused by Margaret; who however was forced to surrender with a show of friendliness. But she herself very shortly took refuge in England.

In 1517 Albany withdrew to France with a view to resuscitating the French alliance; the rivals Arran and Angus were again the two most powerful of the nobles; Margaret returned to Scotland, but quarrelled with her husband. In 1520 Albany was still in France which he probably found more cheerful than his own country. Angus got the better of Arran, who fled to France. There however Francis was still aiming at close alliance with England; and under such a combination of favourable conditions the truce between England and Scotland, entered upon in 1514 and now about to terminate, was extended for a couple of years. But Margaret herself being now hostile to Angus, there was every prospect that, should Albany return to Scotland, Wolsey would have to reckon seriously with the anti-English party there as a factor in his diplomatic relations with France.

[Sidenote: 1520-21 Affairs abroad]

The closing months of 1520 arid the opening months of 1521 witnessed events of importance at the time-and one at least which had very far-reaching consequences. The Emperor's wide do-minions were disturbed by a local outbreak in Germany, a revolt in Spain, and an attempt on the part of the claimant to the throne of Navarre to recover that territory. The Diet of the Empire met at Worms, and Martin Luther was cited before it; with the result that the Empire was practically divided into two camps, Charles ranging himself on the papal side. As Henry VIII. was so far a loyal son of the Church, wielding an anti-Lutheran pen in theological controversy, while the French King's reverence for the papacy was under suspicion, the present tendency of this event was favourable to the union of Charles and Henry with the Pope against Francis. On the other hand there was very little question that the troubles in the Emperor's dominions were fostered by Francis, who was preparing for an Italian expedition. Had Charles and Wolsey trusted each other, their alliance would certainly have been drawn closer; but Wolsey was not the man to take up Charles's cause without securing an adequate return, while Charles wished to involve England on the strength of promises which he expected subsequently to find no necessity for carrying out. Charles found his justification in the unexpected success of his arms in Navarre, in Spain, and in Germany. Good fortune relieved him from the more pressing need of English aid, and thus the prospect of a close and active alliance faded.

[Sidenote: 1521 Buckingham]

In the late spring of 1521 there occurred in England a domestic episode which must have impressed both Charles and Francis with the power wielded in England by Henry; the first notable instance among the numerous executions marking the reign for which treason was the pretext.

[Footnote: Unless we except that of Edmund de la Pole, Earl of Suffolk, in 1513.] The Duke of Buckingham stood at the head of the nobility; accepted as representing the House of Lancaster, next in order to the Tudors. [Footnote: The Staffords of Buckingham on one side descended, like Henry, from the Beauforts. They were also the representatives of Thomas of Woodstock, the youngest son of Edward III. See *Front*, and p. 9, note.] The Duke no doubt had a sufficiently strong dislike to Wolsey, and had used very incautious language about him, and the Cardinal was popularly held responsible for his downfall, though there is no evidence that this was actually the case. Buckingham had consulted soothsayers, and was reputed to have used compromising expressions about tyrants and the succession. At any rate, he suddenly found himself arrested for high treason. The King had made preliminary inquiry on his own account—not in the presence of Wolsey—and had made up his own mind that Buckingham was to die. The peers were summoned to try him on May 10th, under the presidency of Norfolk. The depositions of the witnesses against the Duke were read; there was no cross-examination; he denied the charges, but was not allowed counsel. The decision was of course a foregone conclusion. One by one the peers pronounced him guilty; he was condemned to death, and executed. No one was found to challenge the justice of the sentence, though on a review of the evidence it is almost incredible that any human being could have honestly endorsed it. The world at large however knew nothing about the evidence, and merely accepted the judgment as final and indisputable. By a single ruthless act, Henry had practically established his own right to judge cases of treason on the hypothesis not that guilt had to be demonstrated but that the accused must prove his own loyalty or suffer the extreme penalty. For the King to entertain an accusation was tantamount to condemnation. Even to plead on behalf of such a one was dangerous: to maintain his innocence would have been a short way to the block.

[Sidenote: Wolsey's diplomacy]

By the execution of Buckingham, Henry vindicated his own authority in England while popular opinion laid the responsibility on the Cardinal's machinations. In the meantime, an impetus was given to the anti-French policy of Charles by the death of his Burgundian minister Chievres. As the summer advanced, the prospect of keeping the peace between the rival monarchs grew fainter. The parties however agreed to hold a conference at Calais, at which Wolsey should act as mediator. But matters looked as if England would be forced to take a side in a European war; and if she did so the balance of advantage to her lay on the side of the Emperor.

In August the conference met. Ostensibly with a view to obtaining from Charles himself more concessions to France than his envoys would allow, the Cardinal visited him at Bruges; where however he was really engaged in coming to comparatively satisfactory terms as to the conditions upon which Charles should receive English assistance. These included the deferring of actual participation in hostilities, and indemnification for the inevitable loss of the Tournai purchase-money, of which France had paid only a part. Wolsey returned to Calais with a secret treaty, and the conference continued, the Cardinal still making every effort to avert war; but towards the end of November it became clear that his endeavours must be fruitless, and the conference was broken up. He was followed to England by the news of Imperial successes both in Italy and in Picardy—which went far to justify Charles in his refusal to postpone hostilities for his own part. Henry, whose own predilections were in favour of war, was very well pleased with the result, and rewarded his minister by presenting him to the vacant and lucrative office of Abbot of St. Albans. Such were the conveniences of being served by an ecclesiastic.

[Sidenote: 1522 A papal Election]

The year closed with an event of importance. Leo X. died unexpectedly and there was an election to the papacy. There is no doubt that Wolsey desired the papal crown; and both Francis and Charles in courting his favour had held out as a bait the influence they were prepared to promise on his behalf. But he had not allowed these offers to influence his actions. Charles now gave him fair words, but evidently intended his real support to be given to some candidate whom he expected to be more pliant. The man he would have chosen was the Cardinal de Medici, afterwards Clement VII.: but Italian party spirit among the Cardinals ran too high for this to prove practicable, and Adrian VI. who had been tutor to Charles was the new Pope. Wolsey can hardly have been disappointed, and never gave undue weight to the Emperor's promises: but the event was not calculated to increase his confidence or his goodwill. The present fact however of the alliance between the Emperor and England, with the corollary that England must before long be at war with France, remained unaltered.

[Sidenote 1: War with France]
[Sidenote 2: Scotland]

By the end of May the war could no longer be postponed, and was duly declared. It was still some months before Surrey took the field in France at the head of the English forces—conducting his campaign on the general principles of Anglo-Scottish border warfare—ravaging, burning, and rousing the hatred of the country population, but striking no blow. If Henry seriously contemplated the idea of reviving old claims to the French crown, he could have adopted no worse policy. Charles of course gave no practical assistance, and the allies each blamed the other for the futility of the operations. Albany on the other hand had been back in Scotland for some months; and in opposition to Angus—in conjunction therefore with Margaret —threatened an invasion as soon as the French expedition started. The ingenious Lord Dacre however by sheer bluff—there is no other word— succeeded in procuring an armistice when the English border was all but defenceless. After this exhibition, Albany found it as well to retire to France; while Wolsey used the occurrence to urge upon Charles that Scotland required too much attention to allow French expeditions to be practicable.

[Sidenote: 1523 Progress of the war]

With 1523 events took a turn more favourable to Charles. The Duke of Bourbon, Constable of France, turned against the King, on the ground of insults more or less fancied, and of a genuine attempt to deprive him of his inheritance by legal process. The idea was revived in Henry's mind that in alliance with some of the French nobility he might make himself King of France as Henry V. had done; so Wolsey had to develop an active policy against France. His hand being thus forced, the Cardinal devoted his energies to making the combination against the French King really serious, coercing Venice into the coalition. The military operations however were not in train till the autumn; Suffolk, whose military skill was extremely limited, commanded the English expedition, and marched into the interior instead of falling on Boulogne as Wolsey had advised; Bourbon did nothing useful; Charles's troops gave their attention to Fontarabia instead of to a combined operation. From the English point of view the whole campaign was a complete fiasco. Wolsey had been set to carry out a policy of which he disapproved, with instruments of whose incompetence he was fully conscious; and the results were probably neither better nor worse than what he and the cooler onlookers like Sir Thomas More expected. The one thing that Wolsey could do, he had done: he had placed Surrey on the Northern border to deal with the inevitable return to Scotland of Albany with threats of invasion. Surrey was successful: Albany having advanced into England was obliged to fall back, and the border country was subjected to the usual process of raiding and harrying.

[Sidenote: Election of Pope Clement VII.]

Once again, the closing months of the year witnessed a papal election; and for the second time Wolsey was disappointed. The reign of Adrian closed in September. It had been brief, well intentioned, and honest: but ineffective. The Pope's efforts at reform had been met by the solid *vis inertiae* of the ecclesiastical world. His successor, the Medici, Clement VII., was destined to play a much more important part in history, and, buffeted by forces which he could not control, to become the instrument whereby England was severed from Rome. In this election Charles played the same part as before. He promised Wolsey his support, wrote letters to Rome which were delayed till too late, and actually expended his influence on behalf of Medici. Again, though Wolsey's anxiety to achieve the papacy has probably been much exaggerated, he would have been more than human if he had not inwardly resented the Emperor's behaviour. It is to be noted in connexion with this election that Wolsey actually proposed the employment of armed coercion to secure a convenient choice—a rather gross method of condemning the theory that the Conclave reached its decision by Divine guidance.

[Sidenote: 1524 Wolsey's difficulties]

The year had but six weeks more to run when Clement was finally elected. In 1524 the belligerents were all desirous of ending the war, but none was willing to make concessions to hasten that end. The allies had good reason to suspect each other of trying to make separate terms with Francis; each hoped to extract concessions from the French King as the price of defection. Wolsey in fact was neither able nor willing to carry on active hostilities. England had gone into the war with a light heart; but when Parliament was called upon in the summer of 1523 to vote the necessary funds, the light-heartedness was modified, and the funds were voted with extreme reluctance, under something very near akin to compulsion; and the collecting of the taxes aroused angry complaint—the blame being as usual laid on the Cardinal. He was well aware that any increase in the burden would be a dangerous matter to propose, and very dangerous indeed to try and carry through; yet without more funds an active campaign was impossible. Therefore, as concerned the Continent, Wolsey on the one hand sought to induce Charles to assent to a fresh conference where England should mediate as to the claims and counter-claims of Charles and Francis; and on the other made private overtures to Francis.

[Sidenote: Intrigues in Scotland]

In Scotland, the game of intrigue was actively carried on. Albany retired permanently to France soon after the failure of his invasion. While he was in Scotland, Margaret had sided with him; now she began to fall in with the English policy, and was eager for the "erection" of her son—that is for his recognition as actual King though he was barely twelve years old. Throughout the summer, schemes were on foot for a peace conference—the real object being the kidnapping of Beton, the Archbishop of St. Andrews, coadjutor of Albany, Chancellor of Scotland, and the most resolute opponent of the Anglicising party and policy. Wolsey is quite explicit on this point in a letter to Dacre, though Surrey, who had just succeeded to the Dukedom of Norfolk by the death of the victor of Flodden, never grasped this peculiar method of diplomacy. Beton declined to be trapped; still, the "erection" was carried through. [Footnote: *L. & P.*, vol. iv., part i., 549. *Cf.* Lang, *Hist. Scot.*, pp. 405, 406. Beton was to have a safe-conduct, and the kidnapping was to be done by Angus, at the time in England, quite as a private personal matter. Angus had come to England from France, whither he had been removed by Albany.] By dint of bribery, many of the anti-English party had now changed sides along with Margaret, with the curious result that Angus, who was bound to be in opposition to his wife, allied himself to Beton. Next year, however, the French or anti-English party in Scotland suffered a serious blow when the French King was vanquished and taken prisoner at the battle of Pavia.

[Sidenote: 1525 Pavia]

Meantime, Wolsey had found Francis not too ready to accept his overtures, and had therefore set about making a show of pursuing a more actively antagonistic policy in conjunction with Bourbon. The Cardinal however, whose object was to make Francis think it necessary to conciliate him—not to be forced into expeditions and armaments—intentionally made his conditions to Bourbon such as the Constable would not agree to; while obtaining the desired result of moving Francis to enter seriously on negotiations. He even felt that matters were progressing favourably enough to justify a "diplomatic episode"—the interception of the Imperial ambassador's dispatches, his virtual imprisonment, and the lodging of a protest against his conduct with the Emperor. But the battle of Pavia wrecked Wolsey's schemes, as well as those of his adversaries in Scotland. For the disaster to Francis wakened anew in Henry's breast the belief that the French crown was still attainable: and the minister found himself forced to seek means to provide war-funds, while he was alive to the practical impossibility of persuading Parliament to grant them.

For Wolsey to protest would have been vain. He did not in any way dominate Henry, who was ready enough to follow his advice or allow him to carry out his own policy so long as it fell in with the royal views. But if the King chose to lay down a different policy, the Cardinal had to carry it out as best he could—or else to retire in disfavour. And he could not afford to retire in disfavour, since, if the royal countenance were once withdrawn, the malignity of his many enemies would be given rein, and his utter ruin would be inevitable. Therefore, while watching for any opportunity to convert the King from his martial designs, he made a desperate effort to fill the exchequer.

[Sidenote: The Amicable Loan]

Two years before, when Parliament had been called, it had been induced to vote the money asked for. But (according to Hall) the Speaker, Sir Thomas More, had taken the opportunity to resist Wolsey's high-handed methods, to insist on parliamentary privileges, and to refuse to debate the matter in the Cardinal's presence, though he actually exerted his influence in favour of the grant. To repeat the demand now would be to risk rebellion; at the best, to court an inevitable refusal. Therefore Wolsey reverted to ancient precedents, and demanded an "Amicable Loan," on the ground that the King was going to lead his armies, and must therefore go fittingly equipped. The loan was to amount to about one-sixth of a man's property. Very soon however it became clear that this was more than the country would endure. Wolsey revoked the demand and called for a "Benevolence". London replied that benevolences were illegal, by reason of the statute of Richard III. Wolsey protested against appealing to the laws of a tyrant; but the Londoners remarked that the fact of Richard having been a tyrant did not annul the excellence of good laws when he made them. In Norwich the aggrieved populace assembled in force, and presented their case allegorically, but convincingly, to the Duke of Norfolk, who was sent to deal with them. The Cardinal's attempt to raise money was a failure. The King grasped the situation and remitted the demand, taking all the credit for his clemency, while his minister had the odium for the proposal. For the first time, Wolsey had failed to carry his master's wishes through, for the simple reason that the task set him was an impossible one. The soundness of his own antagonism to the French war was conclusively demonstrated, since without the funds war could not be waged: but the cost of the demonstration was the increase of his unpopularity, and an appreciable diminution of Henry's favour. He did what he could to mollify the King by presenting him with his palace of Hampton Court—a present graciously accepted.

[Sidenote 1: A diplomatic struggle]
[Sidenote 2: 1526-27 Success of Wolsey]

Now, however, a *rapprochement* with France was again possible. Charles and Wolsey returned to the attitude of mutually desiring nothing so much as to prove their complete accord, their own anxiety to fulfil all obligations, provided only that the other would reasonably recognise his own obligations in return. Each wanted to extract what he could from Francis without regard to his ally: each wanted an excuse for evading his contract with that ally—the Emperor because he now perceived the more immediate pecuniary profit of the Portuguese marriage. In the diplomatic contest Wolsey had the advantage, that Charles, in spite of Pavia, could not bring the necessary pressure to bear on his captive, if the support of

England was felt to be withdrawn. He had something to lose by an open breach: Wolsey had not—provided the responsibility for the breach could plausibly be laid on Charles. Moreover, although the French King was the Emperor's prisoner, the French Government was much less bitterly opposed to the English demand for money than to the Imperial demand for territory. Thus by the end of the year Wolsey achieved his end—a treaty with France, involving the payment of two million crowns to England, and including Scotland in its terms. Charles being isolated made his own peace with his prisoner in the following February (1526); but Francis, before signing, declared that his promises were extorted and not binding, and after his release repudiated their validity. The Cardinal in fact had extricated England from a very awkward situation, recovered her position as arbiter, and once more made the rival European monarchs feel that they could neither of them afford to have her definitely ranged as an enemy. As the year advanced, the tendency for the French alliance to draw closer, and for the Imperial alliance to dissolve became more marked. Charles, in his desire to dominate Italy, allowed a Spanish force to enter Rome and terrorise the Pope—though he disavowed their actions. In 1527, while he was continuing this policy, and preparing for the sack of Rome and the seizure of the Pope's person in May, Wolsey was carrying through a new French alliance, by which Orleans (afterwards Henry II.) was betrothed to the Princess Mary, and France not only bound herself to make heavy payments but also surrendered Boulogne and Ardres. It seemed as though the isolation of Charles was about to be completed, his opponents becoming the champions of the papacy—while his own antagonism to the Pope had been emphasised at the Diet of Spires by the withdrawal of the anti-Lutheran decrees, and the temporary recognition of each State's right to adopt or reject the Reformer's doctrines in its own territories.

[Sidenote: 1527 A new factor]

But in 1527 Henry had developed a single purpose; he had set his mind on one object to the achievement whereof every political consideration was to be subordinated. The state-craft of the great minister was dominated by and subjected to the king-craft of a master who never brooked opposition to his will; and Wolsey, failing to carry out that will, was hurled without remorse from his high estate. The Cardinal's fall, the breach with Rome, the defining of the shape which the Reformation was to take in England, were all the outcome of Henry's resolve to be released from the wife to whom he had been wedded for eighteen years. Hitherto we have made only incidental allusion to the Reformation; it is now time to examine the development of that movement, down to the moment when Henry took into his own hands the conduct of it within his own realms.

CHAPTER VI
HENRY VIII (ii), 1509-32—BIRTH
OF THE REFORMATION

[Sidenote: The Reformation in England]

Down to a comparatively recent date, the popularly accepted accounts of the Reformation in England treated it as a spontaneous outburst of the deep religious spirit pervading the mass of the people; a passionate repudiation of the errors of Rome, born of the secret study of the Bible in defiance of persecution, and of repulsion from the iniquities of the monastic system. Then there arose a picturesque historian, who recognised in Henry VIII. and Thomas Cromwell the men who created the Reformation; and having once imagined them as the captains of a great and righteous cause, succeeded in interpreting all their actions on the basis of postulating their single- eyed devotion to reform as their ever-dominant motive. A view so difficult to reconcile with some other stereotyped impressions has invited criticism; and it is not unusual now to be told that the changes effected by the Reformation were small, except in so far as the Church was robbed by the destruction of the monasteries.

[Sidenote: Its true character]

As a matter of fact the change which took place was very great and very far-reaching for the nation, though it is easy to exaggerate the deviations from Roman doctrine imposed by it on the clergy of the Anglican Communion. But the movement was one in which many factors were at work. Moralists, theologians, and politicians, all had their share in it; some who were prominent promoters of it in one phase were its no less active antagonists in another; and not infrequently were guided by purely personal ambitions and interests throughout. In its essence however the Reformation was a revolt against conventions which had lost the justification of the conditions that had brought them into being, and had become fetters upon intellectual and spiritual progress instead of aids to its advancement. Each group of reformers was ready enough to impose on the world a new set of conventions of its own manufacture, but no group succeeded in dominating the aggregate of groups; and thus in the long run toleration became the only working policy, though its practice was by no means what the Reformers had set before themselves. After long years, religious liberty was the outcome of their work; but few indeed were the martyrs whose blood was consciously shed in that great cause. The men who died rather than submit their own convictions to the dictation of others were for the most part ready, when opportunity offered, to sit in judgment on those who would not accept their own dictation.

[Sidenote: Religious decadence]

The prevailing conditions of the Church at the dawn of the Reformation were exceedingly corrupt, with the corruption of worn out institutions; but they appeared to be part of the necessary order of things. Hitherto, occasional heretics had arisen, but (superficially at least) they had been suppressed without serious difficulty. The State, in England and elsewhere, had entered upon conflicts with the priesthood; secular monarchs had even challenged the authority of the Pope; but such quarrels had ended in compromises formal or practical. Moral reforming movements like that of St. Francis had arisen within the Church herself; they had not been antagonistic to her, and they had thriven and decayed without producing revolutionary results. Clerical abuses had been for centuries the objects of satire, but the satirists rarely had any inclination for the role of revolutionaries or martyrs. The recent revival of learning had developed a scepticism which was however habitually accompanied by a decent profession of orthodoxy. That there was prevalent unrest had long been obvious; that there was risk of disturbing developments was not unrecognised; but that these things were the prelude to a vast revolution had been realised neither by Churchmen, Statesmen, nor literati.

[Sidenote: The Scholar-Reformers]

It did not appear, then, that the revolt of Wiclif in England and of Huss in Europe was about to be renewed: though they had in fact prepared the soil to receive the new seed. Lollardry had been driven beneath the surface. Still, so far at least as it represented anti-clericalism rather than a theological system, its secret disciples were accorded a considerable measure of popular sympathy; though it numbered few professors among the cultivated classes, it had semi-adherents even among the wealthier burgesses of London; it was active enough to cause some alarm to Convocation, and to excite reactionary bishops. But it was not in this quarter primarily that any notable movement seemed likely to arise. The demand for Reformation during the first quarter of the century was formulated by scholars who were not heretics—Dean Colet of St. Paul's; Thomas More; the cosmopolitan Erasmus, who was but a bird of passage in this country, yet one who was warmly and generously welcomed.

To men of this school, a schism in the Church never presented itself as a desirable end. Luther had not yet burned Pope Leo's Bull when Colet died; Lutheranism changed More into a reactionary, as, centuries later, the French Revolution changed Edmund Burke; Erasmus would not range himself beside the stormy controversialists of Germany and Switzerland. To the scholars, the Roman system was not irreconcilable with truth; its defects were accidents, excrescences, curable by the application of common-sense and moral seriousness. In the eyes of Luther and Zwingli, the corruption of Rome was vital, organic, incurable. Ecclesiastical Authority was the corner-stone of the Roman system: Colet and More never attacked it; Luther attacked it because it maintained opinions which he held to be fundamentally false; but in England it is possible to doubt whether the attitude of More and Colet would ever have been officially discarded, had it not been for the political and personal considerations which led Henry and Cromwell to trample ecclesiastical authority under foot. Nevertheless, by their attacks on ecclesiastical abuses, Colet and More helped intelligent people to perceive that the abuses were intolerable, and to acquiesce even in the extreme remedy of schism rather than continue to endure the burden.

[Sidenote: Ecclesiastical demoralisation]

It is not disputable that the existing corruption was so serious that some kind of Reformation was absolutely necessary. Where the head is corrupt, there cannot be much general health. If the spiritual head of Christendom were unworthy of his office the ecclesiastical body was certain to suffer; nor could much spirituality be looked for therein, if it habitually acquiesced in the election of Popes in whom spirituality was the last quality recognisable. The climax was perhaps reached when a Borgia— Alexander VI.—was raised to the papal throne; a man who revelled in the practice of every imaginable vice, and shrank from no conceivable crime. The mere fact that such an election was possible is sufficient proof of the utter absence of religious feeling in the ruling ranks of the clergy: nor was its presence compatible with the appointment either of his free living and warlike successor Julius II. or of Leo X. who followed—a person of no little culture, a patron of art and of letters, whose morals were not exceptionally lax as compared with those of the average Italian noble, but in all essentials a pagan. With few exceptions, the princes of the Church owed their position to their connexion, by birth or otherwise, with great families; not a few of them were territorial lords of considerable dominions, for whom it was a sheer necessity to be politicians first, whether they were scholars, ministers of the Gospel, or mere pleasure- seekers afterwards. Italians completely dominated the college of cardinals, looking upon the control of the Church as a national prerogative. The characteristics of the ecclesiastical princes were shared in due degree by bishops and abbots. The fact that until recent years learning had been practically a clerical monopoly necessarily made the clergy the fittest instruments for carrying on much State business, thereby withdrawing many of the better men from the service of religion to the service of politics. In brief, the whole system tended to entangle the able members of the ecclesiastical body in the temptations not so much of the Flesh and the Devil as of the World.

[Sidenote: Monastic corruption]

Further, the monastic system had utterly fallen away from its pristine ideals. It had served a great purpose. Born as it was when the world was just emerging from paganism, and the Roman civilisation was being engulfed in the flood of barbarian invasion, the men and women who withdrew from the desperate turmoil without to the sheltering walls of the monastery or the convent, invested with a sacrosanct character which was at least in part respected, found therein the opportunity for prayer, meditation and study which was denied them elsewhere. They could maintain a standard of piety, and keep a rudimentary education from altogether dying out. For centuries they were the only source of alms and succour to which the afflicted and needy could turn; and so long as the rules of the Orders were observed in the spirit and in the letter, they were a genuine help towards a life of self-devotion, of self-abnegation whereof the ultimate motive was not always a subtle form of self-seeking. But as time passed, the monasteries became the recipients of the bounty of pious benefactors. Their inhabitants, in spite of ascetic regulations, found that life was none so hard—at least in comparison with that of serfdom or villeinage; luxuries were not less available than to the laity. The privileges of the sacred office gave increasing opportunities for vicious indulgence when once corruption had entered a Religious house. Promotion became the prize of intrigue instead of the recognition of piety; till it came to be no scandal when a political priest was rewarded for his services by presentation to the rule of a wealthy abbey, with which he was connected only as the chief recipient of its revenues, as when Wolsey had St. Albans bestowed on him in return for his diplomatic labours. Apart from the diatribes of zealots and the evidence of interested informers, apart also from the inclination to generalise from well authenticated but extreme examples, it is evident that, in the absence of a positive religious enthusiasm, the system was peculiarly liable to grave degeneration; and it was long since there had been any active spiritual revival to counteract that tendency.

[Sidenote: The proofs]

To these general considerations we have also to add the direct positive evidence in connexion with Cardinal Morton's visitations of the Monasteries in the reign of Henry VII. It was neither shown nor attempted to be shown that the Religious houses *en bloc* were hotbeds of vice. But it was shown beyond question that even among the great Abbeys there were to be found appalling examples of corruption and profligacy, where the heads were the worst offenders and the rank and file imitated their superiors; and that small houses were not infrequently conducted in the most scandalous manner— for the simple reason that, when once corruption had found an entry, there was no supervising external authority sufficiently interested to intervene vigorously.

Mutatis mutandis, what was true of the Monasteries was also true of the Mendicant Orders. The class of men who had no desire to dig, and no shame about begging, found the friar's robe a useful adjunct to the latter occupation. Long after enthusiasm had ceased to draw any large numbers into the ranks of the friars, they were increased and multiplied by crowds of ignorant and idle rogues, who were subjected to no adequate control.

[Sidenote: Corruption of doctrine]

But the corruption of the clerical body fostered also the degeneration of popular religious conceptions. The actual teaching of the clergy was a grotesque distortion of the doctrines they professed to expound. The intelligible doctrine of absolution following on repentance and confession, and accompanied by penance, had been transformed into that of absolution purchasable by cash. Reverence for the relics of saints and martyrs had been degraded by their spurious multiplication. The belief that such relics were endowed with miraculous properties had been utilised to convert them into fetishes, and pampered by fraudulent conjuring tricks. The due performance of ceremonial observances was treated as of far more vital importance than the practice of the Christian virtues. The images of the Saints had virtually come to be regarded not as symbols, but as idols possessed of various degrees of power, the assistance of one and the same saint proving more or less efficacious according to the shrine favoured by his suppliant.

[Sidenote: Evidence from Colet and More (1512-18)]

These facts are not disputable. They were fully recognised by Reformers of the type of Colet and More, who would have had the Church reform herself by reverting to the primitive and orthodox expression of the doctrines of which these deformities were a corrupt latter-day misrepresentation, and to the ideals of life and conduct which had been overlaid by ceremonial observances. The primitive doctrines they accepted without question; as regarded the ceremonial observances, they objected to them not in themselves but only so far as they obscured in practice the much higher value of moral ideals. In the view of such men the remedy for heresies lay in the hands of the clergy: would they but bring their lives into some conformity with primitive ideals, surrendering the pursuit of place, profit, or pleasure to tread in the footsteps of the apostles, heresy would perish of inanition.

[Sidenote: Later evidence]

When Colet was preaching at St. Paul's, when More was imagining the *Utopia*, when Erasmus was preparing his *Praise of Folly* and his edition of the Greek Testament, the name of Luther was still unknown. Their aim was the active propagation of reform; not to exercise thereon a restraining influence, which at that time would have seemed superfluous. The only reason they could have had for understating the existing corruption would have been fear of the authorities, a fear from which both Colet and More always showed themselves conspicuously free. Colet's most vigorous exhortations were addressed to prelates and persons in high places; More never throughout his career hesitated to oppose Chancellors, or even Tudor Kings, when a principle was involved. We are therefore entitled to assume that they neither over-coloured nor deliberately toned down the prevalent conditions. A decade later, when fanaticism had broken loose, the anathemas hurled at the clergy by irresponsible pamphleteers, or zealots who were sheltered in the Lutheran States of Germany, were of a much more sweeping character. Later, again, the reports of the Commissioners for the suppression of monasteries formed an appalling indictment. Later still, when the Protestant party won the upper hand after a season of relentless and embittering persecution, the pictures they painted of the past were lurid in the extreme. But the evidence of such witnesses could not be other than passionately biassed, just as the evidence of persecuted monks and nuns must have been biassed on the other side: whereas the evidence of Colet, of More in his earlier days, and, with certain reservations, of Erasmus, is that of honest and high-minded men of great intellectual capacity, speaking without prejudice of conditions with which they were in direct contact. Their assertions, and the fair inferences from their assertions, are a safe basis from which we can ascertain both the gravity and the limits of the corruption which existed in England.

[Sidenote: Dean Colet]

John Colet was appointed to the Deanery of St. Paul's four or five years before the death of Henry VII., being transferred thither from Oxford, where he had won high repute, not merely for character and learning, but as the initiator of a new and rational method of Scriptural study in place of the old scholasticism. At St. Paul's the Dean proved himself a great preacher, exercising also in private life a powerful influence on all who came in contact with him, alike from the splendour of his intellect and the large-hearted purity of his character. His outspoken sermons were by no means to the liking of his bishop; but some of the leading prelates, notably Warham of Canterbury and Fox of Winchester, were well disposed to the new school of learning and exposition and to higher moral standards, as Cardinal Morton had been. When the young King ascended the throne in 1509, his accession was hailed by all men of the new school as heralding the reign of intellectual liberty and enlightenment.

[Sidenote: Colet's sermon, 1512]

Accordingly, when Convocation was summoned in 1512 to discuss the suppression of heresy, in consequence of some stray reappearances of Lollardry, the prevalence of a wider spirit was shown by the selection of Colet to preach the opening sermon, and by the subsequent ignominious failure of the Bishop of London to have the Dean punished as a heretic. It is to the sermon preached on this occasion that we must turn to see how Colet viewed the situation. It was a direct indictment of the manner of life of the clergy from Wolsey down; a summons to them to amend their ways, to set a higher example to their flock; an appeal to them to fix their eyes on apostolic ideals, and so to remove the real incitement which turned men's minds to heretical speculation. While the positive arguments of the preacher are evidence not only of the purity of his own aims and his courage in supporting them, their reception shows that the substantial justice of the indictment was recognised by the audience at whom it was personally directed, however little disposed they might be to act individually on his appeal. On the other hand however, it is a striking fact that the charges brought are almost exclusively of worldliness, laxity, indiscipline, unbecoming in pastors and in ministers of the Gospel of Christ—though these charges were pressed home relentlessly; not at all of that rampant immorality and vice of which the clergy were so freely accused in later years. From what Colet did *not* say, we may fairly infer a reasonable average of respectability among them.

[Sidenote: Erasmus]

If, in the *Encomium Moriae* or *Praise of Folly*, which Erasmus wrote at about the same period (1511), the vices and follies of the Church were lashed with a mockery still more unsparing, we have to note, first, that the great scholar drew his picture less from England than from the Continent; next, that it had no injurious effect on his appointment to the professorship of Greek at Cambridge. The patronage extended to him by the Primate, and by Fisher of Rochester, the most orthodox and saintly of the English bishops, is a sufficient proof that the authorities were not bigoted enemies of all reform; a proof borne out by the enthusiastic welcome extended to his edition of the Greek Testament in 1518, by Fox of Winchester amongst others.

[Sidenote: The *Utopia*, 1516]

From the *Utopia* of Sir Thomas More we derive precisely the same impression. In 1516, when the work was published, Luther had not yet defied the Pope; the German Peasants' War had not yet broken out, nor the spread of new ideas been associated with Anarchism under the name of Anabaptism. Persecution, which fifteen years later More advocated and practised as the unavoidable remedy for the spread of doctrines which he had come to regard as actively pernicious, was alien to his instincts; in his ideal Commonwealth, men might expound whatever they honestly held, provided they did not deny God and the Future Life. More's nature was tolerant and charitable. But his own convictions were thoroughly orthodox; he had at one time a strong disposition to enter the priesthood himself; he held the priestly office in high reverence. Yet his restriction of the number of priests in *Utopia* shows his vivid consciousness of the evil wrought by their unrestricted multiplication in England; and in the description of English social conditions in the introductory portion of his work, he refers in emphatic terms to the large proportion of "sturdy vagabonds" among them. His whole tone in the section of his book devoted to religious matters implies that he is pointing a contrast between his ideal order of things and that familiar to his readers, wherein non-essentials are so emphasised that essentials are practically forgotten. Yet More, like Colet, makes no sweeping attack on the morality (in the narrower popular sense of the term) prevalent among the clerical body.

[Sidenote: Exaggerated attacks]

The wholesale condemnation of later days has been largely due to the acceptance without qualification of denunciations poured forth in the heat of controversy, in days when men did not mince words and were not given to the careful weighing of evidence. Typical of such works is the *Supplicacyon for the Beggers* produced by one Simon Fish in 1527, which has been seriously treated as a sober indictment. The Clergy, from Bishops to "Somners" are a "rauinous cruell and insatiabill generacion" … "counterfeit holy and ydell beggers and vacabundes" … "that corrupt the hole generation of mankind," committing "rapes murdres and treasons". They are a "gredy sort of sturdy idell holy theues" habitually guilty of every conceivable form of vice and profligacy. The pamphlet teams with arithmetical absurdities. It is simply inconceivable that the growth within the realm of such an organisation as is here depicted would have been permitted; or that, if there, it would not have been sternly repressed by Henry VII.; or that if it had survived the first Tudor, the second would have suffered it to flourish unregarded for eighteen years of his reign. The exaggeration is so flagrant that we can hardly infer from it even a substratum of truth. Such diatribes as this must be referred to, not as being valid evidences against the accused, but as proving the passion of the controversy, and the hesitation necessary before accepting conclusions traceable to the wild and whirling words of such controversialists.

[Sidenote 1: Clerical privileges]
[Sidenote 2: Tentative reforms]

In another respect however there was a serious demand for reform; namely the legal and judicial privileges which the ecclesiastical body had acquired in the course of centuries, and which had gradually become the source of serious abuses. The administration of certain branches of the Civil Law had been absorbed by the Clerics, who were charged with converting their functions into an elaborate machinery for extorting fees; and on the Criminal side, what was known as Benefit of Clergy, as well as the rules of Sanctuary, had become not merely anomalous but an actual encouragement to crime. Any criminal or accused person who succeeded in reaching Sanctuary was safe from the secular arm; and any one who could produce evidence, even of the flimsiest character, that he was a cleric could claim to be tried by the ecclesiastical instead of the secular courts. Originally these privileges had been of very great service in the wild days when judicial treatment was at least more readily obtainable from the Clergy, when trial by ordeal was common, and the merciless punishments of the ordinary law gave place to the milder but not ineffective penalties of Ecclesiastical discipline. Even the legal fictions by which evildoers were allowed to claim Benefit of Clergy as Clerics had their justification. But when even murderers could escape with a moderate penance as Clerics, because they could read, the general public were hardly the better. A beginning of reform in this direction had been made when Henry VII. obtained a Bull diminishing the rights of Sanctuary in cases of treason; and again in 1511 when the rights both of Sanctuary and Benefit of Clergy were withdrawn from murderers. It was noteworthy however that there was a protest against even this made by the Clergy in 1515; when one Dr. Standish, for justifying the measure, was attacked by the Bishops in Convocation. Warham and Fox both supported the old privileges. The temporal lords on a commission appointed to enquire into the matter sided with Standish, and declared that the Bishops had incurred the penalties of praemunire. Wolsey tried to persuade the King to refer the question to the Pope, but the King asserted the rights of the Crown in uncompromising terms. The Bishops had to submit to a sharp rebuke, and Standish was made a Dean not long after. The episode was a premonition of future events.

[Sidenote: The Educational Movement]

It does not appear that the writings or the preaching of the scholars had any marked effect on the conduct of the clergy, or aroused any general reforming zeal. But in one direction, that of education, they exercised a very material influence on the intellectual attitude of the younger generation. Dean Colet is known to-day to many even of those who take little interest in his times, as the founder of St. Paul's School, where he endeavoured to make the teaching of the young a real training instead of a drill in pedagogic formulae. And as he set the example which was by degrees followed in other grammar schools, so the example he had already set at Oxford was followed both there and at Cambridge by his disciples. To him, more than to any other man, was due the practical application of the new knowledge of Greek to the study of the New Testament, resulting primarily in the treatment of the Pauline Epistles as organic structures; as connected treatises, instead of collected texts according to the custom of the schoolmen; who, dragging phrases from their context, expanded, interpreted and harmonised them with other phrases for fresh expansion and interpretation; neglecting the apostolic argument to illustrate their own theses or those of the mediaeval doctors. Fox, of Winchester, when he founded Corpus Christi College, Oxford, Fisher in the Lady Margaret foundations at Cambridge, put into them men of the new school. Wolsey himself had evidently been influenced by the new methods, for his active connexion with Oxford had not ceased when Colet was there; and when in later years he founded Cardinal College, afterwards Christ Church, the men he appointed to it were chosen from the disciples of the school of Colet and Erasmus. To this higher ideal of University education, perhaps the strongest impulse was given by Erasmus himself, during the brief time about 1512 when he was Professor of Greek at Cambridge, where he proved himself the most brilliant exponent of the principles which in part at least he had imbibed from the Dean. Cranmer, his great rival Gardiner, and many others among the protagonists in the coming religious struggle, received their training under the new conditions— conditions very markedly affected by that edition of the New Testament, to which reference has already been made, issued by Erasmus from Basle in 1516 after he had left England: a work in which the Greek text appeared side by side with a new Latin translation, in place of the orthodox "Vulgate" whereof the stereotyped phraseology had acquired, through centuries of authorised interpretation, a meaning often very far removed from that of the original.

[Sidenote: Wolsey and the Reformation]

Thus what the Scholars accomplished was not Reform but the preparation of men's minds for Reform. What Wolsey the Statesman might have done, if foreign affairs had not occupied the best of his energies, we can only guess. His point of view was that of a Politician, not that of a man of religion. Such reforms as he might have been prepared to introduce would not have been the outcome of any lofty idealism, but only such as seemed to be dictated by public decency. As a Statesman, he was alive to the advantages of education, desired much of the wealth of the Church to be turned into that channel, and founded colleges, which he staffed with men of the new school and financed in part from the proceeds of suppressed religious houses. He went so far as to procure a papal Bull for the abolition of all Houses numbering less than seven inmates. But it may be doubted whether the real motive of the suppression was not rather the appropriation of funds for his favourite schemes than zeal for monastic morality. As Cardinal and Legate and an aspirant to the Papacy, he could never have lent himself to a policy calculated to weaken the ecclesiastical organisation; he could never have associated himself with Colet's campaign against clerical worldliness, of which there was no more conspicuous example in the kingdom than he. Having children himself by an illicit union, he could hardly have taken high ground as a reformer of morals. In brief, he must have confined his treatment of the situation within the limits of the work of a politician with educational leanings. What he actually did was to renew the monastic visitations set on foot by Cardinal Morton, to suppress some few small houses as corrupt or superfluous, and to encourage the new school of teaching which no one of authority had hitherto condemned as heretical. As to actual heresy, he looked on it with the eyes not of a theologian but of a politician; as a thing to be suppressed if it threatened public order, but otherwise negligible. He sought also to diminish the abuses connected with the ecclesiastical courts by the establishment of a Legatine Court of his own. But there is no sign that he was ever alive to the volcanic forces at work; or recognised that sooner or later the revolution which Luther initiated in Europe would have to be reckoned with in England also. Even at the time when the great Cardinal fell from power, there were but slight signs within the realm of the coming revolt, mutterings of a growing storm. No prophet had arisen denouncing the evil of the times convincingly, no statesman propounding drastic remedies; only the scholars had been preaching amendment, and occasional zealots had been bringing discredit on the cause of reformation by the violence of their incriminations. The far-reaching political effect of the religious differences was long in being realised on the Continent; in England it was still longer in making itself felt. Yet the Lutheran revolt was destined vitally to influence both the international relations and the internal order of every State in Christendom.

In 1517 Pope Leo X. was in want of money: and one of the recognised methods of obtaining it was the sale of Indulgences—that is to say, remissions in the duration of Purgatorial sufferings, ratified by His Holiness, and purchasable for cash. The whole thing being simply a commercial transaction, the Indulgences were offered at popular prices. There was nothing new in the method. The Lay Princes had no objections to the sale in their territories, since they could demand a share in the profits as the condition of their permission. The system moreover had been held up to ridicule before. But on this occasion, there were two novel features: one, the unprecedented scale on which the transaction was to be worked, the other the nature of the opposition it aroused. Doctor Martin Luther, an Augustinian monk and Professor at the University of Wittenberg in Saxony had been coming to the conclusion that the practices of the Church were not what they should be, and that much of her teaching was false. The affair of the Indulgences brought things to a head; and when Tetzel the Papal Commissioner was approaching Saxony, Luther drew up a counterblast in the form of a series of propositions which he nailed up publicly on the Church doors. Moreover he received unexpected support from the "Good Elector" Frederick, who forbade Tetzel to enter his dominions.

Leo was occupied with political affairs, which seemed for the time to be more important than the heretical vagaries of an obscure monk. Wolsey's diplomacy was working up to the point at which in 1518 he attached France to England in the alliance which culminated in the "Universal Peace," the Cardinal having supplanted the Pope as the moderator in the disputes of the great Powers. Then Maximilian died, and the Imperial Election absorbed political attention, with the ensuing complications described in a previous chapter. Meantime however, Luther was waxing increasingly determined; instead of quailing at threats, he was fully resolved to maintain his convictions and fight the matter out. As to what he had done, he appealed to a General Council; what he was going to do he made clear by exhorting the German Princes to stop their tributes to Rome. The advice had a natural attraction for the German Princes though they might lack enthusiasm on questions of theology. Leo issued a Bull condemning Luther. Luther answered by publicly burning the Bull (December 10th, 1520).

The young Emperor, fresh from his coronation at Aachen, was about to hold the Diet of the Empire at Worms. It was his policy to maintain friendly relations with Rome; and Luther was summoned to the Diet under a safe-conduct. The precedent of Huss showed how little such a safe-conduct was worth; but the great Reformer was undaunted. Frederick of Saxony, encouraged by Erasmus, was known to be on his side. He faced the Diet, reaffirmed his heresies, and emphasised his flat repudiation of Papal Authority. He had fiery supporters and fiery opponents. His life was in the gravest danger, and his death would have been followed by a bloody collision between the two parties. The disaster was averted by the Elector Frederick who kidnapped him for his own sake and carried him off to a secure retreat in the Wartburg: where he remained for nearly a year, working at his translation of the Bible. The Diet however confirmed an edict condemning Luther and his doctrines. The English King moreover, who accounted himself no mean theologian, issued a refutation of the Lutheran heresies which won for him from Pope Leo the title of Defender of the Faith.

At this time, and for some time to come, the Papacy regarded Francis I. with hostility, and looked upon his Italian ambitions as dangerous to itself. Hence there was a natural tendency to alliance between Rome and the Emperor. 1521 was the year of the ineffectual Conference of Calais, followed by the death of Leo X., the election of the (Imperial) Pope Adrian in the next year, and the embroilment of England in the European wars. Charles was sufficiently occupied with these high political matters, and was personally withdrawn from Germany, whose affairs were more or less controlled by an Imperial Council in which Frederick of Saxony was the guiding spirit; popular sentiment was on Luther's side, and the Worms edict was practically a dead letter. But the seclusion of the great Reformer threw the movement largely into the hands of extremists such as Carlstadt and Münzer to whose anarchical theories he was opposed as vehemently as to Rome.

[Sidenote: 1524 The German peasant rising]

Now we shall presently see that in England itself there was strong ground for discontent with the prevailing social order and the relations between the peasantry and the landed classes: but in Germany matters were very much worse. In England there had always been a tendency for the religious reformers to associate their movements with demands for social reform; and so it was now to an exaggerated degree in Germany. Social revolution was no part of the scheme of Luther and his lieutenant Melanchthon; but in defying the authority of Rome they had awakened the revolutionary spirit. Fired with religious fanaticism, the demagogues acquired a new character, a devouring zeal, a reckless courage. At last in 1524 the peasants rose demanding redress for their grievances. What they asked was indeed bare justice according to any intelligent modern view; yet the granting of their demands would have been completely subversive of the existing social order. The upper classes were united against them, Luther and his associates denounced them. The fiercest passions broke loose: there were ghastly massacres and ghastly reprisals, ending in the slaughter of scores of thousands of peasants, and the complete suppression of the rising.

[Sidenote: Its effect in England]

The Lutherans proper had emphatically dissociated themselves from the zealots who stirred up the "peasants' war," which did not alter the general attitude of the Germans on the religious question. But in England, these things had a serious effect. The Lutheran heresies were condemned as heresies in this country before the outbreak, and a considerable number of heretically inclined Englishmen took refuge in the German States, where they looked to find countenance. Being for the most part men of extreme tendencies, those tendencies were quickened; whence it resulted that in importing the new religious doctrines from Germany they combined them more or less with the doctrines of social revolution. Thus the distinction between the two movements was lost sight of, and the profession of the new doctrines was regarded as not merely heretical but in itself anarchical—a thing which must be suppressed in the interests of public order. Hence we find the curious paradox of Thomas More, the one-time advocate of a toleration which was obviously in accord with his instincts, becoming in course of time the advocate and agent of a rigorous intolerance and a relentless persecution.

[Sidenote 1: 1525 The Empire and the papacy]
[Sidenote 2: 1527 The sack of Rome]

The Peasants' Revolt was crushed in the summer of 1525. Before this end was accomplished, the Good Elector passed away—a wise, kindly, tolerant man who had exercised an immense moderating influence by simple benignity, shrewdness, and force of character. A little earlier, the ambitious schemes of Francis I. had been shattered by the disaster of Pavia. In effect, the whole European situation was changed completely since the death of Leo X. in 1521. His successor Adrian was a man of good intentions but limited purview; the great issues at stake were beyond his grasp, and his attempts at disciplinary reforms were made nugatory by the stolid immobility of the hierarchy. After a brief reign he was succeeded by Clement VII., a man of considerable talent and inconsiderable ability: a man shifty and fearful, not fitted to cope with the stubborn wills of the reigning princes and their ministers, or with the moral and intellectual forces which were threatening the supremacy of the historic Church. The collapse of the French in Italy gave Charles a power which filled Clement with alarm, since his friendliness was no longer of political moment to the Emperor, while sentimental considerations would certainly not suffice to retain the active support of Wolsey and England. In 1526 the insecurity of his position was emphasised by the attitude of the Imperial Diet held at Spires, where Charles through his brother Ferdinand withdrew from the position of anti-Lutheranism to adopt that of impartial toleration, and it was decreed in effect that each Prince might sanction what religion he would, within his own territories; thus cancelling the Decree of Worms. The capture and occupation of Rome by troops mainly Spanish in the same year, despite the Emperor's repudiation, was another alarming symptom; which received a terrifying confirmation in 1527, when the Imperial troops, Spanish and German, headed by the "Lutheran" Frundsberg and the Constable of Bourbon, turned their arms upon the Holy City, stormed it, sacked it with a savage thoroughness unparalleled since the days of Alaric, and held the Pope himself a prisoner.

[Sidenote: 1530 Diet of Augsburg]

Thus the Pope himself was now not merely dominated by the Emperor but actually in his hands. The successes of Charles however urged Francis — who had been liberated in 1526 — to renewed activity, and for a time it seemed not unlikely that he would recover his ascendency in Italy, a consummation as little to Clement's taste as the Imperial dominance. But the French King misused his opportunities and his armies met with fresh disasters. In 1529, the Pope and the Emperor were reconciled, with the result that at another Diet of Spires the Worms edict was revived and the last Spires edict revoked, in face of the protest of the Lutheran Princes which earned for them the title of Protestants. That party however was sufficiently strong to prevent its opponents from enforcing the decree over the Empire. At the Diet of Augsburg next year (1530) the decree was confirmed: the Protestants replying by drawing up the Confession of Augsburg, formulating their doctrines, a document which became the definite expression of Protestantism in the least general sense of the term — while they bound themselves for mutual support in the League of Schmalkald. The two parties seemed to be on the verge of war; but the sentiment of nationality in face of the threatening of a Turkish advance and of the non-German leanings of Charles — a sentiment most zealously preached by Luther who was a typical German patriot as well as a religious reformer — deferred the rupture till after Luther's death.

[Sidenote: The Swiss Reformers, 1520-1530]

The active aggressive Reformation began in Germany with Luther's attack on Indulgences. In France it made no headway for many years; in Spain and Italy none at all; in England none, till the meeting of Parliament in 1529. But the movement in Switzerland was as marked as that in Germany, and hardly less important in the influence ultimately exercised by the Swiss teachers, though of less direct political weight. Nor is it possible to follow the course of the Reformation in England, unless the separate existence of the Swiss School is duly appreciated. Switzerland was not a Political entity which could rank effectively as a make-weight in international rivalries; but its geographical conditions preserved it from interference, and permitted it, so to speak, to work out its own salvation. The country was a federation of small democratic States or Cantons, with no Princes and no nobility. It followed that when once the question of ecclesiastical reform was raised, the theories of Church Government which would find acceptance would be democratic in principle: and accordingly it was from Switzerland that the vital opposition to Episcopal systems sprang. But the main fact to be observed at this stage is, that the Swiss Reformers were not the outcome of the Lutheran movement; their movement was spontaneous, independent, and parallel. Their leader Zwingli anticipated rather than followed Luther. But an agitator who appealed to Germany and an agitator who appealed to Switzerland seemed to be of very different degrees of public importance. Hence comparatively speaking Zwingli was ignored by the authorities. Half Switzerland might—and did—revolt from the Pope, without greatly exercising the Papal mind. But in the process Zurich became hardly less important as a teaching centre and an asylum for heretical refugees than Wittenberg; and in many respects, the teaching of Zurich departed from the teaching of Rome more seriously than did the teaching of Luther. The element of Mysticism, to which the German genius is generally prone, had no attraction for the Swiss mind, while it was essential in the eyes of the Wittenberg school; so that Luther and the Zurich Reformers assailed each other with hardly less virulence than they both lavished on the Papal party. It was a long time before the term "Protestant" was extended so as to include the disciples of Zurich and Geneva.

[Sidenote: English heretics abroad]

Alike to Switzerland and to the German States which may by anticipation be called Protestant, there gathered during these first years an appreciable number of Englishmen, who were either already touched with Lollardry, or found themselves in revolt against prevailing doctrines or practices, or were discovering by the light of the New Learning discrepancies between the teaching of the Gospels and the current interpretation. In these territories they were for the time assured of such liberty as enabled them to issue pamphlets, dissertations, and commentaries, which found their way into England and not infrequently received effective advertisement by being publicly condemned and burnt, with the result that the few copies which escaped acquired an adventitious interest and influence. Considering the violence of the invective often conspicuous in them, and the extravagance of the controversial methods usually adopted, the treatment they met with can hardly be condemned as oppressive; whether it was politic is another question. The modern English view generally is that such repressive acts tend to defeat their own ends. On the whole however it would seem that it was the manner rather than the matter of these productions which caused the authorities to treat them and their authors with such severity, though it was done largely at the instigation of theological partisans. Thus Tindal's translation of the Bible was attacked as being *per se* dangerous; but it was the accompanying commentary which ensured its suppression.

[Sidenote: Contrasted aims]

The fundamental fact, however, which must be borne in mind in the early stages of the Reformation in England is this: that whereas the cause to which both Luther and Zwingli devoted themselves was primarily a revision of dogmas and of the practices associated with them, the work which Henry VIII. and Thomas Cromwell were to take in hand was the revision of the relations between Church and State—of the position of the Clerical organisation as a part of the body politic; not the introduction of Lutheran or Zwinglian doctrines. Such countenance as was given to Lutheranism was given for purely political reasons. Luther's was a Religious Reformation with political consequences: Henry's was a Political Reconstruction entailing ultimately a reformed religion.

CHAPTER VII
HENRY VIII (iii), 1527-29—
THE FALL OF WOLSEY

[Sidenote: "The King's affair"]

The whole prolonged episode concerned with the "Divorce" of Queen Katharine is singularly unattractive; the character of almost every leading person associated with it is damaged in the course of it—save that of the unhappy Queen. Unfortunately it is an episode which demands close attention and examination, because its vicissitudes exercised a supreme influence on the course of the Reformation initiated by the King, besides bringing into powerful relief the nature of that strange historical phenomenon, the Conscience of Henry VIII. Moreover it has received from the pen of a particularly brilliant writer a colouring which is so misleading and so plausible that the evidence as to facts requires to be presented with exceptional care.

[Sidenote 1: Story of the marriage]
[Sidenote 2: Anne Boleyn]

It is not till 1527 that the project of a Divorce emerges definitely, so to speak, into the open; but the evolution of the project had its origin at a considerably earlier date. We have to begin with a review of the conjugal relations between the King and the Queen. Arthur, Prince of Wales had celebrated his marriage with Katharine, daughter of Ferdinand of Spain and aunt of the infant who was to become Charles V. A few months later he died. The young widow was thereafter betrothed to Henry; a dispensation being obtained in 1504 from the Pope, Julius II, since marriage with a brother's widow is forbidden by the laws of the Church. Henry VII. however, who never liked to make any pledges without providing himself with some pretext by which they might be evaded, instructed his son to make a sort of protest at the time. The second marriage was not carried out till Henry VIII. was on the throne: the bride being robed in the manner customary for maidens, not for widows, on such occasions. She was older than her husband, and not particularly attractive; but they lived together with apparent affection. It is uncertain how many children were actually born; but none lived long after birth until Mary (1516), when the King showed himself conspicuously fond of his infant daughter. Henry does not in fact seem to have displayed that extreme licentiousness which characterised most of the monarchs of the time, though one illegitimate son was born to him, three years after Mary, by Mistress Elizabeth Blount—"mistress" being the courtesy title of unmarried ladies. The Court however was undoubtedly licentious, and many of his favourite companions were notoriously profligate. In 1522 Anne Boleyn, then an attractive girl of sixteen, the daughter of Sir Thomas Boleyn, came to Court. At what time Henry became seriously enamoured of her is uncertain; but from 1522 her father became the recipient of numerous favours; and in 1525 was made a peer. It was a symptom of alienation between Henry and his wife that the six-year-old son of Elizabeth Blount was at the same time created Duke of Richmond and Lord High Admiral, with much pomp. [Footnote: Brewer, ii., 102. L.& P. iv., 639.]

[Sidenote: 1527 The King prepares]

Apart from expressions in letters of 1526 which can only be reasonably interpreted as having reference to a contemplated divorce, letters of Wolsey's and the King's in the early months of 1527 prove incontestably that Henry had at that time determined that he would marry Anne, and that Wolsey [Footnote: Brewer, ii., 182, 184; S. P. Henry VIII., i, 194. L. & P., iv., 1467.] was elaborating a case, for presentation to the Pope, against the validity of the dispensation under which the marriage with Katharine had been contracted.

What, then, was the King's attitude? In April 1527, he had made up his mind to break with Charles, Katharine's nephew, and concluded a treaty with France; but under this the French King's second son, the Duke of Orleans, was to marry the Princess Mary. It is difficult to believe that when this was done, the King was actually intending at a later stage to have Mary declared illegitimate. He would hardly have proposed to alienate Charles and Francis simultaneously. Possibly he anticipated no difficulty in legitimating Mary while annulling her mother's marriage—as was ultimately done. It may be noted that it is absolutely impossible to maintain that *both* Mary and Elizabeth were born in lawful wedlock; yet the country accepted both as legitimate without demur. But this French treaty darkens rather than illuminates the problem.

The only fact definitely apparent in the papers of 1527 is that Henry had determined to make Anne his wife. There is no hint of the conscientious scruples or the patriotic motives afterwards alleged, though that of course does not preclude their having been present. Those two alleged motives require to be examined merely as *a priori* hypotheses.

There was one possible plea, then, for urging that a divorce was necessary: namely that political considerations made it imperative for the good of the nation that the King should take to himself a wife who might bear him a male heir to the throne. And there was one possible plea for demanding a formal enquiry into the validity of the dispensation: namely a conscientious doubt on the part of the King or Queen whether the union with a brother's widow was contrary to the Moral Law. No doubt existed as to the Pope's power of abrogating a law, made by the Church for the public good, in a specific case; but it was not claimed that he could abrogate the Law of God in like manner. If this was a case in which the Pope possessed the dispensing power, the dispensation held; if it was not, the marriage was no marriage however innocently the parties entered upon it. One or other of these pleas must be made the pretext of any public action.

[Sidenote: The need of an heir]

The plea that Henry must have a male heir is so absolutely conclusive in the judgment of Henry's great apologist that he feels it necessary to offer excuses for the womanly weakness which blinded Katharine to her obvious duty. It may also have appealed with considerable force to a statesman who regarded all pledges and bonds as being in the last resort dissoluble on grounds of national expediency. England had suffered enough from disputed successions; and while it is not probable that a title so incontrovertible as Mary's would have been directly challenged, it is evident that disastrous complications might have been involved by her union with any possible husband, or by her death. It may have been that it was Henry's own wish to act directly on this view, and to declare his marriage null, arbitrarily, on the ground of public expediency. But whatever were Wolsey's views on expediency, and on the desirability of nullifying the marriage, such a course would have been too flagrant a violation of the universally accepted belief in the sanctity of the marriage tie to meet with his support. Moreover the offspring of a new marriage contracted under such conditions could hardly escape having his legitimacy challenged when opportunity offered. The security of the succession could not therefore be obtained by this method. Yet the burden of discovering some way to enable Henry to marry again was laid upon the Cardinal's shoulders.

[Sidenote: The plea of invalidity]

A pretext was forthcoming, whether devised by the Cardinal or another. The marriage with Katharine might be held invalid on the ground that the dispensation under which it was contracted was invalid, as being *ultra vires*. [Footnote: *Cf.* however Wolsey's letter, Brewer, ii., 180. Katharine argued that since she had remained a maiden, no actual affinity had been contracted, therefore the re-marriage was not contrary to God's Law. Wolsey was prepared to reply that in that case, the dispensation was invalid; since it specified only the impediment of "affinity" but not that of "public honesty" created by a contract not consummated, and so failed to cover the admitted circumstances. It appears from the complete context that this plea was hit upon only as a rejoinder to this particular plea of Katharine's. But see Taunton, *Thomas Wolsey*, chap., x., where a different view is taken; the whole context, however, is not there cited.] This was the line that Wolsey advised, and to which the King committed himself. It should be clear that it finally precluded the other line of arbitrary dissolution, since it rested on the inviolability of a marriage once validly contracted. If the Pope could not set aside the bar to re-marriage with a dead husband's brother, the King could hardly set aside his own marriage, if it had been itself lawful. Stated conversely; if the King could, so to speak cancel a living wife on the ground of public expediency, the Pope had surely been entitled to cancel a dead husband on the same ground.

[Sidenote: Conjunction of incentives]

When Wolsey had propounded the theory that the validity of the dispensation was doubtful, it is easy enough to see how Henry might have persuaded himself that his conscience must be set at ease. What if the death of all his male children had been a Divine Judgment on an unlawful union? The wish is father to the thought. From this point, it was a short step to a conviction that, whatever any one might say, the union was unlawful. Thus Henry could with comparative equanimity adopt the role of one who merely felt that his doubts must be set at rest, while he would be only overjoyed to be finally certified that they were groundless. It is not till this professed hope is in danger of being realised that the mask is dropped and the King's determination to have a divorce by hook or by crook is avowed.

On this view of the policy pursued, passion and patriotism may have combined—in uncertain proportions—to make the King desire a new marriage; obedience and patriotism may have likewise combined to produce the same desire in the Cardinal. But it is extremely difficult to doubt that the King's conscientious scruples were an after-thought, since they had not overtly troubled him for eighteen years of married life; while the Cardinal's position was painfully complicated by an intense aversion to the particular marriage in contemplation. The Boleyns were closely associated with the group of courtiers who were most antagonistic to Wolsey; while on the other hand, Katharine had for long regarded him as her husband's evil genius.

[Sidenote: The Orleans betrothal]

There is a single feature of the situation in the spring of 1527 which might be taken as pointing to a belief on the King's part that the validity of the marriage would be confirmed: namely the betrothal of his daughter to Orleans. This however would completely negative the activity of that patriotic motive by which Mr. Froude set so much store. Moreover, it is flatly contradicted by the letter to Anne [Footnote: *L. & P.*, iv., 1467.] in which Henry unmistakably declares his determination to marry her: and by Wolsey's [Footnote: *S. P.*, i., 194. Brewer, ii., 193 ff.] letter to him, stating the case for the divorce.

[Sidenote: Conclusion]

The only possible conclusion is that the one motive which really actuated the King was the desire to gratify an illicit passion. Other subsidiary motives he may have called in to justify himself to himself, on which he dwelt till he really persuaded himself that they were genuine. For it was his unfailing practice to do or get done whatsoever served his personal interest, and to parade some high moral cause as his unimpeachable motive—or if this proved quite impossible, to condemn a minister as the responsible person. Yet however difficult it is to reconcile such avowed motives with the known facts, the avowal always has about it a tone of conviction which can only have been the outcome of successful self-deception.

[Sidenote: The first plan (May)]

It was the Cardinal's task then to procure by some means a formal and authoritative pronouncement that the Papal Dispensation was invalid. The first scheme was that he should hold a Legatine Court before which the King should be cited for living in an unlawful union with his brother's widow. Since the Legate was also the King's subject, the royal assent had to be formally given. This was duly arranged in May, the affair being conducted with the utmost secrecy; but after the first beginnings [Footnote: *L. & P.*, iv., 1426.] these proceedings were dropped: presumably because, if they had been carried through, Katharine might have appealed to the Pope and Wolsey would have had no voice in the ultimate decision. [Footnote: The Pope in that case must either have decided the case himself, or have given full powers to a Legatine Court to act without appeal. In the latter event, Wolsey could not have been appointed, since Katharine's appeal would have been an appeal against his previous decision.]

In the same month the world learnt with amazement that the troops of Bourbon and the Lutheran Frundsberg had stormed and sacked Rome; and that the Imperial troops held Clement himself a prisoner in the castle of St. Angelo. The Pope was thus completely in the Emperor's power: the Emperor was Katharine's nephew and would most certainly veto the divorce.

Moreover, Katharine had now an inkling that steps to obtain a divorce were being projected; and, unknown to Henry, Mendoza the Spanish ambassador had already warned the Emperor.

[Sidenote: The second plan (June)]

Thus the difficulties of Wolsey's task were increased; since the next move must be to get a Papal Commission appointed which should be under Wolsey's control. To that end, the ecclesiastical support of the English Bishops and the political support of Francis were requisite. Wolsey played upon the guilelessness of Fisher of Rochester, till he persuaded the saintly bishop that the confirmation of the marriage was the one thing desired — that the Queen's opposition was due to an unfortunate misconception, and entirely opposed to her own interests. The same course was pursued with Warham of Canterbury. [Footnote: Brewer, ii., pp. 193 ff.] The necessity for the enquiry was fathered upon the Bishop of Tarbes, a member of the French embassy which had settled the betrothal of Orleans and Mary, who was said [Footnote: There is some reason to suppose that this story of the Bishop of Tarbes was merely concocted by Wolsey and Henry. It appears to have been referred to only in Wolsey's communications with Warham and Fisher.— Brewer, *Henry VIII.*, ii., 216. But *cf.* Pollard, *Henry VIII., sub loc.*] to have questioned the validity of the dispensation, and by consequence the certainty of the princess's legitimacy.

In July Wolsey proceeded to France, ostensibly for the settlement of details in connexion with the recent treaty: actually, that Francis might be induced to bring pressure to bear on Charles for the release of the Pope—in the somewhat desperate hope that Clement in his gratitude would thereupon grant Henry's wishes. Should the Pope's release be refused, Wolsey had the idea (soon to be abandoned) that the Cardinals might be summoned to meet in France, on the ground that the Pope was being forcibly deprived of the power of action. [Footnote: *S. P.*, i., 230, 270. Brewer, ii., 209, 219.]

[Sidenote: Knight's mission (Autumn)]

The treaty of Amiens, cementing the union between Francis and Henry, was signed late in August without reference to divorce. Now however Henry began to conduct operations independently of Wolsey, sending his own secretary Knight to Rome with private instructions, the object of which was to evade the ultimate submission of the question to Wolsey's jurisdiction. Under the influence of the Boleyn clique, and knowing Wolsey's aversion to the Boleyn marriage, the King may have suspected that his minister would play him false if he lost all hope of averting that conclusion to the divorce. Or he may merely have resolved that it was time to check any development of his minister's authority. On Wolsey's return to England, instead of being received in privacy according to precedent, he was summoned on his arrival at Richmond Palace to meet his master in the presence of Anne Boleyn.

[Sidenote: Its failure (Dec)]

Knight's mission was a failure. In December, Clement escaped in disguise from his Imperial guards: Knight found him at Orvieto. It was evident that the secret plan of getting the Pope's permission to marry again without upsetting the existing marriage [Footnote: Brewer, ii., 224, 234-239. Both the Conscience of the King and the need of an heir, are dwelt on in the instructions.] was out of the question. So the Secretary presented a form for a dispensation, and for a Commission which was to give Wolsey power to decide summarily against the validity of the dispensation granted by Pope Julius, without appeal; and power to declare Mary legitimate at the same time. The dispensation was to enable Henry to marry thereafter in despite of difficulties which might be raised on certain specified grounds—intelligible only if those difficulties applied in Anne Boleyn's case: and implying the truth of allegations subsequently made as to relations between Henry and Anne's mother and sister. Knight was outwitted by a Cardinal, Lorenzo Pucci, who redrafted the documents so as to make them useless for Henry's purpose. The deluded envoy returned to England under the impression that he had achieved a diplomatic triumph. But the King saw that he must leave the management of such delicate matters to Wolsey.

[Sidenote: The Pope and the Cardinal]

It is evident that the Pope's one desire was to evade all responsibility in the matter; as it was Wolsey's, on the contrary part, to fix the ultimate responsibility on him. Clement wanted the support of England and France; but, though now no longer actually the Emperor's prisoner, he was distinctly in greater danger from him than from the other Powers. Moreover for one Pope to be invited to nullify the proceedings of another was a somewhat dangerous precedent: as implying that a papal decision was not necessarily unimpeachable. The Cardinal however required the Pope's authority. The divorce was not popular in England, where the general inclination was towards the Imperial alliance. Besides, Katharine was firmly convinced that Wolsey was the moving spirit; so was the general public. If the divorce were carried through by any method which seemed to bear out that theory— if it could be looked upon as a political job of the Cardinal's—Henry too would come in for a share of the odium, and might be trusted to visit that misfortune on his minister. So Wolsey would have nothing to say to the suggestion that the King should act on his own account without the Pope, and take his chance of an appeal.

[Sidenote: 1528 Gardiner's mission]

Early in 1528, the negotiations were again on foot. This time they were in the hands of Wolsey's own men—Steven Gardiner and Foxe, the King's almoner. Their instructions were to obtain a commission with absolute authority, in which a legate—Campeggio for choice—should be associated with Wolsey; failing that, a legate without Wolsey but one on whom Wolsey could depend; finally, as least desirable, the commission was to consist of Wolsey and Warham. If the Pope continued recalcitrant, he was to be given to understand that the results for him might be very awkward. Gardiner in fact did not hesitate to indulge in threats which were more than hints. England's goodwill was at stake. If Clement had so little faith in his own authority that he dared not exercise it in a manifestly righteous cause, Henry might repudiate papal authority altogether. Nevertheless, in spite of all Gardiner's skill and vigour—and he showed himself deficient in neither—the result was unsatisfactory. A commission was obtained for Wolsey with Campeggio; but it was not absolute. The decision they might arrive at could not take effect till referred to Rome for confirmation.

[Sidenote: Wolsey's critical position]

Although the purpose of Gardiner and Foxe was not completely achieved, it certainly appeared at this time that Wolsey had practically won over the Pope; in other words, had made sure that the King should get his desire under cover of law, and of the highest moral sanctions, without any breach with the Church, defiance of Authority, or association with heresy. So far, the credit was the Cardinal's, who had dissuaded his master from following a much more arbitrary course. Nevertheless indications were not wanting that the Boleyn influence was at work in a manner very detrimental to Wolsey; that Henry was fully alive to his minister's unpopularity; and that if occasion served he might take the popular side. Thus when Wolsey appointed a suitable person to be Abbess of Wilton, instead of a very unsuitable person who was connected with the Boleyns, the King reprimanded him in his most elevated style—taking occasion at the same time to be scandalised at the subscriptions to Wolsey's educational schemes provided by monasteries which had pleaded poverty at the time of the "Amicable Loan". It was at least tolerably evident that "the King's matter" as the divorce was generally called would have to be brought to a speedy and successful issue if Wolsey was to retain the royal favour.

Clement VII. however was a dexterous procrastinator. Campeggio got his Commission in April. But he did not start from Rome till June: he did not reach French soil till the end of July: in September he got as far as Paris. Meantime, the French troops in Italy were not doing so well, but the Pope was strongly suspected of Imperial leanings. The French King formed the opinion—which he transmitted to his brother of England—that Campeggio's object was to induce Henry to change his determination.

[Sidenote: Campeggio and Wolsey (Autumn)]

When at last Campeggio reached London, still suffering seriously from the gout which was the ostensible cause of his dilatory journeying, Wolsey was explicit. He warned the Legate that the business must be put through promptly. The need of a male heir was imperative; the King was convinced that his wedlock with Katharine was contrary to the Divine law: if he were not quickly released, the respect hitherto shown for the Church by the Defender of the Faith would certainly vanish; while Wolsey himself, whose influence had hitherto kept his master loyal in the face of strong temptation, would no longer be able to restrain him. From Campeggio's letters, [Footnote: Brewer, ii., 296.] it is evident that the King had mastered his own case thoroughly, and knew the legal aspects better than any one else: also, that the intention was to declare Mary his heir unless there should be male issue of the new marriage. The Legate let slip that in view of the determined attitude of Henry and Wolsey, he would have to await further instructions from Rome; whereupon he was again threatened with the secession of England from the Roman Obedience. Next, the two Cardinals tried to induce Katharine to accede to a divorce without a formal trial; on the ground that thereby she would ensure that save on the single point of the re-marriage any demand she might put forward would be granted, and much scandal would be averted. The Queen took some days to consider her reply: but was absolutely obdurate. She was Henry's wife; she could not and would not profess that she was not. On every ground, she would fight to the last.

Campeggio did his best to impress the Pope with the urgency of the case: but Clement was more than ever afraid of Charles, and persisted in the first place that proceedings were to be postponed and prolonged by every effort of ingenuity, and in the second that no verdict adverse to the marriage was to be pronounced without his ratification.

[Sidenote: Henry's attitude]

Henry for his part, learning or knowing before that Ferdinand had received from Pope Julius a confirmation of the dispensation in ampler terms, urged upon Katharine the necessity of obtaining this document in her own interests—hoping that there would be a chance of repudiating it as a forgery. Also he instructed his agents at Rome to persuade the Pope to give him a dispensation for re-marriage, without a divorce, if Katharine retired into a nunnery; [Footnote: *L. & P.*, iv., 2157, 2161. Brewer, ii., 312, 313, and note. Such a marriage was admissible according to some of the

Lutherans.] or even for an openly bigamous union. Moreover about the same time, Henry openly separated himself from his wife, and began to treat Anne Boleyn publicly as his partner-elect on the throne.

[Sidenote 1: 1529]
[Sidenote 2: The trial]

The Pope's one object was to evade the responsibility of any pronouncement. The Imperialist cause in Italy was progressing: Charles was growing steadily stronger. Clement dared not pronounce in Henry's favour; he was only less afraid of pronouncing against him. He told the agents that the King should act on his own responsibility on the ground of dissatisfaction with Campeggio's conduct; whereas the King was quite resolved to act, but also quite resolved to force the responsibility for his action on Clement. There was a limit to the possibilities of procrastination, but it was not till June 1529 that the Court opened proceedings, citing the King and Queen to appear. Fisher of Rochester, appearing on behalf of the Queen, boldly declared that the marriage was valid and could not be dissolved. Standish supported him, less vigorously. The Queen challenged the jurisdiction of the Court, and appealed from it to the Pope. She regarded Wolsey as the source of her woes; Anne believed that the procrastination was due to his machinations; the King was quite capable of crushing the Cardinal to relieve his own feelings. Popular sentiment was entirely on the Queen's side, but held the Cardinal to blame rather than the King: though even in Court Henry declared, in answer to Wolsey's appeal, that the minister had not suggested but had deterred him from the course adopted. Campeggio prorogued the Court in July. At about the same time, Clement, acting under Imperial pressure, formally revoked the case to Rome. Before the revocation reached England, a desperate attempt was made to persuade Katharine to place herself in the King's hands: it failed. A sharp public altercation between Wolsey and Suffolk showed how the current was setting.

[Sidenote: The storm gathers]

During the following months, Wolsey's loss of the royal favour became increasingly evident, and the opposition to him on the part of the nobility more and more open. Steven Gardiner, who had proved his conspicuous ability, was made the King's private secretary, and became the normal medium of communication—the close personal intercourse hitherto prevalent was at an end. Wolsey's European policy was thrown over by Henry, who allowed Francis and Charles to come to terms without his claiming any voice in the negotiation. A treaty of amity was signed at Cambrai, which terminated all prospect of Francis being induced to assist

Henry in bringing pressure to bear either on the Emperor or the Pope, and released Clement from serious alarms as to the results of his accepting the Imperial policy. England had deliberately vacated the position of arbiter, because Henry was too thoroughly engrossed with the divorce to care about anything else. Since both Francis and Charles were for the time satisfied to restrict their ambitions so as not to collide with each other, there was no further demand for the Cardinal's diplomatic genius. The best to which Wolsey could now look forward was that he might be permitted to turn his vast talents to the reform of administration, ecclesiastical, legal, and educational, which he had always postponed to what he regarded as the more vital demands of international politics.

[Sidenote: The storm breaks (Oct.)]

It was not long before even these hopes were destroyed. At the beginning of October, Campeggio departed from England. At Dover, his baggage was ransacked by the King's authority, in the hope of discovering documents which would enable Wolsey to deal with the divorce in his absence. The documents were not forthcoming. Wolsey was of no more use to his master. The day after Campeggio reached Dover a writ was demanded by the King's attorney against the Cardinal for breach of the statute of Praemunire in acting as Legate.

[Sidenote 1: Wolsey's fall]
[Sidenote 2: 1530]
[Sidenote 3: Wolsey's death (Nov.)]

The fatal blow had been struck. From that hour, the Cardinal's doom was sealed. He ceased absolutely to be a political force and became merely an object for the King, and for every enemy he had raised up against himself, to buffet. A week later, on October 16th, the Dukes of Norfolk and Suffolk demanded the seals from Wolsey as Chancellor; he was deprived of all his benefices and retired to his house at Esher, where he abode in poverty. This contented Henry for the time, and he sent gracious messages—but restricted them to words. Even Thomas More, who succeeded him as Chancellor, is said to have acted so far out of character as to speak of him publicly in insulting terms. Parliament had been summoned for November; a bill depriving him for ever of office was introduced in the Lords: in the Commons, it was boldly resisted by Thomas Cromwell who won thereby great credit for his loyalty; and it was dropped—not against the wishes of the King, who was as yet disinclined to deprive himself of the chance of resuscitating the great minister. In February Wolsey was restored to the see of York, whither he departed to act in the novel capacity of a diocesan devoted solely to his duties—duties which he so discharged as to change bitter unpopularity into warm affection. The King kept a firm hold on his forfeited properties, Gardiner was advanced to his see of Winchester: the college at Ipswich was dissolved. Wolsey was rash enough to attempt to open secret communications with Francis I., in the hope that his influence might be exercised to restore to favour the man who had done so much for him. But Norfolk, in power, had to cultivate Francis; and Francis, finding him a much simpler diplomatic antagonist, had no wish to reinstate the Cardinal. The attempted correspondence became known, and in November, without warning, Wolsey was arrested for high treason. Sick and worn, he started on his last journey towards London; but was stricken with mortal illness, and could travel no further than Leicester Abbey where the end came.

[Sidenote: Wolsey's achievement]

So died the great Cardinal who for nearly twenty years had mainly swayed the destinies of England. Henry VII. had slowly recovered a place among the nations for a country brought low by long years of reckless civil strife. His son's minister again raised her to be the arbiter of Europe, holding the scales between the two mighty princes who virtually ruled Christendom: not by deeds of arms like Edward III. or Henry V., for no English soldier of real distinction arose in his time; but by a diplomatic genius almost without parallel among English statesmen. In this field, the superiority of his abilities to those of his contemporaries made his position with his master absolutely secure, so long as foreign relations were the primary consideration; for though the ends the minister himself had in view were always the same, he was ready to exert his powers to the full, even at the expense of those objects, in carrying out any policy on which Henry himself might determine; and as a general rule the King's wishes did not run counter to his own.

[Sidenote: Appraisement of Wolsey]

His absorbing aim was to magnify England and the King of England in the eyes of Europe: nor was personal ambition lacking, but it was subordinate. That he desired the popedom is clear, and that Henry desired it for him; but he was above the temptation of allowing that desire to dominate his national aims, and had he achieved it, he would have regarded the alliance of the Ecclesiastical Power with England as the real prize secured. His personal weight in the Counsels of Europe would hardly have been increased; and he cared more for Power than for the appearance of it, though he had a possibly exaggerated perception of the practical value of magnificence in securing both national and personal prestige. In part at least this was the cause of that habitual display which, while impressing, also roused the anger of the nobles, who regarded him as an upstart, and of the satirists of ecclesiastical ostentation and luxury. Secure in the confidence of the King, he never attempted to conciliate either popular sentiment or the rivals whom he deposed.

But at all times, if he magnified his own office, it was as the King's right hand. If the King's will, even in opposition to his own, necessitated unpopular measures, he carried those measures out, and took the odium for them on his own head, preserving his master's popularity at the price of his own. He ruled the country on autocratic principles, and the increase of his power was the increase also of the King's. And the King rewarded him after his kind.

But for the all-absorbing interest of diplomacy, his vast abilities as an administrator and organiser might have achieved great things. He would at least have pruned ecclesiastical abuses; and would have forced upon the clergy as an ecclesiastic those reforms which they were always on the verge of introducing when they found themselves anticipated by the drastic action of the temporal Power. Reform was the inevitable corollary of Education, and the development of Education was of all schemes the nearest to Wolsey's heart. Yet whether, if the Divorce question had never arisen, he would have played an effective part in the Reformation is open to doubt, for at bottom the Puritan movement in these islands, the Lutheran movement, and the Counter-reformation, were all the outcome or expression of Moral ideals, not of state-craft; and for Wolsey morals were subordinate to state-craft. It is probable that in any case the assertion in England by the State of its supremacy over the Church would only have been deferred; but Wolsey might have deferred it. As it was, Henry willed otherwise. The great statesman, failing to carry out his master's demands, was hurled from power. The battle of the Reformation was to be fought under other captains.

NOTE.

The term "Divorce" has been employed above, because, although a misnomer, it is universally applied. Properly a divorce is the cancellation of a legally contracted marriage. What Henry sought was a *declaration of nullity*—that no valid marriage had ever taken place.

CHAPTER VIII
HENRY VIII (iv) 1529-33—THE
BREACH WITH ROME

[Sidenote: 1529 No revolt as yet]

It will have been observed that when Wolsey found that the divorce was inevitable, his energies were concentrated on the single purpose of securing it under papal authority. For this he had two reasons—one, that without that authority the King's act would appear in all its arbitrariness, causing grave scandal: the other that if that authority were refused, he foresaw the cleavage between England and Rome which did eventually take place. Apart however from the divorce, there had not been up to the time of Wolsey's fall any hint of an opinion in high places that such a cleavage was *per se* desirable or desired—although both Wolsey himself and Gardiner had given Clement fair warning that Henry was likely to reconsider the papal claims altogether unless the Pope complied with his wishes. The revocation of the cause to Rome immediately brought the execution of this threat into the sphere of practical politics.

In the second place there had been no tendency to encourage or allow deviations from recognised orthodox doctrine. The new criticism had been so far admitted as to produce a rigid section and a liberal section among the orthodox, such leading prelates as Wolsey himself, Warham, Fox, Fisher, and Tunstal, all favouring the new learning in various degrees, and being supported therein by such learned laymen as Sir Thomas More. Their toleration however had not extended to anything censurable as heresy, and their attitude had been somewhat stiffened by the course of the Lutheran revolt on the Continent. The increased licence within the Empire, following the edict of Spires in 1528, led to an increased activity in the suppression of heretics and heretical publications in England, first under Wolsey and then under his successor in the Chancellorship.

[Sidenote: Growth of anti-clericalism]

In a third direction however, though not much had been done in the way of measures, an *anti-clerical* party had been growing up: a party which sought to diminish clerical jurisdiction, clerical privileges, and clerical emoluments. Among the ecclesiastics themselves there were not a few who desired to improve clerical administration from within, but without diminution of ecclesiastical authority; the anti-clericals were laymen who wished the reforms to be forced on the Church from outside, reducing ecclesiastical authority in the process. These two policies were in direct opposition, seeing that antagonism to Wolsey—emphatically a reformer of the prior class—was the leading motive with the nobility who headed the second class; while the Commons in general desired primarily to be freed from the exactions by which the clergy benefited, and from which they did not believe the clergy would of their own initiative cut themselves off. Wolsey had begun the internal amendment, by his visitation and suppression of the smallest monasteries and the appropriation of ecclesiastical property to educational purposes, and by some substitution of the superior organisation of the legatine court for that of the Ordinaries; but the latter step had been cancelled by his fall and by the ominous appeal to the statute of Praemunire against legatine jurisdiction. On the other hand, the anti-clerical action had been practically confined so far to the modifications as to Benefit of Clergy; unless we include the publication of pamphlets and rhymes attacking the ecclesiastical body in general, or Wolsey in particular as the incarnation of their shortcomings.

Some years were still to elapse before any material changes from orthodox theological doctrine were to be entertained. But in 1529, the suspension of the Trial was forthwith followed by the adoption of a policy—as yet only provisional—setting aside the Pope's authority; and the assembly of Parliament in November was marked by an immediate attack on ecclesiastical abuses.

[Sidenote: Thomas Cranmer]

In the last six months of this year the King discovered two instruments consummately adapted for executing his will. It appears that the idea of obtaining the opinions of the Doctors at the English Universities had already been mooted, and that one of those selected [Footnote: Strype, *Memorials of Cranmer*. Hook, *Life of Cranmer*.] at Cambridge was Thomas Cranmer, a learned and amiable divine with marked leanings towards the New Learning; who in his early graduate days had fallen under the influence of the teaching at Cambridge of Erasmus; in scholarship subtle and erudite, in affairs guileless and easily swayed; timorous by nature, but capable of outbreaks of audacity as timid persons often are: a gentle and lovable man, but lacking in that robust self-confidence needed by one who would take a resolutely independent line; a man intended to be a student and forced by an unkind fate to assume the role of a man of action. Such a character, brought under the direct influence of a powerful will and a magnetic personality, is readily led to see everything as it is desired that he should see it, and at the worst to differ from the master-mind only with submission.

[Sidenote: Appeal to the universities]

When Campeggio suspended the sittings of the Commission the, King withdrew to Waltham Cross. Steven Gardiner and Foxe the King's almoner, who were in his suite, met Cranmer who had left Cambridge on account of an outbreak of the sweating sickness. They had, as was natural, a conversation on "the King's affair"; when Cranmer propounded the theory that if the Universities of Europe—that is, the qualified divines—gave it as their opinion that the union with Katharine had been contrary to the Divine Law, the King might follow the dictates of his conscience and pronounce the marriage null without recognising Papal jurisdiction. This was clearly quite a different thing from producing the judgment of the Doctors merely as an expert opinion which must carry weight with the Judge at Rome. It was practically an assertion that the Pope's judgment was not of higher authority than the King's; an answer to a question as to jurisdiction; a suggestion of replying to the Pope's revocation of the case by a counter-revocation. Foxe reported the conversation to Henry, who caught at the new method of giving a constitutional colour to an arbitrary proceeding. Cranmer was summoned to court, attached to the Boleyn household, set down to write a thesis on the point of conscience, and sent off early in 1530 in the train of the Earl of Wiltshire (to which dignity Sir Thomas Boleyn—had been raised) on an embassy to the Emperor at Bologna. Moreover his plan for consulting the Universities was actively taken in hand.

[Sidenote: The new Parliament]

In the meantime, in November, Henry's most famous Parliament had opened session. The last, called six years before under Wolsey's regime to obtain supplies, had shown a qualified submissiveness. The new one, whether packed or not, displayed prompt signs of activity. Known to fame as the "Seven Years'" or "Reformation" Parliament, it consistently displayed three characteristics: it was anti-papal and anti-clerical; it endorsed the Royal will; but it refused dictation where its pocket was concerned. Its first session lasted only a few weeks, but was marked by an attack on clerical abuses, and by the sudden prominence achieved by Thomas Cromwell.

[Sidenote: Thomas Cromwell]

Concerning Cromwell's early years, much is reported and little is known. The common rumour declared that he was the son of a blacksmith—as it declared Wolsey to be the son of a butcher. He is said to have tried various trades, among others those of man-at-arms in the mercenary troop of an Italian nobleman, wool-merchant and usurer at Antwerp, usurer and petty attorney in England. On all these points the evidence is scanty and inconclusive. About 1520, he found his way into Wolsey's entourage, and was a member of the 1523 parliament. Wolsey found him an apt man of business, and entrusted him with a good deal of the financial management of his educational schemes; in the course of which it is at least probable that he applied the twin practices of bribery and blackmail, which not without reason were attributed at a later date to his servants. Yet, however unscrupulous he may have been in his dealings with others, to the master whose service he had followed he was always loyal. Wolsey made him his secretary; and when the Cardinal fell, the secretary's position seemed exceedingly precarious. Whether from an admirable fidelity or through amazingly astute hypocrisy, he boldly and openly took up the cudgels in parliament on behalf of the stricken minister, apparently challenging imminent ruin for himself. Action so courageous won him applause and good-will instead of present hostility. More than that, it immediately marked him in the eyes of the King — an exceedingly shrewd judge of men — as an invaluable prospective servant for himself. A combination of audacity and fidelity with shrewdness, resourcefulness, and unscrupulosity, was precisely what he wanted and precisely what he had found. The Cardinal's secretary became the King's secretary, and forthwith identified himself with the policy of establishing the Royal autocracy in a stronger form than it had ever before assumed in England. Whether or no Thomas Cromwell learnt his political principles as an adventurer in Italy, he became himself the living embodiment of those doctrines of state-craft which were systematised by Macchiavelli in his treatise "The Prince".

[Sidenote: Pope, Clergy and King]

In the reconstruction of the relations between Church and State which covers more than nine-tenths of the Reformation under Henry VIII. there were three parties concerned; the Pope, the Sovereign, and the Clerical Organisation in England. From time immemorial, Popes and Kings had striven periodically with each other in asserting antagonistic control over the ecclesiastical body; and the ecclesiastical body had made common cause, now with the Pope and now with the King, in resisting encroachments by the rival authority. If the clergy submitted to one or the other, it was always with a reservation that submission to physical force could not impair the inherent rights of the successors of the Apostles. Similarly, if the Pope gave way to the King or the King to the Pope, their respective successors regarded the claims surrendered as rights not cancelled but in abeyance. The prevailing conditions at any given time were always looked upon as a *modus vivendi* liable to readjustment when any of the three parties felt impelled to claim a larger freedom of action or a larger power of control. In the past however the Spiritual Powers had drawn effectively upon their armoury of excommunications and interdicts in the conflict; it was now to be seen whether these ancient weapons had become obsolete. If they could be defied with comparative impunity, there could be but one end to a struggle between the Spiritual and the Temporal forces.

[Sidenote: Double campaign opens]

By the appeal to the Universities, Henry gave warning of a possible anti-papal campaign: in which he could look for a considerable degree of clerical support up to a certain point, more particularly because the clergy generally were ready to be released from the financial exactions of the Holy See, as well as from its practical exercise of patronage. Parliament opened an anti-clerical campaign, but its measures at first were confined to dealing with almost indefensible and obvious abuses. Bishop Fisher recognised the familiar thin end of the wedge, and charged the Commons with desiring "the goods, not the good" of the Church; but the opposition was slender. In the six weeks of the first session, there were passed, the Probate and Mortuaries Acts, abolishing, reducing, or regulating fees, and the Pluralities Act, forbidding the clergy in general to hold more than one benefice, and requiring Residence—a very inconvenient arrangement for papal nominees. The general value of the Act however was impaired by a schedule of exemptions. Fisher's protest had its counterpart in the protest of Convocation, not against the avowed objects of this legislation but against Parliament as its source: the position being that Convocation was itself preparing legislation with the same ends in view, and was the proper body to do so.

[Sidenote: 1530 Answers of the Universities]

During 1530, Parliament remained inactive. The Earl of Wiltshire's embassy to Bologna, of which the object was to induce Charles to withdraw his opposition to the divorce, naturally proved abortive. The consultation of the Universities however went on apace. The theory propounded for their acceptance was that Katharine had been in actual fact the wife of Henry's brother; that this being so her marriage with Henry was contrary to the Law of God; and that by consequence the second contract was actually not only voidable but void, the dispensation being under those circumstances a dead letter. On the other side it was maintained that whatever validity there might be in this argument, it fell to the ground if—as was asserted on the Queen's behalf—her first marriage had been ceremonial only. The answers of the Universities were inconclusive, some declaring the marriage valid, others declaring it void, and others, including Oxford and Cambridge, declaring that it was against the Law of God without pronouncing the dispensation of Julius *ipso facto* invalid. Moreover, had the opinions given been decisive in themselves, the method by which they were obtained would have destroyed their moral value. Francis, finding that England's friendship was in the balance, dictated a favourable reply to the French Universities. Those in England knew they were not free agents. Clement professed to give those in Italy a free hand, but in that country Charles was the dominant power. In Germany the Lutherans were hostile to Henry personally on account of his own anti-Lutheran pronouncements. Nowhere was a judgment on the simple merits of the case procurable.

[Sidenote: Preoccupation of the Clergy]

In the meantime, the clergy in England had been mainly occupied with a campaign against heresy, and with the suppression of dangerous literature; [Footnote: According to Mr. Froude, Henry only assented with reluctance to the suppression of Tindal's Testament on condition of the preparation of an authorised version being agreed to. But even Hall, whom he cites, only says that both proposals were adopted after long debate.—Froude, i., p. 298 (Ed. 1862).] but willingly or not found themselves committed to approving the preparation of an authorised translation of the Scriptures—the one movement under Henry which tended definitely, in effect though not of set purpose, to a revision of Doctrine.

[Sidenote 1: Menace of Praemunire]
[Sidenote 2: 1531 "Only Supreme Head"]
[Sidenote 3: Proceedings in Parliament]

In December of 1530, however, the Church was to receive a rough reminder that the Defender of the Faith was a stickler for the rigidity of the statutes. He had already struck at Wolsey because, urged thereto by himself, the Cardinal had obtained and exercised legatine powers contrary to the Statutes of Praemunire. Such was the King's reverence for the Law that after it had been transgressed with his sanction for ten years he felt it his duty to penalise the transgressor. After another twelve-month, he felt it his further duty to penalise all who had submitted to the illegal authority. The clergy were informed that they lay one and all under the royal displeasure for breach of praemunire (of which they had in fact been technically guilty), and could only hope for pardon by purchasing it for something over £100,000—practically equivalent to about a couple of millions now. Convocation, alive to the futility of resistance, apologised for its iniquity and admitted the justice of the punishment. Thereupon, in the preamble to the bill by which they were to mulct themselves, the King required the insertion of a clause which designated him "Protector and Only Supreme

Head of the Church and Clergy in England". This roused general resistance. Convocation proposed conferences, and sought some compromise which they could reconcile with their consciences. The King would have no compromise, demanding instant submission. At last Warham hit upon the expedient of one of those saving phrases which might mean everything or nothing, and yet could not be objected to on the face of it; inserting the words "so far as the laws of Christ permit": the precise degree to which the said laws did permit being susceptible of unlimited argument, as the royal claims or the clerical conscience might respectively demand. Even so had Becket in the past shielded himself with the words "Saving the rights of my Order". For the time being, this diplomatic evasion or pitiful subterfuge, as the advocates and contemners of the clergy respectively call it, saved the situation. At the time, it must be remarked, Henry did not intend the title to be read as repudiating the Papal Supremacy, which had not hitherto been formally called question. On the face of it, it looks like a touch of Cromwell's; in a thing designed to force the hand of the Clergy in the future if the Papal Supremacy should be directly challenged. The clause was accepted (for the Province of Canterbury) on March 22nd; six weeks later it was also accepted by the Convocation of York, with a protest from Tunstal, now bishop of Durham, who had been distinguished by his diplomatic services under Wolsey's régime. During the corresponding session (January-March 1531) no anti-clerical measures were introduced in Parliament; which registered the Royal pardon and received the formal announcement of the decision of the Universities. The "stern and lofty moral principles" [Footnote: Froude, i., 307, 310 (Ed. 1862). The historian's enthusiasm may seem to require some qualification. The retrospective creation of crimes is a dangerous practice: and the penalty applied might even be considered savage.] of the nation were however vindicated, in consequence of the wholesale poisoning of the bishop of Rochester's household, attributed to an attempt to make away with Fisher himself. By a special enactment, the essentially un-English practice of poisoning was retrospectively classified as high treason, and the criminal sentenced to death by boiling.

[Sidenote: 1532 Parliament]

In the beginning of 1532 the campaign was renewed with vigour; whether from the laudable desire of reforming abuses, or with the object of terrorising the Church into complete subservience. Incidentally it is to be observed that so far as the activity of the Commons was directed against the payment of extortionate fees, the Church had a part only, not the whole, of their opposition. They logically and manfully resisted a "Bill of Wards" legalising claims of the Lords in sundry cases of the marriage of wards. This has been jibed at [Footnote: Moore (Aubrey), *Hist. of the Reformation,*

103.] as showing that they cared for cash and not for principle. As a matter of fact it appears to prove the first, but to have no bearing on the second. It also proves that when they did care, they could be obstinate, for the Bill was dropped: which illustrates the tact with which the King could yield on a point unimportant to him personally.

In especial however this session was signalised by three Acts, dealing with Mortmain, Benefit of Clergy, and Annates: and by the "Supplication against the Ordinaries" which took partial effect in the "Submission of the Clergy".

[Sidenote: Supplication against the Ordinaries]

The Supplication [Footnote: Mr. Froude, i., 211 (Ed. 1862), dates this 1529, but without apparent reason. *Cf.* Dixon, i., 77, note.] was in effect a statement of grievances, directed against the powers of Convocation in the way of ecclesiastical legislation, and the conduct of the ecclesiastical Courts and their fees. Under this second head it was simply the expression of a popular outcry, which had already begun to take effect in the legislation of 1529; an outcry so far justified that the clergy themselves met it, in part, by declaring that they were giving independent attention to the abuses complained of. As an indictment its weakness lay in the inadequate support by specific instances of the general charges of miscarriage of justice. Under the first head it has the appearance of being inspired by Cromwell, of whose policy a main feature was the concentration of all effective legislative power in the King.

[Sidenote: Resistance of Clergy]

The Supplication was presented, and laid before Convocation for an answer. The answer was given on the lines that, as concerned the grievances in general, so far as they were real they were in process of removal, and that as concerned miscarriage of justice it was impossible to answer effectively unless the charges were made specific. As to ecclesiastical legislation it was replied that this was a function of the Clergy, and that their canons were in accord with Scripture and therefore not antagonistic to the Civil Law; to which was added an appeal to the King as the Protector of the Faith. They were informed that this answer was "too slender"; so sent a second in which appeal was made to Henry's own book against Luther, and an offer was added that they would publish no ordinances without the royal assent excepting on matters of faith. In both answers Gardiner, now bishop of Winchester, is reputed to have been the guiding spirit—thereby showing that Henry could not count upon his assistance in reducing his Order to subservience.

This attitude however was by no means sufficient for Henry and Cromwell. It is in fact clear that they had made up their minds to put an end to an anomalous condition of affairs. Hypothetically, the Church and the State had been making laws independently of each other side by side. The two sets of laws might involve incompatibles; the King's lieges might be harassed by the canons of the Church, and loyal churchmen might be embarrassed by the laws of the realm. The time had come when one ultimate authority must be recognised. There was no manner of doubt which of the two that ultimate authority was to be. Yet for the attainment of this end, the Clergy must be required to surrender what they had always accounted a right inviolable, sacred, vested in them by divine commission. The Clergy had to surrender or take the risk of martyrdom: and they elected to surrender—in effect to recognise that they were beaten *de facto* if not *de jure*. They struggled hard for a compromise which would salve their collective conscience. Finally (May) they agreed to enact no new canons without the Kind's authority, and to submit to a commission such of the existing canons as were contravened. The wording of this "Submission of the Clergy," as it is called, does not leave it absolutely clear whether the entire canon law or only a portion was to be subjected to the revision of the commission—which was to consist of thirty-two members, half laymen and half clergy—but the balance of opinion is in favour of the partial theory. The defeat was a crushing blow to the aged Warham who never recovered from it and died three months later; and it caused the immediate resignation of the Chancellorship by Sir Thomas More—a *rara avis* among statesmen of the day, with whom conscience actually had the last word, not the King's will.

[Sidenote 1: Mortmain and Benefit of Clergy]
[Sidenote 2: Annates Act]

The other Acts referred to above were passed before the Submission of the Clergy was completed. The Mortmain and Benefit of Clergy Acts were respectively in limitation of bequests to the Church and of privileges of clerical criminals. They were merely normal steps in the reform of abuses. The Annates Act however demands closer attention. Every bishop on appointment to his see paid the first year's income to Rome—whether on an original appointment, or on translation from one see to another. Obviously this was a tremendous tax on the bishops and a source of large income to Rome. There had been frequent complaints, and suggestions that the Pope should reduce his claim. Very recently, Gardiner had been obliged to borrow heavily to meet the exaction on becoming bishop of Winchester. The Bill provided that five per cent. only should be paid, by way of compensation for expenses of papal Bulls, the ground taken up being that the papal claim was contrary to the ruling of the General Council of Basle, and that the payment, being an alienation of the property of the See, was contrary to the bishops consecration oath. The Bill was passed, the bishops—according to letters of the foreign ambassadors in London—dissenting; a course perfectly natural on their part as a protest, not in favour of the payment, but against the authority of the temporal power to intervene. Yet it is frequently stated as a matter of common knowledge that the clergy themselves were the prime movers, and that the Bill was brought in on their petition. This belief would seem to rest exclusively on the misinterpretation of a document attributed by a later historian [Footnote: Strype, *Eccl. Memorials* I., ii., 158. Froude, i., 361 ff. (Ed. 1862). But *cf.*. Gairdner, *English Church*, p. 116. The present writer fell into the usual error in a previous volume on *Cranmer*; and has to thank Mr. Tomlinson for correcting him.] to Convocation, but almost certainly of parliamentary origin.

The Act however was not put in immediate execution: but the English agents in Italy were instructed to hold it *in terrorem* over Clement's head.

[Sidenote: The European Powers and the Divorce]

The subsequent methods of procedure were largely the outcome of the diplomatic situation on the Continent. In the first place, the idea of calling an Oecumenical Council had been much in the air. Each of the three great monarchs was desirous of calling one, on his own terms; so were the Lutherans. But for each the terms must be such as should ensure practical subservience to his own dictation: while to the Pope the proposal, so long as it was hypothetical, was a thing he could produce as either a sop or a threat, as circumstances might commend. In the next place, for the time Charles dominated the Pope; but while he was making terms with the Lutherans, under pressure of the advance of the Turks on the east, whereby his loyalty to the papacy was made doubtful, he was also on the other hand, Katharine's unyielding champion. Thus any positive declaration on the divorce from Clement was tolerably certain to finally alienate either Charles or Henry. Now the rivalry of Charles was the great obstacle to Francis: whose object had come to be to utilise England so as to obtain for himself the concessions he wanted from the Emperor; extorting them as the result of joint pressure on the part of France and England or as the price of a separation between France and England. The thing he most feared was a compromise between Henry and Charles. Thus his policy was, by associating himself with Henry, to detach the Pope also from Charles, by the menace of a joint Anglo-French schism from the Roman obedience. Therefore in the summer and autumn of 1532 Francis was ostentatiously friendly to Henry and the cause of the Divorce. Conferences to which Henry was invited to bring Anne Boleyn as his Queen-elect were arranged, and took place at Calais and Boulogne.

Henry thereafter made up his mind to a decisive step and on their return to England in November or perhaps in the following January he married Anne privately. Francis however had successfully avoided committing himself unequivocally to an uncompromising English alliance.

[Sidenote: 1533 The crisis arrives]

In December, the Pope and the Emperor both being at Bologna, Clement professed to the English agents a more amenable spirit, suggesting that the divorce should be held over for a General Council, or that Henry should agree to have the trial held outside his own realms; propositions, however, to neither of which the King could be lured to assent. But the year 1533 had hardly opened when Charles was enabled to publish a Papal warning of excommunication against Henry unless he restored Katharine to her full rights as his wife (Feb.); while he detached France from England by the promise of concessions restoring her position in Italy.

Clement might now defer a pronouncement in favour of Katharine; there was no practical room for hoping that he might still pronounce against her. Henry stood alone; if the Pope were finally driven to choose between defying the King or the Emperor there could be no doubt which of the two he would rather have for an enemy. It only remained for Henry to put it beyond question that the declaration must be made, and that his own enmity would take an energetic form. His reply to the Pope was decisive. Early in April, parliament passed the great Act in Restraint of Appeals, which was virtually the announcement of the repudiation of the Roman allegiance; before the end of May, the new Archbishop of Canterbury in his court pronounced the marriage with Katharine void *ab initio*, and the recent marriage with her rival valid.

[Sidenote: Restraint of Appeals]

In form, the Act in Restraint of Appeals was not a fresh piece of legislation but a declaration of the existing law; a flat assertion that any appeal to the jurisdiction of Rome from the English courts brought the appellant under the penalties of praemunire, the "spiritualty" of the country being competent to deal with spiritual cases, and the sovereign recognising no jurisdiction superior to his own. It did not raise the question of authority in matters of doctrine; nor was it a formal declaration of schism from Rome. Its meaning however was clear. The constitutional theory of independence, put forward on many occasions as the warrant for legislation, was henceforth to be acted upon in its most ample interpretation: though, as with the Annates Bill, the final confirmation was suspended to leave Clement a last chance of surrender. Taken on its merits the Act laid down principles entirely acceptable to all parties who claim or claimed independence of Rome: yet it was quite obviously issued with the direct purpose of setting aside the Pope's authority in a particular case already referred to him.

[Sidenote 1: Cranmer Archbishop]
[Sidenote 2: The decisive breach]

It is in fact doubtful whether Henry could have procured a judgment from Warham; but Warham was dead, and the successor appointed was Thomas Cranmer, who already before he had been dragged into public life had committed himself to the sufficiency of the judgment of the English courts. Since taking part in Wiltshire's embassy in 1531 he had been for the most part in Germany on diplomatic affairs, associating with Protestants and imbibing their views. The most pronounced and definite of his doctrines was that of the supremacy of the crown; and on his installation as Archbishop in March, he had qualified [Footnote: Moore (Aubrey), *Hist. of Reformation*, 109, finds a proof in this of "servility and dishonesty," which terms appear to be in his view equivalents of Erastianism.] his oath of allegiance to Rome accordingly. Other ecclesiastics, from Becket to Gardiner, had been appointed to bishoprics under the impression that they were going to support the secular arm against the claims of their Order, and had falsified expectation. Cranmer maintained as Archbishop the theories of clerical subordination which he had adopted as a University Doctor. Convocation was called on to express an opinion on the marriage; and whether from conviction or despair, it supported the King by a majority. The Archbishop obtained the royal licence to convene a court. Katharine, refusing to appear, was declared contumacious; and the Court pronounced her marriage void while confirming Anne's. The Pope rejoined by pronouncing the judgment void. Henry retorted by confirming the Acts in Restraint of Annates and Appeals; and himself appealed against the Pope to a General Council. Until, in March of the next year, Clement himself definitely pronounced judgment in favour of Katharine, there remained a shadow of a chance of a reconciliation tantamount to the submission of the Holy See; but the chance was not accepted. Practically the judgment of Cranmer's court marked the definite schism from Rome.

CHAPTER IX
HENRY VIII (v), 1533-40—
MALLEUS MONACHORUM

[Sidenote: 1533 Ecclesiastical Parties]

WE have noted that a proportion of the higher clergy were at least not unwilling to be freed from the domination and the financial exactions of Rome; this attitude being either the cause or the effect of the line they took as to the divorce. When, however, it was borne in upon them that the price of escaping the yoke of the Popedom was to be the subjection of the Church, in form to the lay monarch, and in fact to the State, the bulk of them endeavoured to protest against the newly imposed subordination. With the "Submission of the Clergy" and the appointment of Cranmer as Warham's successor, it became entirely clear that to protest or resist would be worse than useless. Accordingly we shall now find this section of the clerical body, including such prelates as Gardiner of Winchester, Stokesley of London, and Tunstal of Durham, devoting themselves to evading or rendering nugatory the directions of the Temporal power and its instrument Cranmer, under colour of obedience, while dissociating themselves from the more rigid of the Old Catholics such as Fisher of Rochester, More, the London Carthusians and others. On the other hand, the newer school, who were much more antagonistic to the papacy, such as Cranmer, Latimer and Barlow, found more personal favour with the King and with Cromwell, though their leanings towards the doctrinal tenets of Continental reformers were checked from time to time with sufficient rudeness.

[Sidenote: Pope or King?]

A very peculiar situation however soon resulted from the Royal rejection of the Papal supremacy. To hold the opinion that the Pope was head of the Church implied the recognition of a divided allegiance, casting a doubt on the holder's loyalty to the Secular Sovereign, and easily translated into treason; since the papal party were bound to maintain in theory the validity of the marriage with Katharine, and the rights of her daughter Mary. Henry never lacked a plausible theory to justify his most tyrannous actions. Modern historians however who carry their support of Henry to the extreme point ignore the two facts, that to hold an opinion which if acted on would lead to treason is not in itself treason; and that it was quite logical to maintain the supreme authority of the Pope in matters spiritual, without admitting his power to depose a recalcitrant monarch or to determine the line of succession—which was in fact the position adopted by Sir Thomas More.

[Sidenote: 1534 Confirmatory Acts]

The Spring session of Parliament in 1534 was devoted mainly to the passing of Acts in confirmation and extension of what already been done. The Submission of the Clergy and the Restraint of Appeals were re-affirmed in one Act; but with the important difference that the whole of the Canon law was to be subjected to the Commission when appointed, [Footnote: See p. 128, *ante*]. till which time the clergy would be acting at their peril in enforcing any rules which might subsequently be condemned as against the Royal Prerogative. This was accompanied by an Act in confirmation of the Annates Act, coupled with the *congé d'élire*, assuring to the King the right of nomination to ecclesiastical appointments under the form of permitting the Chapters to elect his nominee. A third, the "Peter Pence" Act, abolished the remaining contributions to the Papal Treasury. At the same time the "exempt" monasteries—those, that is, which had not been subject to the supervision of the bishops—were conveyed to the King's control, still without episcopal intervention. A fourth Act, not *prima facie* ecclesiastical in character, was the Act of Succession, declaring the offspring of Anne Boleyn (the princess Elizabeth had been born in the previous September) heirs to the throne.

[Sidenote: The Pope's last word]

While these proceedings were in progress, the last attempt to subdue the Pope by diplomacy was failing. At the end of March, Clement gave the long deferred judgment on the divorce, pronouncing the marriage with Katharine valid, and that with Anne Boleyn void. Clement survived but a short time. His successor Paul III. had at one time been in Henry's favour; but reconciliation was now outside the range of practical politics, and the new Pope soon found himself more definitely antagonistic to the English monarch than his predecessor had been.

[Sidenote: The Nun of Kent]

The prevailing superstitions of the day and their reality as factors even in public life are curiously illustrated by the story of the "Nun of Kent" —a story concluded by her execution about this time. The "Nun" was a young woman named Elizabeth Barton of humble birth, who was subject to fits or trances, presumably epileptic in character, in which trances she gave vent to utterances which were supposed to be inspired, being generally religious in their bearing. Having acquired some notoriety and a reputation for sanctity, her prophesyings before long took the form of denunciation of the divorce, at that time in its earlier stages. She was exploited by sundry fanatical persons honest or otherwise—in such cases it is seldom possible to fathom the extent to which mania, intentional deception, conscious or unconscious suggestion, and mere credulity, are mingled. In those days, there were few people who would venture to attribute such phenomena to purely natural causes. Such a man as Thomas More, who was eminently rational as well as deeply religious, was not easily beguiled; but the more credulous and equally honest bishop of Rochester was unable to regard the prophesyings as mere imposture, as was also the case with Warham; and being thus countenanced, when the Nun's utterances reached the point of denouncing the wrath of Heaven upon those who consented to the Divorce, she became really dangerous. She and her associates were charged with treason and executed, while Fisher was necessarily to some degree implicated. Before her death the Nun made a confession of elaborate imposture, but too much weight should not be attached to confessions made under such conditions. Given a certain degree of mental aberration, the case is not without parallels pointing to an absence of conscious fraud. But whether in her case it was fraud or mania, the important fact remains that there were numbers of people who attributed her utterances neither to the one nor the other but to inspiration; numbers more who were in doubt on the point; and that those utterances were to some extent utilised in a seditious propaganda; for to declare as a message from on high that the King and his advisers had brought upon themselves the curse of the Almighty must be recognised as effectively, even if not intentionally, preaching sedition.

[Sidenote 1: The Act of Succession]
[Sidenote 2: The oath refused]

The proceedings against Elizabeth Barton had been accompanied by revelations of more or less suspicious conduct on the part of the Countess of Salisbury and of Poles, [Footnote: The Countess of Salisbury's children. The de la Poles were now extinct. The Nevilles were the Countess's kinsfolk, her mother having been a daughter of the Kingmaker. See *Front.*] Courtenays and Nevilles, while the Princess Mary declined to regard herself as illegitimate. This was made the pretext for adopting a very irregular course in connexion with the Act of Succession. The Act not only established the order of Succession to the throne, but in the preamble asserted the invalidity of Katharine's marriage, it was accompanied by an authority to exact an oath of obedience to the Statute, the form of the oath not being laid down. Commissioners were appointed to exact the oath, which was drawn up in a form accepting the entire terms of the Act, not merely promising adhesion to its provisions. Presented to them in this form, both More and Fisher refused to take the oath. Both were prepared to swear to maintain the succession as laid down; neither would avow a belief that the marriage with Katharine was void *ab initio*. More laid down definitely the doctrine that it was in the power of the State to determine the succession, and the duty of the citizen to accept its decision; but that obviously does not involve an opinion that the reasons for its decision are sound. Cranmer would fain have persuaded the King to accept the oath thus modified as sufficient—not realising that the primary object of Henry and Cromwell was to drive the opponents of the divorce into a public recantation of their opinion. More and Fisher were resolute, and were sent to the Tower, though in form an indictment ought first to have been brought against them in the courts. Cromwell expressed and no doubt felt a very genuine regret at the failure of the plan; but it was ever Cromwell's method to strike at the most influential opponents of his policy. If they would bend, well: if not, they must break. The device of the oath would force the surrender or else the destruction of the best members of the high Catholic party. Three of the most zealous and most irreproachable monastic establishments—the London Carthusians, the Richmond Observants, and the Brentford Brigittines—were inveigled or cowed into temporary submission, but later reverted to the position of More and Fisher, and suffered accordingly. The Greenwich Observants refused submission altogether, and were dissolved.

[Sidenote: "The Bishop of Rome"]

Before the administration of the oath, the news of Clement's decision had come from Rome, with a Bull of Excommunication to follow. It was well for Henry that Francis could be relied on to keep Charles in check; for the foreign ambassadors, whether well-informed or mainly because the wish was father to the thought, were reporting serious disaffection in the country, which otherwise might have led to armed intervention by the Emperor. The answer to Rome however took the emphatic form of a declaration by Convocation and the Universities that "the Bishop of Rome has no more authority in England than any other foreign Bishop"; in addition to the Acts of Parliament already recorded.

[Sidenote 1: Parliament (Nov.)]
[Sidenote 2: Treasons Act]

Before the end of the year (1534) Parliament was again in session. The argument submitted to the Pope before the passing of the Annates Act— that it pressed with undue severity on the bishops—was shown in its true character by a new Annates Act which appropriated to the King the funds of which the Pope had been deprived. The relief of the bishops was ignored. By the "Act of the Supreme Head," Parliament also professedly confirmed the declaration of Convocation in 1531; but omitted the saving [Footnote: See p. 125] clause; and by a fresh Act of Succession, regularised the treatment of More and Fisher, enforcing the oath in the form in which it had been submitted to them, retrospectively. Then came the Treasons Act, the coping stone of Resolute Government; bringing into the category of Treason not only the specific overt actions to which it had been limited by the Act of Edward III., but also "verbal treason" and even the refusal to answer incriminating questions. It is easy to see what vast opportunities were thus given for fastening a practically irrefutable charge of treason on any victim selected, when the recognised principle was that the *onus probandi* lay with the accused. An irresistible instrument of tyranny was created, justified of course by the usual argument that without such powers it was not possible to deal adequately with the abnormal dangers of the situation. It need only be remarked that where there is practically no check on the abuse of such powers save the scrupulosity of the persons in whom they are vested, the risk of flagrant injustice becomes almost incalculable. Since the days of Edward III., no monarch had occupied the throne with less risk of serious treason than Henry VIII. Under all save Henry V. there had been active rebellion, and under him there was at least one serious plot. Yet the treason statute of Edward III. had under them been held sufficient. The new Act was in truth but one step in the systematic development of autocracy under constitutional forms to which the policy of Thomas Cromwell was devoted.

[Sidenote 1: 1529-34 The New Policy]
[Sidenote 2: Cromwell]

When Wolsey fell in 1529 the Duke of Norfolk became ostensibly the King's most powerful subject. But it is impossible to trace to him or to his following among the nobility the formulation of any sort of definite policy. Nevertheless, a quite definite policy had been initiated after a short lapse of time. Starting with the checking of palpable ecclesiastical abuses, it had gone on to assert with steadily increasing rigour the subjection of the entire clerical organisation to the Supreme Head, and to embody the assertion of the theory in practical legislation, and dictation to Convocation. It had threatened the papacy, till the threats issued virtually in an ultimatum followed by repudiation of papal authority. It had placed papal and ecclesiastical perquisites under gradual restrictions, till by the last Annates Act it began transferring them openly to the Crown. In many instances, the initiative had been ostensibly taken by Parliament; in others, the King had exercised direct pressure on the clergy, but had obtained from Parliament a ratification of the ecclesiastical concessions. The whole trend of the policy, culminating in the Treasons Act, was to concentrate effective control in the hands of the sovereign, by consent of Parliament. And now Cromwell emerges as the man who was to give that policy tremendous effect, and by inference at least as its probable creator and organiser from the close of 1530. It is not till 1535 however that he becomes openly and indisputably first minister; Wolsey's successor in Henry's confidence—and to Henry's gratitude.

[Sidenote: 1535 More and Fisher]

Before the prorogation of Parliament in February (1535) the two recalcitrants in the Tower, More and Fisher, were attainted High Treason for maintaining their refusal to take the prescribed oath under the Act of Succession. It was perhaps in the hope that the King might hesitate to proceed to extremities, in the face of a very marked expression of sentiment, that the new Pope, Paul III., proceeded to nominate Fisher a Cardinal. It ought to have been obvious that the very contrary effect would have been produced: the step was naturally looked upon as a challenge. More and Fisher were condemned to death and executed in the summer—martyrs assuredly to conscience. The whole of their offence consisted in the single fact that they could not and would not recant their belief in the validity of Katharine's marriage. Had they sought to make converts to that opinion, or to make it a text for preaching sedition, there might have been some colour of justice in their punishment. As it was, such danger as there might be in their holding that view lay entirely in the advertisement of it by insistence on the oath. All Europe shuddered, and half England trembled at the demonstration of ruthless power, when those two were struck down— the aged bishop whose spotless character and saintly life had for many a year given the lie to those who included all the higher clergy in a universal condemnation; and the ex-chancellor, the friend of Erasmus, whose wide learning, kindly wit, intellectual eminence, and unswerving rectitude had won for him a European reputation greater than that of any other Englishman of his time. The Carthusians, Brigittines, and Observants who had been induced to give way on the question of the Oath reverted to the position of More and Fisher. Their heads also were put to death, and the houses broken up.

The wrath of the Pope was expressed in a Bull of Deposition; which however on second thoughts he found it advisable to hold in suspense till three years later.

[Sidenote: Cromwell made Vicar-General]

When More and Fisher opposed themselves obstinately to the King's will, there was no doubt that the King would see to it that they paid the penalty. But we may suspect that it was not Henry's brain but Cromwell's which devised the policy of presenting them with the fatal dilemma. Before they were put to death, the minister's supremacy was already established by his appointment as Vicar-General, with full power to exercise on the King's behalf all the rights vested in the Supreme Head of the Church: rights which—however it might be asserted that they were and had been at all times inherent in the sovereign—were now to be interpreted in a novel and comprehensive spirit. But besides the development alike in extent and intensity of the attack on the clerical organisation, we now find foreign policy taking a new direction for which Cromwell was assuredly responsible.

[Sidenote 1: The German Lutherans]
[Sidenote 2: Overtures]

Hitherto, since the fall of Wolsey, the Emperor had been in steady antagonism to the English King: so had the Pope, except when he had hopes of the Imperial pressure on him being removed. France had on the whole given support to England, usually of a lukewarm character. But it does not appear that, until this time, Henry had learnt to look upon the German Lutherans as an available political force: while his active hostility to the Lutheran theology seemed to preclude anything in the nature of a *rapprochement* with the Protestant princes. Yet the Lutherans, like Henry, had repudiated papal authority. Recently the French King had taken up the idea of bringing about a compromise between the Pope on one side, and the Lutherans and English on the other, which would place Charles in dangerous straits. The prospect however was unpromising at the best; a reconciliation with Rome was really impossible. Cromwell, then, conceived the idea of a Protestant league, which would suggest to Francis the advantage of following Henry's lead in throwing off the Roman allegiance, and ranging himself with the Lutherans and the English. Henry's own theological predilections stood in the way, and the Lutherans regarded him with suspicion: but Cromwell looked to political expediency as a potent salve for healing controversial differences. Thus in the late summer of 1535, the first advances were made in the direction of seeking a mutual understanding with the German Protestants—not without hints that Henry had an open mind on the subject of the Augsburg Confession. The Germans however were in no haste to accept Henry as a brand plucked from the burning; rather, they had a not unnatural suspicion that he merely wanted to make use of them. They propounded conditions, which Cromwell submitted to Gardiner, at this time ambassador at Paris. Whatever Gardiner's views were as to papal ascendancy, he was no Lutheran; and he pointed out that to accept the terms would deprive England of her ecclesiastical independence. Thus the negotiations fell through—as might have been expected. Nevertheless, the desire for the Lutheran alliance remained at the back of Cromwell's policy; not avowed but latent; and it was in an attempt to entangle Henry irrevocably in that policy that he committed, not five years later, the blunder which cost him his head.

[Sidenote: Visitation of the Monasteries]

In the same Autumn—1535—Cromwell as Vicar-General opened his great campaign against the monasteries; actuated, according to the historians on one side, by a determination to remove a cancer which was destroying the morality of the nation; according to the historians on the other side, by the vast opportunities afforded for plunder.

[Sidenote: 1536 Suppression of Lesser Houses]

Heretofore the visitation of "exempt" monasteries had lain with the Superiors of their respective orders, except when special authority had been granted by the Pope to a Morton or a Wolsey. In other cases it had been deputed to the bishops, each in his own diocese. At the time of the recent Peter Pence Act (1534) the exempt houses had been formally subjected to the King. Cromwell now took upon himself the right of visitation, not only of the exempt monasteries, but of the others as well, suspending the jurisdiction of the bishops while his enquiries were going forward, and thus emphasising the doctrine that that jurisdiction was derived from the King. Commissioners were appointed—Legh, Leyton, Bedyl, and Ap Rice—to investigate and report upon the conduct and the finances of the various houses. In a period of about three months (Oct.-Jan.), they made their investigations and prepared their report, keeping up an active correspondence with Cromwell in the meantime. On the strength of this report, a bill was laid before Parliament and passed in February (1536), suppressing all houses with less than £200 a year, 376 in number—of which however 31 were reinstated later in the year as having been well conducted. In part, their inmates were to be redistributed among the greater houses; in part they were to be released from their vows; and in part they were to receive some compensation.

[Sidenote: The evidence discussed]

Now it is clear that in the time at their disposal, the commissioners could not possibly have sifted thoroughly the evidence brought before them. In many cases there was enough that was gross, palpable, obvious, to warrant condemnation at sight. But the scandalous levity and domineering insolence with which they carried out their task must have suggested to the ill-conditioned members of every community that slander and false-witness might lead to favour and profit, and were not likely to be too carefully tested: while it is easy to see how the insulting interrogatories would be angrily resented, and answers be refused, or given in the most injudicious manner, by perfectly innocent persons; while demands for inventories of valuables were met by prevarication and concealment, when the object of the commissioners was suspected of being spoliation. The letters of Leyton and Legh convey the impression that the fouler the scandals unearthed or retailed, the more enjoyment and humour they discovered in their occupation. There can be no doubt that the state of things they found was in general bad; but by their own statement it was by no means universally so; and it is also clear that they accepted adverse witness almost without examination and wilfully minimised all that was favourable.

[Sidenote: The Black Book]

Also, it is very doubtful whether the "black book" of monastic offences was ever laid before parliament. The preamble to the bill set forth, luridly enough, the conclusions arrived at by the King and the vicar-general, and summed up the grounds for them. But it seems by no means improbable that parliament simply accepted the statement thus laid before it. The black book itself disappeared. The Protestant historians of Elizabeth's reign said that Bonner destroyed it; the Roman Catholics affirm that it was the other party who took care that the evidence on which they acted should never be made known. The actual surviving evidence is to be found in the partial summaries known as the Comperta and in the letters of the commissioners to Cromwell. The examination of these can hardly fail to leave the reader with a conviction that the methods of the Commissioners were atrociously iniquitous, but that a strictly judicial investigation would still have revealed a state of things often appalling, not seldom vicious, and commonly reprehensible, without the elements which might have made effective reform possible: while it is beyond a doubt that especially among the younger monks and nuns, the desire to escape from the bonds of monastic rule was common.

[Sidenote: The Consequent Commission]

In favour of the monasteries however, it is to be noted that these 376 minor houses were suppressed not as having been individually condemned, but on the theory that the report pointed to the system of maintaining minor houses as bad. Mixed commissions were now appointed to continue the visitation, carry out the suppression, and recommend exemptions when it was desirable; and the reports of these commissions were of a far less unfavourable character, though (as we have seen) only 31 houses were actually reinstated. It is to be observed also, in a somewhat different connexion, that the further visitation was accompanied by the issuing of Injunctions for the conduct of monastic establishments which may have been designed solely with a view to enforcing a pure and pious manner of living, but are undoubtedly open to the suspicion of having been deliberately calculated to make the monastic life insupportable and so to encourage the religious houses to efface themselves by voluntary surrender—a course which was not infrequently adopted.

[Sidenote: The policy discussed]

There was sufficient precedent for laying the Church under heavy contributions to the exchequer. The idea of deliberately confiscating Church property had before now been seriously put forward. There had been previous suppressions of monastic establishments; but in these cases the funds, ostensibly at least, had been diverted to other purposes recognised as ecclesiastical, such as Wolsey's schools and colleges. The differentiating feature of Cromwell's confiscation was that the funds were for the most part withdrawn from any ecclesiastical purpose whatever. [Footnote: There was precedent for the proposal however in Parliamentary petitions of Richard II.'s reign; but these had not taken effect in legislation.] The monastic lands passed to lay owners by grant or purchase; they enriched the King or his friends or those whom Cromwell thought fit to enrich or to gratify. The evidence that in the public interest it was time for the religious houses to go is convincing; the method of proceeding against the smaller houses first was tactically shrewd, as evoking less opposition at the outset; but even if it be conceded that the Church had forfeited her property, it is impossible to find any excuse for the application of the spoils to other than public objects. The Church might simply be looked upon as a vast corporation, holding its wealth in trust for the nation, and rightly deprived of that wealth when it failed to fulfil the trust. But on that view, the wealth was bound to be handed over to another body, to administer as a trust for the nation. The fact that this was not done makes possible only one conclusion as to the motive of the suppression. The Church was both the wealthiest and the least dangerous victim available for bleeding, besides being open to the charge of deserving to be penalised.

[Sidenote 1: Anne Boleyn threatened]
[Sidenote 2: Her condemnation and death]

In January 1536 the deeply-injured Katharine died; to be followed ere many months had passed by her supplanter. Ostensibly, Henry had married Anne Boleyn, because a male heir was needed to secure the succession; but she had borne him only a daughter and a still-born son. Henry was disappointed in her. Moreover, his passion had for some time been cooling: nor was her character—even on the most favourable reading—calculated to retain affections that had begun to wane. She was frivolous and undignified; her arrogance and her assumption had left her few friends. She was jealous of the attentions paid by her husband to Jane Seymour, who had been one of Katharine's ladies-in-waiting—attentions which she received with a becoming reserve. Suddenly it appeared that Anne had been guilty of gross misconduct. Sundry gentlemen of the court, including her brother Lord Rochford were charged with sharing her guilt. One of them ultimately made confession—true or false. There were stories, flatly denied, that she had been contracted to Northumberland: that she had actually been his wife when she married Henry. There were stories that the marriage was void, because of earlier relations between Henry and her mother and sister. Whether the queen was guilty or not, the judges of course did what they were expected to do; she was tried for treason and condemned. Cranmer was torn between an affectionate conviction that she was really a good woman and an inability to believe that the King could be misled, much less do her a deliberate and conscious wrong. But some sort of admission which she made before him was interpreted by the Archbishop as involving the nullity of the marriage. Anne was executed: next day, the King married Jane Seymour; the marriage with Anne was officially declared to have been invalid; Elizabeth being of course de-legitimatised, and so occupying precisely the same position as Mary. Thus Henry was left with three illegitimate children (the third being the Duke of Richmond who died not long after), and no legitimate heir— truly an ironical outcome of that divorce which his apologists defend as having been demanded by the need of a successor with an indisputable title to the throne!

[Sidenote: The Succession]

Within three weeks of Anne Boleyn's execution (May 19th, 1536), a new parliament was sitting; for that which had commenced its sessions at the end of 1529 had been dissolved in the spring of this year. The first business was formally to ratify the late proceedings, and fix the succession on the offspring of the new queen; the second was formally to authorise the King himself to lay down the order of succession thereafter. Incidentally we may note that the actual legitimate heir presumptive [Footnote: See *Appendix B*, and *Front.*] to the throne was now the King of Scotland, the son of Henry's elder sister Margaret. The claims of a child of Jane Seymour could alone on legitimist principles take precedence of his, if the judgments invalidating the two previous marriages held good. It is only by admitting the power of parliament to fix or delegate its power of fixing the succession, that James's claim to be heir presumptive could be challenged. But there was no sort of doubt that it would be in actual fact challenged, simply because the English would not take a King from another land. There was not much room in England for advocates of the doctrine of Divine Right. Neither Henry IV., and his successors, nor Henry VII., nor Elizabeth, could have maintained a plausible claim to the throne apart from their title by Act of Parliament. Of present importance however was the fact that both Katharine and Anne were dead before the marriage of Queen Jane; there could therefore be absolutely no ground for challenging the legitimacy of any children of hers, while any conceivable claims on behalf of either Mary or Elizabeth would necessarily yield precedence to the claim of Jane's son, should she bear one. Moreover, since there was now no Katharine to claim rights as a queen, and her supplanter had died a traitor's death, Mary might without risk be reinstated as a Princess on sufficient grounds. Thus a door was opened for a renewal of amity with the Emperor.

[Sidenote: Punishment of Heresy]

The aims and objects of the Reformation in England had been entirely political and financial. There had been no official movement towards a new doctrinal standpoint. On the contrary, the suppression of heresy had been not less active after Cranmer's accession to the primacy than before. The prosecutions however do not at any time appear to have originated with the clergy: and the Ordinaries habitually endeavoured to procure the recantation of heresy rather than the exaction of its penalties. But the most advanced of the clergy, even those who like Latimer were continually verging on doctrines which their stricter brethren regarded as heretical, showed as little mercy as any one to the upholders of Anabaptism; whose theology was usually combined—or supposed to be so—with perverted views on the political and social order. To this class belong most of the martyrs of the period; with the notable exception of John Frith. Frith was a young man of great piety and learning, who would probably never have been arrested but for his association with the distributors of forbidden literature. Being arrested, he maintained—in spite of earnest efforts to persuade him to recant—the Zwinglian doctrine of the Lord's Supper: but further he stood almost alone in declaring that to hold a correct opinion on this point of doctrine could not be essential to salvation. Frith was the first and almost the only martyr (July, 1533) to the theory of toleration, to which neither Romanists nor Protestants, Anglicans nor Zwinglians, were yet ready to give ear.

[Sidenote 1: Progressive Movement]
[Sidenote 2: The Ten Articles]

Although, however, there had been no revolt from orthodox doctrine the course of the Reformation abroad could not be without influence in England. There was a growing inclination to think and speak of minor questions as being debatable; an increasing suspicion on one side that the spread of knowledge and of discussion tended to heresy and to irreverence—on the other, that they tended to edification. In theory the leading ecclesiastics agreed that an authorised translation of the Bible would be good, but half of them were afraid that it would lead to novel and dangerous interpretations. The general attitude may be regarded as one of uneasiness. Hence the commission appointed under Cranmer's auspices did little; and Cranmer himself, whose heart was really in the scheme, was overjoyed [Footnote: Dr. Gairdner (*Eng. Church*, p. 192) thinks however that it was Matthew's Bible, issued next year, to which Cranmer's expressions of satisfaction were applied.] when Coverdale produced a rendering to which an authoritative *imprimatur* could be given. The general sense of unrest, aggravated perhaps by some alarm lest the Augsburg Confession should attract adherents—especially since the Lutherans had been told that there might be room for its discussion—led to the enunciation of the first of the Anglican formulae of Faith, known as the Ten Articles "for establishing Christian Quietness," in July 1536: professedly prepared by the King's own hand. These Articles contained no deviation from orthodox dogma; but their most notable feature lay in the distinction drawn between institutions necessary and convenient, with the implication that the latter were liable to modification.

[Sidenote: The Lincolnshire rising]

The issuing of these Articles with the sanction alike of King, Parliament, and Convocation, was probably intended to counteract the alarm attendant on the visitation and suppression of the monasteries. Those institutions, though not popular in cities, and viewed with jealousy by the secular clergy, provided in many country districts the only existing charitable or educational organisations; and moreover, whatever their defects were in the eyes of the Economist, they were much more lenient landlords than the average lay landowner. It would have been strange indeed if some of the dispersed monks had not allowed their tongues to wag, to the stirring up of alarm and discontent. In the autumn of this year, the effect of these things were seen in a rising in Lincolnshire. This was promptly suppressed without any undue tenderness either of speech or action; but it was very soon followed by the much more significant and formidable insurrection in the North, known as the Pilgrimage of Grace.

[Sidenote: The Pilgrimage of Grace]

The insurgents were headed by a very remarkable man, a lawyer named Robert Aske of a good North-country family. He had taken no part in inciting rebellion; but the position of leader was thrust upon him, and as it would seem not unwillingly accepted. His abilities were great: the rising was organised with much skill, and with wonderful system and discipline. Yet Aske's very virtues unfitted him for his office under the existing conditions. He was honest himself; he wished to avoid bloodshed: what he sought was the remedying of genuine grievances. As with the Lincolnshire insurgents, this meant the restoration of the monasteries, the removal of evil councillors, notably Cromwell, the removal of the advanced bishops, such as Cranmer and Latimer, the remission of a tax granted in 1534 which a commission was collecting, the repeal of a recent land-act ("Statute of Uses") which had increased the difficulty of providing younger sons with sufficient endowments, the restoration to the Church of revenues lately attached by the Crown. All over the North, cities and strongholds fell into the hands of Aske's followers without a blow. With thirty thousand well equipped and fairly disciplined troops he advanced to the Don, where he was faced by Norfolk with a far smaller force.

[Sidenote 1: Aske beguiled]
[Sidenote 2: 1537 Suppression of the rising]

It was then that Aske committed his fatal but noble error. Had he struck then, he could in all probability have marched triumphantly to London and have dictated his own terms. But he did not wish to strike. He sought a conference, and laid his proposals before Norfolk. Norfolk temporised, and referred the proposals to London. The insurgents were allowed to believe that they would be pardoned, and their demands be essentially conceded. The nobles and gentry among them were appealed to privately; Norfolk even sought to get Aske betrayed into his hands. Aske still would not give up the hope of a peaceful solution. At last in December the King gave Norfolk powers to concede a free pardon and a Parliament at York; but there is no doubt that Norfolk's statements to the insurgents gave the totally different impression that they could count upon the fulfilment of their demands. By the King's command the leaders went South to be personally interviewed, and returned in sanguine mood. But their army was breaking up, and it was very soon apparent that in fact the North was being rapidly garrisoned for the King. The pardons were accompanied by a new oath of allegiance which showed very clearly that the grievances were not going to be remedied. Wild spirits broke out again in deeds of violence. By this time, the royal armies were in a position to strike. It was declared that the conditions of the pardon had been violated; the insurgents had now no prospect of making head in the field. Hangings were freely resorted to; Aske and other leaders were seized and executed: an impressive series of abbots and priors was among the victims. And so, early in 1537, ended the one formidable insurrection of Henry's reign.

[Sidenote: The rising turned to account]

Not only had half the nobility and gentry of the North been seriously implicated in the rising; the clergy had taken active part in fomenting it. Being followed up by a visitation from Cromwell's most energetic commissioners, such guilt as there had been was presented in the strongest colours and was made a new ground for Suppression, or the application of the drastic regulations which induced voluntary surrender; and at the same time pains were taken to impress the Ten Articles on the public mind. These were supplemented by the publication of the "Institution of a Christian Man" otherwise known as the "Bishops' Book"; in which some points which had been omitted or left vague in the Articles were laid down with a more defined orthodoxy, though the prelates of every shade of opinion had their share in the work. On the other hand, the preparation of an authorised version of the Scriptures was going forward. In spite of Cromwell's Injunction that the Bible should be set up in English and Latin in the Churches, Coverdale's work had not been adopted; and though this was followed by "Matthew's Bible," a combination of Tindal's and Coverdale's, in 1537, it was not till the issue of the revised version, known on account of its size as the Great Bible, more than a year later, that the injunction was given general effect.

[Sidenote: 1533-36 James V.]

Abroad, the reluctant but anxious desire to maintain friendly relations with England which attended the domination of Wolsey had practically disappeared since the Cardinal's fall. From 1529 to 1536, there had been no prospect of a reconciliation between Henry and Charles; Francis had only at intervals been disposed to make advances; the demeanour of the Lutheran princes had been cold at the best. In Scotland, the young King, who only attained his majority in 1533, displayed that lack of confidence in the disinterested generosity of England which seems to be always a cause of pained surprise to the English politicians and historians. In fact it was his firm and extremely natural conviction that his uncle was responsible for keeping the whole border country in a perpetual state of unrest, fomenting the rivalries of the Scottish nobility, and generally promoting disorder, in order to bring about the subordination of the Northern to the Southern kingdom. The clerical body in Scotland, which had always been most energetic in maintaining resistance to England, was of course rendered more Anglophobe than ever by Henry's ecclesiastical policy; and its influence was strong, since it had done a good deal in the way of fighting James's battles with his nobles. Henry proposed a conference with his nephew, to be held at York, in 1538; James had at first welcomed the proposal, but presently evaded it in the belief that his uncle would kidnap him, as he had before designed to kidnap Beton. Instead he went to France, to arrange a marriage with a daughter of Francis; and on his return was reported to have given encouragement to the North-country rebels.

[Sidenote: 1536-37 Naval measures]

Meantime, in the Channel, the estimation in which England was held had been shown by the increasingly piratical proceedings of French, Spanish, and Flemish ships; since of late Henry's hands had been too full for him to give clue attention to naval affairs. Now however the opportunity was taken to devote some of the monastic funds to coast defence. A series of forts was raised, commanding the principal harbours on the south coast; and a few ships, secretly prepared, were suddenly sent out under competent captains, to teach the channel pirates a lesson in English seamanship; which was very effectively accomplished.

[Sidenote 1: 1537 Birth of Prince Edward]
[Sidenote 2: Marriage projects]

The problem of the succession to the throne was at last settled by the birth of a prince in October (1537). There was now an heir whose claims if he lived would be unassailable. But within a few weeks the queen died; and there was still only the life of one baby to shield the country from anarchy, in case Henry himself should die. With probably genuine reluctance, the King agreed that he would marry again if a suitable wife could be found for him; and the whirligig of intriguing for his union with one or another foreign princess was set in motion; princesses related to Charles, or to Francis, or to one of the Lutheran chiefs. Two years elapsed before the choice was made which, led to Cromwell's downfall. And in the meantime Mary of Guise (or Lorraine) was withdrawn from the lists by her marriage with James V., whose Queen Madeleine had died a few months after the nuptials: while the Duchess of Milan, a youthful niece of the Emperor, was for some time utilised by Charles as a diplomatic asset. The risk of an Anglo-Imperial alliance was employed by him in negotiations with Francis; and when these negotiations were brought to a successful issue the proposed alliance was gradually allowed to drop.

[Sidenote: 1538 Diplomatic moves]

During 1538 however, this marriage was being dangled before Henry, accompanied by the hope that it might cause a rupture between Charles and the Pope, from whom a dispensation would be necessary—a question which could not now be raised without the kindling of explosive materials. Further the English quarrel with Rome was being embittered by a campaign against spurious relics, miracle-working shrines, and the like, involving a particularly virulent attack on St. Thomas of Canterbury, the type of defiant ecclesiasticism. Moreover, the arrival of a deputation of Lutheran divines in England was ominous of the closer association of the bodies which had revolted from Rome. Reginald Pole, a member of the house which stood high in the Yorkist line of succession [Footnote: See *Front.*], who had been not long before raised to the Cardinalate, had for some time been carrying on from the Continent a violent propaganda against Henry. Pope Paul's Bull of Deposition was again being talked of, though there is some doubt as to whether it was actually published.

[Sidenote 1: The Exeter Conspiracy]
[Sidenote 2: Cromwell strikes]

Under all these circumstances, it is scarcely surprising that a new and formidable conspiracy, essentially Yorkist, was brought to light. In fact the whole country was sown with spies, and there was not much difficulty in obtaining information of treasonable speeches, when hasty expressions of discontent counted for treason. Now outside the offspring of Henry VII., the Marquis of Exeter, Edward Courtenay, was a grandson of Edward IV.; the Poles were grandsons of his brother, Clarence, whose daughter, their mother the Countess of Salisbury, was living still. The theory that a tyrant might be deposed and another scion of the royal house substituted, had ample precedent; and it is in no way improbable that the Courtenays, who were all-powerful in the West, might have been ready enough in conjunction with the Poles to make a bid for the throne, if they could have found or created a favourable opportunity. The Cardinal had warning from Cromwell that the safety of his kinsmen was jeopardised by his diatribes; while Lord Montague, the head of the family, was on very close terms of friendship with Exeter. Exeter's own conduct on the occasion of the Pilgrimage of Grace had been suspicious. Out of these materials there was no difficulty in constructing a damning case against as many members of these Plantagenet houses as might be considered advisable: since there was no need to prove that rebellion was actually organised. It was enough to have a record of the use of disloyal expressions, or even of the concealment of the knowledge that such expressions had been used. Finally it was notorious that there was no love lost between Cromwell and the suspected nobles. Cromwell, having collected sufficient evidence for his purpose, struck. Geoffrey Pole, a younger brother, learned that the blow was coming in time to turn informer. How far there was anything really deserving the name of a conspiracy the evidence produced did not show; but the existence of treason under the Treasons Act was indisputable. The policy which had struck down Buckingham nearly a score of years before was repeated even more ruthlessly. The materials for formulating a Yorkist rising were destroyed; there was no figure-head for one left when Exeter and Montague had been executed (Dec.), even though the old Countess of Salisbury's doom was deferred. And men realised afresh—if there was need that they should do so—the irresistible machinery that Cromwell had prepared for the certain annihilation of any one worth annihilating.

[Sidenote: 1539 Menace of Invasion]

The warning was perhaps necessary; for in the beginning of 1539 the attitude of the foreign Powers was menacing. The Pope was planning a sort of crusade, with invasion and insurrection in Ireland as its basis. The marriage of James of Scotland to Mary of Guise would make matters the more dangerous if France assumed a definitely hostile attitude; and the pretence of negotiating the union between Henry and the Duchess of Milan had been ended by the reconciliation of Charles and Francis. A combination including the Emperor was threatening. Wriothesly the English ambassador in the Low Countries, did not believe on the whole that there would be a breach of the peace, unless the Imperialists felt that their victory would be assured. Nevertheless, a great armament was assembled in the Dutch harbours. England, however, had awakened to the need of defence in the Channel; fleets were assembled and forts manned. The solidarity of the country had been demonstrated by the easy suppression of the Courtenays and Poles. If an invasion was contemplated—which can hardly be doubted—the invaders thought better of the situation, and the armada dispersed without any overt hostilities taking place.

[Sidenote 1: The King and Lutheranism]
[Sidenote 2: The Six Articles]

The Lutheran conference of the previous year had been without direct results: but it had the effect of forcing to the front the settlement of the official position as to several points of doctrine. The advanced bishops were distinctly inclined to admit the Lutheran views: the other powerful body within the English Church was in strong opposition. Theologically, the King was in agreement with the latter section, although he retained a particularly strong and persistent personal affection for Cranmer—apparently the only persistent affection of his life. The result was the production of the Six Articles Act, pronouncing in favour of Transubstantiation, clerical celibacy, auricular confession, communion in one kind only for the laity, prayers for the dead, and the permanence of vows once taken. On the first head there was not as yet any real difference of opinion. As to the second, Cranmer was actually a married man when he became archbishop, and many of the clergy, especially in country districts, had wives, in spite of the fact that the law did not recognise the relationship: so that an awkward situation was created. Considering the abolition of the monasteries, the Article concerning vows was remarkable. But on all these doctrines the views of the reformers were not yet sufficiently crystallised to prevent their submission when the Jaw demanded it, though it justified a determined opposition to the passing of the law; in this Cranmer was particularly conspicuous, and two of the bishops, Latimer and Shaxton, lost their sees. That the Act should have been passed is not surprising; but the ferocity of the attendant penalties is best explained by the fact that, on an attempt being made to apply the statute in a wholesale fashion, the accused were promptly pardoned and set at liberty. The object was not so much to punish as to silence the advanced section.

[Sidenote: Final Suppression of Monasteries]

At the same time two other Acts of grave import were passed. One was the Act for the suppression and forfeiture of those religious houses which had not been accounted for in the Act of 1536. The new Act was merely the logical corollary of the old one. The distinction in morals between the lesser and greater monasteries was not marked: and to the old charges of the commissioners were added the new charges of complicity in the rebellion of the North and in Exeter's conspiracy, and of fomenting disloyalty generally. The measure was carried out with great harshness, and especial severity was shown in the cases where abbots and monks attempted to conceal the monastic treasures. The aged and beloved abbot of Glastonbury was found guilty of treason and put to death. The great estates became for the most part the prizes of the nobility. Some few of the houses were converted into Chapters. There was a scheme for constructing twenty-one new bishoprics out of the proceeds of the suppression, but the twenty-one dwindled to six. [Footnote: Chester, Peterborough, Oxford, Gloucester, Bristol and Westminster.] A fraction of the money was expended on the Channel defences. But broadly speaking the vast bulk of the spoils went to no national or ecclesiastical purpose but to the enrichment of private individuals. Still the amount realised by the National Exchequer did no doubt relieve the present necessity for taxation in other forms, which would have been a more fruitful source of murmuring and discontent than sympathy with the dispossessed monks.

[Sidenote: Royal Proclamations Act]

The second measure was the Royal Proclamations Act, giving to Royal Proclamations made with the assent of the Privy Council the force of law. This was the coping stone of that edifice of absolutism built up by parliamentary enactments of which Cromwell was the Architect: an adaptation of the system initiated by Henry VII. and developed by Wolsey; springing now from the assertion of the doctrine of the Supreme Head, continuing with the novel practical interpretations of that doctrine in matters ecclesiastical, and buttressed by the Treasons Act, which effectually translated discontent into Treason. Now the King was left in such a position that his will became formally law unless his Privy Council opposed him.

[Sidenote: Anne of Cleves]

Cromwell had shattered the ecclesiastical power of resistance: he had shattered also the dangerous elements among the nobility: he had systematically secured parliamentary confirmation for every step. But he wished to carry still further the anti-clericalism which was part of his policy. He desired the domination in England of the Lutheranising section of Churchmen, and the central idea of his foreign policy was the construction of a Protestant League. In these respects he went beyond his master, and in the attempt to carry his master with him, he made ship-wreck of himself. The question of another marriage for Henry was still unsettled; if more children were to be hoped for, it must be settled soon. Cromwell fixed upon Anne of Cleves as politically the wife to be desired. By wedding with her, Henry would be drawn into closer relations with the Protestant League of Schmalkald. He painted for the King a misleading picture of the lady's charms: the King consented to his plans; the negotiation flowed smoothly.

[Sidenote 1: 1540 The Marriage]
[Sidenote 2: Fall of Cromwell]

Early in the year (1540) the bride came to England; bringing disillusionment. Matters had gone too far for the King to draw back, and the marriage was carried out; but his wrath was kindled against its projector. The blow fell not less suddenly than with Wolsey. The Earl of Essex—such was the title recently bestowed on Cromwell—was without warning arrested and attainted of high treason. The instrument he himself had forged and ruthlessly wielded with such terrible effect was turned as ruthlessly against him. He had over-ridden the law. He had countenanced and protected anti-clerical law-breakers. He had spoken in arrogant terms of his own power. As it had availed Wolsey nothing that his breach of praemunire had been countenanced by the King, so it availed Cromwell nothing that the King had seemed to support him. If the King had done so, in each case, it was merely because he in his innocence had been misled by his minister, so that in fact their crime was aggravated. For the merciless minister, there was no mercy. That the process against Essex was by attainder and not by an ordinary trial is of little moment. His fate would have been the same in any case; nor was he so scrupulous in such matters that he can claim sympathy on that head. No voice but Cranmer's—in lamentation rather than protest—was raised on his behalf. The mighty minister, the most dreaded of all men who have swayed the destinies of England, found himself in a moment as utterly helpless as the feeblest of his victims had been. He was flung into the Tower;

his stormy protests were unheeded by the King; on July 28th, his head fell beneath the executioner's axe.

[Sidenote: Nemesis]

Cromwell had learned his ethics and his state-craft in that school whose doctrines are formulated in "The Prince" of Macchiavelli. He had applied those principles with remorseless logic, untinged by the fear of God or man, to the single end of making his master actually the most complete autocrat that ever sat on the throne of England. His loyalty was as unfailing as it was unscrupulous; his work had been thorough and complete—the King was placed beyond further need of him. His reward was the doom of a traitor. Unpitying he lived, unpitied he died. Regardless of justice, he had swept down each obstacle in the way of his policy: regardless of justice he was in turn struck down. By his own standards he was judged; his end was the end he had compassed for More and Fisher. History has no more perfect example of Nemesis.

CHAPTER X
HENRY VIII (vi), 1540-47—
HENRY'S LAST YEARS

[Sidenote: 1540 Katherine Howard]

The complaisant and very plain lady who had been the cause of Cromwell's downfall had no objection (subject to compensation), to being discarded on technical grounds by her spouse. Before the minister was dead, the marriage had been pronounced null: not without compensatory gifts. But her brother the Duke of Cleves was less easily pacified, and all prospect of an alliance with the Protestant League was at an end. A new bride was promptly found for the King in the person of Katharine Howard, a kinswoman of the Duke of Norfolk—a marriage which marked the renewal of the ascendancy of the old nobility in alliance with the reactionary Church party.

[Sidenote: The King his own Minister]

Thirty-one years had passed since Henry, in the first flush of a manhood exceptionally rich in promise, but untried and inexperienced, had taken his place on the throne of England as the successor of the most astute sovereign in Europe. For nearly twenty years thereafter Wolsey had served him with such latitude of action that nearly every one except the Cardinal believed that he dominated the King. After a brief interval, for nearly ten years more the same statement would have applied to Cromwell. While those two great ministers held office, each of them towered immeasurably above all his fellow-subjects: though each knew that the brilliant boy had hardened into a masterful King who could hurl him headlong with a nod. But when Cromwell had fallen, none took his place; there is no statesman who stands out conspicuous. Edward Seymour, Earl of Hertford, brother of Jane Seymour, showed some military capacity; Paget proved himself an astute diplomatist; Cranmer and Gardiner led the rival Church parties, but neither the parties nor their leaders exercised any semblance of control over the Supreme Head. Abroad, Henry's battle with the Pope was won: at home his autocracy was established alike as temporal and spiritual head of the nation. There was no one left who needed crushing. Cromwell had seen to that before he was dispensed with. After that revolutionary decade, there were no more marked changes. There were incidents in the now slowly moving course of the reformation; there was even an unimportant insurrection; but the chief interest of Henry's closing years is once more to be found mainly in foreign relations, and more especially in those with Scotland.

[Sidenote: England and the European Powers]

On the continent, the two leading Powers, France and the Empire, were in a chronic state of antagonism only occasionally veiled: while the Pope was in permanent opposition to England. This situation was complicated by the Schmalkaldic League of Protestant German Princes. When Charles was disposed to religious toleration, the League were his very good subjects, the Pope became antagonistic, and a Franco-papal alliance threatened. When Charles leaned to intolerance, the Pope grew favourable to him, and Francis turned a friendly eye on the perturbed Protestant League. Charles, Francis, and the League, would each of them have been pleased to make use of England, but none of them wished to be of service to her: and now Thomas Cromwell's great desire of bringing about a cordial relation between England and the League had been frustrated instead of furthered by the affair of Anne of Cleves. The risk of this alliance had forced Charles into a conciliatory attitude towards Francis; relieved from it, he could now revert to his normal attitude. At the end of 1540, the Emperor and the French King were almost within measurable distance of hostilities, while the relations between the latter and Henry were becoming seriously strained by his neglect to pay the instalments of cash due under past treaties. For the time being, however, there was no immediate likelihood of a breach of the peace.

[Sidenote: Cardinal Beton]

In Scotland, James Beton Archbishop of St. Andrews, the most consistent enemy of England, had died in 1539, and had been succeeded, both in his office and his influence, by his nephew, the still more famous Cardinal, David Beton. The Cardinal was the last of the old school of militant ecclesiastical statesmen; a foe to the English the more deadly because of Henry's anti-clerical policy, as well as on account of traditional views, and of the specific grounds of distrust for which Henry himself had been responsible during twenty years past—including the proposal to let Angus kidnap James Beton [Footnote: Cf. p. 81.] under a safe-conduct. He was moreover a zealous persecutor of heretics; which greatly intensified the bitterness with which all the historians of the reforming party treated not only the man himself but the whole policy which he was supposed to have instigated. In Scotland, religious reformers were almost of necessity Anglophiles, since Henry did all he could to encourage their doctrines.

North of the Tweed, English writers have relied so much on the statements of John Knox and Buchanan that the persistent hostility not only of the King and the clergy but also of the Scottish Commons to Henry's overtures is generally represented as mere frowardness. It was in fact due to a distrust sufficiently accounted for by the English King's undeniable complicity in the deliberate fostering of disorder, and more than justified by his re-assertion in public documents of the English claim to suzerainty which had been finally and decisively repudiated at Bannockburn—a repudiation confirmed by treaty [Footnote: It is true that this had not prevented Edward III. from re-asserting the claim.] in 1328.

[Sidenote: Scotland and England, 1541]

In 1541 the attempt was renewed to bring about a conference with the Scots King at York; again it failed, after James had seemed to commit himself. Henry was indignant, and recriminations passed on the subject and on that of border raids, which culminated in the following summer in the affair of Haddon Rigg when an English party was very badly handled. It is a curious illustration of Henry's notions of honour that—although the two countries were nominally at peace—Wharton, one of the English Wardens of the Marches, proposed to take advantage of James's 1542 roving propensities and arrange to have him captured and brought prisoner to England; a scheme which Henry apparently approved, but fortunately for his own credit referred to his Council, whose consciences were less adaptable. In October, the English indulged in a week's invasion of Scotland, and the Scottish King would have responded in kind but that his nobles thought better of it.

[Sidenote: Solway Moss (Nov.)]

The counter-invasion however was not long delayed. The popular accounts of it are mainly derived from the narrative of John Knox; according to whom the Scottish army, ill-led and disorderly, was utterly routed with immense slaughter by three or four hundred English yeomen who succeeded in gathering together and smiting them after the analogy of Gideon. But the dispatches of Wharton [Footnote: *Hamilton Papers.* Lang, Hist. Scot., i., 455. Froude, iv., 190 (Ed. 1864), follows Knox picturesquely.], the Warden of the Marches, show that, acting on some days' information, he had ready a force of from 2,000 to 3,000 men, with whom, having watched his opportunity, he fell upon the very badly organised Scottish levies and entangled them in the morass called Solway Moss. The completeness of the disaster has not been over-rated; but it was an intelligible operation of war, not a miracle. James was prostrated by the blow. In three weeks time (December 14th, 1542) he was dead, and his week-old daughter Mary inherited the woful burden of the Scottish crown.

[Sidenote: Intervening events]

In the meantime, there had been a futile insurrection in the North, headed by Sir John Neville, in the Spring of 1541; which led to the execution not only of Neville himself, but of the old Countess of Salisbury—niece of Edward IV., mother of the Poles, and grandchild of the "King-maker". Not long after this, the Norfolk interest suffered a severe shock at Henry's court from the discovery of flagrant and confessed misconduct on the part of the monarch's fifth spouse, Katharine Howard; she was attainted and beheaded, in February, 1542, and succeeded by Katharine Parr; who was fortunate enough to outlive her husband.

[Sidenote: 1543 Henry's Scottish policy]

Solway Moss inspired Henry with a fresh determination to invade and chastise Scotland; but James's death suggested a simpler method. For the moment, Beton was in the hands of his enemies. Henry proposed that the baby Mary should be betrothed to his own son Edward, that the government of Scotland should be vested in a Council which he could control, and that sundry English garrisons should be planted in the country. The Scots lords captured at Solway Moss were quite ready to promise support to his plans as the price of returning home: they were also ready to break faith with the English King when they got there; and did so. As soon as the lords were out of Henry's reach, the Scots Estates demanded modifications in the proposed treaty which would have made it nugatory from the English point of view. A Scottish Prince might have been allowed to wed an English Princess; but Scotland would not take her King from England. It was not long before the Cardinal recovered his ascendancy, and, acting in conjunction with the queen-mother, Mary of Guise, sought the aid and alliance of France.

[Sidenote: Alliance with Charles]

The French King was already at war with Charles, and his relations with England were exceedingly strained; whilst he was openly declaring his determination to support Scotland, and French ships were playing the pirate in the Channel. The Emperor on the other hand had quieted the Protestant league by his tolerant attitude at the Diet of Ratisbon (1541); but the Duke of Cleves, Henry's enemy, was defying him. Hence the whole conditions pointed to an anti-French *rapprochement* between Charles and Henry; which took the form of a treaty of alliance early in 1543. If the territories of either Power were invaded, the other was to render assistance: and thereafter neither was to make peace unless his ally was satisfied also. The French King attempted to detach England by offering to meet the bulk of her separate requirements; and considering the prevailing standard of bad faith, it is to Henry's credit that he refused these overtures.

[Sidenote: War with France]

In the early summer Francis invaded Flanders, and an English force, not numerous but in good trim, entered Picardy. The Imperial troops however awaited the arrival of Charles himself from the South, and it was not till August that he took the field, having gathered his army, largely composed of Spanish soldiery, at Spires. But his first objective proved to be not France but Cleves which he brought to rapid submission and treated with great severity. In October he began to concert operations with the English, and a scheme was prepared, to be given effect in the following summer: when the English were to invade France by way of Calais, and the Emperor by way of the Upper Rhine, the two armies converging on Paris.

[Sidenote: 1544 Domestic Affairs]

Though the French campaign was thus deferred, the early months of 1544 were not uneventful. In the realm of domestic affairs, we observe that the King was now resorting with vigour to the worst expedient of bad financiers, a monstrous debasement [Footnote: See *infra* p. 180] of the currency. Also he had recently raised a considerable forced loan, pending the collection of subsidies already voted by Parliament but not yet due. An act was now passed in effect converting the loan into a gift, by reason of the necessities of the war—a measure not practically different from the voting of an additional subsidy. Parliament also had the satisfaction of being invited to lay down the succession to the throne in accordance with Henry's wishes, although he had already been empowered to fix it without appeal—an apt illustration of his preference for following Constitutional forms whenever there was no risk of his objects being interfered with. After Prince Edward and his heirs, Mary was to succeed, and after her Elizabeth. Beyond Henry's own offspring, the claims of the Stewarts through Margaret Tudor were postponed to those of the descendants of the younger sister Mary.

[Sidenote: Intrigues in Scotland]

In Scotland, Beton was in power, carrying out a drastic policy of religious persecution; the nobility were in their normal condition of kaleidoscopic flux, taking sides for or against Henry, the Cardinal, and each other, as the moment's interests might suggest. The Anglicising party made a pact with England to repudiate the French alliance, hand over the baby Queen if they could, and accept Henry's control. Scotland was to be invaded. Certain zealous spirits proposed to assassinate the Cardinal if they could do so under Henry's aegis, but the opportunity passed before he replied to their overtures—to the effect that the scheme was eminently laudable, but that he could not openly move in the matter. The assassination of a tyrant was not looked on as an act deserving of severe moral condemnation; many zealots would have accounted it a virtuous deed, to risk their lives for such an end. But a King [Footnote: Froude, iv., 319 (Ed. 1864), apparently defends Henry on the ground that he regarded Beton as a traitor; and saw "no reason to discourage the despatch of a public enemy".] who encouraged even while declining to hire assassins stands in a different category from such persons.

[Sidenote: Edinburgh Sacked]

In the beginning of May, Edinburgh was startled by the appearance in the Forth of a great English fleet. The idea of an invasion in this form had never presented itself. There was no army to give battle. The Cardinal and his friends fled. The English landed and sacked Leith. Edinburgh was in no condition for defence; the resistance of the citizens, though stubborn, was easily overwhelmed. The city was pillaged; the county for miles round was laid waste; and then, satisfied with his work of simple destruction, Hertford, the English commander, withdrew. Scotland was leaderless and powerless to strike: for months to come, the English Wardens of the Marches were free to carry out a series of devastating raids with practical immunity. Under these circumstances, Henry dismissed the idea of organising a subordinate government: anarchy in Scotland suited him equally well, without involving responsibilities or taxing his resources. His serious attention was given to the Continent.

[Sidenote: The French War]

During May, separate overtures were made on behalf of France both to Charles and Henry with a view to severing their alliance; each however declined entirely to treat apart from the other. More-over, at the Diet of Spires, Charles took a strong line in favour of the maintenance of the ordinances of Ratisbon and generally of deferring all religious differences till the war with France should be over. With the Pope supporting France and advocating alliance with the Turk as a less dangerous enemy to Christianity than the ecclesiastical rebel of England, Charles was not disposed to show favour to the Catholic princes of the Empire.

[Sidenote: Charles makes peace at Crepy (Sept.)]

The time was now at hand for the campaign to commence: and Henry proposed a modification of the original scheme. According to his view, it would be better for the two armies to concentrate in force on the frontiers while a single detachment penetrated as far into France as might seem wise. Charles however insisted on his plan of two separate invasions. Henry could not refuse, but pointed out that his own march on Paris was conditioned by the thorough reduction of the country as he advanced;

notably of Boulogne and Montreuil which would otherwise perpetually threaten his communications. The English proceeded to lay siege to these two places, and the Emperor attacked St. Dizier. Until these strongholds were captured, the two armies were respectively unable to advance. With August, Francis renewed his scheme of making separate overtures accompanied by suggestions to each monarch that his ally was trying to make terms for himself. Each again refused to treat apart from the other. At last St. Dizier fell, and Charles advanced into France, passing by Chalons and a considerable French army which was enabled to act on his line of communications. Hence he very soon found himself in grave difficulties. Thereupon he informed Henry that unless the English marched straight upon Paris, regardless of Boulogne and Montreuil, (which he knew to be strategically impossible) he would have to accept for himself the terms offered by Francis. Boulogne was taken (September 14th) three days after the message was received, but Montreuil held out. Henry had honourably refused to make terms for himself; but on September 19th Charles signed the peace of Crepy—amounting to a simple desertion of his ally.

Boulogne was lost to the French, and though they were now free to concentrate their forces against the English, all attempts to re-capture it were repulsed. Henry felt no disposition to abate his own terms or to resign Boulogne: Francis required him to do both. Charles politely repudiated any obligation to armed intervention, despite the efforts of Gardiner to persuade him—much to the bishop's disappointment, since the Lutheran Princes, alarmed by the Emperor's conduct, were again making overtures to England.

[Sidenote: 1545 Ancram Moor]

In Scotland, the policy of destruction adopted by the English throughout 1544 had driven the country to a temporary rally, and a severe reverse was inflicted on the Southron, beguiled into an ambuscade, at Ancram Moor in February 1545; whereby Francis was encouraged to maintain, and Charles to assume, hostility to Henry: who in turn unsuccessfully sought the Lutheran alliance—a failure due to the persistent distrust of the German Princes, who could never make up their minds whether the promises of the King or the Emperor were the less to be relied on. To the quarrel over the desertion of England by Charles at the peace of Crepy, was added a quarrel over the seizure by the English of Flemish ships carrying what would now be called contraband of war, and the arrest in retaliation of English subjects in Flanders.

[Sidenote: A French Invasion]

The isolation of England was complete: and Francis now looked to effect a successful invasion; to which end a great fleet was collected. But there was now a respectable English navy, supplemented by ships from every port on the southern coast. The threat of invasion raised the whole country in arms. In the latter part of July, the French armada was off the Solent, and a landing was accomplished in the Isle of Wight; but though there were various demonstrations and a few skirmishes, there was no general engagement. The French could not get into the Solent: the English would not come out in force, so long as the lack of a sufficient breeze gave the fighting advantage to the enemy's oar-driven galleys. Finally, plague broke out in the French fleet which retired about the middle of August. Its dispersion allowed of the relief of Boulogne; which was becoming somewhat straitened, being blockaded on the land side by a large army.

[Sidenote: 1546 Terms of Peace]

Thus when the autumn set in, the offensive operations of the French had resulted in complete failure though there had been no important engagement: and in the meantime, the temporary nature of the reverse at Ancram Moor had been demonstrated by renewed ravages in Scotland directed by Hertford. The altered aspect of affairs made Francis ready to treat, and changed the tone of Charles from hostility to conciliation. Negotiations were set on foot; but in the course of them it became clear not only that Henry was determined to keep Boulogne but that Charles had no intention of letting Milan go. England's readiness to continue the struggle was demonstrated by the strength of the forces she threw onto French soil in the following March, and in May Francis proposed terms. Most of the cash claims were to be paid up; part were to be referred to arbitration; and Boulogne was to remain for eight years in the hands of the English as security. The financial pressure of the war had been terribly heavy, so that the expedient of debasing the coinage had been repeated in order to supplement taxation. Henry accepted the French terms; and almost simultaneously his hands were strengthened by the assassination of his most resolute opponent in Scotland, Cardinal Beton (May 29th, 1546). The Peace with France was concluded in June.

[Sidenote: 1532-46 Events in Europe]

Before proceeding with the account of the ecclesiastical movement in England during these six years, and with the narrative of the concluding six months of Henry's reign, we must turn aside to observe certain events on the Continent which have not hitherto fallen under our notice, since they did not at the time exercise a direct effect on English policy, and were not immediately influenced thereby. Yet since the treaty of Nuremberg in 1532—

the point down to which, in a previous chapter, we followed the course of the Reformation in Europe—a compromise which served as a *modus vivendi* between the Protestant League and the Catholic subjects of the Empire, important developments had been taking place, which very materially, if indirectly, affected the subsequent course of events in England as well as on the Continent. The period corresponds roughly with the pontificate of Paul III. which lasted from 1534 to 1549.

[Sidenote: The Lutherans and the Papacy]

The idea that the ecclesiastical reconciliation of Christendom was still possible—apart from the banned and recalcitrant sovereign of England— was one of which a considerable body of Churchmen by no means despaired. There were men like Contarini and Pole on the one side and Melanchthon on the other whose doctrinal attitude did not seem to be hopelessly irreconcilable. But while the Lutherans demanded for themselves a latitude of opinion beyond what the Pope would ever have been prepared to concede, the two sides laid down two contradictory propositions as the condition of reconciliation, in respect of the validity of Papal authority. Each was willing, even anxious, for a General Council; but neither would admit one unless so constituted as to imply that its own view was postulated and *ipso facto* the opposing view ruled out of court. The Emperor, though anti-Lutheran, was unwilling either to enforce his view at the sword's point, or to subordinate himself to the Pope. The French King was equally ready to win papal favour by persecuting his own protestant subjects, and to encourage the protestant subjects of the Emperor, according as one course or the other seemed more likely to embarrass Charles. Finally the Pope, while set upon the suppression of the Lutheran heretics, was desperately afraid of the accession of strength to Charles which would result from their complete disappearance as a political factor: and he was almost equally afraid that if a Council could not be carried through, Charles would call a national Synod of the Empire to settle the religious question independently.

[Sidenote 1: 1541 Conference of Ratisbon]
[Sidenote 2: 1542 Council of Trent]

Thus attempts to bring about a General Council failed repeatedly. The nearest approach to reconciliation was achieved when a conference was arranged at Ratisbon (1541) at which there were papal as well as Lutheran representatives and it seemed as if common ground of agreement was in course of emerging. But Luther himself held aloof; Paul III. would not ratify the concessions that Contarini and others were willing to make. The Conference ended in failure; and Charles—always embarrassed in his dealings with the Protestants by his need of their support against threatening Turkish aggression—was obliged, a good deal against his private inclinations, to reaffirm the Nuremberg toleration. The result was a renewal of negotiations between Pope and Emperor for the calling of a General Council; whereof the outcome was that in May 1542 the Pope summoned the famous Council of Trent which did not conclude its sittings till twenty years later. Although the Council was formally called for the end of the year, it did not succeed in holding a working Session till 1546; after the spring of 1547 it was transferred to Bologna; nor did it get to work again (once more at Trent) till 1551. The fundamental point however is that, by its constitution, the Lutheran controversy was prejudged and the Lutheran party effectively excluded. It was not a Council representing Christendom; it stood for the Church of Rome seeking internal reformation for itself and arrogating Catholicity to itself. Hence arose the custom of using the terms Catholic and Protestant as party labels for those within and without the "orthodox" pale, in spite of the objection more particularly of the Anglican body to its implied exclusion from the "Catholic" Church and inclusion in the same category with the Lutheran and Calvinistic bodies. The historian cannot admit that Rome has a right to monopolise the title of Catholic; but during the period when Europe was practically divided politically into two religious camps, it is difficult to avoid using the current labels though their adoption is in some degree misleading.

[Sidenote: 1548 Death of Luther]

With the convocation of the Council of Trent, such hope as there had been for a reunion of Christendom was practically terminated. Its first working sessions in 1546 were contemporaneous with the death of the man who had led the revolt against Rome. But if Martin Luther had been a great cleaving force, in Germany itself his influence had been consistently exerted for national unity. To him more than to any other man it was due that Germany had not as yet been plunged into a civil war. He was hardly gone, when the forces of discord broke loose.

[Sidenote: 1546-49 Charles and the Protestant League]

Charles in fact found the Schmalkaldic League a thorn in his side, and had for some time been resolved on its extinction should a favourable opportunity occur. His war with Francis was terminated by the Peace [Footnote: P. 162, *ante.*] of Crêpy in September 1544; the pressure from Turkey was relaxed; there was no probability that either England or France would commit themselves to helping the League. In the summer of 1546, the League was put to the ban of the Empire; in the following summer it was crushed at the battle of Mühlberg, largely owing to the support given to the Emperor by the young Protestant Duke of Saxony, Maurice. But while this triumph broke up the League, and led Charles to regard himself as all-powerful, it frightened the Pope into an attitude of hostility; the Protestants were not annihilated; the course taken by Charles satisfied neither party within the Empire; and we shall shortly find a new and formidable Nationalist and anti-Spanish movement evolved in Germany with surprising suddenness and effectiveness.

During these years two religious developments had been in progress— one among the Protestants, the other among the Catholics—both destined to play a very large part in future history. These were the rise of John Calvin on one side and on the other the institution of the Society of Jesus familiarly known as the Jesuits.

[Sidenote: The Order Of Jesuits]

This Order was the creation of a Spaniard, Ignatius Loyola. Born in the same year as Henry VIII. he was taking active part as a knight in the wars of 1521, when he was crippled by a cannon shot. He rose from his sick bed a religious enthusiast; with the conception forming in his brain of an association for the service of his Divine Master based on the principles of military obedience carried to the extreme logical point. He devoted many years to training himself, body and brain and soul, for the carrying out of the idea. In course of time he found kindred spirits; at Montmartre in 1534 a little company of seven solemnly vowed themselves to the work. All of them men of birth and high breeding, with rich intellectual endowments and full of an intense devotional fervour, they soon attracted disciples; and in 1543 the new Order was formally sanctioned by the Pope. Utter obedience was their rule, thorough education of their members the primary requirement. Every Jesuit was a consummately cultivated man of the world as well as a religious devotee, responding absolutely to the control of a superior officer as a finished piece of machinery answers to the touch of the engineer; accounting death in the service a welcome martyrdom; shrinking from no act demanded for the fulfilment of orders which might not be questioned. Within a few years of its institution, the Society had developed into one of the most potent organisations, whether for good or for evil, that the world has ever known.

[Sidenote: Calvin]

While Loyola was preparing himself for his work, John Calvin was growing up in Picardy. Having adopted the tenets of the Swiss Reformers, the persecution of the heretics—within French territory—by the Most Christian King compelled him to take refuge in Switzerland. There, when only twenty-seven years of age, he published the work known as the "Institutes," setting forth that grim theology, the extreme logical outcome of the Zwinglian position, which is associated with his name; a system far more antagonistic to that of Rome than was Luther's. His head-quarters, save for a brief interval of banishment, were at Geneva, where he established about 1542 an absolute authority, no less rigorous or intolerant of opposition than the papacy itself; constructing a theory of ecclesiastical government that dominated the civil as the old Church had never dominated the State, and carried the stark severity of its controlling supervision into every detail of private conduct: banishing the comparative tolerance and charity which had distinguished the Zurich school.

[Sidenote: The ecclesiastical revolution in England]

In the meantime the course of the Reformation in England had been almost stationary. The whole movement in fact during Henry's reign took outwardly the form not of a revision of Religion but of a revolution in the relations of Church and State—a revolution already completed when Cromwell was struck down. Until his day, Englishmen—ecclesiastics and laymen alike—recognised the authority of the Holy See, though not always its claim to unqualified obedience. That authority was now finally and totally repudiated: none external to the kingdom was admitted; the Church was affirmed to be the Church of England, coterminous with the State; while a new interpretation was put upon the supremacy heretofore claimed from time to time by the secular Sovereign. Not only was the right assumed by the crown of diverting or even confiscating ecclesiastical revenues and of controlling episcopal appointments—so that it was even held doubtful whether the demise of the ruler did not necessitate re-appointment—but the power was appropriated, (though not in set terms), of ultimately deciding points of doctrine and promulgating the formulae of uniformity. This was the essential change which had taken place: resisted to the point of martyrdom by a few like More and Fisher; submitted to under protest by the majority of the clergy; actively promoted by only a very few of them, such as Cranmer. In asserting the position of the Crown, however, the Defender of the Faith admitted no innovations in doctrine and not many in ritual and observances. Now and again, for political purposes, Henry dallied with the Lutheran League; but in this direction he made no concession.

[Sidenote: 1540-46 Progressives and Reactionaries]

No marked alteration then appears after the death of the Vicar-General. Nevertheless, the contest between the progressive and reactionary parties was not inactive. In one direction alone, however, did the former achieve a distinct success. There was an increasing feeling in favour of the use of the vulgar tongue in place of Latin, not only in rendering the Scriptures but also in the services of the Church. The advanced section had already so far won the contest in respect of the Bible that the reactionaries could only fight for a fresh revision in which stereotyped terms with old associations might be re-instated in place of the new phrases which were compatible with, even if they did not suggest, meanings subversive of traditional ideas—a project which was quashed [Footnote: A revising Commission had been appointed; but was suddenly cancelled, with an announcement that the work was to be entrusted to the Universities; which however was not done. The probable explanation is that Cranmer, seeing the bent of the Commission, influenced the King to withdraw the work from their hands, and it was then allowed to drop.] when its intention became manifest. Measures however were taken to restrict the miscellaneous discussion of doctrine, which had not unnaturally degenerated into frequent displays of gross irreverence and indecent brawling; while on the other hand the use of a Litany in English instead of Latin was by Cranmer's influence introduced in 1544.

[Sidenote: 1543 The King's Book]

A year earlier the third formulary of faith—the two preceding had been the Ten Articles and the Bishops' Book—was issued under the title of the "Erudition of a Christian Man," popularly known as the "King's Book". This was the outcome of a group of reports drawn up by bishops and divines, severally, in answer to a series of questions submitted to them. The reports showed great diversities of opinion on disputed questions; but the book which received the imprimatur of Convocation and of the King was in the main a restatement of the doctrines of the Bishops' Book with a more explicit declaration on Transubstantiation and on Celibacy in accordance with the Law as laid down in the Six Articles. Throughout the preliminary discussions, Cranmer had championed the most advanced views which had hitherto been held compatible with orthodoxy; and, becoming shortly afterwards the object of direct attack as the real disseminator of heresy, he openly avowed to the King that he retained the opinions he had held before the passing of the Six Articles Act although he obeyed the statute. Henry, to the general surprise, refused to withdraw his favour from the Archbishop, and caused much alarm to the opposing party by the manner in which he rebuked the Primate's traducers. The circumstances deserve special notice because they show that Cranmer was not the mere cringing time-server that he is sometimes represented to have been; and also as proving that the King himself was for once capable of feeling a sincere and continuous affection.

[Sidenote: Henry stationary]

The hopes of the reactionary party were in fact somewhat dashed by the "King's Book"; since, despite Cromwell's death, the Six Articles still marked the limit of their influence. A companion volume, known as the *Rationale,* dealing with rites and ceremonies on lines antagonistic to Cranmer, was refused the royal sanction. Henry never lapsed from his professed attitude of rigid orthodoxy. But he showed an increasing disposition to check random and malignant prosecutions for heresy and to give the accused something like fair trial; more especially after the culminating iniquity of Anne Ascue's martyrdom (in the last year of his reign) for denying the doctrine of the Real Presence in the Eucharist. The system of ecclesiastical spoliation was also in 1546 rounded off, by the formal transfer to the crown of chantries which had not been swept away in the dissolution of the monasteries.

[Sidenote: 1546 Attainder of Surrey]

The autumn of 1546 arrived. The King's health was known to be exceedingly precarious, and it was practically certain that there must be some form of regency or protectorate until the boy prince of Wales should attain a responsible age. The most prominent men were on the one side the Duke of Norfolk and Gardiner, on the other the Earl of Hertford and Cranmer. The King's attitude was more favourable to the second of the two parties; the conduct of the Earl of Surrey, Norfolk's son, ensured them the domination. Surrey was entitled to bear on his shield the Arms of England, as a descendant of the Plantagenets; [Footnote: See *Front*. He traced through his mother and the Staffords to Edward III, and also through the other line to Thomas, son of Edward I.] but he assumed quarterings proper only to the heir-apparent. He used language which showed that he counted on a Norfolk regency and might have meant that it would be claimed by force. And he was proved to have urged his own sister, Lady Richmond, to become the King's mistress in order to acquire political influence over him. It was also found that the Duke, his father, long a partisan of France, had held secret conversations with the French Ambassador. These charges were easily construed into treason under the comprehensive interpretation of that term which Thomas Cromwell had introduced. Surrey was sent to the block: his father escaped the same fate merely by the accident that death claimed Henry himself only a few hours after the Act of attainder was passed. The inevitable result followed, that practically the whole power of the State was found to be vested in Hertford and his supporters.

[Sidenote: 1547 Death of Henry]

On the 28th of January 1547, the masterful monarch was dead: to be followed to the grave two months later by one of his two great rivals, Francis. Of the three princes who for thirty years had dominated Europe, only one was left. A greater than any of them—he who, also thirty years ago, had kindled the religious conflagration—Martin Luther, had passed away a twelvemonth before.

CHAPTER XI
HENRY VIII (vii), 1509-47-ASPECTS
OF HENRY'S REIGN

[Sidenote: Ireland, 1509-20]

Affairs in the sister island did not, after the final collapse of Perkin Warbeck directly affect the course of events in England: so that they lend themselves more conveniently to summary treatment. Ireland in fact hardly thrust herself forcibly on English notice until Thomas Cromwell was in power, and even then she only received incidental attention.

[Sidenote: Surrey in Ireland, 1520]

It appears to be generally recognised that when Gerald Earl of Kildare finally made up his mind to serve Henry VII. loyally and was for the last time re-instated as Deputy, he proved himself a capable ruler and kept his wilder countrymen in some sort of order. In 1513 he was succeeded in the Deputyship by his son Gerald, who bore a general resemblance to him, but lacked his exceptional audacity and resourcefulness. It was not long before the Earl of Ormonde—head of the Butlers, the traditional rivals of the Fitzgeralds, and chief representative of the loyalist section— was complaining of disorder and misgovernment; and in course of time, Kildare was deposed and Surrey [Footnote: The Surrey who became Duke of Norfolk in 1524, and was under attainder when Henry died in 1547.]— son of the victor of Flodden—was sent over to take matters in hand (1520). Kildare was summoned to England, where after his father's fashion he made himself popular with the King whom he accompanied to the Field of the Cloth of Gold. Surrey was a capable soldier, and took the soldier's view of the situation. There would be no settled government until the whole country was brought into subjection; it must be dealt with as Edward I. had dealt with Wales. The chiefs must be made to feel the strong hand by a series of decisive campaigns, the whole country must be systematically garrisoned, and the Englishry must be strengthened by planting settlements of English colonists. Half-measures would be useless, and he could not carry out his programme with a less force than six thousand men.

Henry however had no inclination to set about the conquest of Ireland. His own theory, with which it may be assumed that Wolsey, now in the plenitude of his power, was in accord, was more akin to his father's. Moreover, Wolsey and the Howards were usually in opposition to each other. Surrey was instructed to appeal to the reason of the contumacious chiefs; to point out that obedience to the law is the primary condition of orderly government; to authorise indigenous customs in preference to imposed statutes where it should seem advisable. In fact there were two alternatives; one, to govern by the sword, involving a military occupation of the island; the other to endeavour to enlist the Irish nobles on the side of law and order and to govern through them. The first policy, Surrey's, was rejected; the second was attempted. But the Irish chiefs had no *a priori* prejudice in favour of law and order, and something besides rhetoric was needed to convince them that their individual interests would be advanced by such a policy. Henry VII. had prospered by reinstating the old Earl of Kildare; Henry VIII. tried reinstating the young one. But precedents suggested the unfortunate conclusion that a little treason more or less would hurt no one, least of all a Geraldine. Things went on very much as before. Kildare was summoned to London again, rated soundly by Wolsey, suffered a brief imprisonment, and was again restored. Desmond, his kinsman, intrigued with the Emperor, who was in a state of hostility to Henry because of the divorce proceedings; Kildare was accused of complicity, and going to London a third time in 1534 was thrown into the Tower from which he did not again emerge. Henry had just burnt his boats in his quarrel with Rome and was by no means in a placable mood.

[Sidenote: Fitzgerald's revolt, 1534]

Kildare had named his eldest son Lord Thomas Fitzgerald, a young man of twenty-one, to act as Deputy in his absence; moreover he had so fortified his castle of Maynooth and otherwise made military preparations, as to give colour to the idea that he had rebellion in contemplation. Excited by a report that his father had been put to death, Lord Thomas—known as Silken Thomas from a badge worn by his men—burst into the Council at Dublin, threw down the sword of office, and renounced his allegiance; then raised an insurrection at the head of his friends and followers. Dublin Castle was soon besieged by a large miscellaneous force; the Archbishop, a leader of the loyalists, attempted to escape but was taken and foully murdered; bands of marauders ravaged the Pale. The only effective counter-move was made by Ormonde who rejected Fitzgerald's overtures, and, in spite of Desmond's menacing attitude on the South-west, raided the Kildare country, and brought Silken Thomas back in hot haste to defend his own territories.

[Sidenote: 1535 The revolt quelled]

Fitzgerald's rising began in June. Henry had appointed as Deputy Sir William Skeffington, an old soldier who had held that office before during Kildare's last suspension. But his departure from England with his troops was delayed. Fitzgerald was back before Dublin in September, after a vain attempt to win over Ormonde who defied him boldly. Again the Kildare lands were raided, and Lord Thomas had to raise the siege; and now at the end of October Skeffington succeeded in crossing the channel and securing Dublin, while the rebels carried fire and sword through the neighbouring districts. For the rest of the winter Skeffington did nothing but send out a futile expedition, a detachment of which was ambuscaded: while the loyalists fumed. In the spring however he shook off some of this inactivity, whether due to sickness, advancing years, or general incompetence, and besieged Maynooth which was reputed impregnable. The fortress fell before long; owing to treachery as tradition relates, but more probably to the improved siege artillery as the official despatches affirm. Most of the garrison were promptly hanged; a fatal blow was dealt to the insurrection. The "pardon of Maynooth" became a proverb. Skeffington, retaining the deputyship, was replaced in command of the army by Lord Leonard Grey, Kildare's brother-in-law, son of Lord Dorset; to whom ultimately Silken Thomas surrendered under a vague half-promise of lenient treatment. Kildare himself had died in the Tower not long before; Lord Thomas and his principal kinsmen were executed after a little delay; the one surviving representative of the great house which had "ruled all Ireland" was a child, preserved in hiding by loyal friends and retainers. The Geraldine power was at an end.

[Sidenote: 1535-40 Lord Leonard Grey]

Grey himself was now appointed to the deputyship in place of Skeffington, Desmond in the south-west and O'Neill in Ulster carried on the resistance, but were no match for Grey, who followed up his military successes by attempting to carry out the principles of conciliation which Henry had laid down—to the bitter indignation of those loyalists who favoured the methods advocated in the past by Surrey. To this and to Grey's insolent temper were due violent altercations between him and the Council. A Commission was sent over to examine and set matters straight, but instead the commissioners took sides with the Council or with the Deputy. Affairs were complicated by the application to Ireland of the English theory of ecclesiastical Reformation as understood by Henry and Cromwell. The suppression of the monasteries was acquiesced in (though not till 1541); since their condition was undeniably bad, and the distribution of their property convenient for the recipients; but the revolt from Rome was antagonistic to Irish feeling. Disloyalty to England, the natural and normal condition of three-fourths of the island, received a new authority from the sanction of loyalty to the Church. Grey persisted in his policy of domineering over the English party—who would have preferred to do the domineering themselves—and of laying himself open to the charge of favouring and fostering rebels, especially of the Geraldine faction. Another rising of O'Neill and Desmond in 1539 forced him to reassert his authority, but he again allowed it to appear that he was influenced by his connexion with the Geraldines; and in 1540 he was recalled, attainted, and executed. Experience of Henry had taught the conclusion that to fight the charge of treason was useless; but Grey gained nothing by throwing himself on the royal clemency, though his admission of guilt is not under the circumstances very conclusive.

[Sidenote: 1540 St. Leger]

Whatever the extent of his actual guilt, his downfall was due not so much to his professed policy as to the personal methods adopted which in the end had excited almost universal distrust and hostility. The proof of this lies in the fact that St. Leger, his successor as Deputy, carried out the same nominal policy with very remarkable success, and, it would seem, with general approval: mainly because he applied the principles impartially instead of as a partisan. The agent of conciliation was judicious, clear-headed, and tactful, instead of being injudicious, hot-headed, and tactless. The new Deputy distributed titles and monastic lands with a shrewd perception of the value of the services to be purchased thereby; legal commissioners were appointed who were allowed a due latitude in applying native customs and relaxing the rigour of English law; a number of important chiefs were converted into supporters of the Government instead of its more or less open enemies; the Pale settled down into the condition of a reasonably well ordered State. In the last years of Henry there is a complete disappearance of the wonted turmoil. At length he had found a man capable of administering the policy he had enunciated in 1520. The Deputyship of St. Leger gave promise of initiating a new era; but it showed also how completely the working out of the Irish problem would depend on the character and capacity of the men to whom the task should be successively entrusted.

[Sidenote: Henry "King of Ireland"]

One significant change remains to be noted. Hitherto the King of England had borne the title of Lord of Ireland, the theory being that Ireland was held as a fief from the Pope. As marking a final repudiation of every kind of papal authority, Henry, after the suppression of the Geraldine rising, assumed the style of King of Ireland. The fact that the change was needed has some bearing on the opposed papal and royal claims to Irish allegiance. Wales, it may be remarked, acquired citizenship when for the first time she sent representatives to Parliament in 1537.

[Sidenote: Wolsey's work]

Throughout the first half of Henry's reign the figure of the great Cardinal dominates the political field. In two respects at least his work was the extension of what Henry VII. initiated. By his efforts, the personal power of the crown became irresistible; and as the old King raised England from being almost a negligible quantity on the Continent to become at the lowest an effective make-weight in European combinations, so Wolsey raised her still further to a position of equality with the two great Powers which overshadowed all the rest. This he did by the same method of evading serious military operations whenever the evasion was possible, and by the exercise of a diplomatic genius almost unmatched among English statesmen. After his fall, the King's domestic interests withdrew him from a like active participation in the quarrels of Charles and Francis, although in his last years he became involved in a French war.

[Sidenote: The Army]

It is singular however to observe that Wolsey won for England all the prestige of a great military Power, after a period during which that ancient reputation of hers had been all but completely lost, without any single achievement memorable in the annals of war, and without producing any commander even of the second rank. With the sole exception of Surrey's victory at Flodden, due rather to the disastrous blunder of James than to the Earl's exceptional ability, no striking strategical or tactical feats are recorded, and few remarkable displays even of personal valour: nothing at all comparable to the brilliant if sometimes hazardous operations of the great Plantagenets. Nothing more is heard of that once triumphant arm, the Archery: the English bowmen had not, it would seem, lost their cunning, but they could no longer overwhelm hostile battalions. Nor does this seem to have been owing as yet to the displacement of the bow by firearms, though cannon both for defence and destruction of fortresses were improving— as exemplified at Maynooth. In the Scots wars, the border moss-troopers fought after their own fashion: but in the French wars the levies, no longer fighting in bodies following their own lord's flag, and feeling neither a personal tie to their leaders nor any particular bond among themselves, repeatedly displayed mutinous tendencies—as befel in Ireland under Lord Leonard Grey, and earlier with the entire army commanded by Dorset in

1512 and again with Suffolk's soldiery in 1523. The transition period from the era of feudal companies to that of disciplined regiments was a long one, particularly in England. During the whole of that period, English armies accomplished no distinguished military achievement.

[Sidenote: The Navy]

It was otherwise with English navies. All through the Tudor period, the nation was steadily realising its maritime capacities. Whether the strategic meaning of "ruling the seas" was understood or not, the century witnessed the rise of the English naval power from comparative insignificance to an actual pre-eminence. The two Henries fostered their fleets; when Elizabeth was reigning, the sea-faring impulse was past any need of artificial encouragement. But it is noteworthy that coast defence and ship-building were almost the only public purposes to which an appreciable share of the King's ecclesiastical spoils was appropriated. The King's ships were few, but they were supplemented by an ever-increasing supply of armed merchant-craft; and in the French war at the end of Henry's reign is the premonition of the great struggle with Spain, in which one most characteristic feature was the comparative reliance of England on sails and of her rivals on oars. As yet however, naval fighting was still governed by military analogies.

[Sidenote: The New World]

Though Henry was keenly interested in ship-building and naval construction, in the matter of ocean voyages and the acquisition of new realms Spain and Portugal still left all competitors far behind. Albuquerque had already founded a Portuguese Maritime empire in the Indian Ocean when Henry VIII. ascended the throne, and Spain was established in the West Indies. In 1513, Balboa sighted the Pacific from the Isthmus of Darien. In 1519 Cortes conquered Mexico; in 1520 Magelhaens passed through the straits [Footnote: It was still believed that Tierra del Fuego was a vast continent stretching to the South.] that bear his name, and his ships completed their voyage round the globe in the course of the next two years; in 1532 Pizarro conquered Peru; Brazil and the River Plate were already discovered and appropriated. All that England had done was represented by some Bristol explorers in the far North, some tentative efforts in the direction of Africa; and some four voyages to Brazil, the first two under William Hawkins, father of the more famous Sir John.

[Sidenote: Absolutism]

As Wolsey's policy was a development of that of Henry VII. in the direction of raising England's international prestige, so it was also in the concentration of power in the hands of the sovereign: and the process was carried still further though in a somewhat different way when Wolsey had fallen. It is curious to note that Henry VII. for the first half of his reign ruled by a skilful reliance on parliamentary sanctions, in the second half almost dispensing with parliaments. This order was reversed by his son. For the first twenty years, there were hardly any parliaments: from 1529 there was no prolonged interval without one. The economies of the old King sufficed to support the extravagant expenditure of his successor with only an occasional appeal to the purses of the Commons. It was only the necessities of a war-budget that involved such an appeal, so that none took place between 1514 and 1523. Had Wolsey been permitted to maintain his peace-policy unbroken, there would have been no rebuff from the House of Commons in 1523, no trouble over the Amicable Loan two years later. The country, habituated to an absence of parliaments, might have come to accept a monarchy absolute in form as well as in fact.

[Sidenote: The Parliamentary sanction]

But when Wolsey fell, Henry was embarking on a policy in which he knew that he must keep the nation on his side; the support of the body representing the nation must be secured. Whether that support was granted spontaneously, or was encouraged by manipulation, or spurred by the menace of coercion, was comparatively unimportant. The powers which the King was resolved to exercise must ostensibly at least have the sanction of national approval. The thing was managed with such thoroughness that long before the close of the reign the royal absolutism was confirmed by the Act which gave the force of law to the King's proclamations, and by the authorisation for him to devise the crown by will; and with such skill that Henry's and Cromwell's critics are obliged to fall back on the alleged subserviency of the parliaments to account for it, although these same subservient parliaments were quite capable of offering an obstinate resistance whenever their own pockets were threatened. Henry was one of those born rulers who impress their own views on masses of men by force of will. He made the country believe that it was with him. But behind the dominant force of will, he possessed the instinctive sense of its limits, besides being endowed with that final remorseless selfishness which made him ready to make scape-goats of the most loyal servants, to deny responsibility himself and to fling the odium upon them, as soon as he found that those limits had been transgressed.

[Sidenote: Depression of the Nobles]

Alike, then, by his disuse and his use of parliaments, Henry strengthened the royal power, the initiative of all legislation remaining in his hands. To the same end he continued to depress the great nobles and to create a new nobility dependent on royal favour. All who threatened to display a dangerous ambition, from Buckingham on, were struck down; the House of Norfolk survived till the end of the reign, when the Duke was attainted and his son was sent to the block. No ancient House was represented in the Council of Regency nominated under Henry's will. The men who served the King were those whom he had himself raised, and could himself cast down with a word. The edifice of his absolutism was complete, though it was modified by the conditions under which his son and his two daughters succeeded to the throne.

[Sidenote: Parliament and the purse]

The theory of absolutism from Richard II. to Wolsey had been that the King should make it his aim to rule without parliaments; whereas we are confronted with the apparent paradox that Henry was never more absolute than when his parliaments were in almost continual session. The explanation lies in this, that he did not usually call them to ask them for money out of their own pockets; for the most part he invited them to approve of his taxing some one else, by confiscations or the conversion of loans received into free gifts—a much more congenial task. The King had found other methods of raising revenues than by appealing to the generosity of his faithful Commons—methods which in effect relieved them of demands which they would otherwise have been obliged to face. The vast sums wrung from Convocation or from the Monasteries went to relieve the Commons from taxes. The parliament of 1523, summoned to grant subsidies, faced Wolsey with an independence which fully justified the minister in avoiding the risk of similar rebuffs: the Reformation parliament itself offered a stubborn resistance to the Bill of Wards, which touched its own pocket. Independence and resistance vanished when the incentive was withdrawn, and the diversion of the stream of ecclesiastical wealth into the abysses of the royal treasury was acquiesced in with a certain enthusiasm. The King got the credit of the ends secured, his minister the odium for the methods of obtaining them: and so year by year the crown became more potent.

[Sidenote: The Land]

The economic troubles brought about mainly by the new agricultural conditions in the reign of the first Tudor were exaggerated in that of the second, and were further intensified by the dissolution of the Monasteries. The evils at which More pointed in his *Utopia*, when Henry VIII. had been but seven years on the throne, showed no diminution when another thirty years had passed. The new landowners who came into possession of forfeited estates or of confiscated monastic lands continued to substitute pasture for tillage, and to dispossess the agricultural population as well by the reduced demand for labour as by rack-renting and evictions. The country swarmed with sturdy beggars; and the riotous behaviour encouraged when religious houses were dismantled or even "visited" must have tended greatly to increase the spirit of disorder, evidenced by the frequent popular brawling over the public reading of the Bible. The usual remedies of punishing vagabondage, and of attempting to force industry into unsuitable fields and to drive capital into less lucrative investment in order to provide employment, failed—also as usual. The landowners did not emulate the monastic practice of dispensing charity, so that distress went unrelieved. Charity often encourages un-thrift; but its absence sometimes leads not to industry but to thieving; and in this reign, crimes of violence were notably abundant. The economic conditions were therefore in fact unfavourable to thrift. But apart from economic conditions, the practice of that virtue is apt to be largely influenced by social standards. An ultra-extravagant court, and the calculated magnificence of such a minister as Wolsey, went far to induce a reckless habit of expenditure in the upper classes; and the inordinate display of the Field of the Cloth of Gold was merely an extreme instance of the prevalent passion for costly pageantries.

[Sidenote: Finance]

The resulting distress was not compensated in other directions. During the earlier half of the reign, Commerce did no doubt continue to prosper; but the King's financial methods were hardly more conducive to public industry and thrift than his personal example. Wolsey indeed was an able finance minister. In spite of the enormous expenditure on display, his mastery of detail prevented mere waste; and until the pressing necessities of a war-budget arose in 1523, enough money was found by tapping the sources to which Henry VII. had applied, supplemented by the ample hoards which that monarch had left behind. In 1523, the Cardinal's scheme of graduated taxation was sound and scientific in principle, so far as existing methods of assessment permitted. But for the remaining years of his life, the process of raising money to meet the King's requirements was exceedingly difficult and unpopular. After his death, the King discovered an additional and productive source of revenue in the property of the Church; but even this did not suffice for his needs.

[Sidenote: The Currency]

Henry therefore resorted to an expedient as disastrous as it was dishonest—a wholesale debasement of the coinage, which was continued into the following reign and was remedied only under Elizabeth. The first experiment was made as early as 1526; but it was the financial embarrassments of Henry's last years which brought about a debasement that was almost catastrophic. From 1543 to 1551 matters went from bad to worse till the currency was in a state of chaos: and the silver coin issued in the last year contained only one-seventh of the pure metal that went to that of twenty-five years before.

It followed that the purchasing power of the debased coinage sank—in other words, prices went up. On the other hand, the new coin remaining legal tender in England up to any amount, creditors who were paid in it lost heavily, the Royal debtor—and others—discharging their obligations by what was practically a payment of a few shillings in the pound. Also as a matter of course, the better coins, with each fresh debasement, passed out of the country or at any rate out of circulation, the base coins becoming the medium of exchange. Thus the foundations of commercial stability were sapped, while foreign trading operations were thrown into desperate and ruinous confusion.

Nor did the evil end here. For the influx of silver and gold from the Spanish possessions in America, though its effects were felt only very gradually, tended to depreciate the exchange value of the metals themselves. This depreciation, added to the debasement, further increased the rise of prices. But while prices went up, money-wages did not rise in anything like the same proportion; labour being cheapened by the continuous displacement of the agricultural population, which was not attended by an equivalent increase of employment in the towns, and by the dissolution of the monasteries, which at the same time wiped out the sole existing system of poor-relief. The natural Economic transition that began in the previous reign, while producing wealth, was also attended by distress: now, for a vast proportion of the population, Henry's artifical expedients for filling his own coffers converted distress into grinding want, destitution, and desperation.

[Sidenote: Learning and Letters]

The earlier half of the reign promised well for Education; but the promise was not duly fulfilled in the latter portion. The funds which Wolsey would have devoted to that object were wanted for other purposes. The Universities discarded the study of the schoolmen, but their attention was absorbed rather by loud-voiced wrangling than by the pursuit of learning. Nevertheless, in great families at least, the education of the younger members was carried to a high pitch. The King, a man of accomplishments which would have made him remarkable in any station, himself set the example, and in this respect at least his children were not lacking; the literary impulse was at work.

[Sidenote 1: The *Utopia*]
[Sidenote 2: Prose and Verse]
[Sidenote 3: Surrey and Wyatt]

Yet the literary achievements of Henry's time can hardly be called great. One work by an Englishman, More's *Utopia*, alone stands out as a classic on its own merits: and that was written in Latin, and remained untranslated till a later reign. In its characteristic undercurrent of humour, and its audacious idealism, it betrays the student of Plato; standing almost alone as a product of the dawning culture. Partly by direct statement, partly by implication, we may gather from it much information as to the state of England in Henry's early years, much as to the political philosophy of the finer minds of the day. But that philosophy was choked by revolution; More himself so far departed from its tenets of toleration as to become a religious persecutor. Most of the English writing of the reign took the form of controversial or personal pamphlets in prose or verse; such as the extravagant *Supplicacyon for the Beggers*, a rabid tirade against the clergy, or Skelton's rhyme *Why come ye nal to Court*, an attack chiefly on the Cardinal. The splendid raciness of Hugh Latimer's sermons belongs to oratory rather than to letters. The exquisite prose of Cranmer found its perfection in the solemn music of the Prayer-book of Edward VI. The translations of the Bible made no great advance on Wiclif. In the realm of verse, John Skelton was a powerful satirist with a unique manipulation of doggerel which has permanently associated a particular type of rhyme with his name; an original and versatile writer was Skelton, but without that new critical sense of style which was to become so marked a feature of the great literary outburst under Elizabeth. Herein, two minor poets alone, Surrey and Wyatt, appear as harbingers of the coming day. A hundred anonymous writers of Gloriana's time produced verses as good as the best of either Wyatt or Surrey; but these two at least discovered the way which, once found, became comparatively easy to tread. They introduced the sonnet, learnt from Petrarch; Surrey (the same who was executed on the eve of Henry's death) wrote the first English blank verse. The moribund tradition of the successors of Chaucer continued to find better exponents in Scotland than in England, in the persons first of bishop Gawain Douglas—who perhaps should rather be connected with the previous reign—and later of Sir David Lyndsay. But doctrinal controversy does not provide the best atmosphere for artistic expression. The whole literature of the reign, while showing emphatic signs of reviving intellectual activity, is remarkable not for its own excellence, for profundity of thought, intensity of passion, or mastery of form, but as exhibiting the first random and tentative workings of the new spirit.

[Sidenote: Estimate of Henry VII.]

The most arresting figure of the period is that of Henry himself. No English King has been presented by historians in more contradictory colours than he. One has painted him as the Warrior of God who purged the land of the Unclean Thing: to another he is merely a libidinous tyrant. One contrasts his honesty and honour with the habitual falsehood of his contemporaries: to another he appears supreme in treachery. In fact, there is an element of truth in both estimates, however exaggerated.

[Sidenote: His Morals]

In the matter of personal morality, in the restricted sense, it does not appear—in spite of his list of wives—that he compares unfavourably with contemporary princes. He had only one child certainly born out of wedlock—which cannot be said even of Charles V., [Footnote: It should perhaps be remarked that whenever Charles had a wife living he appears to have been faithful to her. His divagations took place in the intervals.] and contrasts with the unbridled profligacy of Francis, the frequent amours of his Stewart brother-in-law and nephew. The stories of his relations with both Anne and Mary Boleyn before the marriage, even if untrue (which is not probable), would never have been told of a man whose life was clean; but it is what may be called the accident of his numerous marriages which has given a misleading prominence to licentious tendencies not perhaps abnormally developed. With the exception of his passion for Anne Boleyn, there is no trace of his amours influencing his general conduct: and it is at least probable that after the death of Jane Seymour he would have remained a widower, but for the desire to make the succession more secure. Yet the story of his reign hinges upon the Divorce; and in the divorce, however much other considerations may have influenced him, the controlling consideration was the determination to make Anne Boleyn his wife since she would have him on no other terms. That fact, with the disastrous termination of the marriage with her, the fiasco of Anne of Cleves, and the catastrophe of Katharine Howard, is responsible for the somewhat mythical monster of popular imagination. The man who divorced two wives and beheaded two more is too suggestive of Bluebeard to be readily regarded as after all to some extent the victim of circumstance.

[Sidenote: His general character]

While Anne Boleyn was the object of his pursuit, Henry was dominated by his passion for her: but that passion cooled quickly enough after possession. Jane Seymour was not his wife long enough to put him to the test: but it would certainly seem that his affections were short-lived and easily transferred. This was manifestly the case with men: at least it never appeared to cause him a moment's compunction to hand over an intimate to the executioner. While a man was rendering him efficient service the King was lavish of praises and rewards; when the need for him was past the services were forgotten. His sentiments were always of the loftiest; it habitually "consorted not with his honour or his conscience" to do otherwise than he did; but the correspondence between his honour and conscience on one side and his personal advantage on the other presents a unique phenomenon. His conscience permitted him to connive at schemes for kidnapping the King of Scots or assassinating his ministers, and his honour permitted him to encourage his own servants in a course of action for which he had subsequently no hesitation in sending them to the block. He could give, prodigally; but what he gave had generally been taken from some one else. He could protest against the cruel burden of the annates, and then absorb them himself. And with all this, it is not difficult to suppose that he constantly persuaded himself that he was an honest man beset with dishonest rogues, since he rarely broke the letter of an engagement except on the pretext of bad faith made manifest in the other party.

[Sidenote 1: His peculiar abilities]
[Sidenote 2: Intention and achievement]

Henry's ethical standards were thus in no way calculated to hamper his actions, owing to his happy capacity for colouring his actions in conformity with them. When he set an end before himself, no influence could make him waver a hair's-breadth in his pursuit of it, and he spared neither friend nor foe in the attainment of it. As a statesman he did not lay down far-seeing designs. But he had the art of maintaining popularity, and a shrewd eye for a good servant. Thus as a rule he gave Wolsey a free hand and very vigorous support. But when he elected to order a change of policy, the Cardinal proved to have been right and the King wrong. His candidature for the Empire, and his dreams of the French and Scottish thrones show him capable of indulging in entirely impracticable visions. The vital achievement of his reign was the severance from Rome; and that was merely—as far as he was concerned—the accidental outcome of the Pope's opposition to the Divorce. In the destruction of the ecclesiastical *imperium in imperio*, the subordination of the Church to the State, it is difficult to tell how far the policy was his own and how far it was Cromwell's; but the King never recognised as Cromwell did that the logical corollary of the whole ecclesiastical policy was a Protestant League. The defiance of Rome, and the subjection and spoliation of the Church, were accompanied by a measure in which Cranmer was the moving spirit, and to which Henry gave full support—the open admission of the Scriptures in the vernacular—which made it no longer possible for the individual to disclaim responsibility on the score that the priesthood alone held the key to the mysteries of religion. This was in truth the keystone of the Reformation, since it entailed upon every man the *duty* of private judgment even though the *right* continued to be denied; yet this was not the effect which Henry contemplated. Hence, out of the four points in the ecclesiastical revolution of the reign: the subordination of the Church to the State was a constitutional change absolutely Henry's or Cromwell's own; the spoliation was the same, but reflects no credit on either; the severance from Rome was an accident; and the creation of the duty, to be ultimately recognised as the right, of private judgment was unintentional. And on the kindred subject, the persecution of innovators labelled as heretics, Henry's policy represented nothing but the commonplace attitude of Authority in his times.

[Sidenote: A Dominant personality]

We cannot, in short, find in Henry a statesman remarkable for far-sighted perceptions or ennobling idealism: but he gauged the sentiment of his subjects and the abilities of his servants acutely and was shrewd enough as a rule to identify himself with the schemes of those whom he trusted. Nevertheless he stands out, with all his faults, as a very tyrannical King yet a very kingly tyrant. If his personal ambitions and desires over-ruled other considerations, he never forgot the greatness of the country he ruled, and his personal ambitions at least involved England's magnification. For good or for evil, his actions were on a great scale. He knew his own mind, and he never shrank from the risks involved in giving his will effect. He defied successfully the Power which had brought the mightiest monarchs to their knees. He had the kingly quality, shared by his great daughter, of inspiring in his servants a devotion which made them ready to sacrifice everything for his glorification. Two of the most powerful ministers known in English history recognised the domination of his personality whenever he chose to exercise it.

[Sidenote: Summary]

Even when he was most feared he maintained his place in the popular affection. His parliaments carried out his will, but his will and theirs were in conformity: while Wolsey ruled, he rarely consulted them, but after Wolsey's fall they were called upon to ratify all the King's measures, and were in frequent session. He promoted a revolution, but while he lived he controlled it; through all the accompanying shocks and upheavals his mastery remained unshaken. The proof of the man's essential force, the greatness we may not deny him, is made manifest by the chaos which followed his death. He was gross; he was cruel; he was a robber; he suborned traitors and was prepared to suborn assassins; but his selfishness, flagrant as it was, did not wholly absorb him; behind it there was a sense of the greatness of his office, a desire to make England great; and therewith he had the indomitable resolution and the untiring energy for lack of which statesmen have failed who intellectually and morally stand far above him, while no monarch has left on the history of England a stamp more indelible than Henry VIII.

CHAPTER XII
EDWARD VI (i), 1547-49—THE
PROTECTOR SOMERSET

[Sidenote: 1547 Jan.-Feb. The New Government]

In accordance with the extraordinary powers granted to him, Henry VIII. laid down in his will both the order of succession to the throne and the method of government to be followed during his son's minority. Under this instrument he nominated sixteen "executors," forming virtually a Council of Regency, giving precedence to none. Superficially, the list represented both the progressive and the reactionary parties. Cranmer was balanced by Tunstal of Durham; Wriothesly the Lord Chancellor was a strong Catholic. But as a matter of fact, the influential men belonged for the most part to the advanced section. Edward Seymour, Lord Hertford, was their leader: but Paget, Dudley (Lord Lisle), Russell, and Herbert, were all of the same way of thinking. None of the rest were of the same weight as these; while Norfolk, the natural head of the conservative nobility was a prisoner in the Tower, and Gardiner, the ablest of the ecclesiastics, was omitted from the list.

Henry died in the early morning on January 28th; the fact was not made public till the 31st; and in the meantime, Hertford had carried the Council, which forthwith nominated him Lord Protector. The next step was a distribution of honours: Hertford was made Duke of Somerset; his brother, the Lord Admiral, (not an executor), Lord Seymour of Sudeley; Dudley became Earl of Warwick, Wriothesly Earl of Southampton, and Parr, brother of the late King's widow, Earl of Northampton. A couple of months later, that lady—who had succeeded in surviving two husbands including Henry—herself wedded Seymour of Sudeley,

Southampton was the one man whose opposition on the Council was to be feared; and he gave himself into his enemies' hands by an act of indiscretion. He issued a commission appointing four judges to act in the Court of Chancery, under the Great Seal, on his own responsibility: and was promptly declared to have forfeited his office which was bestowed upon Rich. This was immediately followed by the granting of new powers to the

Protector, enabling him to act virtually without consulting the Executors: while he was already guardian of the King's person. In effect, Somerset meant himself, as representing Edward, to exercise all those powers which had been surrendered to the formidable Henry. In the meantime, the trend of the ecclesiastical policy to be anticipated was shown by the treatment of the bishops; who—with the approval of Cranmer—were required to receive their commissions anew from the new King as though they had been Civil servants. Cranmer, in the Coronation sermon, made pointed references to Josiah, which could only be regarded as precursors of a war against "images," and the more advanced among the clergy began to express themselves with a freedom which would have been very promptly and unpleasantly dealt with by the late King. Ecclesiastical conventions received a startling shock when it was made known that the Primate himself was openly eating meat in Lent.

To carry the Reformation beyond the stage at which it had been left by Henry in a tolerably peaceful manner was a sufficient task in itself; but the situation which the new Government found that it had to face, by the time Somerset had secured his position, towards the end of March, was complicated by many additional problems—not least among these being the lack of funds.

[Sidenote: Relations with France]

The recent peace with France had given the English Boulogne for eight years as security for the payment of a substantial annual sum. But while this might be looked upon as a valuable diplomatic asset—a means to graceful concession in return for adequate benefits—it remained an incitement to French hostility; the more so when Francis I. followed his great contemporary to the grave after less than two months, and was succeeded by Henry II.; with whom the retention of Boulogne was a particularly sore point, as he had failed in an attempt to recapture it. If England found herself in difficulties it was tolerably certain that France would try to recover Boulogne without waiting the eight years for its restitution.

[Sidenote: with Scotland]

France was not unlikely to find her opportunity in Scotland. There the group who had murdered Cardinal Beton in the previous summer retained the castle of St. Andrews in defiance of the weak government, at whose head were the regent Arran and the queen-mother Mary of Guise, whose family was now the most influential in France. The one means by which an English party could be maintained in Scotland was the giving active support to the "Castilians" as the St. Andrews faction was called; whereas French interference on behalf of the Government would immensely strengthen the anti-English party.

[Sidenote: with Charles V.]

The German situation was more complicated. The Emperor, supported by Maurice of Saxony, was at war with the Lutheran League. As yet the issue of that contest was doubtful; the League had at least a chance of success, but had appealed to England for aid. Charles on the other hand, not wishing for war with England, had declined the Pope's suggestion that he should enforce the substitution of Mary for Edward on the English throne: the Pope was annoyed, because the Schmalkaldic war was being fought on a political and not a theological issue; and he was alienating Charles by withdrawing the Council of Trent from that city, which was within Imperial territory, to Bologna where Italian influences would be predominant. If then England intervened on behalf of the League, she would reconcile the Pope and the Emperor, and possibly unite them with France against herself. If she stood aside, she would lose the chance of creating a powerful Protestant League, while experience had shown that any gratitude Charles might feel would count for less than nothing in determining his future policy. The Government hesitated; and while they temporised, the Emperor by a sudden blow became master of the situation. At the end of April, crossing a river by night, he fell upon the unexpectant army of the League at Mühlberg, crushed it, and secured its chiefs. The League of Schmalkald was irrevocably shattered. No effective counterpoise to his power was apparent within the Empire. Now however the task before Charles was to organise the supremacy which had at last become convincingly actual. This, and his quarrel with the Pope over Trent and Bologna, was likely to keep his hands full for some time. Thus the important thing for the Protector was more emphatically than before to conciliate France and gain over a strong party in Scotland to support the policy of friendly relations with England; whereof the chief corner stone was still the marriage of Edward who was about ten years old to the four-year-old Queen of Scots.

[Sidenote: Somerset's Scottish policy]

But Somerset did not conciliate France, which had recently been further irritated by the construction of so-called harbour works at Boulogne which were evidently intended to be fortified, contrary to the treaty; while in Scotland he was meditating a step which could only drive that country into the arms of France.

Somerset in fact was one of those visionaries who are the despair of more clear-sighted persons who are in sympathy with their objects. He suffered from a permanent incapacity for realising the immense difficulties in his way, and the infinite tact necessary to the accomplishment of his aims. Hence the methods he adopted were invariably calculated to bring into full play every conceivable force that could act in opposition. Sincerely anxious to alleviate the lot of the rural population, he went out of his way to irritate the landlord class into more effective combination. Almost alone in a desire for the widest religious toleration, the moderation of his ecclesiastical laws was discounted by the licence of speech and action allowed to the progressives. In like manner, his theory of Scottish policy was admirable, his practice absurd. The Union of England and Scotland was his ideal, as it was to be the ideal in later years of that most acute of Scottish politicians, Lethington. But he could not appreciate the absolute necessity that the Union should be by consent; and even while endeavouring to procure it by consent, for which he appealed in noble language whereof the sincerity is apparent, he adopted methods which aroused the hostility even of those Scots who were most favourably disposed to Union in the abstract. By making common cause with the Reformers, he might have check-mated France; yet he neglected his opportunity. His own solution of the problem was the marriage of Edward and Mary, which he might have brought about by diplomatic persuasion, or by carrying the Reformers with him. Yet he could see nothing for it but to dictate his terms at the sword's point, the one quite certain way of making sure that they would be rejected, by setting even the Reformers against him. To make matters worse, it was in his mind to re-assert the English sovereignty; to which Henry had indeed audaciously affirmed his claim, though only as a right held in reserve. This intention he had already conveyed not to the Scots but to the French who warned him that they would stand by their old allies: while the mere suspicion of such an insult in Scotland was enough to rouse the fiercest hostility of the whole nation.

[Sidenote: Pinkie (Sept.)]

The natural result was that while Somerset was contenting himself with border raids, instead of espousing the cause of the Castilians, Prance was acting. About the beginning of July a French fleet appeared off St. Andrews; at the end of the month the castle surrendered. English ships might have prevented this, but the Protector elected instead to prepare a great invasion. In September he was over the border, in command of a considerable army, supported by a large fleet. The Scots of all parties mustered in force and were lying between the advancing English and Edinburgh in a strong defensive position not far from the spot made memorable two hundred years later by the rout of Prestonpans. The English ships were in the Forth hard by. The Scots in essence repeated the blunder of Flodden before and of Dunbar later. A successful attack by Somerset, who had the smaller army, was almost impossible; they thought that he was delivered into their hand, and mistook a tactical movement for a retreat to the ships. Abandoning their position and racing to cut him off, their leading troops received and broke a charge of horse; but the mass of the English, who were greatly superior in cavalry and artillery, and whose advance had been concealed by the formation of the ground, were already at hand and fell upon them. The Scottish army was completely shattered; ten thousand dead or dying men were left on the field of Pinkie Cleugh. The English loss was small.

[Sidenote: Effect of Pinkie]

Somerset however merely did very much what he had done before when he sacked Edinburgh in the last reign, ravaging and retiring. Pillage and destruction were arguments which invariably stiffened Scottish defiance, and it was now absolutely certain that the Scots would not consent on any terms to the English marriage. Dictation from England by force of arms was the one method of minimising the internal warring of factions in the Northern Country. Had Somerset been prepared to follow up his campaign by an effective military occupation, his plans might have been dignified with the name of a policy. In practice, they amounted almost to a negation of policy. A month after the battle the only effective result for Scotland was a renewed and intensified bitterness of hatred to England, and a corresponding inclination to amity with France. The practical reply to the invasion was the proposal to France of a marriage between the Queen of Scots and the Dauphin.

For the Protector himself however, the victory of Pinkie was a personal triumph. He returned to England in a halo of military glory and popularity, to receive new compliments and honours, and to assume the rôle of beneficent dictator with self-complacent confidence when Parliament met for the first time in the beginning of November.

[Sidenote: The Progressive Reformers]

In the meantime the progressive Reformers, increasingly guided by Swiss rather than Lutheran ideas, were already hurrying forward with their schemes, acting upon Royal proclamations under the authority of the Council. Injunctions were issued for the destruction of "abused" images which term was liberally interpreted so as to cover stained glass, paintings, and carvings which might conceivably be regarded as objects of idolatry— that is to say, become in themselves objects of worship instead of being recognised as mere symbols: a process which unless conducted with the most studied moderation and caution was absolutely certain to give the rein not only to passionate zealotry but to wanton irreverence. Cranmer obtained an order for the reading in churches of the "Book of Homilies," for the most part in lieu of all other preaching. The *Paraphrase* of Erasmus, done into English, was ordered to be set up in the churches. A commission was issued for a Royal Visitation, superseding the authority of the bishops, though some months elapsed before this was fairly at work. Paget, having the instincts of statesmanship, endeavoured to warn Somerset against keeping too many irons in the fire; but Paget was guided solely by political expediency, not by principle. The one man who did boldly take up his stand on principle was Gardiner. His remonstrances were open. He urged that the intentions of the dead King should be carried out; that no revolutionary changes should be introduced during Edward's minority; that arbitrary proclamations by the Council had no sanction of law; that the personal powers bestowed upon Henry remained in abeyance until the young King should be of age; that aggressive measures in Scotland ought to be similarly deferred. The introduction of the Homilies, he argued, to which authorisation had been refused in the last reign, was in itself unjustifiable in the circumstances; the more so as—mainly by their omissions—they were inconsistent with the doctrinal attitude affirmed by Henry's legislation. Gardiner's remonstrances, supported by Bonner, bishop of London, were of no effect. Matters came to a head when the two bishops refused to submit without qualification to the injunctions. Both were imprisoned in the Fleet, while Somerset was in Scotland.

[Sidenote: Nov. Repeal of more stringent laws; Social legislation]

In November, Parliament met, and began its career of benign legislation. Since Cromwell's day, the land had lain under the grip of ruthless laws. Of these the sternest were repealed as no longer necessary. The Treasons Act disappeared; so did the old Acts against the Lollards; so did the Act of the Six Articles. A curious attempt was made to deal with the problem of vagrancy, the outcome of prevalent economic conditions, which the penalties of flogging and hanging had failed to repress. The vagrant was to be brought before the magistrates, branded, and handed over to some honest person as a "slave" for two years. If he attempted to escape from servitude, he was to be branded again and made a slave for life; if still refractory he could be sentenced as a felon. The intention of the Act was merciful, its effect probably more degrading than that of the superseded statutes. At any rate, it failed entirely of its purpose and was repealed after two years.

[Sidenote: Ecclesiastical legislation]

In matters ecclesiastical, Parliament on its own account abolished the form of the *congé d'élire*, giving the appointments directly into the King's hands. Also the chantries and other foundations which had been conferred on Henry, but had not been suppressed by him, were now—despite the strong opposition of Cranmer, Tunstal, and a few of the bishops— formally subjected to the Council and for the most part abolished. It is to be noted however that of the Church property acquired by the crown in this reign a comparatively respectable though still niggardly proportion was re-appropriated to educational purposes. [Footnote: In most cases, only in the way of restoring pre-existing endowments.]

[Sidenote: 1548]

Convocation, sitting concurrently with Parliament, presented petitions for representation of the clergy in parliament, for the administration of the Communion in both kinds to the laity, for the suppression of irreverent language about the Sacrament, and for sanctioning the marriage of the clergy. The first was ignored; the two next were embodied in Acts of Parliament; the last was deferred for a year. The session was rounded off in January by a general pardon, except for the graver offences; with the result that the imprisoned bishops were for a time released.

[Sidenote: Progress of Reformation]

Between this and the next session of Parliament, in November, the arbitrary method of proceeding by proclamations was in full force. The Reformers did not as yet press advanced doctrinal views. There was a proclamation for the observance of the Lenten Fast—expressly for the sake of the fisheries. Another enforced a new Communion Office, pending the completion of a new Prayer-book; but in this the service of the Mass remained unaltered and in Latin: no doctrinal change was implied, though the Communion in both kinds was ordered to be administered to the laity, in accordance with the recent Act and the recommendation of Convocation. More significant was a further proclamation for the destruction of "images," in which the distinction between "abused" images and others, previously laid down, was cancelled. In the meantime no unauthorised innovations were to be permitted. Cranmer was still striving vainly after his ideal of a conference between leading continental and English reformers, who should come to an agreement upon a common body of doctrine. It was *prima facie* reasonable that while awaiting the new authoritative formularies, now avowedly in course of preparation by a commission on which the Catholic party was not unrepresented, partisan preaching should be discouraged, and all but licensed preachers be confined to the Homilies; it was however unfortunate that the licences for preaching should have been systematically granted both by Somerset and Cranmer—to whom the power was restricted—only to keen and sometimes extravagant partisans of the "New Learning"; a term at that time appropriated to the advocates of Protestantism at large. It is not surprising that Gardiner so far placed himself in opposition as to be called upon to express publicly his approval of these proceedings, nor that he should have found himself unable to do so in terms satisfactory to the Council. Before the summer was over the Bishop of Winchester was relegated to the Tower. More unfortunate still was the encouragement to sacrilegious irreverence given by the personal conduct of the Protector, who pulled down one chapel and began to lay hands on another in order to build himself a new palace.

[Sidenote: Somerset's ideas]

Nor were Somerset's activities confined to the campaign against "idolatry," a term conveniently used to include any observances which, in the eyes of the Swiss school, savoured of superstition. With no sense of the limitations of his own intelligence, no suspicion of the subtle skill in adjustment needed at all times to impose ideals on a materially minded community, unable to realise that though his object might be excellent the methods adopted in achieving it might be fruitful of unexpected evils, he conceived in his arrogant self-confidence that he had but to say the word and difficulties would vanish. He resolved to appear as the Poor Man's Friend, establishing a Court of Requests in his own house so that appeal might be made personally to him from the normal processes of the Law; also, he appointed a commission to investigate and deal with that evasion of the agricultural statutes which he imagined to be the actual cause of the prevailing distress. The end in view was admirable, the method high-handed and unconstitutional: the policy won him popularity for the time among the depressed classes, but roused the enmity of nobility and gentry without achieving useful results.

[Sidenote: The French in Scotland]

Meanwhile, affairs in Scotland were aggravating the tension with France, where the proposal to marry the Scots Queen to the French Dauphin was approved. English troops harried the borders, and in the course of the spring captured and garrisoned Haddington. French troops were landed in Scotland, and the marriage proposal was formally ratified; in spite of a belated offer from the Protector to leave Scotland alone and postpone his own marriage scheme till Edward and Mary were old enough to have views of their own, provided that Scotland would hold aloof from France. French ships, evading the English by sailing round the Orkneys, took Mary on board on the west coast and carried her off in safety to France. A diplomatist would have seized the chance of reviving an English party, when it was found that a violent animosity was growing up between the Scots and the French troops; but the opportunity was allowed to pass, and the animosities were reconciled by some minor successes of Scots and

French together against the English: while privateering operations—in other words, authorised piracy—were going on in and near the Channel, which amounted to something not far removed from a state of war between France and England.

[Sidenote: The Augsburg Interim]

It was fortunate that affairs in Germany continued to preclude that union of the Catholic Powers against England which the Pope desired; since neither Charles nor Paul would bend to the other. Charles, with no one to fear since Mühlberg had witnessed the destruction of the League of Schmalkald, was preparing future disaster by his high-handed attitude within the Empire. Deeming his position absolutely secure, his tone to the Pope was peremptory and dictatorial. The French King encouraged Paul to be equally peremptory. In May 1548, Charles, repudiating the authority of the Council, or section of the Council, sitting at Bologna, took the law in his own hands and imposed the "Interim of Augsburg" on the Germans. It was one of those compromises which satisfies no one; schismatical in the eyes of the Catholics, in the eyes of the Protestants an insignificant concession. Many of the latter, including the moderate and conciliatory Bucer, withdrew to England rather than accept it. The Protector however was secured against any present danger of a coalition between Henry II. and Charles; while the incursion of foreign Protestants of extreme views, especially those of the Swiss school, had a marked influence on the ecclesiastical movement in England.

[Sidenote: Nov. Parliament]

At the end of November, Parliament again met—to reject a first, a second, and a third Enclosures Bill, based on the report of the Agricultural Commission; for the labouring classes were unrepresented in the House. Making the rough places smooth proved not so simple a process as the Protector had imagined. The petition of the clergy for the legalisation of their marriages, deferred from the last session, was given effect, and fasting was again enjoined on economic grounds. The real business of the session, however, was the discussion of the new Prayer-book and the first Act of Uniformity.

[Sidenote: 1549 A New Liturgy]

Hitherto, there had been no uniform Order of Service: a variety of "Uses" being sanctioned. The idea however was by no means new, and had in fact long been theoretically approved, though never pressed with sufficient fervour to pass the stage of theoretical approbation. Cranmer had expended an infinity of learning and labour on the work now to be issued, and to him we owe chiefly the solemn harmonies, the gracious tenderness, of its language. To him too in chief, but partly also to the composite character of the "Windsor Commission" under whose auspices [Footnote: *Cf.* Moore, 183.] it was prepared, is due that conscious ambiguity of phraseology which enables persons of opinions so diverse on points so numerous to find in it a sufficiently satisfactory expression or recognition of their own views. It was possible alike for Day and for Ridley, even for Tunstal and for Hooper, to conform to it. Whether it was actually submitted to Convocation is a moot question, [Footnote: Moore, 186,187.] as to which the evidence is inconclusive, but informally, if not formally, it is clear that it received the *imprimatur* of general clerical opinion. In the discussions, the Archbishop — generally regarded by the Swiss school as sadly backward — won from that section unexpected approval; but his other utterances continued to be so difficult to reconcile with their attitude that it is at least doubtful whether he went so far with them as they supposed. At any rate the book known as the Prayer-book of 1549 was accepted, and in January the Act of Uniformity was passed, compelling the clergy throughout the kingdom to adopt it uniformly under severe pains and penalties for recalcitrance. The Act was to come into force at Whitsuntide. Eight of the bishops however opposed the Bill, including some who had been on the Commission. It may be inferred that while they gave the book itself their sanction, they resisted its imposition on the clergy by lay authority.

[Sidenote 1: 1547-49 The treason of the Lord Admiral]
[Sidenote 2: 1549 Fall of the Lord Admiral]

One other matter was to occupy the attention of Parliament before the close of the session, namely the treason of the Protector's brother, the Admiral, Lord Seymour of Sudeley. He was the King's uncle; he had taken to wife the late King's widow on being refused the hand of the Princess Elizabeth; he was violently jealous of his brother and angry at not having the guardianship of the King entrusted to him — an office which in his opinion ought to be separated from that of Protector of the realm. After marrying Katharine Parr he did obtain from the Council the guardianship of Elizabeth, and from Lord Dorset that of his daughter Lady Jane Grey, who, under Henry's will, stood next in succession to the throne after his own offspring. As Admiral, he had refused to take command of the fleet which accompanied the march to Pinkie; and had entered into secret relations with the pirates who infested the Channel. It had long been palpable that he was intriguing for power, but no one was disposed to take part with him, and Somerset was lenient to him. His principal ally was one Sharington, master of the mint at Bristol, who abused his office by debasing the coinage and pocketing or sharing his nefarious profits: Dorset and probably his brother-in-law Northampton (Parr) favoured him. Thus supported, he had money enough in hand to maintain a considerable armed following should occasion arise, and had established a private cannon foundry. When his wife died, he renewed his pretensions to the hand of Elizabeth, and was not unnaturally suspected of having hastened Katharine's end with that intention. Trusting to the soreness of Southampton (Wriothesly) at his deprivation of the Chancellorship, he tried to win him over, and also Rutland. The attempt failed, and was reported to the Protector; who summoned him to give an account of himself before the Council. Seymour refused to attend, using defiant language; and on January 17th he was arrested. Practically there is no doubt of his treason, and had he then been fairly brought to trial, Somerset would have been free from reproach. But the question was debated in parliament whether the Admiral should be so tried, or attainted, and attainder was decided on after he had refused to answer to the Council; as he was entitled to do. He was allowed to plead before a committee of both Houses in his own defence, but did not take advantage of the permission: virtually he was denied the right of an open trial, and was condemned without such defence as he had to make being heard. Cranmer signed the death-sentence: Latimer defended it. The fact is significant of the chaos into which English ideas of justice and fair play had fallen. The Protector's brother was executed at the end of March.

[Sidenote: Troubles in the Provinces]

From April to September, Somerset's troubles thickened. Formidable insurrections took place both in the western and eastern counties, and the hostilities with France, not yet openly at war, were assuming an aggravated form. The one piece of good fortune for England was that the antagonism between Charles and the French King in other fields still prevented any rapprochement between them.

[Sidenote: The Western Rising]

In the country districts there were two exciting causes of disturbance —one, the general agricultural distress due to the selfish policy of the landowners, the extension of sheep-farming and consequent displacement of labour, the enclosure of common lands and evictions from small holdings; the other, the innovations in religion and interference with immemorial practices to which the people were attached with the persistent conservatism of rural folk. The two types of grievance were associated by the recent abolition of the monasteries, and the transfer of their lands to the most obnoxious class of landlord—a class in the nature of the circumstances popularly identified with the enemies of the old ecclesiastical system, since it was they who conspicuously profited by the change. The North and the West, then and for more than a century to come, were the strongholds of traditional faiths and traditional ideals, as Yorkshire had shown by the Pilgrimage of Grace. Now the main trouble arose in the West. The introduction of the new Service Book at Whitsuntide was met with violent opposition; the men of Cornwall and Devon rose, and demanded the redress of grievances. They would have the religious houses reinstated, and at least half their lands restored. They would have the old services, not the new one which was "like a Christmas play". They would not have it in English which the Cornishmen "did not understand". Elsewhere there had already been disturbances, the peasants anticipating Somerset's efforts to remedy the agricultural grievances by a commission to enforce what was actually the law, and assembling in mobs to level fences and enclosures; whereat the Council was wrath, but the Protector as Friend of the People was disposed to applaud them. A religious revolt however was an attack on the Protector's own policy, and must be put down. Foreign mercenaries were called in, to embitter the quarrel. The insurgents besieged Exeter, and had been for some months in arms before they were at last crushed by the Government forces, in August, after desperate fighting.

[Sidenote: Ket's insurrection]

In the meantime a separate rising came to a head in the Eastern counties, where however the religious question was not involved. In that part of the country, destined to be the head-quarters of puritanism, the new ideas had made early way with the population; and Ket, the leader of the rising, conducted it on the hypothesis that his followers were merely enforcing legal rights because the agents of the Government neglected to do so. A great camp was formed at Mousehold Hill near Norwich; order was strictly maintained; morning and evening the new services were read. There was so much to be said in favour of the insurgents that they were offered a free pardon if they would disperse; but unfortunately Ket cavilled at the word "Pardon" on the ground that no offence had been committed, whereupon the herald called him a traitor. The indignant insurgents, ready enough to disperse before, thereupon changed their tone, assaulted and captured Norwich, and carried off the guns and ammunition. Northampton was sent down in command of the Government forces, but the rebels attacked him with such determination that he had to fly—the insurgents maintaining their policy of abstaining from robbery and violence generally. At last however, at the end of August, Warwick, who replaced Northampton, succeeded by the aid of German and Italian mercenaries in inflicting a crushing defeat on them; Ket himself being taken and hanged soon after.

[Sidenote: Somerset's attitude]

Another rising was also attempted in Yorkshire, but this was easily quelled by the local authorities. It is however of interest to note that the nobility regarded Somerset as the real cause of these troubles, on account of the open sympathy he expressed for the grievances of the rural population, and his public admonitions to the landowners urging them to amend their ways. He was driving the country faster than it was prepared to go in the direction of religious innovations; he was attacking the privileges which the new landowners had usurped; his Scottish policy had been upset, in spite of Pinkie, by the young Queen's escape to France; he was further alienating all but a few of the nobility by his increasing arrogance of demeanour and disregard of advice, as well as by an assumption of powers which had no precedent; he was giving a handle to his enemies by the profusion of his own household, his appropriations of clerical lands and even of the fabric of consecrated buildings to his own use; and finally his conduct of foreign affairs had been so incompetent that while the Emperor declined an English alliance, the position of Boulogne—which remained quite inefficiently garrisoned—was becoming critical, and a French squadron, ostensibly in pursuit of English pirates, attacked the island of Jersey. By the end of September war was declared with France.

[Sidenote 1: The Council attacks the Protector]
[Sidenote 2: Fall of Somerset (Sept.)]

The lords of the Council, headed by Warwick, made up their minds that it was time the protectorate should end, and that one vain-glorious nobleman should not absorb so undue a share of power and profit. Somerset, discovering that there was a cabal on foot, attempted to stir up popular feeling against the Council, and retired hurriedly to Windsor with the King, accompanied by Cranmer and Paget; a journey which is said to have materially shaken the health of Edward, who was in a very delicate condition. But the people did not rise in Somerset's favour; the Council had so far taken no improper action, whereas the Protector had evidently incited to violence by the steps into which panic had led him; Herbert and Russell, returning from the West with the troops employed there to put down the insurrection, declared in favour of the Council; who were of course forced— very much to their own satisfaction—to stand on their right to control the Government, and call the Protector to account, at the same time promising him life and declaring that they had never sought his personal injury. By mid-October, Somerset had fully realised that he was without effective support; he surrendered to the Council, and was sent to the Tower. His deposition from the Protectorate was confirmed by Parliament three months later, and a substantial portion of his estates was forfeited, after which he was again set at liberty. But his control in politics was at an end.

Before proceeding to the second division of Edward's reign, it remains to deal with affairs in Ireland, where Sir Anthony St. Leger held sway, with general approval, during the closing years of Henry's life. St. Leger embodied the policy of conciliation by the method of converting Irish chiefs into responsible supporters of the government in return for honours gilded with spoils of the Church. The method worked well, but the condoning— almost, it might be said, the rewarding—of treason, initiated by Henry VII., carried risks which are obvious. Whether it was that the extension to Ireland of the energetic iconoclasm of the English Reformation in 1547 excited new hostility; or that a repressive policy was anticipated from the new Government; or that death withdrew the loyal influence of the old Earl of Ormonde, whose young heir was in England; or that the chiefs were tired of behaving peaceably after six years; or that all these causes combined: signs of disturbance and rumours of French intrigues arose. St. Leger was recalled, and replaced by Sir Edward Bellingham, a stern and rigorous soldier, who ruled autocratically with a strong hand. Fortresses and garrisons were established up and down the country outside the Pale, among the tribes which had been in the habit of raiding or levying blackmail—very much after the fashion of various Highland clansmen in Scotland; while O'Connor and O'More, two chiefs whose lands lay between the English Pale and the Shannon, were attached for treason. In short, Bellingham asserted the authority of the English government, not, it would seem, unjustly, but certainly with severity, and in a dictatorial fashion which thoroughly re-awakened the normal rebellious instincts of a population never really subjugated. While he was present, his power was feared and respected; but if St. Leger's policy had been taking real effect, that effect was thoroughly cancelled. Bellingham died in 1549, and Desmond told Allen the Chancellor, that the Deputy's methods had reduced all Ireland to despair. [Footnote: A phrase expanded by Mr. Froude, v., 421 (Ed. 1864)—perhaps legitimately— into "despair of being able to continue their old habits".] In any case, no long time elapsed after Bellingham's death before the country was again in a ferment. The fall of Somerset left the new Government, controlled by Warwick, with a normally distracted Ireland on its hands as well as an abnormally distracted England. So long, however, as ferment did not mean active rebellion, the English rulers were not greatly troubled.

CHAPTER XIII
EDWARD VI (ii), 1549-53—THE
DUDLEY ASCENDANCY

When Somerset fell, the state of affairs which his successors had to face was singularly threatening, calling for the most skilful statesmanship both at home and abroad.

[Sidenote: 1549 (Winter) The Situation]

Externally, the chance of maintaining the hold on Boulogne was disappearing: but while it was maintained, the hostility of France was assured. Scotland, defiant, allied with France and helped by French troops, might become actively embarrassing. Within two months of the Protector's fall Pope Paul died. He was succeeded by Julius III. who promptly made friends with the Emperor; to whom there was now hardly any open resistance save at Magdeburg which stubbornly refused to accept the Interim. With the Protestants apparently under his heel, and on good terms with the Papacy, he might assume a hostile attitude to England. The one hope for her lay in buying from France the friendship of the party in that country which, ever mindful of the Italian provinces, might make common cause against the Emperor if the immediate source of friction with England were removed.

[Sidenote: State of the Country]

At home there were the rural discontents and the swelling ardours of religious partisanship to deal with, while the financial position was growing worse from day to day. The natural fall in the value of silver everywhere, owing to the quantities of the metal now beginning to pour into Spain from America, depreciated the purchasing power of wages; and this was made infinitely worse in England by the persistent debasement of the coinage. The rulers of the country rewarded their own very inconspicuous merits with the forfeited spoils of the Church, instead of applying them to the public needs. The Treasury was nearly empty, and was maintained even at its alarmingly low level only by borrowing from foreign bankers at usurious interest. For the time being, the country had lost its moral balance; landowners, merchants, and manufacturers were absorbed in rapid money-making at the expense of their traditional integrity. Religion had fallen into a controversial wrangle between contradictory dogmas; the most earnest of the Reformers have given us the blackest pictures of the prevailing irreligion and moral anarchy, rampant products of theological acrimony. It is true that the Moralists of all ages have usually been engaged in expressing a vehement conviction that the decadence of their own age exceeds that of any other known to history; and within the next decade, the denunciations of Latimer were to be lost in the paean of the martyrs. Had the corruption he depicts been vital, those sublime tragedies would never have taken place. But for the time, chaos prevailed. It is true that some of the subjects of controversy were logically vital ultimately; but it is true also that, absorbed in them, the controversialists lost sight of other matters more spiritually vital immediately. If the Christian is taught that his duty to God is comprised in the acceptance or non-acceptance of dogmas and ceremonial observances, while his duty towards his neighbour comprises the whole of his moral conduct; if then his spiritual guides omit to preach the latter in their devotion to the former subject; his morality is in danger of being entirely neglected. "This ought they to have done, but not to leave the other undone."

[Sidenote: 1550 Terms with France]

In one respect, the new Government recognised the force of facts. It made up its mind that France must be reconciled by the evacuation of Boulogne, if any colourable concession could be obtained in return. France however so obviously held the whip-hand that even Paget's diplomacy could do little to qualify the completeness of the surrender. There was a brave display of preparation for a determined defence, but the negotiators on both sides were fully aware of its emptiness. There was nothing that Henry II. desired more than the termination of strife with his excellent neighbours, provided that they would hand over Boulogne, cancel most of the money claim under the treaty of 1546 for which they held it as security, and withdraw their troops from the forts they still retained in Scotland. The reconciliation might then be sealed by the betrothal of Edward to a French princess, the young Queen of Scots being bespoken by the Dauphin—only nothing considerable in the way of a dowry could be expected. France however would pay within a few months what might pass as a ransom for Boulogne. Such were the terms which Paget, the cleverest statesman in England, was obliged to advise the Council to accept: though the suggested marriage project was dropped. The treaty of peace was signed on March 24th (1550).

[Sidenote: Warwick's Protestant zeal]

On the religious question, Warwick lost little time in showing that he was on the same side as Somerset. For a moment, the Protector's fall raised vain hopes in the breasts of those who supported the Old Learning. Gardiner appealed from his prison: so did Bonner who not long before had not only been incarcerated for the second time, but even, in October, deprived of his see. It was useless. Warwick saw that he must either pose as an enthusiastic reformer, or bring the reactionaries into power. In the former case, he could lead; in the latter, he would have to throw himself on the support of the old nobility. Not only Gardiner but Norfolk also would have to be released from the Tower, and he himself would inevitably drop to the second rank. Warwick, with a fine consistency, never permitted any other motive to influence him when his own aggrandisement was involved in the issues. The first step of the parliament which re-assembled in November (1549) was to pass an Act for the removal of Images. Gardiner, and Bonner, remained in prison. Even an attempt of the whole body of Bishops to have something of their disciplinary jurisdiction restored, in the interests of public morality, was quietly suppressed. Three more bishops of the Old learning were at intervals sent to prison and deprived—Heath, Day, and Tunstal. Every vacancy was filled from the ranks of the advanced reformers.

[Sidenote: A new treasons and felonies Act]

Norfolk, like the bishops, continued a prisoner. Somerset on the other hand, no longer regarded as dangerous, was released in February, the major part of the fine imposed on him was remitted, and after a brief interval he was even re-instated in the Privy Council, and his official reconciliation with Warwick sealed by a family marriage. But while his anti-clerical policy was carried to much greater lengths, his social policy and his relaxation of the treason laws were entirely reversed. Parliament made felony or treason out of assemblages presumed to intend disturbance of the peace, to some extent legalised enclosures, made acts against Privy Councillors treasonable as if they were against the King, and included in the ban assemblies for the purpose of altering the laws.

[Sidenote: Activity of the extreme Reformers]

The peace with France still left opportunities for friction; but Warwick's reforming enthusiasm drove him into the course—manifestly irritating to the Emperor—of interfering with the private devotions of the Princess Mary, who was ordered to give up the Mass: to which she replied that she was bound by the law as left by her father, and would not recognise orders in contravention thereof, as long as her brother was a minor. Charles himself was at this very time reverting to an intolerant policy in the Low Countries, and Protestants were hastening to England from Flanders. The risk that the Emperor might adopt Mary's cause in arms was obvious, and it was known that the Guise party at the French court would miss no opportunity of reviving the war with England in the hope of capturing Calais. In the meantime, the extreme reformers of the Swiss school were steadily gaining weight, in comparison with that section which, like Cranmer, continued to favour less drastic changes. One of their chiefs, Hooper, being nominated to a bishopric, for a long time declined to accept it on account of the vestments ordered to be worn at consecration—an attitude however for which he was condemned by all the cooler heads, including some of the most advanced. Hooper ultimately gave way—a narrow-minded but sincere man, who at the last won the crown of martyrdom. An unsuccessful effort was made to obtain Gardiner's release—the failure being the more pointed because Somerset interested himself on the bishop's part. Gardiner, with thorough consistency, declared himself ready to accept the Prayer-book since it did not preclude his view of the Sacrament; but he would not profess opinions in contradiction of the doctrines formally affirmed in the last reign. In the end, he was not only kept in prison, but deprived of his see of Winchester.

[Sidenote 1: 1551 The Council and the Emperor]
[Sidenote 2: Charles's difficulties]

In the early months of 1551 the friction with the Emperor on the subject of the Princess Mary's Mass was becoming alarming; Charles was refusing to let the English Ambassador in his dominions use the English Communion Service; and the Council went so far as to propose making the Princess personally and alone exempt from Conformity: fortunately, however, for them, affairs in Italy took a turn which gave fresh impulse to the anti-Imperialists in France. The Protestant city of Magdeburg was still holding out against the Imperial troops which were under the command of Maurice of Saxony, and the French King was becoming inclined to give active support to the resistance. The Pope had devoted himself to Charles's interests, and assented to the return of the Council to Trent; and there were hints that Henry might call a Gallican synod, instead of allowing the French ecclesiastics to attend, unless the Lutherans were also represented. The Emperor could no longer imagine himself to be completely master of the situation. In April, the Council felt that he was so far hampered that they could venture to assume a bold front. They informed him that the Act of Uniformity was the Law; that it applied to all subjects, including the Princess; and that they claimed the same freedom for their own ambassador which they were willing to concede reciprocally to his. About the same time the German Diet foiled a pet scheme of Charles, who wished his son Philip (afterwards Philip II. of Spain) to be nominated as his successor to the Imperial crown in place of his brother Ferdinand [Footnote: Charles had ceded the Austrian dominions of the house of Habsburg to Ferdinand in 1522.] who was already King of the Romans. The Germans however preferred the Austrian to the Spanish succession, and rejected the proposal. In June he found that the English and French had come to terms, and had agreed to a French marriage for Edward, on exceedingly easy conditions for France. He still continued to threaten war unless England gave way on the disputed points; but the Council answered only by temporising, and he was soon in no position to threaten. The unrest of the German Protestants and later in the year the assembling of the Council at Trent demanded all his attention. In fact, though he did not suspect it, Maurice of Saxony was even now laying his plans for snapping the bonds which the Emperor was seeking to rivet upon his German subjects. The incompetent hand-to-mouth conduct of foreign affairs in England did not bring disaster on the country, mainly because Charles had not rightly taken the measure of his own strength and of the forces in the Empire adverse to his policy.

[Sidenote: Groups among the Reformers]

The domestic history of England during 1551 is not marked by events of magnitude, but the general trend of affairs is not without significance. No serious attempt was made to deal with any of the existing causes of disorder and uneasiness. Warwick, a man whose entire career presents no evidence of his having possessed any religious convictions whatever, had fixed upon the ultra-protestants as the party whose support would be most valuable to him. Honest enough themselves, these men, typified by Bishop Hooper, were ready to credit with a like honesty any one who talked their particular jargon with sufficient fervour, and to stigmatise as Laodiceans any one who did not go to every length along with them. Cranmer and more positively his right-hand man Ridley—recently made bishop of London in Bonner's room—were now leaning more towards them than when the Prayer-book of 1549 was promulgated; and a considerable personal animus cannot but have entered into their feeling towards Gardiner, whose present unimpeachable attitude of legality was discounted by his participation in the intrigues against Cranmer during the last reign.

[Sidenote: Attitude of Somerset]

It is less really surprising than it seems at first sight to find in Somerset the one man who really interested himself on the side of toleration towards individuals, in the cases both of Mary and of Gardiner. As a matter of fact, although when Protector he had been particularly zealous in the war against images, had carried desecration to abnormal lengths in his private appropriation of spoils, and had grossly transgressed his constitutional powers for the repression of the bishop of Winchester as the ablest of the opponents of his policy: yet he was not generally vindictive, was probably quite satisfied with the compromise of the first prayer-book which did not actually contravene the *King's Book*, and—except when he was commanding troops in Scotland—liked at least the posture of magnanimity. Entirely devoid of statesmanlike qualities, but afflicted with inordinate vanity, he had been an intolerably incompetent ruler: yet his intentions were usually quite commendable; while the government which succeeded the Protectorate had failed in every particular to establish a claim to respect, nor could he be, like the zealots, hoodwinked into a belief in its honesty. Apart therefore from personal considerations he did not favour its extreme policy, and personal considerations suggested that he might once more oust his rival from power. Lacking the capacity to organise an opposition, he still lent himself to intrigues. He was a possible danger to the Government for one reason and only one—that popularity with the commonalty which had been gained by his well-meant but ill-directed efforts to espouse their cause against the oppression of the wealthier classes.

[Sidenote 1: Fresh attack on Somerset]
[Sidenote 2: 1552 Execution of Somerset]

Warwick therefore, endowed with plentiful cunning and no scruples, decided to be rid of him once for all, and put in the mouth of an accomplice a story, with enough truth in it to be plausible, which sufficed for his purpose. In October Warwick, having procured his own elevation to the Dukedom of Northumberland, that of Dorset to the Dukedom of Suffolk, and that of Herbert to the Earldom of Pembroke, arrested Somerset at the Council. The Duke was accused of compassing the deaths of several Lords of the Council, and of preparations for an armed revolt and for appealing to the populace. On the greater part of the specific charges, the evidence was quite inadequate—but finding that Somerset might be held to have gone far enough to incur the death-sentence for felony under the law passed by the parliament of 1549-50, Northumberland (as Warwick must now be called) made a show of magnanimously withdrawing the accusations so far as he was personally affected. Somerset was duly condemned; but it was not till the end of January (1552) that he was actually executed, in spite of the somewhat pathetic demonstrations in his favour of the populace, who refused to the last to believe that the sentence would really be carried out, and lamented his doom with tears.

[Sidenote: Pacification of Passau]

While Somerset's trial was still going on, agents arrived in England from the German Protestants, inviting assistance in the contemplated revolt against Charles—a movement carried out with sudden and triumphant effectiveness by Maurice of Saxony in the following spring. Had Northumberland given his adhesion, the formation of a Lutheran alliance at this juncture might have very materially altered the subsequent course of events. The opportunity however was not taken. Indeed it is scarcely surprising that the signs of the times should have been misread. Maurice had helped Charles against the Schmalkaldic League before; yet everything depended on his discarding the apparently erratic politics of his past career, and displaying in full measure the organising and military genius of which he had given promise, though it still remained to be conclusively proved. He did in fact prove it a few months later, when he all but succeeded in pouncing on the Emperor at Innsbruck. Charles was forced to a hasty flight, and, finding a practically united Germany in arms against him, was reduced to accept the pacification of Passau (July), conceding all that the Lutherans demanded. Maurice's brilliant exploit not only terminated Charles's resistance to the Reformation in Germany; it also released England from all danger of his active hostility.

[Sidenote: England stands aside]

In view however of the uncertainty still, at the end of 1551, attendant on the motives, the aims, and the capacity of Duke Maurice, the decision of the professedly enthusiastic protestants in England to stand aside is hardly a ground for reproach. Disaster had so often been escaped during recent years, through some lucky turn of events abroad supervening on the purely temporising policy of the Government, that they had good reason to hesitate about committing themselves to any irrevocable course; while personal intrigues and the strife of religious parties gave the individual leaders sufficient occupation. Possibly also the influence of the Swiss school, antagonistic as ever to the peculiar tenets of Lutheranism, was not altogether in favour of a too intimate association with German protestantism.

[Sidenote: The Reformation;]

We have remarked upon the increasing influence of this party in the Church; an influence which, as far as concerns the formularies of the Anglican body, was to reach its high-water mark in 1552 and 1553, in the revised prayer-book authorised by Parliament immediately after Somerset's death, and the "Forty-two Articles" promulgated about a year later.

[Sidenote: Its Limits under Henry and under Somerset]

In the reign of the late King, the Reformation which had taken place was almost entirely political and financial—in the constitution of the government of the ecclesiastical body, and the allocation of its endowments. The Sovereign had claimed and enforced his own supremacy, involving the repudiation of papal authority, the submission of the clergy to the Supreme Head, and the appropriation by the Crown of Monastic property. As a necessary corollary, the Crown had also taken upon itself to sanction formularies of belief and to regulate rites and ceremonies; but in doing so it had held by the accepted dogmas, suppressed little except obvious and admitted abuses, and affirmed no heresies. The Archbishop had been in favour of further innovations, but these had not been allowed. All, however, that Cranmer had then advocated, was adopted by Somerset's administration— the extended destruction of images, the liturgy in the vulgar tongue, the marriage of the clergy, the Communion in both kinds; the last being perhaps the most marked deviation from the established order. But though the new liturgy might be reconciled with acceptance of doctrines hitherto accounted heretical, it did not enjoin them; it was still reconcilable also with the *King's Book*. It had aimed, in short at the maximum of comprehension. The result was to include within the same pale the adherents of a very slightly modified Mass and the extremists of the Swiss school, for whom the Communion Service was purely and simply commemorative.

[Sidenote: The extremists dissatisfied]

Until the death of Henry, the English clergy from the Archbishop down had almost without exception held the hitherto authorised view of the Eucharist. Since then however Cranmer had followed the lead of Ridley, under the influence of the foreign theologians, and had adopted personally a conception [Footnote: This conception is expressed in the phrase of the Catechism that "the Body and Blood of Christ are verily and indeed taken and received by the faithful," coupled with the direct repudiation of Transubstantiation, *i.q.* the doctrine that the substance of the bread and wine is changed by the Act of Consecration.] which rejected alike in set terms the Transubstantiation of the Roman Mass, the Consubstantiation of the Lutherans, and, implicitly though not explicitly, the purely commemorative theory of Hooper and the Zwinglians.

[Sidenote: 1552 The Liturgy revised]

Thus the extreme comprehensiveness of the first Prayer-book failed to satisfy the school who could not away with the Mass, and those who regarded the Swiss doctrine as heretical. Greater precision, closer definitions, were called for—by way not of changing doctrines but of removing uncertainties. To this end a revision of the volume had been taken in hand, and now received the sanction of Parliament: a revision favouring in the main the Swiss interpretations, the term "minister" taking the place of "priest," "altar" giving way to "table," and the doctrine of transubstantiation being clearly eliminated. At the same time the instruction that the Sacrament was to be received kneeling conveyed a presumption, though not the necessity, that the rite involved a Mystery, that it implied an act of adoration. This was most unsatisfactory to the ultra-protestants, recently re-inforced by the vigorous presence in the North of England of John Knox the Scottish reformer; and before the volume was issued from the press at the end of the year a determined attempt was made to have the obnoxious instruction removed by order. The Archbishop however with resolute dignity protested against the arbitrary subversion of what Parliament had sanctioned. He carried his point, and the instruction was retained, though an explanatory note (known as the Black Rubric)[Footnote: *Cf.* Dixon, iii., 475 ff.] was appended, with which Knox and his friends were forced, however reluctantly, to be satisfied.

[Sidenote: Nonconformity]

This episode, with that of the consecration of Hooper as bishop of Gloucester, are illustrative of the original sense of the term Nonconformity. Nonconformity, of which Hooper is often referred to as the "father," did not seek separation from the ecclesiastical organisation, but expressed dissatisfaction with particular observances, which it sought to have modified in the Swiss sense: not as being in themselves intolerable, but as tending to encourage superstitious and papistical ideas. So Hooper, after an obstinate struggle, submitted to don the vestments ordered at his consecration; so also Knox, when he was finally worsted in the "kneeling" controversy, submitted to the order though with a very ill grace. The Nonconformists in short may be defined as Puritans who still remained within the pale of the Church. The idea of forming sects outside her borders, of challenging the right to enforce uniformity where points in dispute were not "essential" but "convenient," was still opposed to all recognised principles; the Nonconformists themselves being by no means disposed to surrender the position that if they became predominant they would be entitled to enforce their own views no less rigidly. No one thought of protesting against the burning of one Joan Bocher, in 1550, for affirming a peculiarly unintelligible heresy concerning the mode of the Incarnation.

[Sidenote: Parliament]

The session at the beginning of 1552 was the last held by this, the first, Parliament of Edward VI. Besides authorising the revised Prayer-book, it passed a second Act of Uniformity, of which the novel feature was that penalties were imposed on laymen for non-compliance. In other respects, it did not show itself altogether subservient to Northumberland. A new Treasons Act further reviving some of Henry's provisions was introduced in the Upper House, but rejected by the Commons; who did indeed restore "verbal treason," but pointedly required that two witnesses at least should prove the guilt of the accused to his face-with evident reference to the recent trial of Somerset.

Cranmer had been occupied not only with the Prayer-book, but also with the preparation of Articles of Belief, and of a scheme which, as drawn up, was generally known as the *Reformatio Legum*, elaborating a plan of ecclesiastical administration. The latter appears to have seen the light either in 1551 or 1552, but it was never authorised. The Forty-two articles, substantially the same as the Thirty-nine of the present Prayer-book, certainly did not come before parliament and probably did not come before Convocation, [Footnote: Dixon, iii., 513 ff. Gairdner, *English Church*, 311.] but were sanctioned by almost the last act of the King in Council in 1553.

[Sidenote: 1553 A new Parliament]

The national finances continued in an increasingly chaotic condition, and Northumberland's struggles to raise money during 1552 were attended with such inadequate results that he found it necessary to summon a new Parliament in the spring of 1553. There were not wanting, from the last reign, precedents for bringing royal pressure to bear on constituencies to secure the selection of amenable representatives, and the principle was now applied with a reckless comprehensiveness. Nevertheless the Houses when assembled were by no means prepared to carry out a programme which would satisfy Northumberland.

[Sidenote: Northumberland's programme]

In fact that man of many wiles lacked the art, necessary for one with his ambitions, of securing a devoted personal following. For some time past the probability of the young King's early decease had been recognised, and Northumberland's intrigues had been directed to excluding Mary from the succession, and securing a sovereign whom he would himself be able to dominate. He had had his chance, when the Protector was overthrown in 1549, of taking the line of policy which would bring him into accord with the heir presumptive; he made his election, and thenceforward was committed to the Reforming party and to political destruction if Mary should become Queen. He devoted his attention then primarily to gaining a predominant influence over the young King, with great success-the result, in no small measure, of his posing as a puritan; for the boy had all the uncompromising partisanship natural to the morbid precocity which his ill-health and Tudor cleverness combined to develop. If Edward had lived, no doubt the Tudor penetration would have unmasked Northumberland in due course; but this the Duke would hardly have anticipated in any case, and, as it was, he laid his plans on the hypothesis that Edward would die without leaving an heir of his body. Now the succession was fixed by Henry's Will, ratified by Act of Parliament, first on Mary and then on Elizabeth, though both had been declared illegitimate. If they could be set aside, the first claim by descent would lie with Mary Stewart, grandchild of Henry's sister Margaret; but the country would not take her at any price. The next claimant, confirmed also by Henry's Will, would be Lady Jane Grey, passing over her mother Frances Brandon, daughter of Henry's second sister Mary. Frances Brandon had married Lord Dorset, created Duke of Suffolk at the same time that Dudley became Duke of Northumberland.

[Sidenote: Plot to change the succession]

The Duke's scheme then was to supplant the Tudor princesses, on the score of their illegitimacy once officially affirmed, by Lady Jane Grey; having first secured a dominating influence over his unhappy puppet by marrying her to one of his sons, Guildford Dudley. It might plausibly be argued that, since the courts had definitely declared that neither Mary nor Elizabeth was born in lawful wedlock, no subsequent legitimation could give them precedence over an indubitably legitimate descendant of Henry VII. and Elizabeth of York: while political expediency excluded the sole claimant with a prior hereditary right.

There remained, however, the inconvenient fact that the whole country from the Council down had deliberately and unhesitatingly pledged itself to maintain the order of succession laid down in Henry's Will. Something more than an abstract argument from legitimacy was needed to cancel a decision arrived at and established after mature deliberation. Had Mary made herself feared or detested—had Lady Jane been a popular favourite with an organised following—there might have been some chance for a *coup d'état*. But the treatment of Mary coupled with her dignified and courageous conduct had made her the object of popular sympathy; the only people who feared her were those who had been prominent in attacking the Old Learning, and their following in the country was by no means proportionate to their political and theological activity. Their support—all that Northumberland could hope for—would be quite insufficient for carrying his plan through; while the Duke himself, very unlike his late rival Somerset, was an object of such general aversion that any scheme calculated to maintain him in power would have excited keen popular antagonism.

The marriage of Lady Jane was accomplished early in May (1553); Pembroke, as well as Suffolk, was apparently secured by the marriage [Footnote: After Northumberland's fiasco, this marriage was judiciously voided.] of his son to a sister, Katharine Grey. Besides these Northumberland could count on Northampton. Further, he could be sure that France would go as far as diplomacy permitted to prevent the accession of Mary, on account of her relationship with the Emperor, to whom she had all her life looked for counsel. As Edward's death drew nearer, the Duke prepared his final *coup*. If Henry by Will could lay down the course of succession, his son was equally free to change it. It was not difficult to persuade the dying boy of the woes that would follow when a reactionary monarch was on the throne—though there had hitherto been no sign that the reaction would go beyond a reversion to the position of Henry's last years. Under Northumberland's influence, he devised the crown to the issue of the Duchess of Suffolk who was herself passed over in favour of her eldest daughter. In June this "device" was submitted to the Council, with whom however it found little favour. But in view of the personal danger in which they stood, they gave assent subject to the approval of Parliament, arguing that it was unprecedented for a King, to say nothing of one who was still a minor, to set aside an Act of Parliament by his own authority. The Judges, summoned to the Royal presence, unanimously declared that it would be unconstitutional—in effect treason—if they drew up letters patent in the sense desired without authority of parliament; and the more they examined the law, the more convinced they were of their position. But the King was insistent; and at last one by one, they reluctantly gave way, on condition of receiving positive instructions under the Great Seal and an anticipatory pardon in case their obedience should prove—as they believed it—to be a crime. The Letters were drawn, and at last signed by a number of peers and representative men, Cranmer finally yielding his adhesion after prolonged resistance, on the strength of the assertion that the judges had given their sanction. He was not informed how that sanction had been obtained. Cecil, the Burghley of a later reign, would only sign "as a witness". The signatures were appended on June 21st. The affair was still kept secret—though the existence of some conspiracy to supplant Mary was becoming generally suspected. The interval was spent in making preparations to support the *coup d'état* in arms. On July 4th the rumour that the King was already dead was only partially dispelled by letting his face be seen at a window. On the

6th he actually died. On the 8th the fact began to leak out, and on the 10th Lady Jane was proclaimed Queen in London.

[Sidenote: A memorable voyage]

One incident of note occurred during King Edward's last months—the departure of Chancellor and Willoughby's expedition in search of a North-East passage, an entirely novel direction. Chancellor reached the White Sea, and from thence was conveyed to Moscow, with the result that relations were opened between England and Russia. In other respects there was some private activity in the voyages of this and the ensuing reign, but nothing else demanding special attention.

CHAPTER XIV
MARY (i), 1553-55—THE SPANISH MARRIAGE

[Sidenote: The Marian Tragedies]

From first to last, Tragedy is the note of the reign of England's first Queen regnant: the human interest is so intense that the political and religious issues seem, great as they were, to sink into the background of the picture, mere accessories of the stage on which are presented the immortal figures of Doom. First is the tragedy of the sweet-souled and most innocent child, Lady Jane Grey, sacrificed to the self-seeking ambition of shameless intriguers. Then the tragedy of the Martyrs—of Rowland Taylor, of Ridley and Latimer, of Ferrar and Hooper, of many another of less note, who died for the Glory of God, giving joyful testimony to the faith that was in them; the tragedy of Cranmer, the gentle soul of wavering courage, the man born to pass peaceful days in cloistered shades, torn from them to be the unwilling pilot of revolution, who at the tenth hour fell as Peter fell, yet at the last rose to the noblest height. Last, and greatest, the tragedy of the royal-hearted woman whose passionate human love was answered only with cold scorn; who won her throne by the loyalty of her people only to bring upon her name such hate as attaches to but two or three other English monarchs; who, for the wrongs done to her personally, showed almost unexampled clemency, yet, shrinking not to shed blood like water in what she deemed a sacred cause, is popularly branded for ever amongst the tyrants of the earth; who, sacrificing her own heart in that cause, died in the awakening knowledge that by her own deeds it was irreparably ruined. No monarch has ever more utterly subordinated personal interests, personal affections, all that makes life desirable, to a passionate sense of duty; none ever failed more utterly to work anything but unmixed woe.

[Sidenote: 1553 (July) Proclamation of Queen Jane]

Northumberland's plans had been carefully laid. The military forces were at the service of the Government. The whole Council—with varying degrees of sincerity and reluctance—had endorsed his scheme; the persons of its members were apparently at his mercy; he meant also to have Mary safely bestowed in the Tower before any opposition could be organised.

The foreign ambassadors, and their masters, hardly dreamed that there was any alternative course to submission. Neither they nor Northumberland realised the intensity of the general feeling in Mary's favour, or its practical force; nor did they appreciate the capacity of Henry Tudor's daughters for rising to an emergency. On the day of Edward's death, Mary was on her way to London, when she was met with the secret warning that all was over. She turned and rode hard for safer country, just escaping the party who had been sent out to secure her. Jane Grey, the sixteen-year-old bride of a few days, was summoned to the throne by the Council; every person about her implored her to claim what they called her right and fulfil her duty in accepting the crown: what else could she do? Yet, child as she was, they found to their indignant astonishment that she would not move a hair's-breadth from the path her conscience approved. She knew enough to refuse point blank the notion that her young husband should be crowned King. The men of affairs, of religion, of law, having unanimously affirmed that the heritage of royalty was hers, she could not dispute it; but no one could pretend that the heritage was his. Her refusal was of ill omen for Northumberland's ascendancy, and the ill omens multiplied.

[Sidenote 1: The people support Mary]
[Sidenote 2: Collapse of the Plot]

The refusal was given on the evening following the proclamation of Lady Jane as Queen: even at the proclamation, a 'prentice was bold enough to remark aloud that the Lady Mary's title was the better. That same night, a letter arrived from Mary herself, claiming the allegiance of the Council in true queenly style. They were not yet prepared to defy Northumberland, and a reply was penned the next day affirming Lady Jane's title. Two of the Duke's sons were already in pursuit of Mary, and a general impression prevailed that they had captured her and were on their way to London. They had indeed reached her, but their whole force promptly acclaimed her as queen, and the Dudleys had to fly for their lives. The Eastern midlands and the home counties were gathering in arms to her support. It was necessary to take the field without delay, but of those members of the Council who were fit to command there was none on whom Northumberland could rely, when once out of his reach. The Duke must go himself. On the eighth day after Edward's death, the fourth after the proclamation of Lady Jane, he rode gloomily from London at the head of a force which he mistrusted, without a plaudit from the populace which, for all its Protestantism, listened with apathy two days later to the declamations of Ridley at St. Paul's Cross. Northumberland was hardly on his way before news came that the crews of the fleet had compelled their captains to declare for Mary. He had not advanced far before his own followers in effect followed suit. In the meantime, the Council reinstated Paget; who had always been in ill odour with Dudley as being a friend of Somerset, and had been recently dismissed from office and relegated to the Tower. On the 19th came news of further reinforcements for Mary. On that day several members of the Council, who had hitherto been practically under guard in the Tower, escaped, and, headed by Pembroke, declared for Mary. One party returned in arms, to demand surrender; another marched to Paul's Cross and proclaimed Mary amid enthusiastic acclamations. That night they dispatched a message to Northumberland at Cambridge ordering him to lay down his arms. Before it reached him, he had thrown up the struggle. The messengers arrived to arrest a cringing traitor. The stream of his repentant supporters was already hastening to sue for pardon.

[Sidenote: The Queen's leniency]

Never did rebellion collapse more ignominiously; never were rebels treated so leniently. The conspicuous but calculated clemency of the seventh Henry pales in comparison with the magnanimity of his grand-child. Those who had been most active and prominent in word and deed were arrested; but after a brief interval the majority even of these were pardoned. Some, including the innocent figurehead of the rebellion, the nine days' queen, her husband, and Ridley, were detained, in ward; but even Suffolk was allowed to go free; and it was only in deference to the remonstrances of every adviser that the Queen ultimately consented to the execution of the Arch-traitor Northumberland with two of his companions.

[Sidenote: Meaning of the popular attitude]

Mary's triumph, swift and bloodless, in defiance of all prudent presumptions, requires some explanation; which is not to be found in the theory of a sweeping Catholic reaction. London and the eastern counties were the strongholds of the new ideas, yet they went uncompromisingly in her favour. But it seems to prove that the country had definitely made up its mind some years before to accept a given solution of the problem of the succession, and to abide by it. Mary and Elizabeth might both be illegitimate technically, but each had been supposed legitimate at the time of her birth, and it seemed only fair that both should be reinstated in the line of succession. But the decision had been left to Henry, and had gone precisely in accord with popular sentiment. The English people had no mind to allow their settled conclusions to be set aside at the dictation of the best-hated politician in the country. They would have none of Northumberland, and the attempt to coerce them simply collapsed. The fact that all their sympathies — apart from judgment — were with the hitherto persecuted princess, and were not extended to her helpless rival, is in no way remarkable; for Lady Jane had been brought up in retirement, and her charms of mind and of character, though known to posterity, were quite unknown to the world in her own day. She had lent herself, however innocently, to an outrageous conspiracy; nor would any one have thought of remonstrance if the Queen had followed the advice of her counsellors instead of the dictates of her own magnanimity, and sent the girl with her husband and her father to the block along with Northumberland.

[Sidenote: The Queen's marriage and the Reformation]

A woman more politic and less conscientious than Mary—a woman such as her sister Elizabeth—might now have seized a great opportunity for making herself exceptionally popular. The Roman allegiance had been wiped out by Henry, with the entire approval even of Bonner and Gardiner; but of late years the extreme puritan party had gone much further in imposing their theories than the nation generally approved. They, at least, might now have been bridled without exciting serious opposition. Toleration within reasonable limits was what the bulk of the people wanted. Too many of them had really taken hold of the new ideas for a ready assent to be given to a strong reaction; too many still clung to the old ideas for the censorship of the Knoxes and Hoopers to be acceptable.

No one was more thoroughly alive to the impolicy of religious coercion than the Queen's life-long adviser, Charles V.—who had had his lesson in Germany—and his ambassador at Mary's court, Simon Renard. A policy of judicious toleration was the first condition of domestic peace, and would have met with their entire approval. But there was another question of pressing importance on which counsels were likely to be divided—the question of the Queen's marriage. Popular sentiment was flatly opposed to her union with any one who, being a foreigner, might subordinate England's interests to those of his own country, and drag her into the vortex of continental broils. On these two points anxiety was concentrated when the Queen arrived in London.

[Sidenote: Mary's rivals]

The situation was the more complicated because, however popular Mary might be for the moment, there were at least three possible nominees who might be put forward if she lost her popularity. There was her half-sister Elizabeth, who was a protestant. There was Mary Stewart, whom the French would make every effort to place on the throne. Noailles, the French ambassador, would exercise all his powers of intrigue to shake Mary, on the chance of his master having an opportunity of intervention; indeed, but for the rapidity of the Queen's success, there is little doubt that French troops would have come to Northumberland's assistance—for the time; to turn affairs to their own account as soon as might be. And finally there was still Lady Jane, with a title of a sort.

[Sidenote: Moderate Reaction]

There was immediate alarm, when it was known that Mary intended her brother to be buried with the old rites; and though she was with difficulty dissuaded from carrying out that intention she nevertheless did celebrate a requiem Mass. It was however only natural that her first step was to release and restore the old Duke of Norfolk, young Edward Courtenay, [Footnote: Courtenay, a boy of eleven at the time, had been sent to the Tower when his father was executed in 1538.] son of the Marquis of Exeter, and the imprisoned bishops, making Gardiner her Chancellor: though London did not welcome Bonner. Mary frankly professed her desire that religion should return to the position at her father's death, but she was equally definite about exercising no compulsion without parliamentary sanction. The reinstated bishops had been suspended in the most arbitrary manner; those now dispossessed had been appointed under the new theory that they held office only during the royal pleasure. The prompt departure of the foreign preachers and their English allies was facilitated and encouraged. The imprisonment of Ridley was a legitimate reward for his activity on behalf of Lady Jane, in August, Latimer was arrested for seditious demeanour, but was carefully allowed the opportunity of flight. Cranmer was not touched till the draft of a letter he wrote, courageously repudiating the libel that he had restored the Mass, had been copied and widely disseminated. Then he was removed to the Tower, ostensibly for his support of Northumberland. He, like Latimer, was given ample opportunity to fly, but also like Latimer stood to his colours. In all this there was no savour of injustice, though it filled the Protestants with apprehension: as also did the removal of sundry bishops on the ground that they were married. Mary, like Gardiner, had always denied the validity of legislation during the minority; but to take action on that hypothesis without waiting for parliament was hardly consistent with her declarations. Great pressure was also brought to bear on Elizabeth, to induce her to recant her protestantism; but while she declared herself open to argument, and actually presented herself at Mass though with patent reluctance, she steadily refused to pronounce herself converted—which Renard at least attributed to political not to say treasonable intentions.

These events took place during August, and in the meantime Mary reopened communications with the Pope, resulting in the appointment of Cardinal Pole as legate—though more than a twelvemonth elapsed before he reached England. A matter of still greater importance was the Emperor's proposal, not at first openly put forward, that Mary should marry his son Philip.

Now, the sequence of events of which the Peace of Passau between Charles and the Lutherans was a part had resulted in war between France and the Empire. To Charles, the projected marriage might obviously be of immense value. The French on the other hand desired not Mary's marriage but her deposition to make way for Mary Stewart. National sentiment in England demanded her union with an Englishman, pointing to Courtenay, now restored to the earldom of Devon; he and Reginald Pole being the representatives of the House of York. [Footnote: See Genealogical Table. *Front.*] Pole, though a Cardinal, had never taken priest's orders, so was also eligible as a husband, but had no desire for the position, recommending Mary to remain unwedded. Mary herself was already inclining towards the Spanish marriage, though Paget was almost the only prominent Englishman who favoured it; Gardiner being in strong opposition, and pressing for Courtenay. Noailles intrigued against it; but his object was to use Elizabeth as a stalking-horse for Mary Stewart. Finally, before anything could be done, parliament must meet to give its sanction; and before parliament could meet, the seal must be set on Mary's authority by her coronation. It is curious to note that Mary felt it necessary to obtain the Papal pardon for herself and Gardiner for the performance of the ceremony while the nation was still excommunicate. The Coronation took place on October 1st, and four days later parliament assembled.

[Sidenote: Oct. Parliament revokes Edward's legislation]

It began by abolishing once more all new treasons created since the ancient Act of Edward III., and new felonies since the accession of Henry VIII. It proceeded to declare Mary legitimate, though by so doing it did not invalidate Elizabeth's title as heir presumptive, since that rested on Henry's will, which had ignored equally the illegitimacy of both his daughters. It repealed the whole of the ecclesiastical legislation of the last reign, reverting to the position at Henry's death. As originally submitted, these two bills asserted the validity of the papal dispensation, and repealed Henry's ecclesiastical legislation as well as his son's: but in this form the Commons would not accept them. Some past attainders were also reversed, and the Archbishop, as well as Lady Jane, her husband, and one of his brothers, were attainted, though not, it would seem, with any present intention of inflicting the full penalty. Early in December, parliament was dissolved.

In the meantime the Queen definitely made up her mind that she would marry Philip, and was extremely indignant when the Commons petitioned her to wed, but not to wed a foreigner. So far, parliament at any rate did not ratify the Spanish connexion, though the Lords—including Gardiner—

had practically lost all hope of resisting it, and were giving their attention to introducing into the treaty stipulations for the safe-guarding of English interests.

[Sidenote: 1554 Wyatt's rebellion]

Enough however had been done to raise the anti-Spanish sentiment to a painful pitch; the national nerves being already over-strung with excitement and uncertainty as to the coming course of events, deliberately aggravated by the subtle manipulation of the French ambassador. The marriage treaty was signed on January 12th: within a week, there was a rising in Devon—the Courtenay country—a premature movement in the great conspiracy known as Wyatt's rebellion. The leaders were all strong protestants, and it is likely enough that fear of the reaction was with them the primary motive; but their cry was anti-Spanish, not anti-Catholic, they appealed to the national not the religious sentiment. The rising in Devon forced the hand of the other conspirators, before they were really ready to act. Suffolk, pardoned for his share in Northumberland's plot, ill requited the Queen's clemency by an attempt—futile though it was—to raise the Midlands; but for a time it seemed that Sir Thomas Wyatt, who headed the rebellion in Kent—a county prolific of popular movements against the Government—might actually succeed in dethroning Mary.

[Sidenote: Elizabeth]

Ostensibly, the cry was against foreigners. There is very little doubt that Wyatt really intended to marry Elizabeth to Courtenay, and set her on the throne. Whether Elizabeth herself, now twenty years of age, was in the plot, remains uncertain. There were suspicious circumstances, but no proofs, and Wyatt himself ultimately exonerated her. But the atmosphere was thick with suspicions which later historians have crystallised into facts according to their sympathies. Mary is charged with having desired her sister's death, but on insufficient evidence; [Footnote: Stone, *Mary I. Queen of England*, p. 270. The historian asserts Elizabeth's complicity without proof, while criticising Froude for inventing a proof of Mary's culpability.] double-dealing was not the Queen's way, and her behaviour towards her sister points rather to a desire to believe in her innocence coupled with something like a conviction of her actual guilt. Renard certainly did his best to blacken Elizabeth's character, even while he urged her arrest—a measure to which both Gardiner and Paget were opposed.

[Sidenote: Progress of the rebellion]

The news of Wyatt's own rising arrived on January 26th, some days after Gardiner had frightened Courtenay into betraying at least the existence of the plot. Elizabeth had been summoned from Hatfield to London, but declared herself too ill to travel. While it was believed that the only aim was to stop the Spanish marriage, feeling favoured Wyatt, and it seems as if even Gardiner and his supporters were in no haste to put down the rising. Wyatt and his followers were at Rochester: Norfolk was sent down with guns and a company of Londoners to deal with him, but the men deserted to Wyatt crying "we are all English," and the Duke had to ride for safety. London was in a panic: the Council could only quarrel among themselves. Wyatt advanced towards the Capital. Mary rose to the occasion, and herself addressed the populace, her speech going far to allay the panic. Wyatt found the bridge at Southwark impassable, and after some hesitation marched up the river, crossing at Kingston. The loyalists however had plucked up heart. The insurgents' column, in the advance to London, was cut in two. Wyatt at the head of the leading section made a desperate effort to reach Ludgate with ever dwindling numbers; but when he arrived at the City gates, though he did indeed in his own words "keep touch," his small and exhausted following was in no condition for prolonged fighting. He was taken prisoner without difficulty. Many of his followers were captured. The whole affair was over in less than a fortnight from the first rising.

[Sidenote: Subsequent severities]

The leniency previously shown could not be repeated. It seemed dangerous to leave Lady Jane any longer as a possible centre for plots, and she was executed with her husband and father. Wyatt was beheaded; about a hundred of the rebels were hanged. Elizabeth and Courtenay were both committed to the Tower, but were liberated after some two months. At the worst the punishment meted out may be compared favourably with the proceedings after the Pilgrimage of Grace. It was severe, but could not reasonably be called cruel.

[Sidenote: The Marriage Treaty]

Neither the expectation of leniency nor the experience of severity allayed the antagonism to the Spanish marriage. The treaty however, which came up for ratification in Mary's second parliament—summoned to meet in London at the beginning of April—conceded every safeguard against Spanish domination which could be secured by words; and in addition the succession to Burgundy for the offspring of the union, in priority to Philip's son, born to him of his first wife. The terms could not have been more favourable, but the unpopular fact remained that the connexion would inevitably influence Mary's policy in Europe. It was not till July that it was considered that Philip could safely entrust his person in England, when the wedding was completed.

[Sidenote: Pole, Renard, and Gardiner]

Up to this point at least, the Emperor's influence had been exercised in favour of toleration, and in restraint of any disturbance of the subsisting religious conditions. On the other hand he had taken pains to impress upon Mary that the union itself was a practical step towards reconciliation with Rome, which he knew to be her ideal. But he was afraid of the protestants being so much alarmed as to make opposition to the marriage irresistible. For this reason he raised constant obstacles to the arrival in England of Cardinal Pole, believing that the legate's presence would be an irritant. Pole being also entrusted with the task of endeavouring to reconcile Charles with Henry II., it had not been difficult to find imperative reasons for occupying him on the Continent. But when the marriage was safely accomplished, an effective counterpoise secured to the betrothal of the young Queen of Scots to the Dauphin, and time allowed for the English to become accustomed to the new state of affairs and to settle down, it was no longer so important to exercise a restraining influence. Mary was eager for the country to be once more received into the bosom of the Church: and Gardiner, who was bent on the restoration of the old worship, had now come fully to the conclusion that the maintenance of it was conditioned by the restoration of the Roman obedience, although twenty years before at the time of the schism he had been one of Henry's most useful supporters. Still however it was necessary to ensure that the Pope would consent to leave the holders of former Church lands in undisturbed possession, as they might otherwise be relied on to become ardent protestants. It was not till these conditions were assured that the legate was allowed, in November, to set sail for England.

[Sidenote: Public tension]

Between the Wyatt rebellion which collapsed in February and the arrival of Pole in November, the great event was the royal marriage, but there were several other occurrences not without significance. Sir Nicholas Throgmorton, who had certainly been in communication with Wyatt, was nevertheless unanimously acquitted by a jury, and the result was hailed with acclamation by the populace though the jurymen were summoned before the Star-Chamber and fined. Renard, and, if Renard's accusations and the general tongue of rumour are to be trusted, Gardiner also, did their best to persuade Mary to strike at her sister; but Paget and the Council generally were stoutly opposed to the idea, and Mary herself declared that Elizabeth should not be condemned without full legal proof, which was not forthcoming. After some two months she was released from the Tower but kept under surveillance at Woodstock. A Romanising preacher at St. Paul's Gross was fired at, and the culprit was not given up. On the other hand, not only married Bishops but married clergy in general were deprived, though some were restored on doing penance and parting with their wives. These are said to have numbered about one-fifth of the beneficed clergy, a computation which does not seem excessive as Convocation had itself petitioned for the permission of marriage. Cranmer, Ridley, and Latimer, were taken from London to Oxford to hold a disputation on those doctrines as to which their views were held to be heretical. The ecclesiastical condemnation of their argument was of course a foregone conclusion. The parliament, however, which ratified the marriage treaty, was chiefly remarkable for following Paget in refusing assent to bills excluding Elizabeth from the succession and restoring the Six Articles Act and the old Act against Lollards. Paget acquired considerable strength from the fact that William, Lord Howard of Effingham, who was in command of the fleet, was known to be in agreement with his views. The parliament was dissolved in May. It is noteworthy also that France was affording harbourage to many gentlemen of the West Country who had been more or less implicated in the January rising.

[Sidenote: Nov. Reconciliation with Rome]

Mary's third parliament—in which the nation by its representatives was to be formally reconciled to Rome—was called in November. Its first task was to reverse the attainder against Pole which was of ancient date. The Cardinal had distinguished himself in Henry's time by the vehemence of his opposition (from abroad) to the divorce and to the King's subsequent ecclesiastical proceedings, and his brothers as well as his mother had all been found guilty of treason in connexion with real or manufactured conspiracies. The reversal of the attainder was required to legalise his position. On the 25th he landed with official pomp at Westminster. On the 29th, the Houses agreed—with but one dissentient in the Commons—to a "supplication" entreating for pardon and the restoration of the nation to communion with Rome. The next day was performed the ceremony of presenting the supplication to the Legate and receiving his solemn Absolution. Two days later, Gardiner from the pulpit confessed the sin of which he in common with the nation in general had been guilty in the great schism, and declared himself a loyal and repentant son of the Church. Since loyalty and repentance did not involve restitution of Church property, most of his countrymen were equally ready to declare themselves loyal and repentant. Yet were there not a few who would by no means repent.

[Sidenote 1: Reaction consummated]
[Sidenote 2: 1555]

The Reconciliation of the Authorities to Rome was complete. It remained to compel her erring children to return to the fold. During the month following the submission, two fateful Acts were passed; one, almost without discussion, reviving the old acts, "*De heretico comburendo*" and others, which had been restricted under Henry and abolished under Somerset; the other repealing all the anti-Roman legislation since the twentieth year of Henry (1529), with a proviso, however, securing the alienated wealth of the Church to its present holders. On this there was more debate, and it was not actually passed till January 3rd. The former authority of the bishops and of the canon law was restored. It is to be observed that in all this legislation, the Commons were a good deal more amenable than the Lords; and this was even more markedly the case with the purely political measures. An Act was passed to secure the regency to Philip if there should be a child and Mary herself died, it being supposed at the time that the Queen was *enceinte*. But the suggestion that the succession should be secured to Philip was emphatically rejected, and the regency was by the Lords made conditional on his residence in England. He bore the title of King of England, but his Coronation was refused. Parliament was dissolved on January 16th.

CHAPTER XV
MARY (ii), 1555-58—THE PERSECUTION

Here we reach the turning point of the reign; the point at which the great persecution began. If anything like justice is to be rendered to the leading actors in the ensuing tragedy, it is necessary to differentiate between these two divisions of Mary's rule.

[Sidenote: Mary's policy, 1553-4]

We must remark that throughout these first eighteen months, Mary had proved herself to be the reverse of a vindictive woman. Her leniency in the case of Northumberland's accomplices had been almost unparalleled. A second rebellion when she had been barely six months on the throne was treated with no more than ordinary severity, though a very few of those implicated with Northumberland, who would otherwise have been spared, were executed in consequence. The advocates of the old religion had come into power, but their power had certainly not been used more oppressively than that of the opposition party under Warwick or even under Somerset: and there was more excuse for the treatment of Cranmer and Ridley at least than there had been for that of Gardiner and Bonner. If Latimer and Hooper, Ferrar and Coverdale, were imprisoned, it was no more than Heath and Day and Tunstal had suffered. The deprivation of the married clergy was certainly a harsh measure, since the marriages had been made under the aegis of the law; but that appears to be the one measure which had hitherto savoured of bigotry—at least, which had gone beyond the bounds of even-handed retaliation. What, then, was the change which now took place? And how may we account for it?

[Sidenote: 1555 The persecution]

The sanction of parliament had at last been obtained by the Acts just passed for the enforcement of the old religion by the old methods. There was nothing novel about the procedure or the penalties; but practically a reversion to the pre-latitudinarian line of demarcation between heresy and orthodoxy. All or very nearly all of the martyrs of the Marian persecution would have been sent to the stake under Henry for making the same profession of faith. The crucial question was acceptance of Transubstantiation, for the denial of which several victims had perished within the last twenty years, whose doom both Cranmer and Latimer had at the time held to be justified. But in the interval, the conditions had changed. A large proportion of the most learned scholars had adopted the new doctrine, and the legislature had sanctioned it. The methods which were usually efficacious in stamping out sporadic heresy, methods which only involved an execution here and there, lost their efficacy when the heresy had ceased to be sporadic. Hecatombs were required instead of occasional victims; and even the sacrifice of occasional victims had already begun to revolt the public conscience before Henry's career was closed. But this did not alter the vital postulate. Falsehood was none the less falsehood because it had been sanctioned for a time, none the less demanded drastic excision. Gardiner, standing for the old order, saw nothing revolting in applying again the principles which had been consistently applied before he became an old man. It is probable also that he expected immediate success to result from striking fearlessly and ruthlessly at the most prominent offenders—the rule of action habitually adopted by Henry and Cromwell—a rule generally maintained while Gardiner himself lived: that he never anticipated the holocaust which followed. It is remarkable that in his own diocese of Winchester there were no burnings. Mary had already sufficiently proved her own freedom from vindictiveness; it cannot fairly be questioned that she was moved entirely by a sense of duty however distorted.

[Sidenote: Whose was the responsibility?]

From the Spaniards [Footnote: See Renard's correspondence, *passim*. But the numerous citations therefrom alike in the Anti-Catholic Froude and the Catholic Stone (*Mary I.*) are sufficiently conclusive on the point.] there was no incitement to persecution, but the contrary—not that Philip had any abstract objection, but both he and Renard were concerned entirely with the present pacification of the country and its reconciliation to the Spanish marriage; both were aware that persecution would have the opposite effect. The demand for the suppression of heresy did not take its rise among the lay nobility, of whom the majority were prepared to accept whatever formulae might be most convenient. The theory [Footnote: Moore, p. 221, asserts this view.] that they rather than a section of the clergy were the moving cause has no foundation in the evidence, beyond the fact that the Council officially as a body urged Bonner and others forward. Paget and his associates certainly resisted the enactments at first. Still neither they nor the Commons can be freed from responsibility. The persecution was not however a move of one political party against the other; no section was so committed to protestantism as to be exposed to serious injury: no political motive can be even formulated. Vindictiveness, or a moral conviction of the duty of stamping out heresy, alone can make the proceedings intelligible. Of the former there is no fair proof, while the latter is entirely consistent with the prevailing spirit among the zealots on both sides, and with the known character of the persons who must be regarded as the principal instigators. Its source lay with Mary herself, a passionately devoted daughter of the old Church, and with a few ecclesiastics. Since there is no doubt that from the time of Pole's arrival, his influence predominated with her personally, he, more than Gardiner, must share with her the ultimate responsibility.

[Sidenote: Comparison with other persecutions]

Of old, an occasional example had sufficed to hold heresy in check; the changed conditions were not now realised. The case had ceased to be one of checking; nothing short of up-rooting would now be of any avail. For Mary, with her intense conviction of the soul-destroying effect of heresy, no sufferings in the flesh would have seemed too severe to inflict if thereby souls might be saved. But a persecution such as she initiated was absolutely the most fatal of all courses for the end she had in view. Tens of thousands among her subjects had assimilated the new ideas, and were prepared to die rather than surrender their hope of Heaven. These the martyrdom of a few hundreds could not terrify; and the heroic endurance of the martyrs changed popular indifference into passionate sympathy. Applied on this scale, the theory of conversion by fire, hitherto generally acquiesced in, brought about its own condemnation. Such a persecution, on the simple issue of opinion, has never again been possible in England. Catholics or Covenanters might be doomed to death, but the excuse had to be political. Religious opinions as such might be penalised by fines, imprisonment, the boot or the thumbscrew, the imposition of disabilities; still the ultimate penalty had to be associated at least with the idea of treason. In Mary's time, heresy as such was the plain issue. The status of all but some half dozen of the early clerical victims precludes any other view: and the first movement against the heretics in January 1555 was contemporaneous with an amnesty for the surviving prisoners of the Wyatt rebellion. The immediate practical effect was that every martyrdom brought fresh adherents to protestantism, and intensified protestant sentiment while extending the conviction that persecution was part and parcel of the Roman creed. That any of those responsible, from Mary down, took an unholy joy in the sufferings of the victims, appears to be a libel wholly without foundation; for the most part they honestly believed themselves to be applying the only remedy left for the removal of a mortal disease from the body politic; Bonner, perhaps the best abused of the whole group, constantly went out of his way to give the accused opportunities of recanting and receiving pardon. The fundamental fact which must not be forgotten in judging the authors of the persecution is, that the general horror of death as the penalty for a false opinion was not antecedent to but consequent upon it. What they did was on an unprecedented scale in England because heresy existed on an unprecedented scale; and the result was that the general conscience was awakened to the falseness of the principle. The same ghastly error for which Christendom has forgiven Marcus Aurelius was committed by Mary and endorsed by Pole, both of them by nature little less magnanimous and no whit less conscientious than the Roman emperor, though the moral horizon of both was infinitely more restricted.

[Sidenote: Gardiner]

The Marian persecution lasted for nearly four years. During that time, the number of victims fell little if at all short of three hundred, of whom one-fourth perished in the first year. The striking feature of the year is the distinction of the sufferers. One only of high position went to the stake after Gardiner's death—which took place only a few days after the burning of Ridley and Latimer, in November—that one, the highest of all, the whilom head (under the King) of the English Church. And he had then already been doomed. These facts point to the definite policy pursued by the Chancellor—the application of the principles which had proved so effective under Henry and Cromwell. Every prominent leader of the Reformation party who had not elected to conform was either dead or doomed or in exile within a twelve-month of the revival of the Heresy acts. After his time there was no process of selection; the victims were simply taken as they came. To find a sort of excuse in the conviction of an imperative duty to crush out the poison of heresy at any cost is in some degree possible. The attempt to explain the matter as in fact a crusade against Anabaptism [Footnote: *Cf.* Moore, P. 220.] as a social and political crime makes the thing not better but incomparably worse; while the endeavour to compare it with any other persecution in England is absurd. Henry before and Elizabeth afterwards could be ruthless; but while one reigned thirty-eight years and the other forty-five, yet in neither reign was the aggregate of burnings or executions for religion so great as in these four years of Mary's.

[Sidenote: Some characteristics]

In London itself, in Essex, and in the dioceses of Norwich and Canterbury, many informations were laid. Some five-sixths of the deaths were suffered within this restricted area, nearly half of these falling under the jurisdiction of Bonner; so that he was naturally looked upon as the moving spirit, and his conduct was imagined in the most lurid colours. As a matter of fact there is little sign that he initiated prosecutions—indeed he received a fairly strong hint from the Queen and Council that he was less active than he might have been; he certainly tried hard to persuade the accused to recant and escape condemnation; in several cases where he had hopes he deferred handing them over to the secular arm. But protestants were very disproportionately numerous in his diocese; if the accepted principle were sound at all, he of all men was most bound to strictness with the persistently recalcitrant, and that fact of itself sufficed to encourage heresy-hunters. Moreover in London, it must also be remarked, heresy was particularly defiant and audacious, and was not infrequently accompanied by acts of gross public disorder which merited the sharpest penalties quite apart from questions of orthodoxy. Acts of ruffianism were done in the name of true religion, [Footnote: *E.g.* the notorious cases of William Branch or Flower, and John Tooley.] and the doers thereof were enrolled among the martyrs. Moreover among the genuine martyrs for conscience' sake—by far the majority of those who suffered—not a few were zealots who took up their parable against the judges when under examination in a fashion calculated to enrage persons of a far less choleric disposition than the bishop of London. In short if once the postulate be granted that to teach persistently doctrines regarded by authority as false is deserving of the death penalty, the manner [Footnote: The popular impression is derived mainly from accounts based on Foxe's *Book of Martyrs*. Stripped of picturesque adjectives and reduced to a not superfluously accurate statement of facts resting on easily accepted stories by a strongly biased reporter, his evidence against Bonner and Gardiner is not very damnatory.] in which Bonner and his colleagues conducted their task is not to be greatly censured. In Ireland, and in several English dioceses, there were no actual martyrdoms.

[Sidenote: The first Martyrs]

The new year, 1555 had barely begun before the revived heresy laws were set in operation. For Cranmer, Ridley, and Latimer, all now at Oxford, there was to be some delay; for the chief prisoners elsewhere there was none. These were headed by Hooper and Ferrar, both bishops; Rogers, commonly identified with the "Matthew" of *Matthew's Bible*; Rowland Taylor of Hadley, a man generally beloved; Bradford, who had begun life as a rogue, but becoming converted, had lived to make restitution, so far as was possible, for the wrong doings of his youth, a very genuine instance of a striking reformation. Most of them belonged to the school of Ridley rather than of Hooper; but on the question of Transubstantiation, all were equally firm—and all were now in the eye of the law undoubtedly heretics. Had they recanted, they would have suffered but lightly. They were urged to do so, but steadfastly refused. It must even be admitted that they challenged martyrdom, for before they were brought to trial, the London group, including most of those above named, had issued an appeal which was practically a solemn reproof to those whose opinions differed from their own. Rogers was the first to suffer; after brief intervals all of those named went to the stake.

[Sidenote 1: Trial of Cranmer (Sept.)]
[Sidenote 2: Martyrdom of Ridley and Latimer (Oct.)]

Cranmer, Ridley, and Latimer, were all condemned as a result of the disputation held at Oxford in 1554: but since this preceded the reconciliation with Rome, it was not accounted sufficient. On the old Catholic theory, the Metropolitan of England could only be condemned by the authority of the Pope himself—direct, or delegated *ad hoc*. The first move was made against him in September, before a court whose business was not to adjudicate, but to lay its conclusions before the Pope himself. Cranmer declined to recognise the authority, answering the charges brought against him not as a defendant on trial but as making a public profession of his views. Judgment however could not be passed till the results were submitted to the Pope. In the meantime, Ridley and Latimer were condemned under legatine authority, and were burnt at Oxford in November. Cranmer is said to have witnessed the martyrdom from his prison. The aged Latimer's exhortation to his companion at the stake rang like a trumpet note through the Protestant world. Ridley was the learned theologian and keen controversialist who more than any other man had moulded the plastic mind of the Archbishop since he had been released from the thraldom of Henry's moral and intellectual domination: who had led the campaign against "idolatry" but stood fast against the extravagances of the Nonconformists: who had without hesitation opposed Mary's accession. No one could have murmured against his punishment for treason two years before; but he died a martyr, for denying Transubstantiation and the Papal authority. Latimer was no theologian; but he was a pulpit orator of extraordinary power, an enthusiastic if erratic moralist, who had suffered for his own freely expressed opinions in the past and shown scant consideration for false teachers—a quixotic but heroic figure.

[Sidenote: Fate of the Archbishop 1555-56]

The condemnation by the court which tried the Archbishop carried with it no penalty; that was reserved for the Pope to pronounce—by implication, in handing him over to the secular arm, and explicitly by sentence of degradation, which was notified in December. Until this time Cranmer remained steadfast; but about the new year, he displayed signs of wavering, and was said to have been influenced by the arguments of a Spanish friar, Garcia. Possibly he attended Mass; certainly, about the end of January and beginning of February (1556) he wrote three "submissions" recognising the papal authority. These did not avail to save him from public degradation, in the course of which ceremony he produced a written appeal to a General Council, which was ignored. Two more "submissions" followed, but in neither did he go beyond the admission that the papal authority was now valid, since the Sovereign had so enacted. Nevertheless, on February 24th the writ committing him to the flames was issued. There is no reason to suppose that the idea of sparing him was ever entertained; but, wherever the blame lay, he was led to believe that a recantation might save him; and he did now at last break down utterly, and recant in the most abject terms. Had this won a pardon, the blow would have been crushing; the Court in its blindness suffered him to retrieve the betrayal. His doom was unaltered. While the fagots were prepared, he was taken to St. Mary's Church to hear his own funeral sermon and make his last public confession; but that confession, to the sore amazement and dismay of the authorities, proved to be the cry of the humble and self-abasing sinner repenting not his heresies but his recantations. And in accordance with his last utterance, when he came to the fire he was seen to thrust forth his right hand into the flame, crying aloud "this hand hath offended"; and so held it steadfastly till it was consumed. The chief prelate of the English Church was struck down at the bidding of a foreign Ecclesiastic; the recusant had been gratuitously glorified with the martyr's crown. It is likely enough that he won less personal popular sympathy than his fellows; but the moral effect must have been tremendous.

[Sidenote: Cranmer's record]

It is natural but hardly just that Cranmer should be judged on the basis of the impression created by his last month of life. That the protagonist in a great Cause should recant in the face of death seems to argue an almost incredible degree of pusillanimity, and suggests that pusillanimity and subservience are the key to his career. Nevertheless, but for that short hour of abasement nobly and humbly retrieved, the general judgment would probably be altogether different. And that breakdown does not appear to have been characteristic. Twice in the reign of Henry he had bowed to the King's judgment, acknowledging that Anne Boleyn and Thomas Cromwell must be guilty since Henry was convinced: but there was no man in the country who took the part of either. To have defied the King would have been heroic, and there is a wide interval between failing of heroism and being pusillanimous. He withdrew his resistance to Northumberland's plot; but he resisted on the ground that it was illegal and withdrew only when he was assured that the Judges had unanimously affirmed its legality. He changed his views on Transubstantiation; but to surrender an abstruse dogma is not a crime. He repeatedly maintained opinions in opposition to

Henry as well as to Mary at the risk of losing royal support and favour—
which loss would certainly have meant delivering himself into the hands of
his enemies. In practice he conformed to the restrictions laid upon him, but
it was only on points of expediency that he personally gave way, though
he would fain have allowed to others a larger latitude of opinion than he
required for himself.

[Sidenote: His character]

Yet the virtues of Thomas Cranmer fail of recognition. The extreme
Anglican joins with the Roman Catholic in condemning the ecclesiastical
leader of the Schism; the puritan condemns the advocate of compromise;
and the advocate of compromise, at least within the clerical ranks, condemns
the Erastian cleric. In his day, and in Elizabeth's, the lay statesmen were
Erastians to a man; that is forgiven to them; but the ecclesiastic who
adopts and preaches without reservation the theory that the Church—its
organisation, its administration, even its doctrines—is ultimately subject to
the secular sovereign, essentially and not owing to the accidental sanction of
force—such a one is inevitably regarded as a traitor to his order; that he was
guided by honest conviction seems incredible. Cranmer was a man of peace,
driven to do battle in the front rank; an academic, forced to take a leading
part in exceedingly practical affairs; a student, compelled so far as he might
to control a revolution. Yet to him, more than any other single man, it is
due that the Church of England allows a larger latitude of opinion within
her borders than any other, and that she possesses a liturgy of unsurpassed
beauty. A man so weak, so lacking in self-reliance, can hardly be called
great; yet one who, despite his weakness, has carved himself so noble and
so lasting a monument can hardly be denied the epithet.

For the rest of the persecution it is sufficient to say that year by year the
number of victims did not diminish; neither sex nor age brought immunity;
but as they were of less standing, an attempt was made to intensify the effect
by putting them to death in larger batches—which increased the horror. The
laymen of station, it may be remarked, with one accord conformed, at least
outwardly.

[Sidenote: 1555 Philip's policy]

The Parliament which passed the Heresy Acts was dissolved before
the end of January. Rogers was burnt some three weeks later. Symptoms
of unrest were quickly apparent, and Philip felt it necessary to dissociate
himself publicly from the persecution. On this point Renard was urgent,
and he was also anxious about the succession. If the Queen's hopes of a
child should be disappointed, neither Mary Stewart nor Elizabeth would be
satisfactory. The only thing to be done was to secure a convenient husband

for the latter, and a project was on foot (not with her approval) for marrying her to the Prince of Savoy, which might incidentally make the English more disposed to join in the war with France, which was in occupation of Savoy. But by April the belligerents were thinking of holding a conference to discuss terms of peace, with an English Commission to mediate.

[Sidenote 1: Pope Paul IV.]
[Sidenote 2: Mary has no child]

The death of Pope Julius, however, promptly followed by that of his immediate successor Marcellus, caused the election of the Cardinal Caraffa who became Paul IV. On both occasions, Reginald Pole had been perhaps the favourite candidate: but the election of Paul was a victory for the French, the new Pope being an austere zealot with a violent anti-imperial prejudice. Having thus secured the papal alliance, Henry of France was by no means disposed to so easy a compromise as had been looked for. The conference collapsed. If Philip really had hoped, as rumour said, to be enabled by the peace to introduce Spanish troops into England for his own ends, he was doomed to disappointment. So it was also with his hopes of an heir to secure him the English succession. Mary had been misled partly by the symptoms of what proved to be a fatal disease and partly by hysterical hallucinations. It became certain that there was no prospect of her ever having a child at all; which necessitated a complete reconsideration of the Spanish prince's policy. Possibly also the expectation that the Queen's life could not be a long one led the nobles with protestant inclinations to acquiesce in the prolonged persecution rather than countenance a danger of civil war. Neither they nor Elizabeth could be implicated in any of the abortive conspiracies which cropped up periodically during the remainder of the reign.

[Sidenote: Effect on Philip]

In August, Philip left the country, not to return again till more than eighteen months had passed; and then only for a very brief sojourn. Already his father was meditating abdication in his favour, and Philip was pondering how he might secure at least a preponderating influence with Elizabeth, whose ultimate accession he regarded as inevitable. Thus the Spanish counsels were now directed largely to securing favourable treatment for her—a complete reversal of Renard's earlier policy. It may be that the idea of marrying her himself after her sister's death was even now present in Philip's mind.

[Sidenote: Oct. A new parliament]

In October, about the time of the martyrdom of Ridley and Latimer at Oxford, a fresh parliament was summoned, which was called upon to grant a subsidy. The diminution in the royal revenues from normal sources, which had been growing steadily more serious throughout the last twenty years, made the appeal necessary; the more so as the Queen had been honestly struggling to pay off the debts bequeathed to her. The subsidy was granted in part at least owing to the exertions of Gardiner, who in spite of mortal illness attended the opening of parliament.

[Sidenote: Nov. Gardiner's death and character]

It was his last public act. A few days later he followed Ridley and Latimer to the grave; dying stoutly, in harness almost to the last. He was of the old school of ecclesiastical statesmen. Five and twenty years before, he had been statesman first, churchman afterwards; but when he found that the ecclesiastical organisation as well as the Pope was the objective of Henry's attack, he took his stand by his Order, though stubbornly loyal to the King. In Henry's later years, he tried a fall with Cranmer and was worsted through the King's favour. All through the reign of Edward, he watched with continual protest—mostly from prison—the toppling over of the fabric which Henry had established; himself, as he judged, the victim of unconstitutional oppression. Released and restored to power by Mary, he repented what he conceived to have been his initial error, the repudiation of Roman authority, and was not averse to exacting the full penalty from those who had dealt hardly with him; was zealous to restore the power of the Church and to stamp out heresy. But to the last, he stood for the Law, and for English freedom from foreign domination, and to the last he fought for his Queen. His wildest panegyrist would not call him a saint; but according to his lights he was rarely cruel or even unjust, though often harsh; the records of his life have been written almost entirely by bitterly hostile critics; [Footnote: This applies not only to the Protestant historians, but also to the correspondence of Renard (on account of the Chancellor's anti-Spanish attitude), and of Noailles who detested him personally.] and his name deserves more honour and less obloquy than is usually attached to it.

[Sidenote: Mary's difficulties]

An embassy to Rome earlier in the year, which had been charged with the formal announcement of the reconciliation, had also intimated Mary's intention of restoring to the Church such of the alienated property as still remained in the hands of the Crown. The new Pope was with difficulty restrained from demanding more. Parliament however, when a bill was proposed for the restoration of "first-fruits and tenths" displayed so much resentment at the suggestion that it was so modified as only to authorise the Queen to dispose personally of the "tenths" actually remaining in her hands. Even this was not carried without vehement opposition. An impoverished exchequer which required replenishment by a subsidy could not afford to surrender a solid portion of revenue to Rome. The hostility to any such tribute was no less active than it had been twenty-five years ago: and the Pope's attitude served only to intensify the feeling, and to stir up general animosity towards the Papacy. The Opposition was so outspoken that some of the members were sent to the Tower. Parliament was dissolved before Christmas.

[Sidenote: 1556; The Dudley conspiracy; Foreign complications]

In January, Charles abdicated—his Burgundian possessions he had resigned to his son three months before—and Philip became King of Spain. Next month, the peace of Vaucelles was signed between France and Spain; but with a consciousness that war was likely to be renewed at the first convenient opportunity. Philip's hands were full, and the French King did not cease from intrigues in England, while French soil continued to be an asylum for English conspirators. In March, Cranmer closed the tragedy of his life, and Pole, who had long ago been nominated to the Archbishopric, was immediately installed. Before Easter, a plot on the old lines was discovered. Elizabeth was to be made Queen and married to Courtenay (now in Italy where he died soon after); France was to help. A number of the conspirators were taken and put to death after protracted examination; others escaped to France, including a Dudley, a connexion of the dead Northumberland, who gave his name to the plot. Most of them were hotheaded young men, who did not appreciate, as did their shrewder elders, the danger of relying on French assistance which would only be granted for ulterior ends. As the year went on, the violent temper of Paul IV. involved him in war with Philip; France naturally took up his cause; and it was more difficult than ever for Mary to escape being dragged into the imbroglio—a singularly painful position for so fervent a daughter of Rome; while the English refugees checkmated their own party at home by their readiness to pay any price-even to the betrayal of Calais-for French support. But for timely reinforcements, the English foothold in France would probably have been captured by a *coup de main* before the close of 1556. Meantime in England the severity of the persecutions was increased.

[Sidenote 1: 1557, June: the War with France]
[Sidenote 2: 1558, Jan: The loss of Calais]

In the spring of 1557, France and Spain were again at open war, and Philip paid his last brief visit to his wife to obtain English co-operation. Anti-Spanish feeling was strong; but when one of the refugees, Sir Thomas Stafford, [Footnote: A grandson of Buckingham] starting from France, landed in Yorkshire, captured Scarborough Castle, and attempted to raise a rebellion, jealousy of French interference proved an effective counterpoise. The rebellion collapsed at once, and war with France was declared in summer. The success of Philip's troops, which included a considerable English contingent, at St. Quentin in Picardy compelled the French to withdraw from Italy; and the Pope, thus deserted, was forced to a reconciliation with Philip. His animosity however, now aroused against England, was not easy to remove: and it was an additional source of grief to Mary and a great vexation to the Cardinal that Paul deprived him of his Legatine authority. The contest between Philip and Henry of France continued. It is curious that after the experience of the previous year the English authorities still did not realise the precarious position of Calais, and allowed the garrison to be weakened again—though the strain of maintaining its strength with the depleted exchequer would have been almost impossible. The natural result followed. At the end of December, Guise appeared before its walls: on January 6th 1558 it surrendered. Calais was lost for ever. A fortnight later, Guisnes, after a desperate resistance by its commandant, Lord Grey de Wilton, was forced to surrender also.

[Sidenote: National depression]

Whatever else was won or lost in France, the maintenance of the English grip on Calais had been a point of military honour for centuries—like the retention of its colours by a regiment. Nothing substantial was lost with its fall; but the wound to the national honour was deep and bitter. For Mary herself it was the bitterest portion in a cup that was filled with little else than bitterness. Talk of recapture was vain. A subsidy was demanded and granted, but only on the theory that the whole was required not for expeditions but to set the home defences in order against invasion. More could not be done without taxation, which the country could not support. In the attempt to fulfil what Mary and Pole deemed a pious and supreme duty—the restoration to the Church of the property whereof it had been sacrilegiously robbed—political considerations had been ignored and the absolutely necessary expenditure on national objects had been diverted into ecclesiastical channels, at a time when the national revenue was already desperately impoverished. The loss of Calais was reckoned as one more item in the account against Rome.

[Sidenote: Mary's death Nov.]

The whole country was in fact in a condition of irritated despondency, sick of persecution, sick of disaster, disheartened by epidemics and bad harvests; without the spirit or the material means to attempt a whole-hearted prosecution of the war, yet too sore to be willing to make peace till Calais should be recovered. And so in despair and gloom dragged out the last months of Mary Tudor's life. The last message she received from her husband was to beg her to make no difficulties about the succession of the sister who, she knew, would seek to reverse her policy. It was not till November that she passed away—to be followed in a few hours by her one trused friend, Cardinal Pole: the most disastrous example on record of one who with conscientious and destructive persistence aimed at an ideal which her own methods made for ever impossible of attainment.

[Sidenote: and character]

From the time of her childhood she was exposed to unceasing harshness; a princess born, she was treated as a bastard; despite it all, her natural generosity survived. Royally courageous, loyal and straightforward; to her personal enemies almost magnanimous; to the poor and afflicted pitiful; loving her country passionately: she was blind to the forces at work in the world, obsessed with the idea of one supreme duty, and she set herself, as she deemed, to do battle with Antichrist by the only methods she knew, though they were alien to her natural disposition, facing hatred and obloquy. She whose life was one long martyrdom, for conscience' sake offered up a whole holocaust of martyrs: she who thirsted for love died clothed with a nation's hate. Where in all history is a tragedy more piteous than that of Mary Tudor?

CHAPTER XVI
ELIZABETH (i), 1558-61—A
PASSAGE PERILOUS

[Sidenote: 1558 Accession of Elizabeth]

On November 17th 1558, the sun had not yet risen when Mary passed away; within a few hours, Elizabeth had been proclaimed Queen. No dissentient voice was raised in England. Heath, Mary's Chancellor and Archbishop of York, announced her accession to the Houses of Parliament; the proclamation was drawn up by Sir William Cecil, the Council's Secretary under Edward VI. From one quarter, and only one, could a colourable challenge come. In the legitimate course of succession by blood, the claim lay with Mary Stewart, Queen of Scots and now Dauphiness of France. But the Will of Henry VIII., authorised by Parliament, was paramount. That Will had given priority to the two children of his body who had both been declared illegitimate—not born in wedlock—by the national courts. The Papal pronouncement in an opposite sense in Mary's case would have made nugatory any attempt on the part of a Catholic to question her rights; but that difficulty did not apply in the case of Elizabeth. As a matter of practical politics, the Scots Queen might waive her claim; as a matter of high theory, no personal disclaimers could cancel the validity of her title; as a matter of English Constitutional theory, Elizabeth's legal title rested on the superior validity of a Parliamentary enactment as compared with the divine right of inheritance. And in the minds of the entire English nation, there was unanimity as to the acceptable doctrine. But the rejected doctrine remained to fall back on if discontent should arise.

[Sidenote: The claim of Mary Stewart]

The English people might settle the antagonistic claims of Mary and Elizabeth to their own satisfaction: but the rivalry also of the very strongest interest to the European Powers. was actually queen of Scotland; prospectively she was also queen of France. If to these two crowns she united that of England, the hegemony of the empire thus formed would inevitably fall to France, and France would become the premier European Power. That position was now occupied by Spain, [Footnote: See *Appendix A*, ii.] which, in the face of such a combination, would lose its naval ascendancy, and be cut off from the Netherlands both by sea and land. For Philip therefore it was absolutely imperative to support Elizabeth at ail costs.

[Sidenote: Strength of Elizabeth's position]

Here then lay the strength of Elizabeth's position, which she and her chosen counsellors were quick to grasp. The only alternative to Elizabeth was the Queen of Scots; her accession would mean virtually the conversion of England into an appanage of France. Of Elizabeth's subjects none—whatever their creed might be, or whatever creed she might adopt—would be prepared to rebel at the price of subjection to France; the few hot-heads who had ventured on that line when Mary Tudor was at the height of her unpopularity had found themselves utterly without support. For the same reason, do what she would, Philip could not afford to act against her—more than that, he had no choice but to interfere on her behalf if Henry of France acted against her. He might advise—dictate—threaten—but he must, as against France, remain her champion, whether she submitted or no. As long as she kept her head, this young woman of five and twenty, with an empty treasury, with no army, a wasted navy, and with counsellors whose reputation for statesmanship was still to make, was nevertheless mistress of the situation. Mary Stewart's claim presented no immediate danger, though it might become dangerous enough in the future.

There were two things then on which Elizabeth knew she could count; her own ability to keep her head, and the capacity for loyalty of the great bulk of her subjects. If either of those failed her, she would have no one but herself to blame. The former had been shrewdly tested during her sister's reign, when a single false step would have ruined her. The latter had borne the strain even of the Marian persecution—nay, of the alarm engendered by the Spanish marriage, which showed incidentally that fear of domination by a foreign power was the most deeply rooted of all popular sentiments; a sentiment now altogether in Elizabeth's favour, unless she should threaten a dangerous marriage.

But the cool head and the clear brain, and unlimited self-reliance, were necessary to realise how much might be dared in safety; to distinguish also the course least likely to arouse the one incalculable factor in domestic politics—religious fanaticism; which, if it once broke loose, might count for more than patriotic or insular sentiment. And these were precisely the qualities in which the queen herself excelled, and which marked also the man whom from the first she distinguished with her father's perspicacity as her chief counsellor.

[Sidenote: Cecil]

Throughout the last reign, Cecil had carefully effaced himself. In matters of religion, though he had been previously associated with the Protestant leaders, he had never personally committed himself to any extreme line, and under the reaction he conformed; as did Elizabeth herself, and practically the whole of the nobility. He had walked warily, keeping always on the safe side of the law, never seeking that pre-eminence which in revolutionary times is apt to become so dangerous. He was not the man to risk his neck for a policy which he could hope to achieve by waiting, and he was quite willing to subordinate religious convictions to political expediency. On the other hand, he never betrayed confidences; he was not to be bought; and he was not to be frightened. Further, he was endowed with a penetrating perception of character, immense powers of organisation, and industry which was absolutely indefatigable. It was an immediate mark of the young queen's singular sagacity that even before her accession she had selected Cecil to lean upon, in preference to any of the great nobles, and even to Paget who had for many years been recognised as the most astute statesman in England.

[Sidenote: Finance]

Secure of her throne, Elizabeth was confronted by the great domestic problem of effecting a religious settlement; the diplomatic problem of terminating the French war; and what may be called the personal problem of choosing—or evading—a husband, since no one, except it may be the Queen herself, dreamed for a moment that she could long remain unwedded. To these problems must be added a fourth, less conspicuous but vital to the continuance of good government—the rehabilitation of the finances, of the national credit. A strict and lynx-eyed economy, a resolute honesty of administration, and a prompt punctuality in meeting engagements, took the place of the laxity, recklessness, and peculation which had prevailed of recent years. The presence of a new tone in the Government was immediately felt in mercantile circles, and the negotiation of necessary loans became a reasonable business transaction instead of an affair of usurious bargaining, both in England and on the continent. Finally, before Elizabeth had been two years on the throne, measures were promulgated for calling in the whole of the debased coinage which had been issued during the last fifteen years, and putting in circulation a new and honest currency. It seems to have been owing to a miscalculation, not to sharp practice, that the Government did in fact make a small profit out of this transaction.

[Sidenote: Marriage proposals: Philip II.]

Philip of Spain and his representatives in England had not realised the true strength of Elizabeth's position, and certainly had no suspicion that she and her advisers were entirely alive to it. On this point they had absolutely no misgivings. They took it for granted that the English queen must place herself in their hands and meekly obey their behests, if only in order to secure Spanish support against France. Philip began operations by proposing himself as her husband, expecting thereby to obtain for himself a far greater degree of power than he had derived from his union with her sister, while inviting her to share the throne of the first Power in Europe. But Elizabeth and Cecil were alive to the completeness of the hold on Philip they already possessed; and Elizabeth, the daughter of Anne Boleyn, would have utterly stultified her own position by marrying her dead sister's husband, since it would be necessary to obtain a papal dispensation, acknowledge the Pope's authority, and recognise by implication the validity of her father's marriage with Katharine of Aragon. To the ambassador's amazed indignation, the Queen with the support of the Council, decisively rejected the honour. Paget, who had in the last reign stood almost alone in commending the Spanish match, would have repeated his counsel now; but he had been displaced, while Cecil and his mistress were entirely at one.

The Queen's argument that the marriage, however attractive to herself or desirable politically, was, from her point of view out of the question, was unanswerable. The Spaniards had to cast about for some other candidate for her hand, whose success would still be likely to attach England to the chariot-wheels of Spain; besides seeking another bride for their own King.

When Philip's hand was definitely declined, three months after Elizabeth's accession, the most pressing danger arising out of the Marriage question was at an end. Thenceforward, dalliance with would-be suitors became simply one of the tactical tricks of Elizabeth's diplomacy, employed by her perhaps not less to the torment of her own advisers than to the perturbation of foreign chancelleries; seeing that whether she knew her own mind or not, up to the last she invariably took very good care that no one else should know it.

[Sidenote: The Religious Question]

One of Philip's main objects was as a matter of course to secure England, through its queen, for Catholicism; and there is very little doubt that at this time the majority of Englishmen—at any rate outside the dioceses of London, Norwich and Canterbury—would have acquiesced much more readily in the maintenance of the old forms of worship than in institutions modelled after Geneva. Elizabeth however, with her trusted advisers, leaned neither to the one nor to the other. They were guided by considerations not of creed but of politics. They had realised that the repudiation of the authority of the Holy See, and the assertion of the supremacy of the sovereign in matters ecclesiastical, were essential. If they were determined not to submit to Papal claims, they were equally disinclined to submit to the claims of a Calvinistic Ministry, posing as the mouth-pieces of the Almighty, demanding secular obedience on the analogy of Samuel or Elijah. As to creed, what the statesmen saw was that the utmost latitude of dogmatic belief must be recognised; provided that it was consistent with the supremacy of the secular sovereign, and with a moderately elastic uniformity of ritual. The personal predilections of Elizabeth might be in favour of what we call the Higher doctrines, or those of Cecil might lean to the Lower; but neither was willing to impose penalties or disabilities for opinions or practices which did not tend either to the anarchism of the Anabaptists, or to the Sacerdotalism of Rome on the one hand or Geneva on the other hand; both were even disposed to remain in official unconsciousness of such individual transgressors as could conveniently be ignored.

[Sidenote: A Protestant policy]

While the Spanish ambassador, De Feria, like his master, had almost taken it for granted that if Philip offered to marry Elizabeth he would be accepted, he was from the first greatly perturbed as to the attitude of the new Government towards the religious question. That Cecil was going to be chief minister, and that he was, in the political sense, a Protestant, were both manifest facts. All the extreme Catholics, and some of the moderate ones, were displaced from the Council; those who were left might prefer the Mass to the Communion, but only as King Henry had done. The new members were definitely Protestants. Heath, Archbishop of York, Mary's Chancellor, though personally esteemed, gave place to Nicholas Bacon (as "Lord Keeper"), whose wife and Cecil's were sisters, and measures were being taken to secure a Protestant House of Commons when Parliament should meet. The number of lay peers was increased by four Protestants; among the twenty-seven bishoprics, Archbishop Pole had omitted to fill up several vacancies, while a sudden mortality was afflicting the episcopal bench. Around the queen, Protestant influences were immensely predominant. It is quite unnecessary to turn to an injudicious letter from Pope Paul to find a motive for the anti-Roman attitude which from the very outset was so obvious to De Feria. [Footnote: *MSS. Simancas, apud* Froude, vii., p. 27. De Feria to Philip.] Whatever prevarications or ambiguities Elizabeth might indulge in to him, it is quite clear that, whether she liked it or not, she felt that her position required an anti-Roman policy, if her independence was to be secured and the prestige of England among the nations was to be restored.

[Sidenote: 1559 Parliament: The Act of Supremacy]

The methods of the new Government however were to be strictly legal; changes must have parliamentary sanction. At the coronation, the authorised forms obtained. But at the end of January, the Houses met; and during the following four months the whole of the Marian legislation was wiped out, as Mary had wiped out the legislation of the preceding reign. The first measures brought forward were financial — as the first step Cecil had taken was to dispatch an agent to the Netherland cities to negotiate a loan — a Tonnage and Poundage bill, a Subsidy, and a First-fruits bill which marked the revival of the claims of the Crown against ecclesiastical revenues. These bills were skilfully introduced, and well-received; for it was expected that the money would be expended where it was needed, on national defence. Next, the new Act of Supremacy was introduced, against which the small phalanx of bishops fought with determination, supported by the protest of Convocation. It was not in fact carried till April; and then the actual title of "Supreme Head," which Mary and Philip had surrendered, was not revived, but a different formula was used, the Crown being declared "Supreme in all causes as well ecclesiastical as civil". The Act once more repealed the lately revived heresy Acts, and forbade proceedings on the ground of false opinions, except where these were opposed to the decisions of the first four General Councils or the plain words of Scripture. Moreover, the refusal of the Oath was not to be treason, as under Henry VIII.; it merely precluded the recusant from office. All save one of the Marian bishops did refuse it and were deprived; most of them doubtless would have done so even in the face of the old penalties. Incidentally it authorised the appointment of a Commission to deal with ecclesiastical offences, which took shape five and twenty years later as the Court of High Commission. But taken altogether, the measure was a long step in the direction of a much wider toleration than had ever been practised before.

[Sidenote: The Prayer-book, etc.]

In the meantime, the Prayer-book had been undergoing a final revision; and here Elizabeth's own wish would undoubtedly have been to revert to that of 1549. The disciples however of the Swiss school were too strong, and the last Prayer-book of Edward was the basis of the new one, though some sentences were so modified as to cause them dissatisfaction, and higher practices in the matter of ornaments and ceremonial were enjoined. The Act of Uniformity, imposing the use of the Prayer-book on the clergy, resulted in resignations which according to the records did not exceed two hundred. To account for so small a number, we must suppose that the regulations were to a considerable extent evaded; if not, the clergy must have been singularly obsequious.

The only remaining Act of importance was that for the Recognition of the Queen, which declared her to be the lawful sovereign by blood, and repealed in general terms all Acts or judgments [Footnote: *Cf.* Moore, p. 241.] passed in a contrary sense, legitimating her without examining the grounds on which her mother's marriage had been declared invalid—a method of settling the question entirely sufficient on the theory of parliamentary sovereignty, but wholly inadequate on the theory of Divine Right.

It was not till some months later that the depletion of the bench of Bishops by deaths or deprivations was remedied. Matthew Parker, a man of moderation and ability, was selected as Archbishop of Canterbury, the consecration being performed by Barlow—who had resigned Bath and Wells under Mary—with Coverdale, Scory, and Hodgekins. The question whether the Apostolic Succession was duly conveyed at the hands of these prelates belongs rather to ecclesiastical history—even to theological controversy—than to general history. It is sufficient here to observe that it turns mainly on the doubt which has been thrown without real justification on Barlow's own ordination as a Bishop. [Footnote: See the Lives of Parker by Strype and Hook; and a brief summary in Moore, pp. 245-247.] After the Archbishop's consecration, the vacant sees were filled up, generally with moderate men, with a leaning towards Zurich or even Lutheranism rather than the old Catholicism or Calvinism, but always in accord with the Acts of Supremacy and Uniformity.

In point of time, however, the story of these last events has carried us a year forward, and we have to return to the first six months of the new reign and the relations of Elizabeth to France.

[Sidenote: France and Peace]

Before Mary's death, an armistice was in operation. England did not mean to conclude peace with France, unless Calais was restored, and Philip could not desert England lest an effort should be made to place Mary Stewart on the throne—on which Henry could not venture while Spain supported Elizabeth. Unsuccessful diplomatic attempts were made to negotiate separately with the allied Powers, and to induce Elizabeth formally to recognise the Queen of Scots as heir presumptive—which however she stoutly declined to do, being aware that the obvious effect of such a course would be to invite her own immediate assassination, to secure Mary's immediate accession. Moreover, Philip was not without a direct interest in England's recovery of Calais, because of its position on the border of the Netherlands. In the event, however, the English felt that, since the Spanish marriage was rejected, the claims on Philip must not be pressed too hard; and in the final terms of the Peace of Cateau Cambresis, France was allowed to retain Calais under promise to restore it after eight years, while she was formally to recognise Elizabeth as lawful queen of England, with the adhesion of Mary and her husband.

Now however, parties and persons in Scotland become so inextricably interwoven with the English queen's policy and her relations with parties and persons in France, that Scottish affairs demand close attention.

[Sidenote: State of Scotland]

In December, 1542, James V. of Scotland had died leaving a daughter just a week old. When Elizabeth ascended the English throne, the Northern country had for sixteen years been governed or misgoverned by regents and Councils of regency. From early childhood, the little queen had been brought up at the French court, under the more particular tutelage of her uncles, the Duke of Guise and his brothers. In 1558, at the age of fifteen, she was married to the Dauphin. Now (and for some time past) her mother, Mary of Guise—not the least able member of a very able family— was Regent of Scotland, supported in that position against the Protestant factions by a French garrison. In the natural course of events, the Scottish Protestant party looked to England for support, and favoured in the abstract the idea of uniting the English and Scottish crowns, though in the concrete they would not admit an English King. All Scottish sentiment, without distinction of party, rebelled against any prospect of Scotland becoming an appanage of any foreign Power, and the idea of subordination to France was only less unpopular than that of subordination to England. Moreover, with their young queen married to the Heir Apparent of France, and with a Guise supported by French troops as Regent in Scotland, this latter danger seemed the less pressing.

Now the extremes of religious partisanship were more general and more deeply rooted in Scotland than in England; partly because the corruption of the clergy had been more flagrant; partly because in a country where deeds of violence were comparatively ordinary, they had been freely committed under the cloak of religion. The French influence had been cast against the Reformation. The Reformers had murdered Cardinal Beton; John Knox had been taken from St. Andrews to the French galleys; and the Preachers were at war with the Regency. The two men who were about to prove themselves along with Knox the ablest statesmen in Scotland—James Stewart, afterwards famous as the Regent Murray, and young Maitland of Lethington—were on the side of the Preachers, and of what was the same thing, now that a Protestant government was restored in England, the English alliance. Moreover it has to be borne in mind that whereas in England the Reformation was imposed, whether willingly or unwillingly, on the Nation by the Government; in Scotland it was a popular movement which a Government, itself half French, endeavoured to repress. Whatever the sincerity of the aristocratic leaders might be, the Scottish Reformers felt themselves to be fighting for their liberties against an alien domination.

[Sidenote: 1559 Religious parties in Scotland]

In the spring of 1559 the quarrel between the party of the Preachers and the Regency assumed a very threatening aspect. After the peace of Cateau Cambrésis, in March, the French King decided in favour of an anti-Protestant policy. In spite of the promise to recognise the title of the English queen, the Dauphin and his wife were allowed to assume the Arms of England, and it seemed that Mary of Guise in Scotland was about to wage a more active war than of late against the heretics; also that more French troops would be sent to help her. On the other hand, Knox, who on his retirement from England had withdrawn to Geneva, to await an opportunity when his presence might be effective, now returned to Scotland in a very unconciliatory spirit. For the party who desired union with England, it was unfortunate that the great preacher while in exile had issued a tract entitled *The Monstrous Regiment of Women*, aimed against the two Maries, but inferentially (though not of set purpose) condemning Elizabeth; who entirely refused to forgive him, while he on the other hand refused to eat his words. The fact undoubtedly increased the difficulty of harmonious accord between the English Government and the Scottish "Lords of the Congregation," as the Protestant leaders entitled themselves collectively.

[Sidenote: Arran as a suitor to Elizabeth]

The situation however produced a new candidate for the hand of Elizabeth in the person of the Earl of Arran, son of the quondam Earl of Arran now Duke of Chatelherault. The Duke was head of the house of Hamilton, and was in fact at this time heir presumptive [Footnote: As descending from the daughter of James II., sister of James III, Albany was now dead.] to the throne of Scotland. If then a legitimate ground could be devised for dethroning Mary—as for instance, if she employed foreign (*i.e.* French) troops against her subjects lawfully maintaining their constitutional rights—the succession would fall to the Hamiltons; and if Arran and Elizabeth were married, the crowns of the two kingdoms would be united. Thus this marriage became a primary object with the Lords of the Congregation; and the Earl was included in the list of those with whose aspirations Elizabeth coquetted.

In July, the French King was killed in a tournament. Francis and Mary became king and queen of France and Scotland, and Mary's uncles the Guises immediately became decisively predominant with the French Government.

The Spanish ambassador was in the greatest anxiety. The one thing his master could not afford was to see the queen of France and Scotland established as queen of England also. But it was only less necessary to avoid war with France on that issue. If the Arran marriage were in serious contemplation, Mary would have very strong justification for asserting her claim to England as a counter-move. What Philip wanted was that Elizabeth should marry his cousin the Archduke Charles, a younger son of his uncle the Emperor Ferdinand who had succeeded Charles V. Then Philip would practically have control of England; France would not venture to grasp at the crown; and Elizabeth would of course have to leave the Scots to themselves. Elizabeth saw her advantage. She prevaricated with the Scots about the Arran marriage, and with Philip about the Austrian marriage. She did her best to make the Lords of the Congregation fight their own battles, a task which they were equally bent on transferring to England. And meantime, Cecil never wavered in his determination of at least maintaining the Scottish Protestants against active French intervention: while the whole body of Elizabeth's more Conservative Counsellors favoured the Austrian marriage and non-intervention in Scotland.

[Sidenote: Wynter sails for the Forth; 1560]

Elizabeth's own procedure was entirely characteristic. She had, it would seem, no sort of intention of marrying either Charles or Arran; but she worked her hardest to persuade their respective partisans of the contrary. Her officers were in secret communication with the Scots, and were supplying them with money, while she was openly vowing that she was rendering them no assistance whatever. Neither Scots nor Spaniards trusted her, but neither altogether disbelieved. Finally—having devoted the parliamentary grants and all available funds to the equipment of her fleet—when it was evident that a French expedition was on the point of sailing for the Forth, she allowed Admiral Wynter to put to sea; with orders to act if opportunity offered, but to declare when he did so that he had transgressed his instructions on his own responsibility. In January, 1560, Wynter appeared in the Forth, seduced the French into firing on him from the fort of Inch Keith, and blew the fort to pieces—in self-defence. Meantime, D'Elboeuf, brother of Guise, had sailed with a powerful flotilla, which was however almost annihilated by a storm. For a time then at least there was no danger of another French expedition to Scotland. Wynter's fleet commanded the Firth of Forth, and the French soon found that, except for an occasional raid, they would have to confine their efforts to making their position at Leith impregnable.

Wynter's protestations that he was not acting under orders can hardly have deceived any one, though the Queen, Cecil, and Norfolk [Footnote: Grandson of the old duke, and son of the Earl of Surrey executed by Henry VIII.]— who had accepted the command on the Border, after refusing it—confirmed his story. The Spaniards were intensely annoyed. Philip proposed that he should himself send an army to Scotland, to put affairs straight; but this was equally little to the taste of the French and the English. Moreover, Philip had not yet grasped the fact that the one way to make Elizabeth definitely defiant was, to threaten her. Hitherto she had repudiated Wynter's action, and refused to allow Norfolk to march in support of the Congregation, though she had secretly given them encouragement and hard cash; now she came to a definite agreement with them, and by the end of March Norfolk was over the Border. The Queen had doubtless drawn encouragement from the latest turn of affairs in France. D'Elboeufs disaster had greatly diminished the present danger of attack from that quarter; while now the conspiracy of Amboise revealed such a dangerous development of party antagonisms in France as to make it unlikely that she would be able to spare her energies for broils beyond her own borders. The aim of the plot was to overthrow the Guises, and place the young king and queen under the control of the Protestant Bourbon princes, Condé and Anthony King of Navarre. [Footnote: See *Appendix A*, vi.] The conspiracy itself collapsed, but it served as a very effective danger-signal.

[Sidenote: Elizabeth's vacillations]

Elizabeth had no sooner allowed the advance into Scotland than she was again seized with her usual desire to avoid becoming involved in active hostilities; and she continued the exasperating practice—for her servants — of sending them contradictory and hampering instructions. The very men who, like Norfolk, had been flatly opposed to the policy of interference were now convinced that, being once committed to it, there must be no turning back. Vacillation would presently drive the Congregation to such a pitch of distrust that they would break with England in despair; whereas the primary object of interference had been to make sure of a powerful party which would be inevitably committed to forwarding Elizabeth's interests. However, Philip again stiffened her by dictatorial messages, which failed to frighten because the essential fact remained true that he dared not facilitate the substitution of Mary for Elizabeth on the English throne. The Queen refused to recall her troops, and explained elaborately that she was not taking part with rebels against their sovereign, but with loyal subjects who were resisting the abuse by the Guises of authority filched from Mary, who in her turn would approve as soon as she came to Scotland and saw the true state of affairs.

[Side note: The English at Leith]

And so the English army sat down before Leith and set about starving it and bombarding it; till the process appeared to be too slow, and Lord Grey de Wilton, who was in command of the operations, was forced by urgent messages against his own judgment to attempt an assault which was repulsed with very severe loss. Elizabeth was shaken, but her Council remained resolute. Then, if she had really been afraid that Philip might actually mean what he threatened, her fears were dispelled by a disaster to his fleet in a battle with the Turks. She became aggressively inclined once more. The position of Leith, despite the valour of its garrison, was becoming hopeless; and in June the central figure of the French and Catholic party was removed by the death of the Regent Mary of Guise—an able woman, who had played her part with unfailing courage, no little skill, and quite as much moderation as could reasonably be expected, under extraordinarily difficult conditions.

[Sidenote: the Treaty of Edinburgh July 6th]

Cecil had already been sent north to negotiate. The terms required were the entire withdrawal of French troops from Scotland, the recognition of Elizabeth's right to the throne of England, the recognition of her compact with the Congregation as legitimate, and the confirmation of their demands for toleration. It was not till after the Regent's death that the arrangement known as the Treaty of Edinburgh was signed; by this instrument the French gave the promise that the demands of the Congregation should be conceded, but without formally admitting that Elizabeth was ever entitled to make a compact with Mary's subjects. The other two points were allowed, and the French departed for ever. Fortunately a dispatch from Elizabeth requiring more stringent terms (which would have been refused) arrived a day too late, after the treaty was signed. It was comparatively of little consequence that Mary declined to ratify the treaty. When the French had gone, the Congregation were masters of the situation; and before the year was out, the French and Scottish crowns were separated by the death of Francis. The Guise domination in France was checked, and while Mary's accession to the English throne remained desirable to the Catholic party in that country, the hope of combining the three crowns under the hegemony of France came to an end.

[Sidenote: Elizabeth's methods]

The whole episode deserves to be dwelt on at length, because it very forcibly illustrates the strength and the weakness of Elizabeth's methods and the character of her entourage. She saw the sound policy; she maintained her confidence in the men who also saw it. Yet she perpetually wavered and hesitated till the eleventh hour to authorise the steps necessary to carrying it out. At the eleventh hour, she did authorise them; and that, repeatedly, because at the last moment an injudicious threat stirred her to defiance. For herself, she could have secured inglorious ease by simply accepting Philip's patronage, but she elected to play the daring game, and won. Her methods were tortuous. She lied unblushingly, but she was an adept at avoiding acts which palpably would prove beyond a doubt that she was lying. The Spanish ambassador lived under a perpetual conviction that she was rushing on her own ruin—that she would drive his master to choose between the deplorable alternatives of fighting on her behalf or allowing the Queen of France and Scotland to become Queen of England also—that the Catholics would rise to dethrone her. But her calculations were sound, and Norfolk himself commanded her armies and served her loyally in a policy which, in his opinion, ought never to have been initiated. She never allowed herself to be bullied or cajoled; but she perpetually kept alive the impression that a little more bullying or a little more cajolery might turn the scale. And she drove the French out of Scotland.

[Sidenote: The Dudley Imbroglio]

All the intriguing at this time about suitors for the hand of Elizabeth is mixed up with the scandals associated with the name of Lord Robert Dudley (afterwards made Earl of Leicester), a son of the traitor Duke of Northumberland. Lord Robert, although a married man, was allowed an intimacy with the Queen which not only points conclusively to an utter absence of delicacy in the daughter of Henry VIII. and Anne Boleyn, but filled the entire Court circle with the gravest apprehensions. It was the current belief that if Dudley could get free of his wife, Elizabeth would marry him, and that this desire was at the back of her vacillation. The affair was brought to an acute stage by the sudden death of Amy Robsart, Dudley's wife, in September; when already for some time past, his innumerable enemies had been hinting that he meant to make away with her. The facts are obscure; but the impression given by the evidence is that she was murdered, though not with the direct connivance of her husband. Still, the suspicion of his guilt was so strong that if the Queen had married him she would have strained the loyalty of her most loyal subjects probably to breaking point. Yet so keen was her delight in playing with fire that it was many months before English statesmen began to feel that the danger was past; while overtures were certainly made on Dudley's behalf to the Spanish Ambassador, De Quadra, to obtain Philip's sanction and support, in return for a promise that the Old Religion should be restored. Sussex alone expressed a conviction that Elizabeth would find her own salvation in marrying for Love. Every one else was convinced that, whatever might be her infatuation for Dudley, marriage with him would spell total ruin for her: and there was a general belief that Norfolk and others would interfere in arms if necessary; while the secret marriage of Lady Katharine Grey (who stood next in succession under Henry's will) to Lord Hertford, son of the Protector Somerset, was suspected of being a move to which even Cecil was privy, for placing her on the throne should the worst befall. At last, when the limit of endurance was almost reached, Elizabeth finally declared that she was not going to marry the favourite. Judging her conduct by her whole career, it would seem that she never really contemplated the commission of so fatal a blunder, but could not resist the temptation of tormenting her best friends, and torturing politicians of every kind with uncertainty—perhaps even of half believing herself that she actually would set all adverse opinion at defiance if she chose.

[Sidenote: The Huguenots]

From one suitor at any rate Elizabeth felt herself freed by the death of the young French King in December. The main interest of France in the Scottish Crown was thereby ended; more than that, the Huguenot Bourbons, who stood in France next in succession to the sons of Katharine de Medici, recovered for the time much of their power. The political arguments in favour of the Arran marriage lost enough of their force to enable the English Queen to brave the wrath of the Congregation and finally decline the Hamilton alliance. It is of interest to find Paget, once again called in to her Counsels, declaring in favour of a Huguenot alliance, in despite of Spain.

[Sidenote: The Pope]

The position of the Huguenots in France, and the proposed resuscitation of the Council of Trent under the auspices of Pope Pius IV., who had succeeded Paul in 1559, had revived ideas of Protestant representation therein; and Elizabeth, after her fashion, played with the hopes of the Catholic party, at home and abroad, that she might be drawn into participation. It was only when it had become perfectly clear that the admission of the Papal Supremacy was a condition precedent, that these hopes were dashed, and the proposal that a papal Nuncio should be received in England, with which the Queen had been coquetting, was definitely declined; while Philip was obliged to intimate to the Pope that he must not launch against the recalcitrant England ecclesiastical thunderbolts which would involve him in war, whether against or on behalf of Elizabeth.

In the meantime however, both the Catholic party in Scotland and the Congregation were hoping to bring Mary back from France, and to control her policy when she should arrive. For the Protestants felt now that without foreign interference they could hold their own. Elizabeth had rejected their scheme for bringing the union of the crowns in reach by the Arran marriage: they were now bent on the alternative course of inducing Elizabeth to acknowledge their own Queen as her heir presumptive. Mary herself was more than ready for the adventure. Elizabeth refused her a passage through England which might easily have been utilised, especially in the North, for the organisation of a Stewart party within the realm; while on the other hand it would obviously be an easy thing for an "accident" to happen while the Scots Queen was running the gauntlet of her ships on the seas. But Mary was nothing if not daring. In August, accompanied by her Guise uncle, D'Elboeuf, she set sail from the "pleasant land of France," and four days later, without disaster, the Queen of Scots landed at Leith.

CHAPTER XVII
ELIZABETH (ii), 1561-68—
QUEENS AND SUITORS

[Sidenote: 1561 The Situation]

On August 19th, 1561, Mary Stewart returned to Scotland; in May 1568, she left her kingdom for ever. During those seven years, what she did, what she was accused of doing, what she was expected to do, what she intended to do, formed the subject of the keenest interest and anxiety in England at the time; and the problems and mysteries of those years, never unravelled to this day, never with any certainty to be unravelled at all, continued to perplex English statesmen and to complicate the situation in England for nearly nineteen years more. We shall have to follow them therefore in much greater detail than would *a priori* seem justifiable in a volume ostensibly dealing not with Scottish but with English History.

During these same years it may be said that the great antagonisms were formulated, which were to rend the two great Continental monarchies for forty years to come. Thus in order to follow the subsequent story efficiently even from the purely English point of view, we must devote what may seem somewhat disproportionate attention to foreign affairs, which do not appear at first sight to have a very intimate connexion with events in England. For France these events may be summed up as the opening of the set struggle between Catholics and Huguenots; for Spain, as the preliminaries to the revolt of the Netherlands: while for all Europe, the effective sessions of the Council of Trent laid down finally the sharp dividing line between Protestant and Catholic—terms which have a well defined political meaning, in neither case identical with their original or correct theological import, in which latter sense half the Protestant world continued to assert its claim to membership in the Catholic Church.

[Sidenote: (1) The Council of Trent]

That Council reassembled under the auspices of Paul's successor, Pius IV., in January 1562. While the Protestants could not recognise it as a Catholic Council, in the sense of representing the whole Catholic Church, it claimed that character for itself, and those who maintained its authority appropriated the name, which thus became a party title. In the course of its sessions, it rejected doctrines, notably that of Justification by Faith, which had been strongly favoured even by such men as Pole and Contarini, so narrowing the bounds of orthodoxy. But while cutting off all possibility of reconciliation with the Protestants, it marked a strong tendency to reformation not of dogma but of practice; while an increased intolerance of what was stigmatised as error, an intensification of the spirit which demanded the most merciless repression of heresy, was accompanied in other respects by an elevation of the standard of ecclesiastical morals, and a zeal for the Faith more pure and less influenced by worldly considerations, if narrower, than in the past. From this time, as the exemplar both of the new discipline, and of the new warfare against heresy, the Order of Jesuits takes its place as the dominating force. The Council terminated in 1563; in 1566 the Pope died and was succeeded by Pius V., the nominee of the most rigid section of the Church.

[Sidenote: (2) France: Catholics, Huguenots, and *Politiques*]

In France, from the days of Francis I., the tendency had been to persecute the followers of the reformed doctrines, who were for the most part disciples of Calvin rather than of Luther. On the other hand, the political attraction of alliance with the German Lutherans had served to keep the mind of the court open, and throughout the sittings of the Council of Trent there had been and continued to be threats that the Gallican Church might follow the Anglican in claiming independence of the Pope. In France however the opposition lay between the Catholics and the Calvinists, who by 1561 had acquired the general name of Huguenots: in England, the Reformation was carried through under the auspices of a middle ecclesiastical party. In France the middle party was purely political, not aiming at a compromise tending to amalgamation, but rather at holding the two parties balanced.

Before the death of Henry II., the Guise brothers were recognised as the heads of the Catholic faction. The Duke, Francis, was the popular and successful soldier who won back Calais from England: his brother, the Cardinal of Lorraine, was one of the ablest of living ecclesiastics and statesmen. There were four more brothers, all men of mark; and their sister was the mother of Mary Stewart. On the other hand, the family came from Lorraine only in the time of Francis I., and though the first Duke of Guise married a daughter of the house of Bourbon, they were regarded with jealousy by a considerable body of the French nobility, who, partly in consequence, threw their weight in favour of the Protestants. At the head of these now were Anthony of Bourbon, nominal King of Navarre in right of his wife, his brother Condé, and Admiral Coligny, with his brother the

Cardinal Chatillon. When Henry II. died, the Guises—uncles of the new Queen (Mary Stewart)—assumed unmistakable supremacy; but when Francis also died, and was succeeded by his younger brother Charles IX., the Queen-mother, Katharine de Medici, obtained for herself the regency, which would naturally have fallen to Navarre as next Prince of the Blood, and the control passed not to the Huguenots but to the "*Politiques*". [Footnote: The name for the "Middle" Party, which was not however generally adopted till a later date.] It may be remarked that this century is noteworthy for the number of women who made their mark in history as politicians; for Isabella of Castile was still living when it opened, and Elizabeth of England when it closed; Katharine de Medici and Mary Stewart were of ability not much inferior; while Mary of Guise, regent of Scotland, and Mary Tudor in England, were both striking figures; and the women of Charles V.'s family were conspicuous as Governors of the Netherlands.

[Sidenote: Religious war in France 1561-68]

The rule of the Politiques was, unlike that of the Guises, favourable to toleration—as a matter not of conscience but of policy. Katharine's was the controlling spirit, and her chief supporters in the policy were the Chancellor L'Hôpital and the Constable Montmorency, a connexion of Coligny's but an orthodox Catholic. In January 1562 a large extension of toleration was granted to the Huguenots, which roused the fanaticism of the other party and drew the Constable over to their ranks. Navarre was induced to go over to the Catholics, leaving the Protestant leadership to Condé. Some of Guise's followers massacred a number of unarmed Huguenots at Vassy; Paris, frantically anti-Huguenot, gave a triumphal reception to Guise, who held Katharine and the boy-king practically prisoners. The Huguenots rose in arms; Navarre was killed, leaving a boy—afterwards Henry IV.—as his heir and the hope of the Huguenots; for his mother Jeanne of Navarre had not followed her husband in his apostasy. A great battle, indecisive in result, was fought at Dreux, in which each of the commanders, Condé and Montmorency, fell into the hands of their antagonists; and then, in February 1563, Francis of Guise was assassinated by the fanatic Poltrot. About the same time died two of his brothers, D'Aumale and the Grand Prior. The result was the termination of the war by the Peace of Amboise, practically confirming the recent edict of toleration. Katharine still refused to adopt the policy, urged on her by Spain as well as by the Guise faction, of suppressing the Huguenots by the sword. The Huguenots, however, believing that Katharine was merely actuated by motives of expediency, and would seek to crush them if a favourable opportunity offered, organised with a view to enforcing their demands in arms, and again took the field in 1567, thereby deciding the Regent in the policy which they had—up to this time perhaps erroneously—attributed to her. For the time being, however, the war was closed in the spring of 1568, by a treaty confirming the terms of the previous Peace of Amboise.

[Sidenote: The Netherlands and Spain]

The Netherlands or Low Countries was the general title of a group of provinces, corresponding in area roughly but not accurately to the modern States of Holland and Belgium. These provinces, originally independent States, but latterly associated in a loose federation, had owned allegiance to the Dukes of Burgundy, and so had passed in due course to Charles V., who in turn transferred them to Philip shortly before his own abdication of the Spanish crown. The institutions within the provinces varied, as did the character and race of their populations: but in general their industrial development was of a high standard, and their wealth was of great importance to the Spanish monarchy. At the hands of Charles, who was brought up as a Netherlander, they enjoyed considerable favour; but Philip, by instinct and training, was a Spaniard, who looked on them as a paying appanage of Spain, had no sympathy with them, and no regard for their political organisations, and did not set foot among them after 1559. Before that year, most of his time since his marriage with Mary had been spent there; but in 1559 he departed, leaving as Governor his sister Margaret of Parma, and ignoring the nobility of the country.

The Reformation doctrines had obtained a very extensive hold, more particularly in the Northern provinces; but had been suppressed with considerable rigour by Charles, who early established the Inquisition in the country. By Philip the severities were increased, and the government of Margaret of Parma was conducted on the like intolerant principles: her chief adviser being Philip's nominee, Cardinal Granvelle. The native nobles—at whose head were Egmont, Horn, and William (the Silent), Prince of Orange [Footnote: William was a Netherlander in virtue of the lordship of Breda.] and Count of Nassau—as well as the burghers, were indignant at the encroachment on the constitutional liberties of the provinces by the appointment of foreigners to offices of State, and by the presence of Spanish troops; and the removal of both was demanded. The multiplication of bishops and endowment of the new bishoprics constituted another grievance. The troops had to be withdrawn, and in 1564 Granvelle left the Netherlands to join his master in Spain; but Philip's determination to bring the whole country into the system of Spanish despotism remained unchanged: and whereas the whole population was in favour of general religious toleration, he insisted, in the face of remonstrance, on intensifying instead of relaxing the edicts against the Reformed doctrines. To avoid the persecution, multitudes of Flemish weavers left the country, to be welcomed by Elizabeth in England, which was rapidly supplanting the commercial supremacy of the Low Countries.

[Sidenote: 1566 Resistance in the Netherlands]

In 1565 it was generally believed that Katharine de Medici was concerting measures, with the Duke of Alva on behalf of Spain, for the suppression of heretics; and this brought matters in the Netherlands to a head. In 1566 a League, widespread though not openly supported by the greatest nobles, was formed for the abolition of the Inquisition, an institution, introduced forty years before by Charles V., which had worked as mercilessly as in Spain. The supporters of the league included Lewis of Nassau, brother of William of Orange; it was known as the Compromise, and its adherents were nick-named the *Gueux*, or beggars. The general ferment resulted in violent anti-"idolatry" riots, accompanied by great destruction of Church property. The disturbances were quieted down by the exertions of Egmont and William of Orange; the Governor, Margaret of Parma, promising the concessions they advised. Philip however was enraged, repudiated the concessions, and in 1567 sent Alva with an army of Spanish and Italian veterans to restore order. Margaret, finding herself virtually superseded, retired. Alva's conception of order was the enforcement of the worst type of combined military and ecclesiastical tyranny. Egmont (a Catholic), and Horn, though both had rendered the Government conspicuous assistance, were arrested; Orange escaped by retiring to his German dominions. Not Protestants only, but even Maximilian who now occupied the Imperial throne in succession to Ferdinand, remonstrated; yet Philip obstinately encouraged Alva to go on his way. William of Orange avowed himself a Protestant; and in the spring a mixed army of Netherlander, Huguenots, and Germans, took the field under Lewis of Nassau. The revolt of the Netherlands may be reckoned as dating from the first engagement, at Heiligerlee, in May 1568. The Spaniards were worsted, and as an immediate consequence, Egmont and Horn were sent to the block.

[Sidenote: Elizabeth, Mary, and their Suitors]

The arrival of Mary Stewart in Scotland brings her personality into more intimate relation with that of Elizabeth than before. The problem of finding bridegrooms politically and personally acceptable to the two queens becomes particularly prominent. Arran, flatly declined by Elizabeth, becomes for a time one of her cousin's actual suitors. The Archduke Charles becomes a possible candidate for either. Dudley, still looked upon as Elizabeth's favoured lover, is offered by her to Mary as a husband. Now, too, we first meet with Henry Stewart, Lord Darnley, [Footnote: See Appendix A, iii.] whose mother, Lady Lennox, was daughter of Margaret Tudor by her second husband, the young man himself being a possible successor to the English throne. Being an English as well as a Scottish subject, brought up in England and therefore not, like Mary—whatever her claims by descent—an alien, that technical ground for disputing her succession did not apply to him. He too was mentioned as a possible suitor both for Elizabeth's and for Mary's hand. Then there was Don Carlos, son of Philip of Spain by his first wife, to whom Mary had a political inclination; or again there was for her a possibility of marrying her dead husband's brother, the boy-king Charles IX. of France. Mary herself, it must be remembered, was still some months short of nineteen when she landed at Leith. And it was a matter of grave political importance to Elizabeth, who should be the man to share the Scottish throne.

[Sidenote: 1562 Mary in Scotland]

Mary's reception was austere not to say brutal on the part of Knox and his friends; but the Earl of Murray (as Lord James Stewart soon after became) and Maitland, confident now in the security of Protestantism, were not disposed to subordinate polities to zealotry. They were ready for a degree of toleration. Their ultimate goal was the union of the crowns; and they wished Mary to repose her confidence on them. They would not press her to ratify the Treaty of Edinburgh, at any rate unless she was formally recognised as heir presumptive of England. Mary, for her part, though holding by her own faith, was not slow to perceive that for the present at least she must not challenge the Reformers. Her first business was conciliation.

The year 1562 was not far advanced when the first Huguenot war broke out in France. Condé was soon making overtures to Elizabeth, and her Protestant counsellors, headed by Cecil, were zealous that she should lend his party active support; with the restoration of Calais to England as the price. Philip of Spain, bent on suppressing the Netherlands heretics, was strongly on the side of the Guises, and threatened Elizabeth if she should venture to intervene. The house of the Spanish Ambassador in London was the centre of much Catholic intriguing; and much of what was going on was betrayed to Cecil by a secretary. Elizabeth was angry enough, but could not afford an open rupture with Philip, who, now that Mary was no longer Queen of France, might find it in his interest to support her pretensions to the English throne. On the other hand, the French Queen-mother could not now view with complacency the succession of Mary with her Guise connexions, coupled with the possibility of her matrimonial alliance either with the Spanish Don Carlos or the Habsburg Archduke Charles. Elizabeth's own desire now was to be in amity with Mary, and to have her married to some one who would not be dangerous. For a long time she dallied with the idea of meeting Mary with a view to a settlement as to the ratification of the Edinburgh treaty and her recognition as heir presumptive; and Catholic hopes ran high. But the successes of the Guise party in France forced her hand by alarming the Protestants. She had to decline the meeting with Mary, and at least to make a show of enforcing the laws against attendance at Mass more energetically. She had, in fact, been letting herself believe that she could indulge her personal predilection for the more ceremonial worship of the old faith; but as usual when a crisis seemed, really imminent, her personal predilections were suppressed for the time.

[Sidenote: 1562-63 Elizabeth and the Huguenots]

As the year went on, the intrigue with Condé reached a point at which the Huguenot leader actually handed over Havre to the English, and promised the restitution of Calais; and before the autumn was far advanced, the town was garrisoned, and a troop of English—ignoring instructions from home—went to join Condé. The colour for Elizabeth's action was that the Guises had usurped the government, and that they palpably and avowedly directed their policy to the injury of England; also that she was entitled to take measures to ensure the restoration of Calais, promised by treaty. The fighting went steadily against the Huguenots, and Elizabeth made the mistake—in which the country supported her even with passion—of holding Condé to his promise as to Calais, instead of applying herself to the establishment of the Huguenots as a powerful Anglophil anti-Guise party. Throwing over the method which had so successfully cleared Scotland of the French, she staked everything on the recovery of Calais, forced half Condé's friends to look upon him as something very like a traitor, and alienated Huguenot sentiment completely. The battle of Dreux in December, followed early in the next year by the murder of Guise, led to the truce of Amboise, in April, between the warring factions; England was left in the lurch. A desperate effort was made to retain the grip on Havre, but an outbreak of the plague among the garrison ruined all chance of success. It fell, and with it the last hope of recovering Calais (July 1563). It was not till the spring of 1564 that the French war was formally terminated by the treaty of Troyes, when the English, after much vain haggling, found themselves obliged to accept the French terms.

[Sidenote: The English Succession]

Near the end of 1562 the Queen had been stricken with smallpox and her life all but despaired of; so that the grave problem of the Succession assumed a momentary prominence. Henry's Will had never been set aside; but no one would have viewed with favour the claims of the Greys. Mary of Scotland, the heir by inheritance, was an alien, and abhorrent to the Protestants. Darnley was the only remaining claimant of Tudor stock;

[Footnote: Except the Clifford or Stanley branch, junior to the Greys. See *Front.*] while the House of York had still representatives living, in two grandsons of the old Countess of Salisbury executed by Henry—the Earl of Huntingdon and Arthur Pole, the latter of whom did actually become the centre of a still-born plot. What would have happened had the Queen died at this juncture it is impossible to guess: happily for England, she recovered. But the interest attaching to Mary's course was intensified.

The Scots Queen had in the meantime ostensibly given her support to Murray and Maitland, accompanying her half-brother on an expedition to crush Huntly, the head of the Catholic nobility. Murray and Maitland did their best during the early months of 1563 to force the recognition of their Queen as Elizabeth's heir by the menace of her marriage with the Prince of Spain; Elizabeth in turn did her own best to induce Mary to marry Dudley, whom she later on raised to the rank of Earl of Leicester. This union however was one which neither Mary herself nor any of her counsellors would accept; and when the year closed, Knox and the extreme Calvinists were grimly assimilating the to them portentous probability that she would end by marrying either Don Carlos or the young King of France—either event threatening the restoration of the Old Church in Scotland.

[Sidenote: 1564 Darnley and others]

The civil war in France ended, as we saw, in the triumph of the Politiques. The corollary was the treaty of Troyes with England in the spring of 1564. The French court was now disposed to be friendly towards Elizabeth; the Guises had lost weight by the death of the Duke; Philip of Spain saw nothing to gain by further embroilments; so the chances of Mary's marriage either with his son or with Charles IX. were small. The Scots Queen began to give Darnley a leading place in her own mind, feeling that a marriage with him would give a double claim to the English succession, and one in favour of which the whole of the English Catholics would be united. So far Elizabeth had only urged her to marry an English nobleman, with an implication that Leicester [Footnote: Dudley was not in fact raised to the Earldom till the year was well advanced.] was intended. Mary tried to extract approval for Darnley, but with the result only that Leicester was definitely and explicitly nominated. Yet even on behalf of her favourite, the English Queen would not commit herself on the subject of the succession. On the other hand, with the exception of Maitland of Lethington who was not actually opposed to the Darnley marriage on condition of Elizabeth's public approval, the Scottish Protestants were very unfavourable to that solution. So the year passed in perpetual diplomatic fencing, Mary trying to draw Darnley to Scotland, while Elizabeth kept him at her own court, to which he with both his parents had been attached for many years past. It is not a little curious to find all this intriguing crossed by a proposal from Katharine de Medici that King Charles should marry not Mary but Elizabeth, who was eighteen years his senior: while Elizabeth herself was trying to revive the idea of her own marriage with the Archduke Charles, whose brother Maximilian had just succeeded Ferdinand as Emperor. In February 1565, Elizabeth found it no longer possible to prevent Darnley's return to Scotland, and in April it was tentatively announced that he was to be Mary's husband.

[Sidenote: 1565 The Darnley marriage]

It is not impossible [Footnote: The case for this view is effectively put in Lang, *Hist. of Scotland*, ii., pp. 136 ff.; and *cf.* Creighton, *Queen Elizabeth*, p. 87.] that privately Elizabeth had expected and desired that Mary should jeopardise her position precisely in this manner, counting on the animosity to the marriage not only of Knox's party but of all the adherents of the rival house of Hamilton. If so she was justified in the event. But publicly she expressed a strong disapproval, which took colour from the risk that the marriage might serve to rally the English Catholics in support of the joint Stewart succession. At any rate, whether Mary merely miscalculated the political forces; or, weary of the shackles which preachers and politicians sought to impose on her, determined to take her own way at last at any cost; or allowed herself to be swayed by an unaccountable fancy for the person of her young cousin, a spoilt, arrogant, and vicious boy; marry him she did, at the end of July: in defiance of the sentiment of all her Protestant subjects, half of whom were really afraid of the attempted revival of Catholic domination, while the rest foresaw, at the best, the gravest political complications, and the revival of internecine clan and family feuds and intrigues. Mary however had not taken the step until she was sure in the first place that there was no prospect of her marriage with Don Carlos, and had in the second place received assurances of support from Philip [Footnote: *Cf.* Hume, *Love Affairs of Mary Queen of Scots*, p. 262. Mary was aiming at a Catholic combination under Philip, with the active co-operation of Rome. Cecil and Elizabeth however had good reason from experience to count on Spain's immobility, and may very well have counted also on Darnley's imbecility. They knew him.] if she married Darnley. For a girl of two and twenty, working single handed, it was an exceedingly clever move—on the hypothesis that Philip was capable of taking open action, and Darnley of acting with common decency and common intelligence.

[Sidenote: Mary and Murray]

The Protestant lords however were not unanimous. Maitland and the Douglases did not join Murray and the Hamiltons who, even before the actual marriage, were practically in open rebellion. But Mary was now playing for her own hand; if she had any trusted counsellor it was her deformed Italian secretary, David Rizzio. She dropped diplomatic fencing. Elizabeth, who had been privately sending money to Murray, remonstrated on his behalf; but Mary asserted her right to deal with her own rebellious subjects. Now, as always, she maintained that she had no intention of subverting the Protestant religion, though she desired the same freedom for Catholics as for Calvinists. But she would not submit to dictation; and any promises she was willing to make were conditional on the recognition first of herself and her heirs and afterwards of Lady Lennox's heirs, as Elizabeth's successors. At the end of August she marched against Murray and the insurgents; they however avoided battle. On October 6th Murray and his principal adherents crossed the Border. A little later he was allowed to present himself at the English court, where Elizabeth [Footnote: Froude, viii., pp. 213 ff. (Ed. 1864): with which cf. Lang, *Hist. Scotland*, ii., pp. 150 ff., and authorities there cited.] publicly rated him, and declared that she would never assist rebels against their lawful sovereign. Murray, who had just written to Cecil that he would "never have enterprised the action but that he had been moved thereto by the Queen" of England, accepted Elizabeth's lecture without protest.

[Sidenote: The murder of Rizzio, 1566]

The expulsion of Murray from Scotland did not hinder the coming tragedy; perhaps it had the contrary effect. The lords round Mary were bitterly aggrieved by Rizzio's influence; Darnley long before he was six months married, chose to be jealous of the secretary, a sentiment carefully fostered by the lords. The common hatred united them in a "band" for the murder of Rizzio, of which Sadler, the English envoy, was cognisant; Murray probably knew just so much as he chose to know. The plot was carried out in March. The conspirators broke into Mary's room at Holyrood, and butchered Rizzio almost before her eyes.

[Sidenote: Kirk o' Field, 1567]

It may be doubted whether Mary ever forgave any one who was implicated or supposed to be implicated in that outrage. For her husband, as the offence in him was foulest and the insult from him to her deepest, she assuredly conceived and cherished a bitter loathing. But there was one man who had always been ready to champion her cause, the daring, reckless, ruffianly James Hepburn, Earl of Bothwell, who nevertheless was no mere swash-buckler, but according to Scottish standards of the day, a man of education [Footnote: Lang, *Hist. Scotland*, ii., p. 168.] and even, it would seem, of some culture. From this time, Bothwell was her one ally. She had the policy and the self-control to profess a desire for reconciliation even with

Darnley: to receive Murray and even Lethington into apparent favour. But Darnley's brief rapprochement with the lords was soon over; his intolerable arrogance was made the worse by his contemptibility. Three months after Rizzio's murder, the envy of the Virgin Queen of England was roused by the birth of a son to Mary. The history of the following months becomes a chaos of which there are a dozen conflicting versions. The one clear fact is that another "band" was formed to put Darnley out of the way. There were pretences at attempted reconciliation between Mary and Darnley, while the Queen's relations with Bothwell were so intimate as to produce rumours no less scandalous than those which had prevailed about Elizabeth and Dudley. Darnley fell ill; a better appearance than usual of reconciliation was patched up. The sick man was conveyed to Kirk o' Field, a house near Edinburgh, where Mary joined him. Thence one evening she went to Holyrood to attend a bridal masque. That night the house was blown up; Darnley's unscathed corpse was found in the garden.

From the tangled mass [Footnote: The evidence has been discussed in many volumes. The most judicial examination with which the present writer is acquainted is that in Mr. Lang's *Mystery of Mary Stewart*, summarised in his *History of Scotland*, ii., pp. 168 ff.] of letters, narratives, and confessions, it remains, and will for ever remain, impossible to ascertain more than a fragment of the real truth. As to many of the documents, it is hard to say whether the theory of their genuineness or of their forgery is the more incredible. For the confessions, every man had a dozen good reasons for sheltering some of the guilty, implicating some of the innocent, and garbling the actual facts. That the thing was done by Bothwell is absolutely certain; it is hardly less doubtful that both Maitland and Morion helped to hatch the plot; there is no conclusive proof that Mary was active in it. No single act can be brought home to her which was necessarily incompatible with innocence—or with guilt. It is the accumulation of suspicious circumstances which makes the presumption lean heavily to guilt; but it remains no more than a presumption; no jury would have been justified in convicting. Her accusers had a strong case; but they tried to strengthen it by inventing or suborning additional evidence palpably false, with the result of discrediting the whole—and her friends adopted the same tactics. That both Mary and Murray knew that *some* plot existed, and that neither of them stirred a finger to frustrate it, is hardly an open question.

Guilty in the fullest sense or not guilty, Mary's detestation of Darnley was notorious; and within three months of the murder she was the wife of the man whom the whole world accounted the murderer. Naturally, the whole world believed that she was Bothwell's accomplice in the act, and his mistress before it. There was a show at least of the marriage being brought about by force. A formal attempt at investigation into the murder had collapsed. Bothwell had his supporters; he kidnapped the Queen and Maitland—*not* one of his supporters-with her. A scandalous divorce was pronounced between him and his wife, and Mary wedded him. The only credible explanation is that she was over-mastered by a passion for the daring ruffian who at least had always stood by her. The lords—accomplices in the murder with the rest—were almost immediately in arms to "rescue" the Queen, who took the field by her husband's side. The opposing forces met at Carberry Hill; Bothwell, seeing the contest to be hopeless, fled; Mary surrendered.

[Sidenote: Mary made prisoner]

The Queen was forthwith imprisoned in Lochleven Castle; and just at this time the famous casket of letters from Mary to Bothwell was seized, in the custody of a servant of Bothwell's. Of the documents subsequently produced as having formed part of that collection, the experts are totally unable to prove decisively whether any or all are genuine, or forged, or a mixture of forgeries and transcripts from genuine originals; though on the whole the last hypothesis is the least incredible of the three.

[Sidenote 1: Murray made regent]
[Sidenote 2: 1568 Mary's escape to England]

All this took place in June. Elizabeth was now suggesting that the baby prince James should be sent to her safe-keeping: there were similar hints—*mutatis mutandis*—from France. The Scots lords played off French and English against each other, and kept the child in their own hands. There was a strong desire in some quarters that Mary should be put to death; she was actually compelled, at the end of July, to sign her abdication in favour of the infant James. Soon after Murray arrived from France, whither he had gone shortly after the murder, and she assented to his appointment as Regent—indeed begged him to undertake it, having virtually no other course open. Both he and Lethington probably desired to protect her. Meantime however, Elizabeth was demanding her release, the successful rebellion of subjects against their lawful prince being by no means to her liking. Murray, however, felt that such a course could only involve civil war, and if pressed would force him to have Mary executed on the strength of the evidence, genuine or forged, of her complicity in the murder of Darnley. Yet it was universally believed that many of the lords now with Murray were no less guilty; over their heads too the sword was hanging by a thread. Murray as Regent ruled with vigour; and his enforcement of the anti-Catholic laws soon roused the hostility of that section. After many months of imprisonment, the Queen succeeded in escaping from Lochleven in May (1568); but the attempt to rally her followers was desperate. There was a fight at Langside on May 13th; Mary's party were completely routed; she herself fled south; and on May 16th she crossed the Solway; becoming, and remaining from thenceforth, Elizabeth's prisoner.

Thus, in June 1568, there was in France an uneasy truce between Catholics and Huguenots; in the Netherlands, the struggle between the Prince of Orange and Alva was just commencing; in Britain, the Queen of Scots had just fallen into the power of her sister of England—disgraced in the eyes of the world by her marriage with Bothwell, and on almost all hands credited with the murder of Darnley; so that whatever might happen it was certain that no foreign Power would have either the will or the means to intervene on her behalf.

The affairs of Ireland will demand our attention; but, as they did not at the time directly influence English policy, it will be more convenient to treat of them consecutively in a later chapter. The same may be said of the great sea-going movement, which was now active and was in a few years' time to be revealed as a feature of the first importance in the development of "our island story". Here we will merely note that the consideration of these subjects is deferred. The progress however of the religious settlement, always a present factor in the relations of England with other Powers, requires to be treated *pari passu* with the other events of the period; as also do the relations between the Queen and her Parliament.

[Sidenote: England: Protestantism of the Government]

We have already observed that Elizabeth had personal predilections in favour of the ceremonial, if not the actual theological, position adopted by her father. The weightiest of her counsellors however, headed by Cecil and Bacon, succeeded in a more definite protestantising of the bench of bishops than the Queen herself would have desired. The formularies of the Church, confirmed by the Act of Uniformity, were very much easier to reconcile with Calvinism than with what Calvinists called idolatry, and in particular the abolition of the law of celibacy in itself had a very strong tendency to abolish the sense of differentiation between clergy and laity so essential to the old Catholic position. It may have been the consciousness of this which made Elizabeth feel and express with much freedom her own objection to married clerics. But Cecil and his party were alive to the fact that the religious cleavage was everywhere becoming intensified as a political cleavage also; that politically, England would be obliged to declare for one side or the other, or would be rent in twain; that danger to Elizabeth's throne—and this she fully recognised herself— was much more likely to arise from Catholic than from Protestant quarters. Being therefore determined that she should take the Protestant side—whether from genuine religious conviction or from motives of political expediency—they steadily encouraged moderate Protestants of the type of Archbishop Parker, and others who were still more under the influence of the Swiss, or at least the Lutheran, reformers; a course in which they were greatly aided by the direct hostility to Elizabeth of the Guise party in France. In that country, the *Politiques* found themselves driven into the Catholic camp; in England, the Queen, whose personal sentiments were not unlike those of Katharine de Medici, was reluctantly compelled by the force of circumstances to yield to her Protestant advisers.

[Sidenote: Religious parties]

Elizabeth's first Parliament was puritan in its tendencies, and only fell short of that which had approved the second prayer-book of Edward. The bulk of the clergy still no doubt favoured the old religion, but it was the followers of the new lights who received promotion, and it was they who were encouraged by the Act of Uniformity. In many parts of the country, however, and especially in the North, the magnates countenanced a hardly veiled disregard of the new laws: and the Queen's apparent inclination to find a way of recognising Mary as her successor, as well as her favour for crosses and disfavour for married clergy, raised the hopes of the Catholics. The Huguenot war in 1562 compelled her to change her tone, and enabled Cecil to enforce the law against attendance at Mass with greater vigour. The first Parliament had been dissolved in 1559; the second, which met in the beginning of 1563, was not less strenuously Protestant and opposed to the Stewart succession. It was only the determined stand of the Catholic peers which prevented sharp legislation against the Catholics in general; and even as it was, the application of the oath of Supremacy was widened. Then Parliament was prorogued, and the affair of Havre caused the Huguenot alliance to cool. By the winter of 1564-5, the English Queen was irritating the bishops and the clergy, the most capable of whom were increasingly identifying themselves with puritan views, by insistence not altogether successful on obedience to the Act of Uniformity in the matter of vestments; although it was notorious that there was strong feeling against some of the regulations, which in not a few instances were habitually ignored. The feeling was intensified by a lively suspicion that she really wished for the Darnley marriage which actually took place a few months later, though she was professedly urging Leicester's suit, and beyond all doubt encouraged Murray and the Scottish Protestants to rebellion.

[Sidenote: 1566-67 Parliament and the Queen's marriage]

It was not till the autumn of 1566 that Parliament reassembled; more than ever determined to get the Queen committed to a marriage which should end the menace of the Stewart succession. This desire was in some cases the cause and in others the effect of a zealous protestantism. A Bill was introduced, at the instance of the Bishops acting on a vote of Convocation, to compel the clergy to subscribe the Thirty-nine Articles of Religion, a slight modification of Edward's Forty-two Articles; but this was withdrawn after passing the Commons. The Queen was enraged by the audacity of the Commons in discussing the question of her marriage and the succession, and she attempted to suppress debate; but was met with a stubborn insistence, headed by Cecil, on the constitutional rights of the House. Elizabeth had to give way; but while on the question of principle the Parliament was victorious, it did not press the victory and the Queen was enabled to evade the immediate issue. The house voted supplies generously, after which she succeeded in dissolving it with a sharp reprimand and without definitely committing herself on the subject either of her own marriage or of the succession. But this was hardly accomplished, when the murder of Darnley, for the time being at least, divided the party which had hitherto supported Mary's claim to the English throne.

[Sidenote: The Queen and the Archduke]

For some months, the question of Elizabeth's marriage was allowed to fall into abeyance; but the effect of the murder was in some degree counteracted by the imprisonment of Mary in Lochleven the appeal to chivalry of a deserted, helpless, and lovely woman, and the very unattractive character of most of the men now at the head of the Scottish Government. The Stewart cause seemed to be in some danger of reviving, and once again the English Council began to urge the marriage with the Archduke Charles. Elizabeth pretended concurrence, but when she refused to promise that Charles should be allowed the free exercise of his own religion in England, it was no longer possible to doubt that she was merely playing with the idea; while there were certainly a great many of her subjects who entirely sympathised with the ostensible grounds on which the negotiation was broken off. The prospect of a closer union with the House of Habsburg was dispelled, almost at the moment when the Scots Queen fell into Elizabeth's hands, and the standard of revolt against the Spanish system was being raised in the Netherlands.

CHAPTER XVIII
ELIZABETH (iii), 1568-72—THE
CATHOLIC CHALLENGE

[Sidenote: 1568 May, Elizabeth and Mary]

Before crossing the Solway, Mary wrote to Elizabeth throwing herself on her hospitality. She followed hard on the heels of her missive, and awaited the reply at Carlisle, where the Catholic gentlemen of the North rallied to receive her. The situation indeed was a singularly embarrassing one for the English Queen. Mary claimed in fact that Elizabeth should either restore her, or allow her to appeal to those who would do so—that is, to France. To take her part unconditionally had its obvious dangers; not less obvious were the dangers of acceding to the alternative demand. To detain her in England, on the other hand, would inevitably make her the centre of Catholic intrigue. The most convenient arrangement would be to restore her under conditions which would minimise her power of becoming dangerous; and, in the meantime, she was perhaps less to be feared under careful supervision in England than anywhere else. So Elizabeth took the line of informing her that if she cleared herself of the charges of crimes such as made it impossible to support her if she were guilty, she should be restored; which being interpreted meant that there was to be an investigation, and Elizabeth would act on the findings. Murray on the other hand was in effect advised that the English Queen would not countenance him in levying war but that he might read between the lines of her instructions; in view of course of the fear that the party opposed to Murray might seek to procure French intervention.

[Sidenote: A Commission of enquiry]

Elizabeth was in fact in a position to dictate her own terms. Whatever right she might think fit to assume, whatever technical grounds she might assert for that right, Mary was effectively in her power. The Scots Queen— transferred for greater safety to Bolton, away from the dangerous proximity of the Border—indignantly repudiated the jurisdiction, demanded to be set at liberty, asseverated her own innocence. Elizabeth could not afford to set her at liberty; and with some plausibility declared that the innocence must be proved, before her rule could be re-imposed on a nation which had rejected it. Elizabeth quite evidently intended that the investigation should neither clear nor condemn her. Mary's objections were perfectly compatible with innocence. Submission might be taken as implying the recognition of English suzerainty; and if the investigation was to be earned just so far as suited her sister sovereign, if evidence was to be admitted, tested, or suppressed, with a view not to ascertaining truth but to securing a convenient judgment, innocence was no sort of reason for welcoming enquiry. [Footnote: Mr Froude (viii., Ed. 1866) informs us in one breath that Mary was impelled to protest by the consciousness of guilt (p. 253), but admits in the next that Elizabeth had no intention of allowing either her guilt or her innocence to be definitely proved (pp. 262, 270, 277).]

The plan of operations was that a Commission should be appointed, before whom the Scots lords should answer for their rebellion; obviously they would defend themselves on the ground of Mary's guilt of which they professed to hold ample proof in the casket of letters, which if genuine were assuredly damning. On the other hand, Maitland and others of the lords must have suspected at least that evidence of their own complicity in Darnley's murder would be forthcoming. The English Protestants were convinced beforehand of Mary's guilt; they were too much interested in preventing her succession to the English throne to form an unbiased judgment; whereas her condemnation would have been a serious blow to the Catholic party, which included professing Protestants like Norfolk. Altogether, what Elizabeth desired was a compromise between Mary and the Scots lords, by which both should assent to her restoration as queen with Murray as actual ruler, coupled with the confirmation of the unratified Treaty of Edinburgh, and the establishment of the Anglican form of worship as Elizabeth's price. Her real difficulty perhaps was that she did not want Mary cleared to the world by the definite withdrawal of the charge of murder; she wanted the charge to be made and to be left indefinitely not-proven.

[Sidenote: Oct. Proceedings at York]

The commission—Norfolk, Sussex, and Sadler, who had spent many years in Scotland as ambassador—was to sit at York in October. Thither came the Scots lords. Murray was prepared to rely upon the general charges of misgovernment, while privately submitting the evidence as to the murder to the Commissioners. Norfolk was staggered by the letters, and very nearly threw up a scheme which the Catholic party had been hatching for his own marriage with Mary. But Elizabeth's sudden discovery that this scheme existed filled her with alarm, and for the moment she cancelled the Commission.

For the course of events on the Continent was making the outlook more complicated. The initial success of the Netherlanders had been very soon followed by the crushing disaster of Jemmingen, and the country seemed to be under Alva's heel. Catholicism in its most militant and merciless form was predominant; what if Philip, irritated by the practically open piracy of English ships in the Channel and elsewhere, should espouse the cause of Mary? De Silva, the ambassador whose relations with the English court were highly satisfactory, was replaced by the less diplomatic and more aggressive Don Guerau de Espes. The English envoy in Spain was so unguarded in his own religious professions as to give Philip fair ground for handing him his passports. If the English Catholics, irritated by the growth of Calvinism and the increased vigilance of Protestantism in England, founded new hopes on these signs of a changing attitude in Philip, their present loyalty might very soon alter its colour with Mary Stewart in England.

It seemed safer then that the enquiry should be held in London, with a large increase in the number of the Commissioners. Of the Scots lords, Lethington was undoubtedly anxious that the murder charge should be withdrawn. Nevertheless, at the sitting held at the end of November, Murray definitely put in the charge, producing copies or translations of the Casket Letters. These the commissioners examined; later on, they were shown the originals, which they judged to be genuine documents in the Queen's hand. Whether they were competent to test forgeries executed with tolerable skill is at least open to question. The rest of the evidence produced was not only that of interested persons, but contained inconsistencies; neither Mary herself nor her agents were ever put in possession of copies of the incriminating documents; one side only was heard. If it was Elizabeth's object to create in the minds of the English lords a strong presumption that Mary was guilty, that purpose was successfully effected. Under such conditions Mary declined compromises. The Commission was broken up. The farce was over. Murray returned to Scotland: the Queen remained a prisoner in England, to be—with or without her own complicity—the centre of every papist plot till the final tragedy.

So the mystery of Mary Stewart remains a mystery to this day. That she was cognisant of the plot to murder Darnley is the more probable theory, in view of facts which no one denies; yet those facts remain intelligible if she was innocent. There are no admitted facts which preclude her guilt: none which prove it conclusively. The various confessions of interested witnesses, voluntary or extorted, are untrustworthy. The genuineness of the Casket Letters is doubtful. No opportunity was given for cross-examining the witnesses or examining the letters. The world believed that Mary was guilty, however it may have been disposed to condone the guilt. The world was probably right. But to pretend that there was a fair or complete investigation—that Mary's guilt was proved before the Commission—is absurd. That Mary from first to last protested against being brought to the bar of an English tribunal—whose authority she could not acknowledge without implying a recognition of that suzerainty which Edward I of England had claimed, and Robert I of Scotland had wiped out at Bannockburn—was entirely compatible with the innocence of a high-spirited and courageous princess: and would have been so, even if she could have counted on the absolute impartiality of her judges. Knowing that she could count on nothing of the kind, fully aware that Elizabeth herself would in fact be the judge, and suspecting with very good reason that any verdict pronounced by her would be shaped strictly with a view to her own political convenience, it is almost inconceivable that Mary should have acknowledged the jurisdiction merely because Innocence in the abstract ought to invite enquiry. Had Mary been less beautiful, less unfortunate, less of a heroine of romance, it is likely enough that she would find few champions; but the pretence that she had a fair trial would still be none the less untenable.

[Sidenote: Dec. Seizure of Spanish Treasure]

In the meantime, an incident had occurred which shows what an immense change had been taking place in England during the ten years of Elizabeth's reign; how completely the nation had recovered confidence in itself. Throughout these years, English ships had been multiplying, English sailors had been ignoring the Spanish and Portuguese monopolies of ocean traffic, and English captains had been, with only the most perfunctory official discouragement, and under colour of the flimsiest pretexts or of no pretext at all, indulging in what was virtually piracy. Now, the religious struggle, after a few months' smouldering, had again broken out in France. La Rochelle, the Huguenot head-quarters, was a nest of privateers, with whom the English adventurers consorted, and the water-way for Spanish ships to the Netherlands was infested with dangers. Alva was in want of money. Philip borrowed a great sum from the Genoese bankers. The vessels conveying the bullion were forced to put into English ports, in fear of capture. Elizabeth was not ready to declare war in favour of the revolted provinces; but Cecil was extremely anxious to render them all the help possible short of declaring war. The treasure-ships had sailed into a trap. Don Guerau invited Elizabeth to send them on under escort to the Netherlands; she replied that as the money belonged not to Philip but to the

Genoese bankers, who would not object, she intended to borrow it herself. Don Guerau was furious, and sent messages to Alva, who promptly seized all English goods and persons in the Netherlands. With equal promptitude, all Spaniards and Spanish goods were seized in England. The balance of loss was heavily in favour of the English.

It seemed most probable that this astonishingly audacious proceeding must result either in the fall of Cecil, to whom it was due, or in open war with Spain, and the immediate committal of England to the formation of a Protestant League; which might force the English Catholics in their turn directly to espouse the cause of Mary. The reception given in this country shortly before to the Cardinal of Chatillon, Coligny's brother, was a symptom of Cecil's Protestant policy, and he at least was probably willing enough that any tendency of the English Catholics towards revolt should be precipitated rather than delayed.

[Sidenote: 1569 The incident passed over]

Even Cecil however was not anxious for open war, while Elizabeth always shrank from that last extremity. On the other side, Philip had three very good reasons for passing over the affront he had received. First, the Netherlands were giving him enough to do for the time. Secondly, Don Guerau was satisfied that the downfall of Cecil and the reversal of his policy were imminent. Thirdly, the French court would assuredly subordinate religious questions to the political gain of uniting with England against him. A definite league between Condé and the English might have averted that danger, by driving the French Catholics to make common cause with Spain; but any immediate prospect of such a solution of the entanglement vanished when the Huguenots were defeated and Condé himself killed at the battle of Jarnac in May. The result of that event was the immediate prohibition of the English adventurers from joining the Huguenot fleet of Rochelle and sailing under the Huguenot flag; as many of them had been in the habit of doing.

In May, then, the risk of a rupture between the French Government and England, and of the formation of a universal Protestant league, was over for the time at least; and within a few months, in England, the Northern Earls, by a premature rising, inflicted a severe blow on their own party, and decided large numbers of the Catholics to take their stand as in the first place patriots and loyalists.

[Sidenote: The Northern Rebellion]

What we have called the Catholic party included many professing Protestants—*i.e.* men who conformed with entire equanimity, yet would have preferred to see the old worship restored; such as Norfolk. Extreme men saw in the union of the Duke with Mary a prospect of immediately placing the captive Queen on the English throne. The moderate men wanted the marriage, accompanied by her recognition as heir presumptive. There were others outside the Catholic connexion who dreamed rather of Mary under the circumstances conforming to the Anglican faith. Norfolk dallied with all three. There was a moment when Elizabeth herself might have been persuaded to assent; but the Duke missed his opportunity, and she, reverting to a conviction that the marriage would soon be followed by her own assassination, presently forbade it, and summoned Norfolk to answer for his loyalty. After brief hesitation he surrendered himself and was confined in the Tower: but the Northern Earls, Northumberland and Westmorland, believing that they must strike at once if at all, rose and marched to deliver Mary from Tutbury—whither she had been suddenly conveyed to safe keeping, in the expectation of some such event. The rest of the Catholics however were not ready for such a venture; being forced to make up their minds, they resolved to stand loyal. The royal musters were quickly advancing to meet the insurgents, who presently concluded that the cause was hopeless, and fled. Northumberland was subsequently arrested and detained by Murray in Scotland: Westmorland made his way to Spain. Sussex received and carried out orders to punish with a heavy hand those who had taken part in the rebellion; and so without any great difficulty the one serious revolt of the reign was stamped out.

[Sidenote: 1570 Murder of Murray]

The year 1570 had hardly opened when Elizabeth lost one of her most valuable allies by the murder of the Regent Murray, assassinated by Hamilton of Bothwellhaugh. Murray's figure in history is a sombre one, and the sombreness is thrown into the greater relief by the picturesque brilliancy of his hapless sister. It was his fate to fight on the gloomy side; to stand at the head of a nobility conspicuously sordid and unprincipled, half of whom, when not occupied in plotting against the life of a hereditary foe or a political rival, were posing as representatives of the "godly"—an attitude held to be entirely compatible with a total disregard for the decalogue. Perhaps there is no prominent statesman of his times who came through the heavy ordeal of public life with cleaner hands. There is no fair ground for associating him directly and actively with any of the great crimes in one or another of which almost every one of the Scots lords had a share. When his sister married Darnley, he took up arms against her: he did so again when she married Bothwell: and on both occasions he was probably obeying an elastic conscience. While he was endeavouring to fix the odium of the Darnley murder on Mary, he must have been quite aware that both Lethington and Morton, his allies, were steeped in the guilt of it. But he could neither stand aside from the turmoil, nor pick and choose his associates. The political support or countenance of Elizabeth seemed absolutely necessary to the cause of the Reformation in Scotland. A man of a more generous spirit would more than once have felt that the price was too high, that he was accepting a too ignominious position; he stooped to a course which if not exactly dishonourable was perilously near it. But the part he was forced to play was the hardest and the most thankless imaginable; and he played it with a constant effort to be tolerant, to be as just as circumstances permitted, to be true to himself. He was the one man in Scotland who had striven resolutely amid the kaleidoscopic chaos of factions to maintain some sort of order, some sort of liberty, some sort of standard of public spirit. With his fall, anarchy became more rampant than ever. Elizabeth lamented, not without reason, that she had lost her best friend; but while he lived she had not made his task the easier.

[Sidenote: March The Bull of Deposition]

In March, the Pope took the step which paralysed Catholicism as an open political force in England, by issuing a Bull against Elizabeth which virtually declared loyalty to the Queen and loyalty to the Faith to be incompatible; yet since the profession of loyalty was to be condoned, every Catholic was *ipso facto* rendered suspect. The suspicion of disloyalty breeds the disease. Englishmen of the Roman Communion have a right to be proud that so many in those years of storm and stress neither relinquished their faith nor forgot their patriotism; yet when their fellow-subjects had been thus absolved of their allegiance, the Protestants can hardly be blamed for being over-ready to assume that they were in league with the Queen's enemies. The Pope could have done nothing calculated more thoroughly to translate the ordinary sentiment of loyalty into a passion of resentment against its opposite.

[Sidenote: The Anjou Match]

The immediate situation however was fraught with sufficient peril. Mary for the sake of liberty was by this time fairly ready to promise anything, and trust to the chapter of accidents to find some plausible ground for repudiating her promises later. Elizabeth would have been glad enough to get her out of the country if she could by any means be rendered harmless. Once again, to the dismay of Cecil, a restoration, on terms, seemed probable, while the Queen herself showed a tendency to try at any cost to recover the support of the Catholics. In fact however, she would make up her mind to no decided course. But affairs in France suggested to her a new scheme which could be played with indefinitely. In spite of Jarnac, and of another defeat later in the year at Montcontour, Coligny and the Huguenots remained unvanquished in 1570. In the autumn, there was a fresh pacification, and Coligny became once more a power at Court as well as in the country. The younger brother of the young French King, Henry Duke of Anjou, was now old enough to marry. There had been talk of uniting him to Mary. But if he were to marry Elizabeth, who was only some seventeen years his senior, Protestants and Catholics in both countries might make their peace, and all present a united front to Philip and to Papal aggression—for even the Cardinal of Lorraine had dallied with the notion of Nationalism in matters ecclesiastical. Cecil and Walsingham, who had recently come to the front and now represented England in Paris, were keenly in favour of the scheme. As for the Queen she probably intended to use it precisely as she had used all the previous marriage schemes, simply as an instrument for manipulating foreign courts and her own ministers.

[Sidenote: 1570-71 The Ridolfi plot initiated]

Under these conditions, a new plot was initiated for the liberation of Mary, her marriage to Norfolk, and the removal of Elizabeth; to be at last actively if secretly aided by Alva and Philip, on whom the vehement remonstrances of the Pope were now taking effect—in view of the threatened alliance between England and France. The agent was one Ridolfi, who combined cleverness sufficient to deceive even Walsingham for a time with a garrulity and carelessness which proved ruinous in the long run. It was fortunate for Elizabeth that of the two necessary figure-heads for any conspiracy, Mary and Norfolk, one was more than half-believed even by her own party to be stained by the grossest crimes, while the other was nerveless and vacillating.

[Sidenote: 1571 April, Parliament]

At this juncture, need of funds made it impossible for Elizabeth to continue longer without calling a Parliament, which met early in April (1571). The bulk of the peers were still in sympathy with Catholicism and the ideas associated therewith; the lower House, always Protestant, was now more emphatically so than ever. The Puritan element, naturally enough, had come to regard Catholicism as *prima facie* evidence of treason, and was bent on enforcing a more uncompromising conformity, with a greater severity, than heretofore. The Commons insisted on discussing religious matters, and ignored the Queen's attempts to silence them. They gave, what the last parliament had refused, their sanction to the Thirty-nine Articles. The effect of the Papal excommunication was seen in an Act making it high Treason to question the Queen's title, or to call her a heretic, and disqualifying from the succession any one who laid claim to the crown; they sought even to make the Act retrospective, which would have forthwith excluded Mary permanently. They submitted however to some modification of the original harshness of their intentions; whereby it is probable that not a few Catholics, who would otherwise have been fatally alienated, did as matters turned out remain loyal. Finally, a substantial grant of money was made. The Commons in short were thoroughly at one with Cecil, now known as Lord Burghley. They were intensely loyal, and showed their loyalty none the less emphatically because they ignored the Queen's predilections in the manner of doing it.

[Sidenote: Collapse of Anjou marriage]

At the end of May, Parliament was dissolved. In the meantime, and for some months longer, the affair of the Anjou marriage was running the usual course. As mere postponement seemed to become impossible, the old pretended difficulties by which the Archduke Charles had been finally evaded were rehabilitated. Anjou must not have even his private Mass. The Queen's Ministers understood the position, and their one object became the avoidance of a breach with France. By the exercise of much dexterity, Anjou was drawn into taking the initiative in breaking off the match in a quite complimentary manner; and there was even discussion of the substitution for him of his still younger brother Alençon. France, in fact, at this time was swaying strongly towards antagonism to Spain, at any price which would secure English support; the idea of partitioning the Netherlands being part of the programme. Cecil and Walsingham, believing with reason that an accident might again turn the balance with the French government, and painfully distrustful of Elizabeth's endless vacillations, were on tenterhooks till the amicable conclusion of the Anjou affair.

[Sidenote: Developments of the Ridolfi plot]

They had also been on the alert over the Ridolfi plot. In the spring, Ridolfi was concocting with Alva designs for an invasion; in the summer he was in Spain. In the meantime, the capture of an agent, and the liberal use of spies and of the rack, placed important clues in Burghley's hands. At this juncture the famous seaman Sir John Hawkins, in collusion with Burghley, placed himself at the service of Mary and Philip, in the character of an ill-used and revengeful servant of Elizabeth. Yet it was only by another accidental capture, and more use of the rack, that complicity was actually brought home to Norfolk, who was arrested in September. Norfolk once arrested, traitors and spies soon did what else was necessary to reveal the whole plot, in which invasion and assassination were combined. It was no longer possible to account Spain and the Spanish King as anything but mortal enemies to England and the English Queen. Don Guerau was ordered to leave the country; his parting move was a plot for Burghley's assassination, duly detected by spies, Norfolk was convicted for treason, and condemned to a death which was deferred for some months. Mary Stewart expected a like fate. Elizabeth however still rejected the extreme measure. But the *Detectio* of George Buchanan—in other words a complete *ex parte* statement of the case against Mary, including the contents of the Casket Letters—was published.

[Sidenote: 1572 Parliament and Mary (May)]

The effect was seen when a new Parliament met in May. The people of England believed with an absolute conviction in the truth of the whole indictment against the Scots Queen. Nor was there any question that she had appealed both to France and Spain to liberate her; so far at least she was implicated in the Ridolfi plot, even if the assassination proposals had not come within her ken. She was believed to be a criminal, who had forfeited all right to sympathy and consideration; she was palpably a standing menace to the internal peace of the realm, a standing incitement to its enemies abroad. The Commons therefore demanded her attainder; as for the technical right, no sovereign at the time or in the past would have hesitated to ignore or evade the point. The question was outside the range of technicalities. The plea that England had no right to detain her, or to judge her, that she had a right to seek her own release by any available means, was perfectly sound; the counter-plea that the safety of the State forbade her release, and her attempts to procure war against it justified her destruction, was equally unanswerable. But Elizabeth could not resolve to act upon either plea, ignoring the other. So Mary remained a prisoner, and the centre of intrigue. Even an alternative Bill, supposed to have Elizabeth's approval, which merely excluded Mary from the succession, never reached the statute book.

[Sidenote: Lepanto; April Revolt of the Netherlands]

A notable triumph had recently been achieved for Philip's arms, in the crushing defeat of the Turks at Lepanto by the combined Venetian and Spanish fleets commanded by the Spanish King's half-brother, Don John of Austria. To this perhaps may be attributed the less defiant tone of communications with Spain. The narrow seas were swarming not only with English privateering craft, but with Dutchmen commanded by the privateer De la Marck on behalf of William of Orange, who were habitually succoured in English harbours. But though these were now ordered to depart, and the English mariners aboard them were commanded to leave them, there is no doubt that their privy equipment was deliberately connived at, in the flattest possible contradiction to the public declarations. At the close of March, De la Marck's fleet sailed from Dover to fall upon a Spanish convoy; a few days later, it appeared in the Meuse before Brille. The town promptly surrendered. The whole of the Netherlands was seething under Alva's savage rule; trade, already in a fair way to be ruined by the cessation of commerce with England since the seizure of the treasure ships, was being throttled also by the system of taxation which Alva had recently instituted. The capture of Brille fired the train. City after city raised the standard of revolt. The rebellion which Alva fancied he had utterly stamped out was suddenly in full blaze once more; and on the south, Mons, like Brille, was seized by a rapid dash of Lewis of Nassau, operating from French territory.

[Sidenote: The Alençon marriage]

In the meantime also the Alençon marriage project seemed to be advancing, and in April a defensive treaty was struck between England and France, where it appeared that Coligny was paramount at court. Both English and French volunteers were fighting in the Netherlands. Small wonder that Burghley and Walsingham believed that a French marriage would clinch matters, make France a virtually Huguenot Power, and secure a combination which would bring the Pope and the King of Spain to their knees. The approaching marriage of the French King's sister, Margaret, to young Henry of Navarre—now standing next after the King's brothers in the line of succession—pointed emphatically in the same direction.

Walsingham however also knew that, to achieve the desired end, the Huguenots must at once have convincing proofs that they could depend on the English alliance. The marriage, and concerted armed intervention in the Netherlands, were the conditions. But Alençon [Footnote: He was singularly ugly, and Elizabeth who had nicknames for many of her Court, used to call him her "Frog" when he was wooing her, later.] was an incredibly distasteful husband; and however near Elizabeth might suffer herself to be brought to the brink of war, she hung back when the time came. There was very good reason [Footnote: *State Papers: Spanish,* ii., 338.] for believing that even now she was secretly negotiating with Alva, and in a very short time the English and French volunteer contingents in Flushing [Footnote: *S.P., Foreign,* x., 491, 530.] were on the verge of hostilities. The power of the Huguenots was on the surface; fanatics themselves when their religion was not merely political, they were the objects of savagely fanatical hatred. The queen-mother, who had always striven to preserve her own domination by holding the balance between Guises and Huguenots, saw Charles falling more and more under Coligny's influence instead of her own. It may be that if she had felt sure of Elizabeth, she would have gone through with the proposed policy; distrusting the English Queen she resolved to end it. She made a desperate and successful attempt to recover her ascendancy over her weak-minded son. She played upon his terrors, and prepared for one of the most appalling tragedies in all history.

A plot for the assassination of Coligny failed, the Admiral being but slightly wounded. Paris was full of Huguenots, who had gathered for the celebration of Navarre's marriage on August 18th; the attempt on Coligny led to threatening language against the Guises. Katharine stirred her son into a sudden panic. The attack on the Admiral had taken place on August 22nd; with the booming of a bell on the early morning of the 24th, St. Bartholomew's day, the most recklessly devastating mob in the world found itself let loose on its prey, headed and urged on by the Guises and other Catholic chiefs. The Huguenots, utterly surprised, were slaughtered from house to house; with the taste of blood the populace went mad; Paris was a shambles. How many thousands were massacred in that awful frenzy none can tell. The tale of the tragedy flew from end to end of France; all over the country, wherever the Catholics were in a majority, like scenes were enacted. The total of the victims has been computed as high as a hundred thousand; a fourth of that number would certainly not be an exaggerated estimate. In England, all the martyrs for religion in the century did not amount to a thousand, on both sides; in France, twenty thousand at least were slain in a few days' orgy of fanaticism. And the new Pope Gregory sang *Te Deum* in solemn state; and the morose monarch of Spain laughed aloud in unwonted glee; but Charles of France, men said, was haunted to the hour of his death by red visions of that ghastly carnival of blood.

CHAPTER XIX
ELIZABETH (iv), 1572-78—
VARIUM ET MUTABILE

[Sidenote: The Queen's diplomacy]

The picture of Elizabeth and of her surroundings hitherto presented in these pages has been one which rouses rather a reluctant admiration for a combination of good fortune and dexterity than a moral enthusiasm. Statesmen, in fact, had to pick their way with such extreme wariness through such a labyrinth of intrigues that little play was permitted to their more generous instincts; and it is undeniable that Elizabeth herself loved intricate methods, and made it quite unnecessarily difficult for her ministers to pursue a straightforward course. This is the aspect of the national life which is inevitably forced on our attention—the diplomatic aspect in an age when diplomacy was playing an immense part in public affairs. For England, it might almost be said that diplomatic methods had been created by Henry VII., maintained by Wolsey, dropped again for thirty years, and then re-created by Elizabeth. As Wolsey had played France and the Empire against each other, to make England the arbiter of Europe, so Elizabeth played France and Spain against each other, so that neither could afford to go beyond empty threats against her in her own territory; while both governments had recalcitrant Protestant subjects who were a good deal more hampering and disquieting to them than were Elizabeth's Catholic subjects to her. In Scotland, Elizabeth's policy, like her father's, was that of maintaining factions which kept the country divided.

Now the persons with whom Elizabeth had to deal were for the most part perfectly unscrupulous. The Queen-mother in France, the Scots lords, Philip of Spain, and the Spanish ambassadors with the exception of De Silva, were as ready to make and ignore promises and professions as was Elizabeth herself. If they found her fully a match for them at their own game, we can hardly reproach her if we cannot applaud. But it is notable that in England, the arch-dissembler is Elizabeth herself. It is she who manages the undignified but eminently successful trickery of the marriage negotiations. It is she who evades committing herself irrevocably to the Huguenots or to the

Prince of Orange. It is she who preserves Mary's restoration as a possibility, to be held *in terrorem* over Scotland after publishing her accusers' evidence against her.

[Sidenote: The Queen's subjects]

But the success of this supreme wiliness, a quality in which perhaps Elizabeth's one rival was Lethington, was due to the presence in her ministers and in her people of moral qualities which she did not herself display. First and foremost was their loyalty to her. They acted boldly on secret instructions, with entire certainty that they must take the whole responsibility upon themselves; that to be pardoned for success was the highest official recognition they could hope for; that flat repudiation and probable ruin would follow failure. Burghley in particular repeatedly risked favour to save the Queen from herself, when her vacillation, calculated or not, was on the verge of being carried too far; nor was he alone in speaking his mind; yet in spite of merciless snubs his fidelity was unimpaired; none of her enemies ever dreamed for an instant that he could be tampered with. Nor did it ever appear that more than a very few even among the most discontented of her subjects would lend themselves to open disloyalty. In England, there were almost none who would have anything to say to the political assassinations which repeatedly stained the annals of the nations of the Continent and of Scotland: a peculiarity remarked on in the Spanish correspondence.

Again, the religious tone and temper of the country were in striking contrast to those prevailing where the Reformation assumed the Calvinistic model. In France and in Scotland, Protestants and Catholics were ready to fly at each other's throats; in England that inclination was confined to extremists of either party. The bulk of the population was quite content with conformity to a compromise, and was tolerant of a very considerable theoretical disagreement, and even of actual nonconformity, so long as it was not actively aggressive. It was not till Jesuits on one side, and ultra-puritans on the other, developed an active propaganda directed against the established order, that there was any general desire to strike hard at either; nor did even the puritan parliaments display any violent anti-Catholic animus till roused by the insult to the nation of the Bull of Deposition.

[Sidenote: Development of Protestantism]

While the characteristically English love of compromise and devotion to conventions kept the bulk of the population loyal to the established Forms of religion, acquiescent but not enthusiastic, their normal conservatism also disposed them more favourably to teachers of the old than of the innovating school; but other forces were at work, which encouraged the growth of what may be called the Old Testament spirit of militant religiosity directed against Rome and all that savoured of Rome. Stories of the doings of the Inquisition, the enormities perpetrated by Alva in the Netherlands, the fate of English sailors who might, not without justice, have been punished for piracy, but were in fact made to suffer on the ground of heresy, the crowning horror of St. Bartholomew, appealed luridly to the popular imagination. The country was threatened with internal discord by the presence of a Catholic aspirant to the throne, which concentrated the forces of disorganisation on the Catholic side. Protestantism, thereby at once extended and intensified, took its colour from the most active and energetic of the religious teachers, and developed a vehement popular sympathy with the French Huguenots and the revolting Netherlanders; and however politicians might evade official entanglement, English sentiment—at any rate after St. Bartholomew—was always ready to take arms openly in the Protestant cause.

[Sidenote: Katharine de Medici]

When Katharine and the Guises let the Paris mob loose on the Huguenots, they had doubtless no intention of perpetrating so vast a slaughter. They found that it was one thing to cry "Havoc" and quite another to cry "Halt". When the thing was done, they could not have disavowed it wholly, even if they would. Katharine however made desperate efforts to minimise her own responsibility, and to justify what she had done by charges of treason against the murdered admiral and his associates. She had in fact meant to cripple the Huguenots by destroying their leaders, yet to provide a defence sufficiently plausible to prevent a breach with England. Her object had been to recover her own ascendancy in France, not to replace Coligny by the Guises. What she succeeded in doing was to turn France into two hostile camps; since the massacres had not sufficed to destroy the Huguenot power of offering an organised defence and defiance. On the other hand Alva was prompt, and Philip as prompt as his nature permitted, to realise that some capital might be made out of the revulsion in England against the French Government.

[Sidenote: The aim of Elizabeth]

Walsingham, the English Ambassador in Paris, was a sincere Puritan; Burghley's sympathies, personal as well as political, were strongly Protestant. For some time past, both had desired on the mere grounds of political expediency to bid defiance to Spain and frankly avow the cause of the Prince of Orange. They believed that England was already strong enough to face the might of Philip. The moral incentive was now infinitely stronger. That this would be the generous and the courageous course was manifest. Now, too, the English people would have adopted it with a stern enthusiasm worth many ships and many battalions. The course Elizabeth adopted was less heroic, more selfish, safer for the interests of England. That sooner or later a duel with Spain was all but inevitable she must have recognised; but she had seen the power and wealth of England growing year by year, the stability of the Government becoming ever more assured; if an immediate collision could be averted, she calculated that the process would continue, whereas the strain of repressing and holding down the Netherlanders would tell adversely on the power of Spain. The longer, therefore, that the struggle could be staved off, the better.

Fortune favoured her: for the resistance of the Netherlands was very much more stubborn than could have been anticipated. The Protestant fervour in her people, aroused by St. Bartholomew, was kept alive and intensified, as time went on, by other events, and was moreover concentrated upon animosity to Spain. When the great conflict took place, sixteen years later, its result was decisive. It cannot be affirmed with confidence that it would have been so now. From the prudential point of view, Elizabeth was justified by the event. But it is at least possible that the victory would have been equally decisive at the earlier date, and its moral value in that case would undoubtedly have been greater.

[Sidenote: 1572 England and St. Bartholomew]

At the first moment when intelligence of the massacre at Paris was brought to England, the Queen as well as her ministers believed that it was simply the prelude to a Romanist crusade. It was imagined that the plot had been concocted in collusion with Philip and Alva, the outcome of the suspected Catholic League of 1565. Instant preparations were made for war; the musters were called out, the fleet was manned, troops were raised in readiness to embark for Flushing; and immediate overtures were made to Mar—the second Regent in Scotland since the murder of Murray—for handing Mary over to him to be executed. The popular indignation was expressed in bold and uncompromising terms by Walsingham in Paris, in answer to the attempts of the French Government to excuse itself. In England, it was long before the Queen would admit the French Ambassador to audience; when she did so, her Council was in presence; all were clad in mourning; Elizabeth spoke in terms of the most formal frigidity; on her withdrawal, Burghley, speaking for the Council, expressed their sentiments in very plain language. It is abundantly clear that the whole nation from the Queen down was grimly and confidently prepared for war if war should come.

[Sideline: Spain seeks amity]

But war was not to come. Katharine was not in collusion with Philip; she knew well enough that as things stood, in such an alliance France would begin in a subordinate position, and success would only accentuate and render overwhelming the predominance of Spain. Her one desire was to patch up a reconciliation with England. Alva had no illusions about a Catholic crusade; he only rejoiced that the danger of an Anglo-French coalition was scotched; and only desired to make sure that Elizabeth, left to herself, should not make his task in the Netherlands more difficult. Therefore he strove strenuously, and with ultimate success, to impress the same view of affairs on the slowly moving mind of his master at Madrid, who was at first bitten with the idea of effecting a Catholic revolution in England and marrying Mary to Anjou.

So when Mons, with Lewis of Nassau in it, was forced to capitulate, Alva, by way of contrast to the massacre at Paris, allowed the Huguenots to march out with the honours of war—ostentatiously reversing his usual merciless policy: and he pointedly adopted the most conciliatory attitude towards England.

[Sidenote: 1573]

Elizabeth for her part was ready enough to respond. A renewal of the commercial relations in the Netherlands was eminently desirable. The war going on in that country was not to her own taste; politically and theologically she thought the example of the Netherlanders dangerous— one of the real reasons which helped to make her hold back from espousing their cause—and she offered to mediate between Alva and William of Orange, expressing readiness for her own part to have a settlement of all the outstanding grievances between Spain and England. She even went so far as to revive the suggestion of a really representative Council, for the purpose of arriving at a general religious settlement—-a suggestion so entirely impracticable that it was quite safe to make it. Also with regard to some of the grievances, it was tolerably certain that no solution could be offered in which both the parties would acquiesce. But the fundamental thing, both in her eyes and in Alva's, was to revive the old status of amity, officially if also superficially.

[Sidenote: April: A Spanish alliance]

Finally, in spite of the remonstrances of the Pope and the protests of the English Catholic exiles of the Northern Rebellion, who had found an asylum in the Netherlands under the aegis of Spain, a provisional alliance was effected, to last for two years, in April 1573. Spain deserted the English revolutionary Catholics; Elizabeth recalled the English volunteers from Flanders; and commerce was restored. There was a brief lull in the piratical activity of English sailors; and the French were officially left alone to settle the domestic hostilities which afforded them a quite sufficient occupation.

[Sidenote: Scotland: End of the Marians]

By this time, too, the last serious struggle of the Marian party in Scotland was entering on its final stage. There, after Murray's death, the Hamiltons, joined by Lethington and Kirkcaldy of Grange, refused to acknowledge the young King, or the authority of the Regency—-an office in which Murray was succeeded first by the incompetent Lennox, and afterwards by Mar, Lennox being killed in the course of a fight. Finally Lethington and Grange were shut up in Edinburgh Castle, where they continued to bid defiance to the Government. When however overtures were made by England for the delivery of Mary to Mar for execution, the negotiation broke down on the question of Responsibility. Mar would not carry out the extreme measure, unless supported by English troops and by the presence of high English officials. Elizabeth as usual insisted, in effect, that she must be able to repudiate complicity. As the fear of a combined Catholic attack melted away, the English Queen lost her anxiety to be rid of her rival. Mar died; Morton was nominated to the regency. Then also died John Knox, the last of the men who had seen the Reformation through from its commencement; grim to the end.

[Sidenote: The Netherlands, France, and Spain]

When the new year, 1573, came in, Elizabeth, fearing that the Scots lords might, unless they received something besides vague promises, turn to France after all, at length acknowledged the Regent and the King. A compromise was accepted by the Marian lords with the exception of Lethington and Grange in the Castle. But while these held out, the conflagration might be renewed at any time. Elizabeth then reluctantly yielded to the pressure on her from every side. Money, troops, siege- guns, and Drury in command, were sent in April to the help of Morton. After a stubborn resistance, the siege artillery proved too much for the garrison; their outworks were carried, their water-supply cut off, and they were forced to surrender in the last days of May. Lethington survived only a few days; rumour had it that he died by his own act. The craftiest brain in Scotland was stilled but a few months after her sincerest and fiercest tongue was silenced. With Maitland's death, all prospect of reconstructing an organised Queen's-party vanished. It was not many months after these events that Alva, in accordance with his own wishes, was recalled. Conquest did not mean pacification. Haarlem after a prolonged and desperate resistance, fell in July, and the garrison was put to the sword; but there was no hint of yielding on the part of the Hollanders.

When the Spaniards advanced on Alkmaar, they were threatened with the opening of the dykes.

Hardly less significant of the determination of Orange and his following never to submit, at whatever cost, is the fact that they were prepared in the last resort to receive Anjou as their Protector—-Anjou, who was regarded as a ring-leader in the Paris massacre. The same fact is convincing evidence of the overwhelming antagonism of French and Spanish political interests. Had the French been capable of arranging their religious quarrels on the basis of a fairly inclusive compromise, like that in England, so that the moderates could have worked together, such a league as Walsingham had hoped for before St. Bartholomew would have been entirely in the interest both of France and of England. The advantage of it to France was so obvious that, even after the massacre, it was possible for the perpetrators to contemplate friendly relations with foreign Protestants, and for foreign Protestants to regard such relations as possible. Still it was only in the last resort that the Anjou scheme could have been embraced, and perhaps it was now propounded more by way of forcing Elizabeth's hand than for any other purpose. At any rate the project did not deter Anjou from accepting the crown of Poland—-only to drop it and hurry back to assume the sceptre of France as Henry III. when King Charles IX. sank to the grave in 1574.

[Sidenote: 1573-74 The Netherlands, Spain, and England]

Requescens, Alva's successor, adopted a comparatively conciliatory policy. The restoration of the constitutional Government of the States of the Netherlands was offered, on condition of acceptance of Catholicism. In the eyes of Elizabeth, who regarded religious observances as falling entirely to the supreme government to settle, while she could not understand a conscientious objection to outward conformity, the refusal of those terms by Orange seemed quite unreasonable; even Burghley was detached from Walsingham and from those who, thinking with him, still counted the maintenance of Protestantism, and as a necessary corollary hostility to Spain, as the first object which ought to be pursued. This attitude of England, coupled with the irreconcilable character of French religious animosities, which made the prospects of effective French interference a mere will-o'-the-wisp, reduced Orange and his party to a condition verging on desperation.

[Sidenote: 1574 Spain amicable]

Requescens, however, made no haste to crush the stubborn remnant. It was his policy rather to achieve a *modus vivendi* in which the bulk of the Netherlands would concur, and to conciliate England. Alva before him had realised the true danger of the island-nation's hostility. As we shall presently see in more detail, the growth of the English marine had rendered it extremely formidable. Not only had English rovers for years past been giving unspeakable trouble on the Spanish Main and the Ocean highways, but the English fleets also practically controlled the narrow seas: and could make it impossible for any ordinary convoys, whether of transports, or merchantmen, or treasure-ships, to pass up-channel. In other words, England could block the lines of communication between Spain and the Netherlands. Until Spain should bestir all her might, rise up, and annihilate the English shipping, Elizabeth must be kept neutral; whereas, if Orange were pressed too hard, she might be forced even against her will to support him vigorously, if only to prevent France from doing so single-handed, and perhaps thereby capturing the Netherlands for herself.

[Sidenote: Reciprocal Concessions; 1575]

So the Spaniard was polite to Elizabeth, Elizabeth was polite to the Spaniard, and in France the factions fought furiously round Rochelle or rested in temporary truce. The politeness was carried to very considerable lengths. Allen's seminary at Douay, where young English Catholics had been trained to go forth as missionaries and seek martyrdom in their native land, was ordered to remove itself. The refugees who had found shelter at Louvain and elsewhere were required to depart across Philip's borders. Claims on either side for the seizure of merchandise or treasure were balanced against each other. In the spring of 1575, Elizabeth fell upon certain anabaptists with ostentatious severity, by way of demonstrating how narrow after all was the division between Anglican and Catholic in their fundamental ideas. Yet there remained one serious difficulty to adjust; one point, or perhaps we should say two points, on which neither side could or would give way.

[Sidenote: A Deadlock]

On the soil of Spain the dominating force was the Inquisition. Within his own dominions, Philip was absolutely committed to the rigid enforcement of orthodoxy, as understood by the Holy Office. The Holy Office claimed, and the claim was endorsed by Philip, that its jurisdiction extended over vessels in Spanish waters, and it was in the habit of haling English sailors from their ships into its dungeons, as heretics. In this Elizabeth declined to acquiesce; and Sir Henry Cobham was sent to Madrid to demand recognition of the English view, and to propose that resident Ambassadors should again be established, the Englishman to be privileged—as the Spaniard should be in England—to enjoy the Services of his own Church. Further, inasmuch as fortune had so far smiled upon Orange of late that Leyden had triumphantly resisted a determined siege, Elizabeth offered friendly mediation; emphasising the suggestion by a hint that unless Spain could see her way to a pacification, Orange could now appeal with a prospect of success to France; and England could not afford to decline the preferable alternative of an appeal to herself.

On Spanish soil, however, Catholic zealotry was too strong. Alva would fain have made diplomatic concessions, which could be revoked when convenient; Philip was dominated by the extremists, who were scandalised by the presence of a heretic envoy, who in his turn was furious at being called a heretic. The proffered mediation was declined; Philip flatly refused to concede religious privileges to an Ambassador, suggesting only that the difficulty could be got over by sending a Catholic; as to the action of the Inquisition, he was pledged not to interfere.

[Sidenote: 1576 Attitude of the Nation]

With this message Cobham returned, to find that the revolted States were on their part offering the sovereignty of the Provinces to Elizabeth. Walsingham and his allies were supporting the proposal, and under present conditions Burghley too inclined to it. Elizabeth, confident that Spain would not declare war, was ready to carry what we can only call bluff to the extreme limit, though she scolded her Council with energy. The Spaniards took the opportunity to render the Council most effective support, by seizing the crew of another English ship. Elizabeth sent warnings or threats to Requescens; and in February (1576), Parliament was summoned to vote supplies; which it did without hesitation. If the action of Parliament was any sort of index to popular sentiment, the idea that there was any widespread or deep-rooted feeling in the country against a war of religion is certainly fallacious; while there can be no question that the entire sea-going population—which had attracted into its ranks all that was most adventurous, most daring, most energetic, and most capable in the country—was heart and soul hostile to Spain. How much of that feeling was due to enthusiastic Protestantism, and how much to the fact that men hankered after the Spanish El Dorado may be matter of debate; but that the feeling was there is patent. That the attitude of Parliament was not due to any subserviency is emphasised by the open attack in this session on the granting of Monopolies to the Queen's favourites, which sent Wentworth who made it to the Star-Chamber—and found for him early and popular pardon instead of severe punishment.

[Sidenote: The Queen evades war]

Evidently, the force which did really operate against war was the Queen herself. From beginning to end of her reign, she never entered upon any war at all, so long as any possible means could be found for evading it without surrendering some right or claim vital in her eyes either to the nation's interests or her own. On such points she was never prepared to yield: in the last resort she would fight, but at the same time make the most of her reluctance, and relieve her feelings by roundly rating her ministers. Yet repeatedly she went as far as it was possible to go without actually declaring war, relying securely on the certainty that the irrevocable step would not be taken by the other party, and that she could find some plausible though perhaps undignified excuse for not taking it herself.

So it was now. So long as France could be deterred from espousing the cause of Orange, she saw no necessity for her own intervention. If the Inquisition maltreated some of her sailors, others might be relied on to effect reprisals and to collect compensation, on their own responsibility, without her actually applying the grievance as a *casus belli*: it could always be employed to that end, if occasion should arise. Requescens died suddenly, a few days before the prorogation of the English Parliament in March. Elizabeth dismissed the States' envoys, refused all assistance, and threatened open hostility if they appealed to France. The Spanish arms were prospering again, and as the summer advanced, Orange was reduced to such straits that he seriously contemplated a wholesale emigration to the New World, from the two States which remained stubborn, Holland and Zeeland.

[Sidenote: 1575-76 The Huguenots and Alençon]

The involved state of French parties probably accounts for Elizabeth's action. Since the death of Charles IX., the middle party or *Politiques* had been revived, and with this, for some time, both Henry of Navarre and Alençon—now heir presumptive to the French throne—were associated. In the autumn of 1575 however Alençon betook himself to the Huguenots at Dreux. Being thus openly supported by the heir presumptive, the Huguenot position was considerably strengthened. Once more the English Queen resolved to employ matrimonial negotiations, as a means for keeping others inactive and evading action herself. The idea that she should marry Alençon was revived, and found favour at least with the Politiques. The French King approved. In May 1576, a peace was patched up which promised to give neither party undue ascendancy. The great danger of the winter months— that Alençon and the Huguenots would make common cause with the Netherlanders—had passed; and Elizabeth thought she could now afford to decline both the marriage and the entreaties of the revolted States.

[Sidenote: 1576 The States and Don John]

But the impending collapse of the Hollanders was averted. Before a successor to Requescens arrived, the Spanish troops, whose pay was heavily in arrear, mutinied, took the law into their own hands, pillaged in the States which had submitted, and finally perpetrated the sack of Antwerp, known as "the Spanish Fury," when some thousands of the inhabitants were wantonly slaughtered. The result was that the States General, meeting at Ghent, were so alarmed and angered that all the Provinces again united and by the Pacification of Ghent, resolved unanimously to demand the total withdrawal of the Spanish troops before they would admit the new Governor, Don John of Austria, Philip's illegitimate brother, the victor of Lepanto. Vehemently Catholic as were the Southern Provinces, they were even ready to demand freedom of worship for the Protestants, for the sake of political unity in the face of the Spaniard.

[Sidenote: Attitude of Elizabeth]

Don John's military reputation stood exceedingly high; he was known to entertain very ambitious ideas; his brother was gloomily jealous of him. It was more than suspected that in his own mind Don John wished to invade England, raise the Catholics, marry Mary, set her on the throne, and from that vantage ground secure the erection of the Netherlands into a separate kingdom for himself. It was Elizabeth's policy to retain the good-will of Philip, who would certainly hold Don John in check, unless she provoked him beyond endurance. Therefore, while she was ready to lend money but no troops to the States, it was on condition that they would yield on the question of religion; so that she could impress upon Philip that while she must support them in the demands which, after the recent outrages, were obviously reasonable, her influence was being exerted to make them in turn submit to what she did and some of them did not consider reasonable terms.

[Sidenote: The Political Kaleidoscope]

When the new year (1577) opened, Don John saw nothing for it but to accede to the bulk of the States' demands, reserving the question of freedom of worship for Philip. The Catholic Provinces accepted the compromise, and the others had to follow suit. The new Governor was admitted into the Netherlands. Elizabeth sent to Spain a new Ambassador, Sir John Smith, to demand again that the Inquisition should recognise the rights of English sailors. Sir John asserted himself with energy; forced his way into the presence of the Grand Inquisitor, when the two stormed at each other with picturesque vigour; carried his point with the King; and, so far as promises went, returned successful towards the end of the year. In the meantime, the Spanish troops were paid and withdrawn from the Netherlands: but letters to Spain from Escobeda, Don John's Secretary, were intercepted, which showed that the Governor meant after all to reconquer the Provinces, though desiring to postpone that operation to his schemes in England. Also in the meantime, Alençon had been won over to the Guises, and there was a danger of France reviving an aggressively Catholic policy. Once more, circumstances were forcing Elizabeth towards a Protestant alliance, to counteract the schemes not so much of Philip as of Don John.

[Sidenote 1: The Archduke Matthias]
[Sidenote 2: 1577-78 Diverse Measures]

Yet fortune again enabled Elizabeth to put off the evil day. The discovery of Don John's intentions again set the whole of the Provinces against him, but they were divided on the question of leadership. The Catholics of the south, disliking the sovereignty of Elizabeth or the dictatorship of Orange, turned to the Catholic Archduke Matthias, brother of the Emperor Rudolf. The Archduke favoured the proposal; and though the English Queen began by promising help in men and money, before the year was out she had made up her mind that Matthias must look after his own affairs, and that she could afford to continue an interested spectator. Nor did her views change materially when, in January 1578, Don John—having reassembled a number of the recently withdrawn troops—moved suddenly against the forces of the Southern States and shattered them at Gemblours (January 29th). She did indeed send Orange some money, and promised to increase the loan, but declined to do more. Her public policy, however, had not prevented her from privately sanctioning, in November 1577, the departure of Francis Drake on that famous voyage, wherein he circumnavigated the globe, and incidentally wrought much detriment to Spain. Of that voyage, which reached its triumphant conclusion almost three years later, in September 1580, we shall hear more in another chapter.

[Sidenote: 1578 Mendoza]

Since the expulsion of Don Guerau de Espes there had been no regular Spanish Ambassador in England. Now, in accordance with the arrangements effected by Sir John Smith, the complete restoration of friendly relations was to be sealed by accrediting Don Bernardino de Mendoza to England. In March Mendoza arrived. The English Council was as usual much more inclined to war than its mistress. But the Ambassador's instructions were entirely conciliatory. As concerned the Netherlands, Philip could not give way on the point of allowing religious freedom—for which Elizabeth cared nothing —but he would concede all the political demands, even to the withdrawal of Don John in favour of a substitute less dangerous to England.

[Sidenote: Orange and Alençon]

Elizabeth would have been satisfied; but the Protestant provinces were as resolute as Philip on the religious question. The plan of calling in the Archduke had collapsed at Gemblours; but the sovereignty of the Netherlands was still a bait which would tempt Alençon from the Guise alliance; though no one could tell what he might ultimately do if he were received by the States, even that desperate remedy was preferable to submission. Nevertheless, Elizabeth still tried, in despite of her ministers, to force Orange's hand by the singular process of with-holding the bonds by which her last loan to him had been effected. Walsingham, who was sent to overcome Orange's scruples was so disgusted that he thought of giving up his position; naturally his negotiation was a failure. It was announced that Orange would wait no longer and that the arrangement with Alençon would be carried through. Also at this time Don John met with a defeat at Rymenant, mainly owing to the obstinate valour of a battalion of English volunteers commanded by Sir John Norreys. For a moment the Queen was carried away, but immediately reverted to her antagonistic attitude. All she could be induced to do was at last to issue the bonds. The old trick, which had so often served her purpose of suspending action, was to do duty once more. The matrimonial shadow was more alluring to Alençon than the Netherland bone.

[Sidenote: Sept. Death of Don John]

The persistence of happy accidents—of unforeseen events which saved Elizabeth from the disasters which her ministers anticipated, giving her tortuous policy an undeserved success and thereby in the eyes of some historians discrediting the more honourable and straightforward courses which Walsingham and Burghley habitually advocated—is one of the most remarkable features of Elizabeth's reign. Her good fortune did not desert her now. Don John died suddenly, not without the usual suspicions of foul play. The peculiar danger of his association with Mary Stewart, disappeared with his death. No wild schemes were likely to be conceived or encouraged by his successor Alexander of Parma, one of the ablest statesmen and probably the ablest soldier of the day. Moreover about the same time, King Sebastian of Portugal was killed—as was also the English adventurer Thomas Stukely who had been diverted from invading Ireland to take part in this affair— in an expedition against Morocco. Dying without issue, Sebastian was succeeded by his great-uncle Henry, a cardinal whose Orders precluded the possibility of his leaving an heir. Philip of Spain therefore was now, through his mother, claimant to the position of heir apparent. [Footnote Philip claimed as the son of Isabella, sister of Henry and of John III., Sebastian's grandfather. The prior right however really lay with the daughters of their younger brother Edward, of whom the elder, Katharine, was married to John of Braganza and the younger, Mary, to Alexander of Parma. Parma's title was invalidated by Braganza's, and Braganza did not push his own claim. Don Antonio of Crato who did come forward as a pretender was himself the illegitimate son of another brother, Luis. Thus when, later on,

Philip claimed the English throne as the lineal descendant of John of Gaunt, his title, such as it was, was inferior to that of either Braganza or Parma.] The prospect of this further accession to his dominions, and increase of his power and resources, made it more than ever necessary for France to hold aloof from any alliance with him, in which she must play an entirely subordinate part, and to court the friendship of England. The stars in their courses seemed to fight for Elizabeth's policy.

Down to this point the course of events in Ireland does not appear as materially influencing English policy; and it has seemed better, for the sake of clearness to defer its history for consecutive treatment. To this we now turn in the chapter following; after which Irish affairs will be dealt with in the regular progress of the general narrative.

CHAPTER XX
ELIZABETH (v), 1558-78-IRISH AND ENGLISH

[Sidenote: 1549-58]

The Deputyship of Bellingham in Ireland, which terminated just before the fall of Somerset, left the Irish chiefs in a state of angry discontent. As inaugurating a system of severe but consistent government, Bellingham's rule might have been valuable; as matters stood, no doubt he gave the Irish what is commonly called a lesson— from which nothing was learnt. If the Geraldines—Kildare and Desmond— of the South, the O'Neills and O'Donnells of the North, the Burkes and O'Briens in the West, had possessed the slightest capacity for working in harmony, they might have raised such a revolt as the incapable and distracted governments of Edward VI. and Mary could not have coped with. Ormonde however served as a permanent check on the Geraldines, while the young Kildare had neither the inclination nor the opportunity to head rebellions: and the great septs were far too ready to turn on each other for any effective combination. Leix and Offally, the territories of O'More and O'Connor [Footnote: See p. 201, *ante*.] on the west of the Pale, were absorbed into it and partially colonised, becoming King's County and Queen's County; and when Elizabeth ascended the throne, the extent of the Pale corresponded roughly, though not accurately, to the Province of Leinster.

[Sidenote: 1558]

In matters ecclesiastical, religion officially swung with the pendulum in England. Church lands were distributed among the great men under Edward, and within the Pale the clergy generally conformed after a fashion, reverting again under Mary. Outside the Pale no great attention was paid to the orders of the Government. On Elizabeth's accession, the Act of Uniformity was enforced and some bishops resigned. But the new Queen had plenty to occupy her in England, and in Ireland was fain to take the least troublesome course, giving diplomatic sops to the chiefs and spending as little money as possible: Sussex, who was Deputy when Mary died, being continued in that office.

[Sidenote: Shan O'Neill]

The policy was destined to prove difficult. The two great chiefs of Ulster, O'Donnell of Tyrconnel in the West, and O'Neil, created Earl of Tyrone, in the East, had been more or less successfully conciliated by the policy of St. Leger. But Tyrone had a numerous progeny, and the laws of legitimacy were at a discount. The English elected to recognise as his heir a favourite son, Matthew, who certainly was not legitimate. But another legitimate son, Shan or Shane, a man of great if erratic abilities, declined to submit to this arrangement when he grew up. Matthew was killed in a brawl, leaving a young son to claim the succession. Thereupon Shan virtually deposed his father, and in accordance with ancient practice was elected "The O'Neill," head of the clan which claimed that their chiefs were the old-time Kings of Ulster: ignoring the choice of the English Government, and scorning the earldom bestowed by them. Next, no doubt with a view to alliance, Shan married O'Donnell's sister; but when he found that the minor chiefs were disposed to attach themselves rather to him than to O'Donnell, he decided to adopt the policy of breaking his rival in Ulster, as preferable to alliance with him; and his maltreatment of his wife very soon resulted in hostilities.

[Sidenote: The Scots of Antrim]

Now in Antrim there was a considerable colony of Scots from the Islands, whose chief was James M'Connell. Also, a sister of the Earl of Argyle, curiously referred to in the records as the Countess of Argyle, was the wife of O'Donnell. The Antrim Scots were supposed to be in alliance with O'Donnell; whom however Shan's proceedings were now causing to seek English friendship, whereas the Scots were antagonistic to Elizabeth, holding that their own Queen Mary had the better title to the English throne. So Shan got rid of his O'Donnell wife, and married the sister of James M'Connell by way of cementing a union with the Scots; but then proceeded to write to Argyle, suggesting that he should get rid of the M'Connell wife in turn, and that the Countess should be transferred from O'Donnell to himself, on the assumption that this would give him an equal hold on the Antrim Scots. Whereby he merely enraged the Scots and disgusted Argyle. However, a short time afterwards, Shan raided Tyrconnel's country, and carried off the chief and his wife; who seems to have been fascinated by her captor, and willingly became his consort, irregular as the conditions were. M'Connell was somehow outwardly pacified despite the insult to his sister; but the bad blood engendered took effect in due time.

[Sidenote: 1560-61 Shan and the Government]

Before the overthrow of Tyrconnel, O'Neill was already becoming a serious source of alarm to the English. It is the fact that a considerable number of farmers migrated from the Pale into Ulster, feeling greater security under the aegis of O'Neill than under English law; which did little to protect them, while the English soldiery, badly disciplined and badly maintained, were in effect a serious element of disorder. O'Neill, cited to appear in England, wrote a letter to Elizabeth in which he dwelt with some complacency on this testimony to his own superior government, besides arguing very conclusively in favour of his own claim to recognition as head of the O'Neills. But he evaded the journey to London, and made his raid on Tyrconnel instead.

That exploit made Shan more completely master of Ulster than ever. The result was that in the summer of 1561, Sussex marched into the Northern Province. Shan after some preliminary skirmishes surprised his rearguard, and would have cut his whole force to pieces but for a desperate rally. When Elizabeth learned what had happened, she made up her mind that it would be best to concede O'Neill's demands, and induce him to visit England, while Sussex was actually trying to drive a bargain for his murder. The plot fell through, but Sussex received some supplies and was allowed to make another less disastrous expedition before Kildare was sent to negotiate with O'Neill on the Queen's behalf. The chief stipulated for complete amnesty, a safe-conduct, and the payment of his expenses, as a condition of his paying the desired visit.

[Sidenote: 1561-2 Shan in England]

When Shan arrived in London, he made his formal submission, but was informed that though he had his safe-conduct for return the date when that return would be permitted lay with the Queen. He must wait for his rival, young Matthew, to have their claims tried. Meantime Shan, who seems to have adopted Henry VIII. as his matrimonial model, suggested that he should be given an English wife, and that he would manage the government of Ulster admirably in Elizabeth's interests, as soon as he went back—with the Earldom. But as time went on he learned that Matthew was being intentionally kept in Ireland. Then another of O'Neill's kinsmen, Tirlogh, succeeded in murdering Matthew, while Shan in England was vowing that his great desire was to be instructed in English ways by Dudley (not yet Earl of Leicester). Now he remarked on the necessity for his return to keep his kinsmen in order. There was a good deal of ground for believing that he was in fact the only person who could rule Ulster: and after four months (April 1562) he was allowed to return, with promises on his part to be a model ruler and on the Queen's part a concession of something not far short of sovereignty.

Before the end of the year it was evident enough that Shan's promises were not intended to be kept. His murder had been plotted; Sussex had certainly endeavoured to entrap him treacherously; his detention in England had been technically justified by a distinctly dishonourable trick. He did not mean to be tricked again, and if there was duplicity in his conduct the English had set the example. He entered into correspondence with the Queen's potential enemies on all hands, and proceeded to suppress every one in the North whose submission to himself was doubtful.

[Sidenote: 1563 Shan's supremacy recognised]

So in the spring, Sussex made another futile raid, after which Elizabeth thought it best once more to play at conciliation, and to adopt the scheme of formally constituting Ulster, Munster and Connaught into Provinces, with O'Neill as President in the north, Clanricarde (Burke) or O'Brien in the west, and Desmond or Kildare in the south. Shan was to be so completely supreme that he was even to be free to make his own Catholic nominee Archbishop of Armagh. An indubitable attempt to poison O'Neill gave him a moral advantage, though the English authorities indignantly repudiated the perpetrator. Shan was content to allow the affair to be hushed up, and established his own rule throughout Ulster with a combination of barbarity and real administrative ability which to students of Indian History recalls the methods and the ethics of Ranjit Singh or Abdurrhaman. Within the Pale, the exceedingly corrupt administration of recent years was overhauled by Sir Nicholas Arnold; who was no respecter of persons, but outside the Pale regarded the Irish—in his own words—as so many "bears and bandogs" who were best employed in ravaging and cutting each other's throats. And in the south, the Butlers and Geraldines carried out that policy with devastatory results. It is to be noted however that Cecil found Arnold's views very difficult to stomach. [Footnote: *State Papers, Ireland*, i., p. 252.]

It is difficult to avoid the conclusion that in spite of Shan's peculiar views as to marriage and murder, Ulster under his sway was on the whole better off than any other part of Ireland.

[Sidenote: 1565]

In 1565 Mary Stewart married Darnley, in pursuit, as we have seen, of an aggressive policy towards England. In this year, O'Neill was hand in glove with Sir Thomas Stukely, a gentleman-adventurer of Devon, who made the harbours of the west coast his base for piratical cruises in search of treasure-ships. Englishmen at home were devising paper schemes for an ideal government in the sister island, but something very different was required if Shan was not to become strong enough to endanger the very existence of English dominion there. There was considerable risk that Argyle, in disgust at Elizabeth's double-dealing, would sink his differences with the Irish Chief, and give him the active support of the Antrim Scots. Meantime, though Shan himself was careful to render plausible explanations of his very obvious activity, Sir Henry Sidney, a man of very different calibre from Sussex, was appointed to succeed that nobleman in the Deputyship.

[Sidenote: 1566 Sir Henry Sidney Deputy]

Sidney had been in Ireland before and knew the conditions. He said plain terms that he would not accept office, unless he could have the troops and the money needed to compel the success of the military movements of which he foresaw the necessity if order was to be secured. He required in fact that the Government should possess actually the sanction of superior force. The experiment of constituting Munster a Presidency was to be tried, with Ormonde, Desmond, and the other southern lords as a Council. But before he arrived early in 1566, Argyle and O'Neill had already made their new pact, and a crisis seemed to be at hand.

Sidney found the Pale in a state of anarchy, Munster half devastated by the Ormonde and Desmond feud, and O'Neill supreme in the north. Summoned to meet Sidney in the Pale, Shan replied in effect that he knew too much about the traps previously laid for him to run any risks. Sidney employed Stukely to negotiate. Stukely reported that Shan was defiant. Sidney wrote urgently both to Leicester and to Cecil that he mush put O'Neill down and must have money to pay his troops and keep them paid. The Council were willing enough, but Elizabeth kept the purse-strings tight. Moreover she was pleased to rate Sidney for stoutly refusing to settle the Ormonde-Desmond dispute in favour of the former; the Deputy declaring that the questions between them involved complicated points of laws which could only be properly dealt with by lawyers. In April, she sent him half the money he demanded, and dispatched her kinsman, Knollys, to oversee Sidney. Knollys, who was given to speaking his mind, promptly told her that Sidney was entirely in the right and ought to have a free hand. An immediate aggressive campaign against Shan was necessary, especially as the chief was now in correspondence with Charles IX. of France. This was at the time when a general suspicion was prevalent that a universal Catholic League for the destruction of Protestantism was being formed; and Shan wrote as an enthusiastic Catholic.

[Sidenote: 1567 End of O'Neill]

Under extreme pressure then, Elizabeth at last increased the supplies. Unluckily for O'Neill, Argyle's friendship was cooling under pressure from Murray, and the Antrim M'Connells, in spite of recent marriages, did not forget the old feud: while Desmond, encouraged by Sidney's attitude, was deaf to his appeals. Sidney swept Ulster, establishing a strong garrison in a new and well-chosen fort which in course of time developed into

Londonderry, and restored Tyrconnel in the north-west. Sidney himself was seriously hampered by constant reproofs from Elizabeth; but O'Neill was now grievously harassed by the O'Donnells on one side, the M'Connells on another, and by the garrison at Derry. Renewed attempts to obtain aid from the Guises, in February (1567), failed; and though Derry had to be abandoned owing to an outbreak of plague, the death of the commandant, and a fire which destroyed the buildings, O'Neill's fate was already sealed. He marched to meet an incursion of the O'Donnells, but was completely overthrown, and had to flee for his life to seek the ambiguous hospitality of the M'Connells of Antrim; who received him for the sake of subsisting relationships. But the situation was too volcanic. Insults passed over the wine-cup, knives were drawn, and O'Neill was slaughtered. So perished the most formidable challenger of the English rule who had appeared in Ireland; for his one predecessor of equal ability, the old Kildare, had never schemed for the creation of an independent Nation.

The death of O'Neill was followed by a brief period of rest from perpetual warfare: but the peace was not to last for long.

[Sidenote: Irish Catholicism in politics]

From the days of Elizabeth until now the antagonism of the Irish to protestantism has been one of the two great sources of disaffection. As the English power extended, efforts were made to carry out beyond the Pale the principles of the Act of Uniformity, and the cause of Rebellion became more and more identified with the cause of Catholicism. Before the fall of Shan, Queen and Deputies had been disposed to shut their eyes to the open disregard of the Act all over the country. Now, recalcitrant chiefs began to make the preservation of religion the ground of appeal for foreign assistance to cast off the yoke of England. Curiously, however, neither they nor the Catholic clergy grasped the political situation. Irish nationality, *per se*, was profoundly uninteresting to foreign potentates. In England, Scotland, and Ireland, the cause of Catholicism was the cause of Mary Stewart. Unless in support of her, it was impracticable for either France or Spain to move against Elizabeth. The murder of Darnley, three months before O'Neill's fall, destroyed the Queen of Scots' chances, but only for a time. Shan himself had been acute enough to seek Mary's friendship; but now the disaffected prelates and chiefs will be found hoping vainly to place themselves under the dominion of a foreign power, in preference even to a Catholicised English supremacy. Any such scheme would have destroyed the relations between the English Catholics and their friends abroad.

Of the second great disturbing factor, the Land, we have hitherto heard little; but now was about to commence the era of attempts at forcibly establishing an English landed proprietary, displacing the native owners; on the hypothesis that they would be able to keep the population in subjection.

[Sidenote: 1568 The Colonisation of Munster]

The first schemes would probably have been beneficial had they been practicable, as they involved nothing in the shape of forfeiture. But they would have been costly, while offering no temptations to Adventurers. In 1568 a scheme was devised which tempted the Adventurers, made little demand on the exchequer—Elizabeth always argued that Ireland ought to pay for itself—but involved forfeitures on a large scale.

Desmond, who had declined alliance with O'Neill, was summoned to answer charges of treason. He surrendered at once, and was sent to London. Then he tried to escape, and was only allowed to purchase freedom from close imprisonment or worse by surrendering all his lands to the Queen to receive back so much as she chose to grant. A group of Devonshire gentlemen proposed that the titles of other landowners in Munster should be investigated, and that all the lands held under unsatisfactory titles should be handed over to themselves. They would occupy and rule at their own charges, and compel complete submission by the strong hand; a process by which it is quite evident that they intended practical extermination of the Irish. The business was started on Desmond lands; but it was carried to a dangerous point when Sir Peter Carew took possession of Butler property— seeing that the loyalty of the Ormonde connexion was the one source of Irish support which had never been even suspected of failing. There were massacres and reprisals; but fortunately when the other Munster chiefs took the opportunity to petition Philip of Spain to come and take possession, the Butlers still stood firmly to their allegiance.

[Sidenote: 1569 Insurrection in Munster]

An insurrection was headed in 1569 by Fitzmaurice (Desmond's brother); some of the English households were wiped out. The O'Neills in Ulster and the Burkes in Connaught rose. Ormonde declared plainly that if the colonising policy were carried on it would be impossible for him to support the government. Sidney ravaged Munster, and left Sir Humphrey Gilbert in command behind him for a time: but the actual scheme was dropped. There is no evading the fact that the English, who could wax hot enough over the cruelties of Spaniards in America or in Holland, did without compunction or any sense of inconsistency regard the Irish not even as mere human savages but as wild beasts. And many of these were men who in any other circumstances were capable of displaying an admirable chivalry and a heroic valour. Gilbert was a man full of noble ideals, learned, pious, cultivated, valiant, kindly; but if there was a chance of killing an Irish man, woman, or child, he took it.

[Sidenote: Ireland and Philip II.]

In England, 1569 was the year of the Northern rebellion. France was viewing the Scots Queen's pretensions with increasing lukewarmness, and Philip was regarding her with corresponding favour. The Ridolfi plot was developing in 1570 and 1571. In brief, at this period Philip's disposition towards Elizabeth was becoming definitely, though not avowedly, hostile instead of—as hitherto on the whole—friendly. Yet he would not accept the Irish invitation to intervene. But he received at Madrid, and treated with great favour, the very remarkable adventurer Thomas Stukely, already mentioned as a piratical ally of Shan O'Neill's. Stukely had been sent over to England to answer for his miscellaneous misdeeds; but was—perhaps intentionally—allowed to escape to Spain; where he represented himself as an enthusiastic Catholic, and the most influential man in Ireland, and bragged hugely of the coming conquest of that country, of which he was to become in some sort the Prince, with the assistance of Spain. The entertainment of Stukely however summed up all that Philip was prepared to do for Ireland. By September 1572 he was again seeking Elizabeth's amity.

[Sidenote: Experimental Presidencies]

In the meantime, the experiment of constituting Connaught a Presidency had been tried and failed ignominiously. The curse of the English Government—a soldiery whose pay was permanently and hugely in arrear, who were constantly on the verge of mutiny, and lived virtually by pillage—remained unabated; and Sidney, having tried vigorous government first and then, lacking the means to maintain it properly, extirpation as an alternative, but still without success, clamoured to be recalled, and at last got his wish.

Desmond was still detained in England, but the Geraldines in Munster had not been crushed either by Sidney or by Gilbert. Despite the failure in Connaught, the Presidency plan was tried in the southern province, Sir John Perrot being appointed thereto. Perrot blew up strongholds, captured and hanged some hundreds of the population, but could not lay hold of the chiefs or bring the country into subjection. In 1572, Fitzmaurice made his way to Ulster, gathered a force of Scots, and came down the Shannon. The President got his chance of a fight, and shattered the force: but Elizabeth was dissatisfied with the results of an unwonted if still inadequate expenditure, and declared that the whole experiment was too costly. A general amnesty and the withdrawal of Perrot ended it.

[Sidenote: 1573 Essex (the elder) in Ulster]

Yet experiments continued to be the order of the day. The one expedient not attempted was a government supported by obviously efficient physical force, but aiming at the prosperity of the people, and not running violently counter to the customs and the prejudices of centuries. Another inefficient colony was started in Ulster, which only excited popular animosity; Desmond was at last in 1573 allowed to return to Munster with many promises on his part, from which, like O'Neill before him, he considered himself absolved by a breach of faith towards him. Finally Walter Devereux, Earl of Essex, was allowed to try the biggest and perhaps the most disastrous of the whole series of experiments; being virtually granted authority to invade Ulster with a free hand to make laws and generally to do what seemed to him good there—all at his own cost—save only for some provisions safe-guarding the royal prerogative. He went with excellent intentions, romantic ideals, a respectable force, and a sublime ignorance of facts. The Irishmen, mindful of the Munster colonisation, tricked him with an apparently warm welcome at Carrickfergus, permitted him to congratulate himself on roseate prospects, and then at one swoop cleared the district of provisions. They professed to owe allegiance to the Queen, but repudiated the claims of a private adventurer. His own troops were volunteers, with no mind for hardships and no prospects of plunder. In three months he found his dreams hopelessly dissipated, and himself almost deserted, with no remotest chance of carrying out the Utopian projects with which he had started.

[Sidenote: 1574]

The volunteer method having failed thus ignominiously, Essex was made officially Governor of Ulster, and supplied with troops; for the O'Neills were now threatening, and the Deputy, Fitzwilliam, was inactive. Tirlogh O'Neill and his kinsman Sir Brian were very promptly brought to submission. In the south Desmond, between threats and promises, was persuaded to resume an air of loyalty. Essex however had learned to adopt the common view of the Irish in its extremest form. By a ruse which anywhere else he would have counted a piece of the blackest treachery, he seized Sir Brian and his wife and cut up their following when they were actually his own guests; and followed up the performance by a hideous and wanton massacre of women and children and decrepit men at Rathlin off the Antrim Coast; of which things he wrote with a perfect complacency, and for which he was highly applauded. Thereafter he returned to England.

[Sidenote: 1576 Sidney's second Deputyship]

Once more, Sidney was persuaded to accept the Deputyship. It is probable that his honest desire was to govern firmly and justly, although, when denied the means for steady rule he had fallen back on extirpation.

At any rate the Irish themselves, genuinely or not, hailed his return with apparent enthusiasm. The chiefs hoped that after so many experiments had collapsed, the pristine plan of making them responsible for their own districts and leaving them alone might be tried again. But no English statesman could divest himself of the idea that no government was worth having unless it was conducted by English methods. Sidney insisted on reconstituting the Presidencies of Connaught and Munster, Malby taking charge of the former and Drury of the latter. Naturally enough, and with plenty of excuse, they set about hangings on an extensive scale, and where they met with resistance gave no quarter. English methods, as usual in Ireland, promptly degenerated into massacre and devastation. Sidney left the country again two years after he had returned to it—and left it as ripe for rebellion as it had ever been.

And the omens abroad were dangerous. For the Jesuit Sanders was seeking to stir up a Catholic crusade, Stukely was in high favour at Madrid, and the ablest of the Geraldines, James Fitzmaurice, was in Spain. Moreover Philip's indisposition to interfere was on the verge of being seriously disturbed by Drake's great expedition, which had sailed from England in 1577.

CHAPTER XXI
ELIZABETH (vi), 1578-83—THE PAPAL ATTACK

[Sidenote: Union of Utrecht 1579]

The presence of Alexander of Parma in the Netherlands soon resulted in a definite division between the seven northern and the ten southern States. The latter, Catholic themselves, were not inclined to hold out for religious liberty. The rest, being Protestant, and realising that, while William of Orange lived, two at least, Holland and Zealand, would hold out to the very death, resolved to stand together; combining, under the title of the United Provinces, in the Union of Utrecht at the beginning of 1579. Their strength lay in their command of the estuaries of the Scheldt and the Meuse.

[Sidenote: 1578 The Matrimonial juggle]

Elizabeth's great object now was to keep Alençon (otherwise known as Anjou, the title held by Henry III. before he ascended the throne; also very commonly as "Monsieur") dancing in obedience to her manipulation of the wires. In this, as in all the previous matrimonial negotiations, not one of her ministers seems ever to have grasped her policy; the policy, that is, which modern historians attribute to her: a policy of which the successful issue really depended on its never being suspected; which was possible only to one who was entire mistress of all arts of dissimulation; which did in fact succeed completely every time she applied it; a policy however of which no statesman could have dared to recommend the risk. This was, in brief, to make the whole world including her ministers believe that she really intended to marry, to keep that conviction alive over a protracted period of time, and yet to secure a loop-hole for escape at the last moment. She had played the farce for years with the Archduke Charles; she had played it with Henry of Anjou; she had already played it with Alençon once; yet every time she started it afresh, potentates and ambassadors, her own ministers, and the wooer she selected, took the thing seriously, played into her hands, and were cajoled by her boundless histrionic ingenuity. Either she treated the world to a series of successful impositions, carried through, unaided and unsuspected, with the supreme audacity and skill of a consummate *comedienne*; or she was a contemptibly capricious woman whose inordinate vacillations invariably took the turn which after-events proved to have been the luckiest possible in the circumstances. Of these two interpretations, the theory of a deliberate policy is the more acceptable, if only because it is inconceivable that the habitual indulgence of sheer wanton caprice should never once have involved her in some irrevocable blunder, some position from which she could not be extricated. Yet history affords no parallel to such repeatedly and universally successful dissimulation.

[Sidenote: Alençon's wooing]

The comedy had fairly begun three months before Don John's death. In response, as it would seem, to a private invitation, Alençon's envoys came over at the end of July to propose the marriage. Monsieur wanted the affair settled at once, as he must decide whether he was going to help Orange or Don John. After a little formal procrastination, Elizabeth had her answer ready. She was quite prepared to receive him as a suitor though somewhat hurt by his conduct before; still she could not promise to marry any man till they had met, and could really feel sure that they would be happily mated. He had better come over and see her.

Alençon did not want to come over and see her; but his alternative plan, of taking part with Don John, was opportunely spoilt by the Governor's death, coupled with the new Spanish prospects opened up by the death of the Portuguese King. An alliance with Parma under these conditions was not at all the same thing for the French prince as an alliance with the ambitious and somewhat Quixotic schemer who was now dead. Elizabeth, thus strengthened, added a new condition, that he must withdraw for the present from the Netherlands. He could hardly, under the circumstances, support Orange against her will, and he obeyed her behest. Then she consented to receive another representative on his behalf, but held to her declaration that she would settle nothing till she had met Monsieur himself in person.

[Sidenote: 1579 Popular hostility]

At the beginning of the year (1579) Alençon's emissary Simier arrived. In England however practically every one—except apparently the Queen herself—was opposed to the marriage. The traditional animosity to France was strong, and had been intensified by the Paris massacre. The French Huguenots, for whom there was some sympathy, had no confidence in Alençon. The more unpopular the marriage showed itself, the more the Queen seemed to incline to it—since the more reasonably she could also insist to him on the necessity of delay, that her people might first be reconciled to it. Yet however much the Council might dislike it, they now felt bound to advise that Monsieur should be allowed to pay his visit. In

August he arrived, and she could no longer urge the plea that she had not seen him. Mendoza, the Spanish ambassador, thought she would marry him, that a civil war would follow, and the end would be the return of England to Catholicism. On the whole Mendoza was not ill pleased.

[Sidenote: Loyalty to the Queen]

Now however capricious and apparently irrational the conduct of the Queen might be, however her ministers might resent it, condemn it, bewail it to each other, and remonstrate with her, they remained always obstinately loyal. We may cynically attribute the fact to their consciousness that if they deserted her their doom under her rival would be sealed. Were that the true interpretation—were they really guided merely by a more or less enlightened self-interest—it is rather natural to suppose that some of them would have played a double game and secured friends in the other camp, like the Whig and Tory statesmen of the early eighteenth century; that they would have managed their own affairs so that they could change sides. None of them ever did anything of the kind. Whatever the Queen did, they held to their own views, advocated them stubbornly, but obeyed their mistress, even when they thought her caprices were on the verge of bringing them all to ruin. And yet they never seem to have fully realised the extent to which their own loyalty was shared by the people at large. Men may surrender themselves to such a sentiment, without venturing to count upon its influence on others. But Elizabeth reckoned on it in ministers and people alike; and her calculation was invariably justified.

[Sidenote: Yea and Nay]

So it was in this instance. What might have happened if she really had married Alençon can only be guessed. Short of that, popular loyalty was equal to the strain. A passionate pamphlet against the marriage was issued by a lawyer named Stubbs. The Council, confident in the real strength of the country, urged her to take the bold attitude, place herself frankly at the head of European protestantism, and take measures at home to make a Catholic rising impossible. They could see no alternative but the marriage. She stormed at them, burst into tears, vowed that she had expected them all to declare that the marriage would be the fulfilment of all their hopes. They replied that since she would have it so they would do their best to make the marriage acceptable. She had Stubbs and his publisher pilloried, and their right hands struck off—on the strength of a most iniquitous misinterpretation of a law of Queen Mary's. The victims waved their caps with the hand that was left and cried "God save the Queen". The marriage treaty was drawn up (November) but a couple of months were to pass before its ratification, to quiet the public mind. When the two months were over it was still unratified, and the whole negotiation was treated as having lapsed. Burghley at the end of January (1580) was falling back on the leadership of Protestantism as the only alternative to adopt, since France must be regarded as hopelessly alienated.

[Sidenote: The Papal plan of Campaign]

In the meantime the Papal plan of campaign against England—a plan which appears to have been matured early in 1579—was well under way. The Pope himself could not, and Philip of Spain would not, prepare Armadas to bring the recusant island back to the Roman submission. But there were other means to be tried than Armadas. Setting aside schemes for assassination, there was trouble to be made for Elizabeth in Ireland, trouble in Scotland, and trouble in England itself. Ireland was ripe for rebellion; a Catholic faction might be reorganised in Scotland; missionary zeal and martyrs' crowns might still revolutionise sentiment in England. The triple attack was resolved on—war in Ireland, diplomacy in Scotland, in England Seminarists from Rheims (whither Allen's Douay college had migrated some years before) and Jesuits from Rome.

In Ireland we have already seen the scheme taking shape, but scotched for the time by Stukely's diversion to Morocco and his death there, in 1578. In the following summer however, an expedition landed in Kerry, with Sanders as Papal Nuncio, and half the island was soon in a blaze. There, for some little time, such of the wilder spirits of English youth as were not occupied with ventures on the high seas were to find ample employment: and though Philip would not make open war, Philip's subjects were not restrained from seeking to pay back the blows which Drake had been dealing to Spain on the other side of the ocean—the report whereof had already found its way to Europe. In Scotland, the autumn was not far advanced when young Esmé Stewart, Count D'Aubigny, of the House of Lennox, James's cousin, arrived in Scotland to win his way into the boy-king's favour and plot the overthrow of Morton and of the Preachers. In the summer of 1580, Campian and Parsons began to deliver their message to the Catholics of England.

[Sidenote: 1580 Philip annexes Portugal]

In this same summer, the Cardinal-King of Portugal, Sebastian's successor, died. Philip's opportunity for annexation had arrived, and he seized it, expelling with little difficulty another claimant, Don Antonio, prior of Crato, the bastard son of the Cardinal's brother Luis; who however for the next ten years hovers through English politics as a pretender to be supported or dropped at convenience; used as a menace to Philip, much as the enemies of Henry VII. had used Perkin Warbeck. Then, in September, the great English seaman was back on English shores, in the ship that had sailed round the world—back with the spoils of Spain on board.

With this impression in our minds of the leading features of the year 1580, we can turn first to the detailed record of events in Ireland.

[Sidenote: Ireland: 1579 The Desmond rising]

The Expedition which landed in July at Dingle on the furthest south-west coast was small enough; but it brought with it Sanders the accredited representative of the Pope, and Fitzmaurice, cousin of Desmond. It appealed therefore at once to the Catholics at large and the Geraldine connexion in particular. There was no strong or united English force in the country; it was the custom of Elizabeth to provide her officers with the very minimum of equipment. Desmond at first hesitated; but his brother seized an early opportunity to commit him by treacherously murdering two English officers and their servants. Half Munster was up in arms at once, and the new arrivals made haste to fortify Smerwick, in the neighbourhood of Dingle where they had landed. It was expected and declared that reinforcements from Spain would soon be forth-coming. Malby, the President of Connaught, acted with promptitude and energy, marching south with his own troops and some of the Burkes who were at feud with the Geraldines. Fortune favoured them; Fitzmaurice was slain almost at the outset, and the Papal standard captured and sent off to Dublin. Desmond with his immediate following, who had not taken part in the engagement, fell back on Ashketyn, near Limerick; the rest of the insurgents retired on Smerwick. Drury however, advancing from Cork, was less fortunate, his troops being attacked by the Irish and very severely handled, so that he was forced to retreat. He died soon after.

The vigorous Malby assumed control of the Presidency, marched through Desmond's country dealing miscellaneous slaughter and destruction, burnt the town at Ashketyn since the castle could not be carried without cannon, and then went his way into Connaught. When Malby was gone, Desmond sallied forth, marched quietly south to Youghal where there was an English colony, sacked it, put the English to the sword, and burnt the place. Thence, with increasing musters, he marched upon Cork, which however he abstained from attacking. In January the insurgents were encouraged by the arrival of some military stores from abroad, with promises of further assistance in response to messages from Desmond to the King of Spain.

[Sidenote: 1580 Fire and Sword]

Meantime, neither Malby at Athlone nor Pelham in Dublin had sufficient troops to take the field in force. Ormonde, dispatched from England to take the chief command, had neither money nor material allowed him to take the offensive. It was not till March that the Queen was induced to send the urgently needed reinforcements, and Admiral Wynter with a squadron of ships arrived at the mouth of the Shannon. Ormonde from Kilkenny in the Butler country, and Pelham from Dublin, marched in two columns converging on Tralee, burning and slaughtering mercilessly along the route, sparing none. Then they turned on Carrickfoyle, impregnable without artillery, but easily breached by the heavy guns landed from Wynter's ships. The garrison was put to the sword. Desmond at Ashketyn, having no mind for a like fate, withdrew from it, blowing up the castle behind him. But Elizabeth stopped the supplies; the English were again forced to inaction, and parties of insurgents went marauding over Cork and Kerry, taking their turn of murdering. In June the purse-strings were loosened again; Pelham marched into Kerry, and only just failed to surprise Desmond and his people, with Sanders, in their beds. They escaped however, and Pelham went on to Dingle. Ormonde, making his way to the same point, added considerably to the tale of burnings and slaughterings. This loyal earl in 1580 accounted for "forty-six captains and leaders, with eight notorious traitors and male-factors, and four thousand other folk". [Footnote: *Carew Papers.*]

[Sidenote: Development of the Rebellion]

The people in despair were beginning to turn against Sanders and the Geraldines, though persistently loyal to Desmond himself. But a diversion was created by a rising of the Catholics of the Pale. Lord Grey de Wilton had just arrived in Dublin as Deputy. He marched against the rebels, but the greater part of his force was ambushed and cut to pieces in the Wicklow mountains. And on the top of this disaster, the long delayed foreign expedition landed at Dingle—Wynter having withdrawn—and Smerwick was re-occupied by a force mainly consisting of eight hundred Italian and Spanish adventurers. The rebellion seemed to be reviving everywhere. Ormonde, again marching into Kerry with four thousand men, accomplished nothing. But the murderous work of the summer had had effect, and the septs would not openly take the field without immediate cash inducements, which were lacking.

[Sidenote: Smerwick: and after]

In October Grey made a fresh start and marched down from Dublin to Kerry: in the first week of November, Wynter's fleet reappeared, having been held back by stress of weather with the exception of one vessel which had been lying off Smerwick for three weeks. The siege now was brief enough. On the 9th, the garrison, after a vain attempt to obtain terms, surrendered at discretion. The officers were put to ransom; the rest were slaughtered; even women were hanged. The dead numbered 600. Grey doubtless regarded the measure as a just return for the doings of the Inquisition, and the punishment of English sailors as pirates, for his retort to the garrison's overtures had been that their presence in Ireland was piracy. But the whole business illustrates the sheer ruthlessness which characterised both sides, at least where there was a technical excuse for denying belligerents' rights to the vanquished.

It was no longer possible for the rebellion to make head; but for the next two years a guerrilla warfare was kept up, in which English and Irish killed each other without compunction whenever anything in the shape of an excuse offered itself. Most of the English honestly believed that the only practicable policy was one of extermination, and the Irish retaliated in kind. There is nothing so ugly as this history in the annals of a people which, outside of Ireland, has shown a unique capacity for tempering conquest with justice. The very men whose blood boiled, honestly enough, over cruelties to the Indians, adopted to the Irish the precise attitude of mind which so horrified them in the Spaniards. Elizabeth herself, Burghley, Walsingham, and Ormonde, were opposed to the extermination policy; but the bloodshed went on, unsystematically instead of systematically. Sanders, wandering a hunted fugitive, died in a bog. It was not till 1583 that Desmond himself was surprised and slain in his bed. In the meantime, there had been no variation in the story. But the exhaustion of ceaseless slaughters and ceaseless famines had practically terminated the struggle. Sir John Perrot, who became Deputy in 1584, could adopt a conciliatory attitude, without fear that his leniency would be immediately abused—though it led to his recall and condemnation for treason [Footnote: This sentence however was not carried out. It is perhaps worth noting that Sir John was reputed to be a natural son of Henry VIII.] three years later.

[Sidenote: Scotland, 1579-81]

The diplomatic campaign in Scotland need not detain us long. Morton as Regent governed that country with a strong hand, and at least held down its normal turbulence: but while his forcefulness was recognised, he went his own way, quite regardless of the enemies he made. Despite his religious professions, he treated the preachers with scant courtesy, and was unpopular with all parties. D'Aubigny on his arrival promptly found his way into the young King's good graces, was made Duke of Lennox very shortly, and set himself to conciliate the Puritans by professing to have been converted from Popery by James's dialectical skill. In England, there was no doubt that he was an agent in the papal programme, and Walsingham would have had him removed in the usual lawless fashion, failing other means. But Elizabeth, as always, was confident of the practical impossibility of making Scotland united for any purpose except resistance of an English invasion. She made it evident that armed intervention from her need not be looked for; and in December (1580) Lennox (D'Aubigny) struck at Morton by accusing him of complicity in the murder of Darnley. The agent in this proceeding was another James Stewart, an adventurer, now Captain of the Guard, who was shortly after advanced to the Earldom of Arran. Morton was imprisoned, brought to trial in the following June (1581) and executed. The strong hand being gone, the usual chaos supervened. For the time the Papal party was uppermost, but Elizabeth's calculations were correct. The risk of French intervention was brought nearer, but it was counterbalanced partly by the bait of the Alençon marriage, which the Queen managed to keep dangling, partly by the fact that many of the men who had overthrown Morton were anti-papal, and preferred playing for their own hand to encouraging a French ascendancy. By the "Raid of Ruthven" in 1582 James was removed from the influence of Lennox, who had to leave the country; and in 1583 James Stewart Earl of Arran was carrying out a policy which was to make the King himself, with Arran at his elbow, the force predominating alike over preachers and nobles.

[Sidenote: England 1580]

We may now revert to England and Elizabeth in 1580. Throughout the earlier half of the year, it was as usual the Queen's first object to commit herself to nothing, but to persuade Orange that she might yet help him, and Alençon that she might yet marry him. But in July, Philip was master of Portugal, and the Jesuit campaign was beginning in England. In September, Orange's patience was worn out, and the crown of the Netherlands was definitely offered to Alençon; within a few days Drake and the Pelican were home, and Mendoza was demanding restitution; and again a few days later Spanish and Italian adventurers were fortifying themselves at Smerwick.

[Sidenote: The Jesuit Mission]

The Papal Bull of Deposition ten years before had stiffened the attitude of Government towards the English Catholics, but had neither broken down the loyalty of the latter nor led to any serious persecution. On this head, the mission of 1580 was the turning point of the reign. The moving spirit was Allen, of Douay and Rheims; a man of high ability and character who conceived that the recovery of his country for the true Church was the highest of all objects for a patriot, and one to which all other considerations should give way.

[Sidenote: Campian and Parsons]

It cannot be disputed that the aim of the Mission was to sow disloyalty as well as to gain converts, though the allegation that incitement to assassinate the Queen was part of the programme is not quite conclusively proved. Of the two chief missioners, Parsons and Campian, it is at least tolerably certain that the latter, an amiable enthusiast, was quite innocent of complicity in any such design. That certainty does not apply to Parsons. But the instructions were clearly treasonable in character. The Catholics were told that in spite of the Bull of Deposition they might profess loyalty to the Queen, but must assist in her overthrow if called upon. That is to say that if treason were brewing against the *de facto* Government, it was to be a point of conscience and a condition of the Church's approval for all Catholics that they should assist that treason. There is nothing about that instruction which can fairly be called hypocritical; but *ipso facto*, it converted every Catholic, willy nilly, into a potential traitor, who if treason arose could only remain loyal under censure of the Church. Moreover it was the business of the missioners not only to impress on those who were already Catholics this view of their duty; but also, by an active propaganda, to increase the number of such potential traitors; while it was quite certain that under such conditions, converts would be actuated by a zeal which would render them doubly dangerous.

For some months the emissaries travelled the country in various disguises, shifting their quarters secretly, but in favourable districts occasionally appearing quite openly, more or less winked at by the authorities. Their immunity made them the more sanguine, but it also alarmed the Protestants, and before the end of the year, there was a change.

[Sidenote: Walsingham]

Walsingham—a sincere Puritan, a man who never soiled his hands for private gain, who by his outspoken opposition to her political double-dealing provoked Elizabeth's anger more frequently than any other of her many outspoken advisers, of whom more than any other statesman of the day it might be said that he loved righteousness and hated iniquity—had yet the fault of the Puritan character, a certain remorselessness in dealing with the servants of the Scarlet Woman. He would have connived at the murder of D'Aubigny; his organisation of "Secret Service" was as unscrupulous as Burghley's; and he more than any one else approved and fostered the revival of the illegal application of torture as a means of extorting information from recalcitrant prisoners. In this iniquity, however, it is fair to recognise that the rack and the boot were not employed wantonly but, as it would seem, honestly: with the single intention of obtaining true information for the unravelment of plots which endangered the public weal, and only on persons who were known to possess that information.

[Sidenote: 1581 An anti-papal Parliament]

Walsingham then, at the close of 1580, appears to have undertaken the conduct of the operations against the emissaries, several of whom were promptly captured and put to the torture without result, though one or two made haste to change sides to save themselves. The rest showed that magnificent constancy which had characterised alike the Carthusians under Henry and the Protestants under Mary. In January (1581) parliament was called, and passed a very stringent act making it treason to proselytise, or to join the Church of Rome; imposing a heavy fine as well as imprisonment for celebrating Mass, and a fine of £20 per month for exemption from attendance at the Anglican ritual. Drastic as the measure was, and a complete departure from the comparative toleration hitherto prevalent in practice if not altogether in theory, the basis of it was quite manifestly the conviction that as a result of the mission every Catholic must now be suspect of treason, and every convert to Catholicism something more than suspect.

When the parliament had completed its business by voting supplies, it was prorogued. Through the spring and the summer the pursuit of the Emissaries and the oppression of the Catholics under the new Act went on. Campian himself was taken in July, and after some months' imprisonment, in the course of which he was racked, was executed for treason at the end of the year: his martyrdom, with others, producing the usual effect.

[Sidenote: Alençon again]

In the meantime, the acceptance in January of the lordship of the Netherlands by Alençon forced Elizabeth to redouble her pretence of desiring the furtherance of the Alençon marriage—a pretence through which Walsingham alone seems to have penetrated. The French King sent over a magnificent embassy in April, which was magnificently received. Then Elizabeth suggested that a League would serve every purpose. France replied that the League was what it wished for, but the marriage was a condition. Everything was discussed and agreed upon—but the Queen succeeded in retaining her saving clause; the agreement was subject to Alençon and herself being personally satisfied. She was still able to hold off, while she had brought France into such a position that if war should be declared between England and Spain, France must join England. Walsingham was sent off to Paris, with the task before him of evading the marriage, avoiding war while entangling France in it, and all with a full conviction that his instructions would vary from week to week. He believed, and he told her, that France would make the League without the marriage, if her sincerity were only guaranteed by something more substantial than promises; but that if neither the League nor the marriage were completed, she would have Spain, France, and Scotland—where Morton had just been executed—all turning their arms against her at once. But contrary to all reasonable expectation Elizabeth succeeded in avoiding a breach with France and in keeping Alençon still dangling: and however Mendoza—who had quite failed to obtain any compensation for Drake's expedition—might threaten, Philip still refused to declare war openly.

[Sidenote: His visit to England]

The story of the Alençon farce, if it were not unquestionable fact, would be almost incredible. Monsieur was some twenty years younger than the amorous Queen; in person he was offensive and contemptible; his character corresponded to his person, and his intelligence to his character. Elizabeth was eight and forty. Yet the man's amazing vanity made him a perpetual dupe, while it must have taken all her own vanity to persuade the lady that she could play Omphale to his Hercules. Yet she did it. In November she had him back in England. She kissed him before Walsingham and the French Ambassador, [Footnote: *State Papers, Spanish*, iii., p. 226.] and gave him the ring off her finger, declaring that she was going to marry him. But as soon as it came to business, she made one fresh demand after another. When concession was added to concession, she capped the list by requiring the restoration of Calais, an obvious absurdity. Burghley thought the whole thing was ended, and was for conciliating Spain by restoring Drake's booty. Walsingham would have handed those spoils over to Orange. The Queen did neither, but told Alençon that his presence in the Netherlands had now become quite necessary to his own honour—which was true—and that with a little patience unreasonable people would be pacified, and she would still marry him.

[Sidenote: Alençon in the Netherlands]

Thus this most unlucky dupe was once more got out of the country, in February (1582), a dupe still; and the United Provinces swore allegiance to him under the new title of Duke of Brabant—giving him to understand, however, that they accepted him simply as a surety for English support. When he was safely out of the country, Elizabeth became more emphatic than ever in her declarations that she would marry him. After all, however, she was reluctantly compelled to salve her lover's wounded feelings by cash subsidies, real and substantial though secret.

[Sidenote: Exit Alençon]

At the end of March an attempt was made to assassinate the strong man of Holland, William the Silent. He was in fact very dangerously wounded, and Elizabeth became alarmed lest a like danger were in store for her. Orange recovered, but Parma continued his course of gradual conquest, and Alençon bethought him of playing the traitor, seizing the principal towns, and handing them over to Spain as a peace-offering. In the following January he made the attempt; but the capture succeeded only here and there, and at Antwerp, where he himself lay, the *coup* failed ignominiously and disastrously. The city got wind of what was going to happen; the French troops were admitted, and, being in, found themselves in a trap and were cut to pieces. Alençon was deservedly and finally ruined, and no one in France or England could pretend any more that he was a possible husband. The year after he sank to a dishonoured grave, leaving the Huguenot Henry of Navarre heir presumptive to the throne of France.

[Sidenote: Scotland]

Before Alençon's disaster, Elizabeth's policy in Scotland had been justified by results: the raid of Ruthven had placed the King in the hands of the Protestant nobles again, and Lennox was out of the country for good. It is probable that from Elizabeth's point of view, it was not worth while to attempt to obtain the friendship of an Anglophil party, either by force or by bribery. Bribes would have told only just for so long as they were accepted as an earnest of more to follow; while force would have had its invariable result of uniting Scotland in determined resistance. The one thing which would have given reality to the overtures perpetually passing between Scotland and the Guises was an English attempt to grasp at domination. Elizabeth, with Mary a prisoner, had a permanent diplomatic asset in her hands, since she could hint a threat of either executing her, or liberating her, or surrendering her on terms as might seem most convenient at a given crisis. Intrigues which like the marriage projects were never intended to be consummated were more effective than either bribery or force—and cheaper.

CHAPTER XXII
ELIZABETH (vii), 1583-87—THE
END OF QUEEN MARY

[Sidenote: 1583 The Throgmorton Conspiracy]

The collapse of Alençon was the precursor of a comprehensive conspiracy. Before the Raid of Ruthven (August 1582), the Guise faction in France had contemplated a descent on Scotland in conjunction with Lennox's friends there, with a view of course to raising England in favour of Mary. Alençon's relations with Elizabeth had not made the French King or his mother, neither of whom loved the Guises, particularly favourable to the scheme. The Raid destroyed the prospects of the definitely Catholic party in Scotland; on the other hand, the failure of Alençon affected, though only slightly, the objections on the part of King Henry. But any enterprise against England would have to take a somewhat different form. In May, Guise was planning a fresh scheme of assassination and invasion; [Footnote: *State Papers, Spanish*, iii., pp. 464, 479.] while as against the Guise intrigues still going on in Scotland, Elizabeth at the suggestion of the French ambassador was again proposing diplomatically to release Mary [Footnote: *Ibid.*, p. 465.]—on terms.

[Sidenote: Sanguine Catholic forecast]

The English refugees and the Seminarists suffered from the same sanguine conviction that two-thirds of the country was thirsting to throw off the hated yoke of the existing Government, by which Jacobite agents were eternally possessed in the first half of the eighteenth century; and with a good deal less reason. For whereas the House of Hanover had no enthusiastic adherents, while the House of Stuart had many, and the Whig politicians were for the most part ready to transfer themselves to the other side if the other side should look like winning: at this time, the most energetic portion of the population, gentry and commons, including practically all who had practised the art of war by land or sea, in the Low Countries, in Ireland, on the Spanish Main and in Spanish waters, were fierily Protestant, and the Ministers, nearly all irrevocably bound to the Queen, were singularly prompt and alert men of action. Enthusiasts there were on the other side, but they were few. Yet in their prolific imaginations, the enthusiasts multiplied their own numbers pathetically, and believed passionately in phantom hosts only waiting for the word to draw the sword, or at least the dagger, in the sacred cause.

Neither the Spaniards nor the Guises appear ever to have allowed themselves to accept unreservedly the Churchmen's estimate of the state of feeling in England; but the Spanish Ambassadors, one after another, and Mendoza certainly not the least, gave more credence to these impressions than they deserved, placing far too high a value on the assurances of a very small number of the nobility. It is probable also that the Jesuits greatly exaggerated the exciting effect of the martyrdom of Campian and his associates; for these bore no sort of comparison with the burnings of Mary's reign, of which every man nearing forty years of age was old enough to have a tolerably vivid personal recollection. At any rate the advices of Mendoza went far to confirm the declarations of Allen that a determined Catholic rising might be relied on, in case of an invasion which should have for its object the substitution of Mary for Elizabeth and the restoration of the old Religion.

[Sidenote: Divided Counsels]

The counsels however of the plotters were divided. The priests would have kept the French out of the affair altogether. Philip was as reluctant as ever to take an English war upon his shoulders until he had completed the subjugation of the Netherlands. Mendoza, recognising that Guise was not France—for now as always, Spain could not afford to let France dominate England—was willing enough that Guise should head an expedition in which Frenchmen should otherwise play no more than an equal part; on the hypothesis that, when the revolution was accomplished, circumstances would compel the new regime to dependence on Spain. All the parties— Guise, Philip, Allen—were prepared to yield unofficial sanction to the simplification of the problem by assassination. Even when the different interests in the scheme had been compromised, prompt action was obviously essential if the English Government, with its vast network of spies and secret agents, was not to get wind of the plot. Promptitude however was the one thing of which Philip was constitutionally incapable, and Guise was obliged to consent to wait till the following spring.

[Sidenote: The plot discovered]

As a natural result, an active member of the conspiracy, Francis Throgmorton, was suddenly pounced upon in his house in London. He succeeded in conveying sundry important documents to Mendoza, but lists of the English conspirators and other conclusively incriminating documents were found. The rack did the rest. The unhappy man endured through the first application: the second conquered him. He told the whole story—possibly more than the truth, though that is hardly probable; but of course the persons incriminated denied complicity, and there was in some cases no other evidence against them, while the confessions of a victim under torture are—biased.

The main facts at any rate were indisputable—the plan of a Guise invasion, under Spanish auspices, with the complicity of a number of English Catholics, as well as of Mendoza. The presumption that Mary was cognisant of it was supported by Throgmorton's confession, but such presumptions and such evidence fall short of being absolutely conclusive. [Footnote: Mendoza's letters of this period (*State Papers, Spanish*, iii.) implicate Mary *prima facie*: but do not *necessarily* mean more than that her life was endangered by the discoveries.] Under such conditions however, grave and well founded suspicion was enough to justify the severest precautionary measures. Northumberland and Arundel [Footnote: Son of the late Duke of Norfolk. The title came through his mother.] were thrown into prison; several of the seminarists, already in ward, were executed; a number of arrests were made; known Catholics all over the country were placed under strict surveillance, and removed from any commands they might hold. Mendoza was ordered in uncompromising terms to leave the country; fleets were manned, and musters levied. The delay had proved fatal to the combined scheme.

The collapse of two assassination plots, not forming part of the Throgmorton conspiracy, may be mentioned. One was that of an apparently half-crazy person named Somerville, who betrayed himself by bragging; the other, the more curious affair of Parry, who got himself introduced into the Queen's presence several times, but "let I dare not wait upon I would" persistently, till he retired with nothing accomplished; to reappear presently.

[Sidenote: 1584 Death of Orange]

Elizabeth escaped; but death was soon to lay his hand on two personages of consequence. In May (1584) Alençon decayed out of a world in which accident only had allowed him for a time to occupy a very disproportionate share of the political stage. A month later, the most heroic figure of a time when heroes were rare among politicians was struck down by the hand of a fanatic. William of Orange, the head, hand, and heart of the great fight for freedom being waged in the Netherlands, was assassinated by a zealot. More than ever it seemed that the Hollanders must submit to Philip, unless the power of France or the power of England were devoted whole-heartedly to their cause. The death of Alençon made Henry of Navarre the actual heir presumptive to the throne of France. The King and his mother hated and feared Protestantism less than they hated and feared the Guises, and publicly acknowledged Navarre as next in succession.

As usual, Elizabeth's advisers would have had her play boldly for Protestantism; as usual, she herself was bent on evading the open collision with Spain. Her hope was to entangle France in the Netherlands war, and herself to strike in—if she must strike in at all—only when her intervention would enable her to make her own terms. The French King would not be inveigled. If he could have relied on her support, or if the Guises had been somewhat less dangerous, he would have been ready to strike; but his distrust of the English Queen was too justifiably complete. She was in fact saved from the absolute necessity of yielding to the persuasions of Burghley and Walsingham only by the dogged tenacity with which the Hollanders held out. And while they held out, she still held off.

[Sidenote: The "Association"]

In England however, one fact was more universally and vividly present in men's minds than any other. In the eyes of every Protestant, the supreme danger still lay in the death or deposition of Elizabeth and the elevation of Mary Stewart to the throne. Recent events had brought home the enormous risks of assassination; and an Association was formed for the defence of the Queen. A declaration was framed, the signatories whereof bound themselves by a solemn vow not only to pursue to the death all persons concerned in any plot against the Queen, but also any person in favour of whose succession to the throne any attempt should be made against her; to bar any such person absolutely from the succession; and to treat as perjured traitors any of the Association who failed to carry out this oath. It was sufficiently obvious that the declaration was aimed directly against Mary; but it may be said that the entire nation forthwith enrolled itself. And with the bulk of them, the enrolment was anything but an empty form.

[Sidenote: 1584-85 The Association ratified]

At the same time, it was difficult to see how the members of the Association could carry out their pledge without a breach of the law; stronger legal measures for the defence of the Queen and the frustration of assassination as a means to secure the inheritance in any particular quarter were required. Parliament was summoned at the end of November. Ministers wished to have definite provision made for carrying on the Government in case of the Queen's murder; but she would go with them no further than to sanction the Association, with the entirely laudable modification that the person for whose sake the deed was done should not be held *ipso facto* guilty of complicity. The differences of opinion were so strong that the session closed without the passing of any Act. In January however, an accomplice of that Parry already mentioned [Footnote: See p. 330] denounced him for intending to kill the Queen. Threatened with the rack, Parry made a full confession, and was hanged, drawn, and quartered. At the renewed Session in February, it was enacted that an invasion, rebellion, or attempt on the Queen's person, on behalf of any one with a claim to the succession, should disqualify such person from the succession absolutely, if complicity in the attempt should be proved after due enquiry. A commission was appointed to put the Act in execution in the event of assassination; and the Association was sanctioned subject to these provisions. Subsidies were then voted, and parliament prorogued, after an unusually gracious speech from the throne.

[Sidenote: 1585: France: the Holy League]

Meantime the United Provinces, despairing of an English overlordship, were again making overtures to France for a Protectorate, or even annexation if France should insist on that alternative. Relations between the King and Mendoza, now Ambassador at Paris, were so strained that war seemed all but inevitable; Henry seems to have been held back only by the well-founded fear that Elizabeth was intriguing to draw him into the war and frustrate him in carrying it on. But in that fear he declined the offer of the Provinces. In March the Guises produced a new development by the open announcement of the formation of the Holy League, for the exclusion of Navarre from the succession and the enforcement in France of the decrees of the Council of Trent.

But for the unconquerable mutual distrust of Henry and Elizabeth, Henry, relying on English support, would have bidden defiance to the League; but the memories of St. Bartholomew and Elizabeth's character as an intriguer made confidence on either side impossible. The great siege of Antwerp seemed to be on the verge of terminating in a catastrophe for the revolting States, which would enable Parma to co-operate actively with Guise; and Henry found himself threatened with excommunication. Before midsummer he capitulated, and declared for the League. On the other hand, Navarre was not the man to yield, and while Elizabeth again had the chance of playing a bold part and espousing his cause heartily, she judged rightly that he was strong enough unaided to keep the alliance of the League and the Court very thoroughly occupied for some time to come. As a factor in the Netherlands question. France was for the present at least a negligible quantity. So she left Navarre to fight his own battles in France, while she should dole out to the Netherlanders just so much or so little support as might suffice for her own ends.

While the French King was surrendering to the League, the Spanish King took a step which was intended to frighten England, and had as usual the precisely contrary result. He ordered the seizure of all English ships and crews on his coasts. The order was carried out; and England instead of being cowed was forthwith ablaze with defiance. The effect was promptly apparent.

[Sidenote: Agreement with the States]

The United Provinces were again offering themselves to England. In August an agreement was arrived at. The Queen was to hold Ostend and Sluys as well as Flushing and Brille, as security. She was to send over five thousand men with Leicester in command. Some Queen's troops and large numbers of volunteers were shipped off in a few days—too late however to save Antwerp. Still weeks and even months passed before pay or commanders were allowed to follow. But before the year was out, Sidney, Leicester, and others had taken up their commands, the last named representing the Queen of England.

[Sidenote: Drake's raid]

Already, however, an enterprise still more ominous to Spain was in hand—unofficial, like most other great enterprises of the reign. Letters of reprisal for the seizure of the English ships had been promptly issued, and numbers of privateers were quickly in Spanish waters. Among others, Francis Drake fitted out a flotilla, the Queen being an interested shareholder in his venture—though even under those conditions he put to sea before time, lest counter-orders should arrive. The adventurers sailed into Vigo, demanded the release of all English prisoners in the province, which was promised, captured some prizes, and betook themselves to the ocean, with a view to seizing the Spanish Plate Fleet, which was on its way from America. They just missed the Fleet, but proceeded to San Domingo (Hayti) which they held to ransom, went on to treat Cartagena in like manner, and then being attacked by Yellow Fever, came home with the spoils. Whatever fears of a Spanish war might be entertained by Elizabeth herself, the English seamen had no qualms as to their own immeasurable superiority, and desired nothing better than opportunities for demonstrating it.

[Sidenote 1: Elizabeth's intrigues]
[Sidenote 2: 1586 Leicester in the Netherlands]

While Drake was thus congenially employed, Elizabeth was carrying on her system of inaction and double-dealing. She intrigued—behind the backs of her ministers—with Parma, for the surrender to him of the towns she held, on terms which from her point of view were quite good enough for the Provinces, namely the restitution of their old Constitutional Government without religious liberty; although in their own view, religious liberty was primarily essential. Leicester complicated matters for her by accepting, in flat contradiction to her orders, the formal Governorship of the United Provinces: finding in fact that if he was to stay in the Netherlands nothing short of that would prevail against the suspicions of the Queen's treachery. At home, Burghley himself threatened to resign if she would not take a straightforward course. Walsingham wrote to Leicester, with his usual bitterness, of the "peril to safety and honour" from her behaviour. If she had indeed contemplated the surrender of the cities to Parma, that plan was frustrated. Still she stormed at Burghley and Walsingham, flatly and with contumely refused to ratify Leicester's arrangement, and continued to keep back the pay of the troops. Parma, though he too was starved in men and money by Philip, continued inch by inch to absorb the revolted territory. All that Leicester succeeded in accomplishing by the month of September was the brilliant and entirely futile action of Zutphen where in one great hour Philip Sidney won death and immortality (September 22nd). Thereafter, inaction and short supplies continued to be the rule, on both sides. In November, Leicester was back in England, where a fresh situation was developing.

[Sidenote:1585-86 The trapping of Mary]

While the arrangements for armed intervention in the Netherlands were in progress, Walsingham had been busy preparing for the last act in the Tragedy of Mary Stewart. The Secretary was foremost among those who held not only that the captive Queen deserved death, but that her death was more necessary to the welfare of England than any other event. Yet it was quite certain that Elizabeth would not assent to her death, unless she thought she could convince herself and the world that Mary had been actively engaged in treasonous plots. Recently however at Tutbury under the charge of Sir Amyas Paulet, she had been guarded so strictly that no surreptitious correspondence had a chance of passing. Walsingham was confident that if the opportunity were given, a treasonous correspondence would be opened. It became his object therefore to give her the opportunity in appearance, while securing that the channel through which communications passed should be a treacherous one, and the whole of what was supposed to be secret should be betrayed to him. To this end, the Queen was removed in December 1585 to Chartley Manor, avowedly in response to her own demands for a less rigorously unpleasant residence than Tutbury. The instrument of the plot was a young man named Giffard, supposed to be in the inner counsels of the Jesuits, actually in Walsingham's service. Through Giffard, communications were opened between Mary and a devoted adherent of hers in France named Morgan: but every letter passing was deciphered and copied, and the copies placed in the Secretary's hands.

[Sidenote: 1586 Babington's plot]

In the late spring, the great Babington conspiracy was set on foot; whereof the main features were, that Elizabeth was to be assassinated by a group of half a dozen young men who had places at court and occasional access to her person. The two leading spirits were Anthony Babington and a Jesuit named Ballard. Of course a Catholic rising and a foreign invasion were part of the plan, and Mendoza at Paris was playing his own part. Much of the plot was confided to Giffard, who reported to Walsingham. The Secretary and his Queen were satisfied to let the plot develop while they gathered all the threads in their own hands before striking. The correspondence, as copied for Walsingham at Chartley, conveyed not details but general intelligence of what was on foot to Mary, and approval from Mary to the conspirators. In August, Walsingham's moment came: the conspirators were seized; under torture or threat of torture they made complete confession. The Scottish Queen's rooms at Chartley were ransacked, and all her papers impounded. Again, as after the Throgmorton conspiracy, fleets were manned and musters called out. In September, the conspirators were tried and executed, and a Commission was appointed to try Mary herself in October.

[Sidenote: Trial of Mary]

Mary, as before, denied the jurisdiction, professing readiness to answer only before Parliament. She ignored an invitation from the Queen to obtain pardon by a confession of guilt. She assented under protest to appear before the Court, and there avowed that she had consistently appealed to the Powers of Europe to aid her, as she was entitled to do, but flatly denied complicity in the Babington plot. The evidence against her was entirely that of letters—said to be copied from her correspondence, but quite possibly invented in whole or in part—and the confessions of the conspirators or of her secretaries, extorted under torture or the fear of it. Those letters might even have been concocted to suit Walsingham without his actual privity, by the man who had the task of deciphering and copying them. Having heard her denial, the Court was transferred from Fotheringay, where it first sat, to Westminster: and at Westminster, after further examination of the documents and of Mary's secretaries, it unanimously pronounced her guilty. The sentence was left for Parliament and the Queen to settle. The Parliament which had passed the recent Act for the Defence of the Queen was dissolved, and a new one was summoned. On its meeting in November, it petitioned for Mary's execution, in accordance with the terms of the "Association" which Mary herself had offered to join. The publication of the sentence was received with public acclamation: but whether the Queen would assent to it remained to be seen.

What then were the guiding considerations, whether of Ethics or of Expediency?

[Sidenote: The situation reviewed;]

For eighteen years, Mary had been in Elizabeth's power. Elizabeth had held her captive for the sufficient reason—amongst others—that were she outside of England and free from restraint, there was nothing to prevent her from actively agitating the Catholics of Europe to assert her claim to the English throne. No monarch having in his grip a claimant with an undeniably strong title to his throne would have allowed that claimant to escape from his clutches. Few would have hesitated to concoct some more or less plausible pretext for the claimant's death. Half England considered that a sufficient pretext was provided by Kirk o' Field; but even assuming that Mary's guilt in that matter was legally proved, which it assuredly was not, it is sufficiently obvious that the sovereign of England had no jurisdiction. Still any monarch situated like Elizabeth would have maintained, and probably have acted upon, the right to put the captive to death, if proved to be guilty of complicity in treason or subornation thereof. Throughout the eighteen years, Elizabeth had deliberately abstained from seeking to prove definitely that Mary was an accomplice in the various plots on her behalf, while she was no less careful to leave the imputation of complicity clinging to her. But now, if the Chartley correspondence were genuine, the case was decided. The Court, which cannot be said to have been packed, was satisfied. Again it does not appear that any monarch, regarding the captive's death as *per se* desirable, would have doubted the sufficiency of the ground for her execution.

But hitherto the English Queen had not regarded her rival's death as *per se* desirable. Conceivably there was an element of generosity in that view. Certainly there was the fact that Mary was an anointed Queen, and Elizabeth had a most profound respect for the sanctity of crowned heads. But apart from this, there was the purely political argument. Mary living, and in her power, was an asset. She might always be set at liberty on terms. Elizabeth hated parting with a political asset even at a high price, for good value. Hitherto she had reckoned the living Mary as worth more than Mary's death would be: for Mary might simply be replaced as a claimant by James, who was not, like his mother, in her power, and might very well think the crown of England worth a Mass.

[Sidenote: its recent developments]

Now however, a considerable change had come over the situation. Failing Mary the English Catholics were divided as to the succession. James could profess filial affection when it suited him; but for some time past he had dropped that attitude; he had just made a convenient compact with England; and his mother, making up her mind to his antagonism, had by will disinherited him and bequeathed her rights to Philip of Spain, who had a clear claim to the blood Royal of England as descending through his mother Isabella of Portugal from John of Gaunt. [Footnote: See *Front.* Philip's cousins, however, the duchesses of Braganza and Parma, daughters of Isabella's brother, had a better title—as they also had to the crown of Portugal. See p. 303. The exiled Westmorland had a better title still.] The accession of Philip would suit neither France, nor the Pope; the accession of James would be at best an uncertain gain to the Catholics; and so Mary's execution would leave no one claimant for the discontented to rally to. On the other hand, if Mary were allowed to live, her restoration by Elizabeth would be almost incredible. Her value as an asset had fallen, the security given by her death would be much more assured. Political expediency, therefore, entirely favoured her death, unless the execution would bring France or Scotland against Elizabeth in arms. France protested earnestly, but clearly intended nothing stronger than protests, and it very soon became equally clear that no serious trouble need be feared from James.

[Sidenote: 1587 The sentences carried out]

Still through December and January Elizabeth continued to vacillate. The sentiment as to the sanctity of an anointed Queen still influenced her; yet it is sufficiently clear that her real motive for hesitation was the desire, not to spare Mary, but herself to escape the odium of sanctioning the execution. At last however the warrant was signed, and received the Chancellor's seal. Yet she made the Secretary Davison write to Paulet and urge him to put Mary to death without waiting for the warrant. Paulet flatly refused. She used such terms to Davison that he feared on his own responsibility to forward the warrant to the appointed authorities Shrewsbury and Kent. He went to Burghley: Burghley summoned privately all members of the Council then in London. They agreed to share the responsibility for acting without further reference to the Queen. On February 4th, the letters were issued. On the 7th, in the afternoon, Kent and Shrewsbury presented themselves at Fotheringay and told Mary that on the following morning she must die.

[Sidenote: Death of Mary]

It was characteristic of her that during the few hours of life left to her, she forgot neither loyal servant nor victorious foe. Her last written words were to bid her friends remember both. When the morrow came, she mounted the low scaffold in the great hall with unfaltering step, far less moved outwardly than the six attendants whom she had chosen for her last moments, a splendid tragic figure; every word, every gesture those of a woman falsely charged and deeply wronged, majestic in her proud self-control. Was it merely a superb, an unparalleled piece of acting? [Footnote: See Appendix C. Mr. Froude is dramatically at his best in telling the story; but his partisan bias is correspondingly emphasized.] Was it the heroism of a martyr? The voice of England had doomed her; she appealed to a higher Tribunal than England. King or Queen never faced their end more triumphantly. Mary Stewart, royal in the fleeting moments of her prosperity, royal throughout the long years of her adversity, was never so supremely royal as in her last hour on earth.

CHAPTER XXIII
ELIZABETH (viii), 1558-87—THE SEAMEN

As before we postponed the story of Ireland, in order to give a consecutive narrative down to the point at which the interaction of Irish and English affairs became marked and definite, so we have hitherto deferred consideration of the most tremendous factor in the Elizabethan evolution, the development of the Island nation into the greatest Ocean Power in the world. The charter of the Queen of the Seas was drawn by the Tudor seamen, and received its seal when the great Armada perished. It is time therefore to see how it came about that England was able to challenge and to shatter the Power which threatened to dominate the world.

[Sidenote: The New World]

Throughout the Middle Ages, until what we conveniently term, from the English point of view, the Tudor Period, the European peoples were confined to the European Continent and the adjacent islands. In Asia and in Mediterranean Africa the Mohammedan races were a militant barrier to expansion. The discoveries of Columbus and Vasco da Gama opened new fields, whereof the inheritance was destined to the nations who should achieve the dominion of the Ocean. Always important, the capacity for maritime development now became the primary condition of ultimate greatness. The fact was at the first recognised by Spain and Portugal; and an immediate incentive was given to those two Powers, and something of a check to the rest, when Pope Alexander VI., with an authority as yet unchallenged, divided between them the newly found countries and the lands still to be discovered. Acquiescence in the award was limited; with the ecclesiastical revolt from Rome it vanished; but Spaniards and Portuguese were already in full possession of vast territories before their exclusive title to the whole was called in question.

[Sidenote: The English Marine before Elizabeth]

Nevertheless, more than before, the eyes of statesmen were turned to the sea and the eyes of merchants to the ocean. The nucleus of a Royal Navy was formed by Henry VII., and his son very greatly increased the number of the King's ships and built many tall vessels. The merchants of

Bristol and the western ports made daring voyages in hitherto unexplored and half-explored waters, as we have seen; while the general activity of the mercantile marine was greatly increased.

Prosperity, and as a necessary result, enterprise, suffered a check under the disastrous financial conditions prevalent in the reigns of Edward and Mary; yet the closing months of Edward's reign had been marked by the departure of the expedition of Willoughby and Chancellor in search of a North-East Passage; while several voyages to the Guinea Coast—whither William Hawkins had sailed in Henry's day—were undertaken by John Lock and Towerson, during the reign of Mary. We have seen also how the young hot-heads of Protestantism had taken to privateering in the Channel, in the name of Patriotism and true Religion. That course was reprehensible enough; but it led at least to the cultivation of the art of seamanship. On the other hand, that art suffered from a curious draw-back. The partial cessation of the practice of fasting which accompanied the development of Protestantism reacted on the fishing trade, which was the regular school of sailors; insomuch that not only Somerset but Cecil in Elizabeth's time, proposed ordinances in favour of fasting, simply and solely to check the collapse of that industry.

[Sidenote: The Royal Navy]

The Royal Navy developed by Henry VIII. was allowed perforce to decay under his two immediate successors. According to the most authentic lists, [Footnote: Sir W. Laird Clowes, *The Royal Navy*, vol. i., pp. 419 ff. Throughout this chapter, the figures for tonnage are adopted from this work.] in 1548 there were 53 ships in the Fleet, with a total tonnage of about 11,000. In 1558 there were but 26, with a tonnage of little more than 7,000. During the first half of Elizabeth's reign, the numbers were not increased; in 1575 there were but 24 vessels; but the tonnage had risen 50 per cent., and was within 10 per cent, of what Henry had bequeathed to Edward. When the Armada came, in the twenty-ninth year of Elizabeth's reign, 34 ships of the Royal Navy were engaged, which had a slight superiority [Footnote: Clowes, *Royal Navy*, i., p. 561.] of armament over any equal number of the enemy's fleet. The aggregate tonnage is given [Footnote: *Ibid.*, p. 588.] as 15 per cent. more than that of Henry's 53—an average per ship of very nearly double. It is clear therefore that the policy of strengthening the navy was not neglected; but it took the form of acquiring not more ships, but larger and better fighting craft. [Footnote: Corbett, *Drake and the Tudor Navy*, i., pp. 370 ff. It is pointed out (p. 372) that medium sized ships were regarded as better weapons in general than those of the largest size.] The multiplication of smaller craft would have been a far less effective means for achieving the desired end. The Royal Navy, a creation of the century, was not supposed to constitute the naval defences of the country. It occupied a position among the marine fighting force analogous to that of our white troops in India to-day; who form only one-third of the army there while reckoned and intended to be its mainstay.

[Sidenote: Privateering]

It is possible that in the simple legitimate processes of trade, the merchant captains would never have learnt the art of extracting every ounce of value out of their ships as fighting machines; certainly they would not have developed the very marked supremacy in gunnery which was so decisive a feature in the contest with Spain. The mere temptations of successful barter would not have sufficed to attract the fiery and alert young gentlemen of Devon or elsewhere, and the daring mariners who revelled in meeting and overcoming any apparent odds. But the circumstances of the time presented to the men, who in other days would have found no outlet for their energies but in land-service abroad, the opportunity of giving those energies a wider scope in the more exacting but also more inspiring service by sea: where richer prizes were to be won, with greater risk no doubt, but risk which called every faculty of manhood into vigorous play.

[Sidenote: Piracy?]

It has become the common practice to apply the term "piracy" at large to the doings of the Elizabethan seamen; but a single category which embraces Captain Kidd and Francis Drake ceases to imply any very specific condemnation. The suggestion that their acts were on the same moral plane is absurd. The "piracy" of the great Elizabethans was compatible with a clean conscience. At the present day we rightly account a man a murderer who slays another in his own private quarrel; but we do not give that name to one who two centuries ago killed his man in a duel. We decline to recognise the validity of the reasoning by which men justified such acts to themselves; but before the fallacy in that reasoning was understood, the degree of guilt involved in acting upon it was something very different from what it would be to-day. In the same way, a century ago honourable and honest men countenanced smuggling; but we do not classify them with footpads. Yet a similar confusion of thought is involved in this indiscriminate application of the term piracy, unless we emphasize the fact that in this connexion it must be divested of its ordinary moral connotation.

Plain sea-robbers there were, not a few, who had no compunction about seizing and looting any vessel of any nationality except—for politic reasons—their own. The records show clearly enough that there were plenty of these, who found harbourage in the Scillies or on the Irish Coast, or even on the English Channel, or would lie in wait to cut out peaceable traders of any nation almost at the mouth of the Thames. The Government took little enough pains to repress them. They did not attack their own countrymen, and were a useful source for recruiting: but they were indisputably Pirates.

[Sidenote: Volunteers]

Then there were the privateers who had a colour for their depredations; professedly volunteers on the side of recognised belligerents. As it was considered legitimate for troops of English volunteers to fight for the revolted Netherland States, while the Government refused to acknowledge that their doing so constituted an act of war against Spain; so Englishmen were allowed to man ships and sail under the flag of the Huguenots of Rochelle, carrying a commission to wage war on "Papist" ships, French, or others regarded as in alliance with them. This was not piracy in the accepted sense, though it was not perhaps very far removed from it in the majority of cases. The kind of fanaticism which, two hundred years after Elizabeth's accession, elevated Frederick the Great into "the Protestant Hero" could easily, without conscious insincerity, make Religion an excuse for spoiling the Papists in Elizabeth's day; and the privateers who looted a Spanish vessel or one carrying Spanish treasure or merchandise believed as a rule that they were thereby laying up treasure in Heaven as well as on Earth, Their Ethics were derived from the Old Testament; and they looked upon the "Idolaters" very much as the Israelites were told by the prophets to look upon the Philistines, or Amalek, or Ammon.

[Sidenote: Reprisal]

Moreover it must be borne in mind that as concerned the raiding of Spanish ships, the Government balanced the injury done against the grievances of the British sailors and ships seized in Spanish ports by the Inquisition. So long as the Spanish King refused to interfere with the jurisdiction of the Holy Office, the English Queen in effect refused to interfere with acts of reprisal. If these rovers could have been caught and hanged at the yard-arm, she could hardly have protested; but as breaches of international amity the practices were very much on a par. In the technical sense, that they made war on their own account on the ships of a theoretically friendly Power, the rovers of this class were no doubt pirates; what we have to recognise is that the normal condition of affairs was one unknown to the law-books, a state of quasi-war; having no little resemblance to that prevalent for centuries on the Anglo-Scottish border, where it was not to be expected that the Wardens of the Marches on the one side would carry out their duties while the Wardens on the other side were neglecting theirs with the connivance of the Government. And in this case, Philip's connivance at the proceedings of the Inquisition was open and avowed; by consequence, the English Government refused to treat the proceedings of the privateers as piracy; and again by consequence the privateers considered themselves to be acting in a perfectly legitimate, not to say laudable, manner, in treating the enemy's commerce precisely as they would have done under a state of declared war.

No doubt the desire of plunder was usually a stronger incentive than either retaliation or religion. Privateering was not *per se* admirable or praiseworthy. But it was something entirely different from what we understand by Piracy pure and simple. And manifestly it provided a very excellent and efficient school for the sons of a nation which was about to challenge the Colossus of the South for the title to the Empire of the Seas.

[Sidenote: The Explorers]

But while privateering bred in numbers men who knew how to handle and fight their ships, something more was needed to produce a race of great captains; something which was provided by the vast fields opened to exploration. Here was to be found the necessary training in calculated daring, in conquering seemingly impossible obstacles, in defying apparently insurmountable dangers, in rising to overwhelming emergencies, in learning to a nicety what it was possible for seamanship to accomplish.

[Endnote: Spain in America]

At the opening of Elizabeth's reign, Spain and Portugal were practically and theoretically in possession of the inheritance of the explorers and the Conquistadores. The latter Power held complete sway on the African Guinea Coast, and in the Indian Ocean, undisturbed by European rivals; while the Pope had bestowed upon it so much of the New World as lies East of the mouth of the Amazon—in effect, what lies behind the coast-line of Brazil. All that lies west of the mouth of the Amazon he had bestowed upon Spain; and this gift the swords of Spaniards had made good. In the West India Islands, their head-quarters were the Island and port of San Domingo (Hayti). From Florida, north, to the mouth of the Amazon, south, all was Spanish territory. On the Atlantic coast: Mexico had Vera Cruz with its haven of San Juan d'Ulloa; on Darien was Nombre de Dios; on the *Tierra Firma* known to the English as the Spanish Main lay Cartagena and several other ports of varying importance. On the Pacific coast, the most notable spots were Panama, the port whither came the treasure ships from Peru to transport their stores by land to Nombre de Dios; Lima, the great city of Peru, which had its port of Callao; and further south the town of Santiago and the harbour of Valparaiso. The straits of Magellan, the only known entry for ships to the Pacific from the Atlantic, were deemed virtually impassable, while Tierra del Fuego was supposed to be the head of another Continent extending continuously to the south. In all these regions, the Spaniard claimed an absolute monopoly, and the right of excluding foreign vessels and foreign trade from what he regarded as Spanish waters.

It is chiefly with transactions on these seas and territories that we are concerned, in giving some account of the rovers, who first in their private capacity challenged the power of Spain, and then led the English fleets to their triumph over the "Invincible" Armada.

[Sidenote: John Hawkins's early voyages, 1562-1566]

First on the roll stands the name of John Hawkins—greatest of the "sea-dogs" till his fame was surpassed by the mightiest of all, Francis Drake. In Henry's day his father, old William Hawkins, had won high repute, for himself as a sailor and for his countrymen as honourable dealers, by his voyages to the Guinea coast, where the Portuguese were in very evil odour, and to the Brazils. John Hawkins fell as far behind his father in the latter respect as he surpassed him in the former: for he was responsible for initiating the Slave-trade. His first notable voyage was made in 1562, when he sailed to the Guinea coast, purchased or kidnapped from the African chiefs some three hundred negroes, crossed the Ocean, and sold them to the Spaniards in Hayti (or Hispaniola). In 1564 he sailed again with four ships; but on reaching America he was told at Rio de La Hacha and Cartagena that the traffic was forbidden. The Englishmen, however, held that these regulations were invalid, as a contravention of ancient treaty rights of free trade with the Spanish dominions. The Spaniards for their part were willing enough to find an excuse for transgressing their orders, which was given by a slight display of force; and Hawkins came home again with large profits, after visiting Florida where there were Huguenot settlers, and Newfoundland where fishing fleets of all nations congregated. It is noteworthy that while the Queen herself and sundry of her courtiers had a large pecuniary interest in these ventures of Hawkins, Cecil conscientiously declined to have part or lot in them, now or later: lawlessness being to him a thing abominable.

Philip was naturally indignant at the Englishman's method of overriding his trade regulations, and Hawkins had to lie quiet for a time; but in 1567 he sailed for the third time, taking with him his young cousin Francis Drake.

[Sidenote: San Juan d'Ulloa 1567]

For a while all went well. The Spaniards wanted to buy in spite of the regulations; though at Rio de La Hacha Hawkins had to emphasise the advantages of trading with him by seizing the town in force. But when he started for home, contrary winds and storms compelled him to put back to the Mexican port of San Juan d'Ulloa (Vera Cruz) to refit his three vessels. He was well received; but while he was in harbour, a Spanish fleet of thirteen sail arrived. The entry was narrow, and Hawkins could have held them at bay; but his theory was that he was behaving in a perfectly regular and well-conducted manner. For three days there was a peaceful interchange of courtesies; then without warning the Spaniards attacked him. Two of his ships succeeded in escaping, despite the heavy odds against them, taking a number of survivors from the third. But next day they parted company; Hawkins's ship was terribly overcrowded; a hundred of his men, by their own desire, were landed—to fall into the hands of the Inquisition; and Hawkins and Drake finally reached England separately with a remnant of their crews, and the loss of all that had been gained in the first stages of the venture.

[Sidenote: Francis Drake]

Now the Spaniards manifestly had a very good case for arresting Hawkins on the ground of his overriding forcibly the regulations which they were, in their own view at least, entitled to make: but they had chosen to receive him hospitably and attempt his capture by flagrant treachery. When his men fell into their hands, they might have been tried as participators in his lawlessness; but the crime laid to their charge was heresy. It is small wonder then that the feeling inspired by the affair of San Juan d'Ulloa was: first, that the Inquisition, claiming itself to be above international law, was outside international law, a tyranny which should be fought without regard to law: second, that Spain had no more right to the wealth of the New World than any one else; third, that since in the New World she elected to rule not by legal methods but by the high hand, it was legitimate to ignore law in dealing with her. There and then Francis Drake, now twenty-seven years old, made up his mind that he would for his own hand wage war on Spain and the Inquisition in the New World. If to do so was piracy, Drake resolved to become a pirate. But he assuredly did not conceive himself to be a pirate; nor were his motives the same; and his methods were utterly unstained by the blood-thirstiness and cruelty inseparably associated with the title. He was rather an Ocean knight-errant, smiting and spoiling, and incidentally enriching himself, but in knightly fashion and for a great cause: not a miscellaneous robber, but a scourge of the enemies of his country and his faith.

[Sidenote: The Venture of 1572]

Drake laid his plans with care and deliberation, making two more voyages in small vessels to the West Indies to acquire thorough knowledge and information, before starting on the first of his great expeditions. Then in 1572, some months before the *rapprochement* with Spain which followed St. Bartholomew, he sailed for the Spanish Main; his whole force consisting of three small ships of a burden ranging from 25 to 70 tons [Footnote: *Royal Navy*, i., p. 621.] with picked crews numbering in all 111 men. With this small company, arriving by night, he fell suddenly upon Nombre de Dios, a principal port of embarkation on the Isthmus of Darien. The surprise was not complete, and though the resistance of the Spaniards was overcome and a large capture of silver ingots was effected, Drake himself was somewhat severely wounded. One of the ships went home; the other two with the commander remained, and took several prizes. But this did not satisfy him, and he conceived the daring scheme of landing and crossing the Isthmus, to intercept the trains of treasure on their way overland from Panama. In February he got, from a tree-top, his first sight of the Pacific. He succeeded in ambushing a small train of mules laden with gold, and, on his way back, another large one laden with silver. Then where he expected to meet his own ships he found a Spanish squadron; but undaunted by this ill-fortune, reached the shore undiscovered, improvised a raft, put to sea, found his own ships, and returned to Plymouth a rich man: having won golden opinions from the Cimmaroons— escaped slaves of the district—from the contrast between the English and the Spanish methods of treating them.

[Sidenote: 1575 John Oxenham]

This was but the precursor of that most famous of his voyages which made his name more terrible to the Spaniards than that of John Hawkins had ever been. More than four years, however, elapsed before that expedition started; and in the interval one of his lieutenants, John Oxenham in 1575 undertook his own disastrous venture, [Footnote: The details of his story are familiar to all readers of Westward Ho.] which well illustrates the boldness of conception and audacity of execution that characterise the Elizabethan seamen. His plan was a development of Drake's Darien exploit. On reaching the Isthmus, he hid his ship and guns, crossed the mountains as Drake had done, built himself a pinnace, and first of all Englishmen sailed on the Pacific. He captured two treasure-ships, which of course had never dreamed of meeting a hostile vessel; but allowed the crews to depart. Naturally a force was soon in pursuit. Oxenham, with a fourth of their numbers, attacked them: half his men were killed in the fight, and nearly all the rest including Oxenham himself were put to death. Drake had already started before the news reached England.

[Sidenote: Drake's great voyage, 1577]

In December 1577 Drake sailed from Plymouth with five ships; himself on board the largest, the *Pelican*, of 100 tons. His purpose was to invade the Pacific by the straits of Magellan. Therefore, after touching at the Cape Verde Islands, he made not for the Spanish Main but for Patagonia. Here at Port St. Julian occurred the famous episode of the execution of Thomas Doughty, [Footnote: See the examination of the authorities and the evidence in Corbett, *Drake and the Tudor Navy*, i., ch. viii.] on charges which may be summed up as those of treason and incitement to mutiny, wherewith was apparently mixed up a conviction on Drake's part that Doughty exercised witch-craft to bring on bad weather. It is not improbable at least that Doughty was really acting in the interests of that party in England which was opposed to the whole policy of the raid, and believed that he would have at his back Lord Burghley, from whom the objects of the expedition were supposed, erroneously, to be a secret. The Straits were reached at the end of August; but were scarcely passed when a storm parted the ships. John Winter, Drake's second in command, after waiting some while, gave his consorts up for lost and returned home. The Pelican, which Drake had re-christened the Golden Hind, alone remained to carry on the adventurous voyage. The precise course taken by the ships in the storms at this time is uncertain: but it seems clear that in some way or other Drake obtained satisfactory evidence that Tierra del Fuego was only an island, and that the Pacific could be reached by rounding Cape Horn. [Footnote: *State Papers, Spanish*, iii., p. 341. See also Corbett, i., pp. 269, 270.]

[Sidenote: Drake in the Pacific, 1578]

In due time then, when there seemed to be no more prospect of being rejoined by Winter, the Pelican proceeded on its expedition. In December, Drake astonished Valparaiso by sailing in and seizing a prize and stores: no one had dreamed of an English ship in the Pacific. Thence he proceeded, exploring the coast, and creating general alarm, till he reached Callao, the port of Lima; where he secured a prize, with which he started in pursuit of a great treasure ship known as the Cacafuego, which he learnt had sailed a few days before. A couple of ships were sent after him; so he cleared out his prize, left it adrift for his pursuers to recover, and showed them a clean pair of heels. After a long pursuit, and the capture of more minor prizes—which he let go, after taking what he wanted, leaving intact the private property of those on board—he overtook the Cacafuego, securing an immense treasure and some exceedingly useful charts.

[Sidenote 1: Drake in the Northern Pacific 1579]
[Sidenote 2: The return, 1580]

Satisfied, after securing two more prizes, with the damage done to Spain, and the rich spoils collected, he turned his attention to geographical discoveries; for in passing Magellan's Strait he had had two predecessors, but none in the northern regions which he had now reached. Finding harbourage on the Californian coast, he repaired the Pelican thoroughly, and then proceeded on a voyage of circumnavigation; the spring of 1579 being now well advanced. His first idea was to look for that imagined North East Passage, in the search for which Willoughby had lost his life nearly five and twenty years before: and with this object in view he sailed some hundreds of miles further North than any explorers in the Pacific had hitherto gone. Coming, however, to the conclusion that he was not equipped for such a venture as this promised to be, he again returned to California to refit. There he established most friendly relations with the natives, who were anxious to deify him: and thence he started again to find his way across the Pacific to the Cape of Good Hope. After much intricate and dangerous navigation among the Spice Islands-in the course of which Drake made a treaty with the Sultan of Ternate, and the Pelican was all but lost on a reef-she rounded the Cape in January, sailing into Plymouth Sound on September 26th, 1580, a little less than three years from the day when she began her voyage. Drake was the first commander who conducted a circumnavigation from start to finish. His precursors had died on the voyage, and left their ships to be brought home by subordinates.

Luckily perhaps for Drake, he arrived just at the time when Philip's subjects were aiding the Irish rebellion; and the English Queen could claim that her great subject had been doing to Spain nothing so bad as what Philip was countenancing in Ireland. Burghley alone refused to have part or lot in the profits of what he held to be a lawless exploit, but the rigid Walsingham applauded. Drake was knighted, and his name was on every lip. More than that, the whole performance imbued English sailors with an un-conquerable conviction that they were more than a match for all the maritime power of Spain, and with an ardent longing to put that conviction to the proof. Drake was the idol not only of every seaman who had sailed under him, but of the entire English People.

Hawkins after 1567 and Drake after 1580 made no more great voyages for their own hand. Hawkins, a past master in all that concerned ships and shipping, was presently appointed Treasurer and practically controller of the Royal Navy, and brought the Queen's ships to a high pitch of perfection. Drake became, practically if not nominally, the first of the Queen's admirals. Both, with two more among the explorers of whom we have still to speak, were to play leading parts in the fight with the Armada.

[Sidenote: Various Voyages, 1576-88]

Of these two, the more famous is Martin Frobisher, who in the early sixties was one of the captains who made war on Philip's ships in the English Channel. Between 1576 and 1578, he made three voyages in search of the North West Passage-accompanied on two of them by the second explorer referred to, Edward Fenton-visiting Greenland and exploring Frobisher's Strait. [Footnote: Now known to be not a Strait but a Bay.] The ships with which he made the first voyage were of no more than 25 and 20 tons [Footnote: *Royal Navy*, i., p. 624.] respectively. In 1582 Fenton captained another expedition, which seems to have been intended for Magellan but got no further than the Brazils, returning after a successful engagement with some Spanish ships. Another circumnavigation was accomplished by Thomas Cavendish (1586-8), who wrought great damage to the Spanish settlements, burning as well as looting, and brought home considerable spoils; but this expedition was undertaken when England and Spain were technically at war.

Just before Cavendish sailed, John Davis, second to no English explorer save Drake, commenced his series of Arctic voyages, learned much of ice-navigation, and on the third voyage in 1587 discovered Davis' Strait. These Arctic expeditions were of course quite unconnected with the Spanish struggle; but while they exemplified the magnificent spirit of English sailors, they also materially advanced English seamanship.

[Sidenote: Raleigh]

In these years preceding the Armada, there were those who, not content with adventure and exploration by sea, made the first tentative efforts from which in after days was to spring the vast colonial dominion of Britain. There was hardly one of these enterprises which was not directly due to the initiative, the exertions, and the persistence of Walter Raleigh. Others no doubt took their share, whether moved by his arguments or in a miscellaneous spirit of adventure; but Raleigh's was the vision of a New England beyond the seas; a goal to dream of and to strive for through weary years of failure and disappointment: an ideal which appealed at once to an intellect among the keenest and an imagination among the boldest of a time which abounded in keen intellects and bold imaginations.

[Sidenote: Gilbert]

As early as 1578, when he was but six and twenty, Raleigh took part in one such abortive venture, along with his half-brother the enthusiast and dreamer Humphrey Gilbert: the same man whose paradoxical barbarity in Ireland [Footnote: See p. 311, *ante*.] we have already noticed: a barbarity very difficult at first sight to reconcile with the high chivalrous spirit, the odd sentimentality, and the fundamental piety which, besides his absolutely fearless courage, characterised Sir Humphrey in a degree only a little more marked than numbers of his contemporaries. A few years later, in 1583, Gilbert made his second disastrous attempt to establish a colony in "Norumbega," the name given to a vague region in the Northern parts of North America. Five ships sailed. The attempt was a complete failure, and on the return voyage Sir Humphrey went down with the little *Squirrel*, the smallest of his ships, which foundered with all hands. The last time a consort was within hail, he greeted her with the natural expression of his faithful and courageous soul—"we are as near God by sea as by land". The story is worth pausing over, for it is supremely characteristic. We may call these men what we will; they persuaded themselves of the righteousness of acts which shock an age in some respects more sensitive; but they wrought mightily for England, and a main source of their triumphs was their trust in the God whose cause they identified with their own, a faith which was a living, impelling, force.

[Sidenote: Virginia]

Raleigh had not accompanied the expedition though he was one of the promoters. In the following year he dispatched an expedition for exploration and settlement in Norumbega, which took possession of a district in what is now Carolina, naming it Virginia in honour of the Virgin Queen. Thither, again on an expedition of Raleigh's, went Sir Richard Grenville with Ralph Lane and others a year later (1585). Lane remained with a company of a hundred men at Roanoake; Grenville accomplished a characteristic feat of arms against a Spaniard on his way home. But when after another year Raleigh sent succours to his colony, the company was found to have withdrawn, having been taken off by Drake's flotilla after he had accomplished his raid on Cartagena. [Footnote: see p.334, *ante*.] Grenvilie however, reappearing, left a small party. In 1587 Raleigh sent again; Grenville's party had vanished, but a new colony was left. Twice again he sent, in 1590 and in 1602, but both times without success. The colonists, except some half dozen, had been massacred. The path to Empire is whitened by the bones of the Pioneers. In the reign of the Virgin Queen, the attempt to colonise Virginia failed utterly; but the failure was the precursor of ultimate triumph. The United States owe their being to Sir Walter Raleigh.

CHAPTER XXIV
ELIZABETH (ix), 1587-88—THE ARMADA

[Sidenote: 1587 Results of Mary's Death]

If Mary Stewart displayed the most royal side of her character in the hour of her doom, Elizabeth displayed the least royal side of hers in the weeks that followed. She disavowed Davison's act, disgraced him, sent him to the Tower; she would have had him tried for treason but that the judges declared emphatically that the charge could not hold water. She was obliged to be content with the infliction of a heavy fine, and dismissal. She could not trample on the whole of her Council, who had deliberately assumed the responsibility: but to France and to Scotland she clamoured that the deed was none of her doing. There was an elvish humour in the Scots King's reply that he would hold her innocent when she had faced and disproved the charge —accentuated by her answer that as a sovereign she was not amenable to trial; for it was a quite precise reversal of the tone adopted eighteen years before, when Mary was the accused party; and Elizabeth now found herself reduced to the very plea which she had ignored when Mary urged it in her own behalf. The position was ignominious; yet Elizabeth had no one but herself to thank. She might have avowed and justified the Act; disavowing it, the only logical course was to punish those on whom the guilt lay. She tried to evade the dilemma, by crushing the most insignificant one among them and scolding the rest, while protesting on her own part an innocence which was a palpable hypocrisy.

The Scots however might rage; James might find gratification in an argumentative victory; but for more pronounced action he wanted more than a sentimental inducement. Politically Elizabeth had won the game by the method peculiar to herself and her father—of counting on their servants to shoulder the responsibility. While Mary lived there was always the chance that the Catholics of England might be rallied to the standard of a Catholic princess whose legitimacy was indisputable. But they would not rally to that of her Protestant son, or consent to have England turned into a province of the Spanish King. Even Catholic Europe could not view such a prospect with enthusiasm or even equanimity, however much the uncompromising devotees of the Holy See might desire it. In France it was only the extremists of the League who could countenance such a scheme. In England, the death-blow of the Scots Queen was the death-blow also to the chances of a Catholic revolt. Despite the fervid dreams of Allen and Parsons, the entire Nation was ready to oppose an undivided front to any foreign assailant.

[Sidenote: Attitude of Philip]

The time, however, had at last arrived when Philip had definitely made up his mind that the overthrow of Elizabeth must no longer be deferred. This was an end which he had desired certainly for eighteen years past. Whenever he had an ambassador in England, that ambassador had been more or less deeply involved in every plot or attempted insurrection against the throne. But Philip had never concentrated his efforts on that design. He had held on to the theory that the Netherlands must be first crushed. When once they were brought into complete subjection, he would make England feel the full extent of his power. And so year after year passed, the revolted Provinces obstinately holding out in a struggle which year after year it had seemed impossible for them to go on maintaining. More than once advisers had suggested that it would be better to reverse the order; to crush England first, and then finish off the Netherlands at his leisure. But this scheme always involved a danger: he had no alternative, if he succeeded, but to set Mary on the throne in place of her cousin; Mary, once established, even by his aid, might attach herself to France instead of to Spain; and the balance of parties in France was so uncertain — depended so much on the action of the Politiques — that in such an event he might still find that he had a very dangerous Anglo-French combination to reckon with in settling his accounts with the Provinces.

[Sidenote: Attitude of Elizabeth]

On the other hand, whether Elizabeth's policy had been dictated by a most consummate, if by no means elevated, state-craft based upon an abnormally astute calculation of risks and chances, or merely by a desperate desire to stave off an immediate contest, whatever shifts might be involved; whether it was in fact peculiarly long-sighted, or opportunist to the last and lowest degree; it had been actually a complete success. She had given the Provinces just that minimum of assistance or apparent countenance which did enable them to keep their resistance alive. In France she had done just enough, for the Huguenots, to hamper the Guises and no more; and she had kept up the eternal marriage juggle, the eternal menace of an alliance with the French court, which would have doubled Philip's difficulties in the Netherlands, and might have trebled the dangers of a direct attack on England — thereby perpetually driving Spanish diplomacy to seek to detach her decisively from France by professions of a desire for amicable alliance with her. She had replied to the Spanish efforts by perpetual declarations of a corresponding order, and by constant negotiations, always at the last moment rendered futile by the introduction of some condition at the time impossible of acceptance.

[Sidenote: The situation]

At last, however, the endless evasion had ceased to be possible. Leicester's campaign in the Netherlands, feeble as it was, and Drake's expedition to Cartagena, put an end to the theory that Spain and England were at peace. It was known that in the ports of Spain and Portugal Philip was making his slow preparations for a naval attack; his ablest admiral, Santa Cruz, had formulated a vast scheme—vaster indeed than Philip was ever prepared to adopt. The Guises were prepared to go any lengths to prevent the legitimate Protestant succession in France; and the French King had publicly thrown in his lot with the Guises. Now also Mary Stewart was not only out of the way herself, but before her death had declared against the succession to her own claims of her son, and had acknowledged Philip, [Footnote: *State Papers, Spanish,* iii., p. 581; and *ante,* p. 338.] a legitimate descendant of John of Gaunt, as her heir. At last in Philip's mind the suppression of Elizabeth acquired precedence over the suppression of the Provinces.

The near approach of a life-and-death struggle made no difference whatever in the English Queen's methods. Eighteen months before, she had struck one hard blow by sea, when she dispatched Drake on the Cartagena expedition, but otherwise had merely played at helping the Netherlanders, by sending an army and paralysing it for action. She did exactly the same thing now.

[Sidenote: April: Drake's Cadiz expedition]

Drake, with a squadron not large either in numbers or in tonnage but exceedingly efficient, had orders to sail from Plymouth to "singe the King of Spain's beard," as he phrased it. Drake knew his Queen, and got himself out of port before the appointed day, on April 2nd. The expected counter-orders arrived in due time—when he was out of reach. Elizabeth possibly knew her Drake and reckoned on his premature departure, while she had secured her loop-hole for shuffling out of the responsibility. He carried out the singeing business most effectively. Making for Cadiz, where it was known that stores and ships were accumulated, he stood into the harbour, sunk one ship of war there, cleared out so much of the stores as he could accommodate, and fired the bulk of the shipping, cutting the cables. Drake then captured the Sagres forts at Cape St. Vincent, intending to lie in wait for an expected squadron from the Mediterranean; but departed after a short interval, being minded to sail into the port of Lisbon where the Admiral Santa Cruz lay with the bulk of the Armada. This exploit, however, he was obliged to forgo, [Footnote: Corbett, *Drake and the Tudor Navy*, ii., pp. 97 ff. The account there given is followed here. The author points out that Froude and others have been misled by the almost certain misdating of a letter of Drake's which he attributes to 1589.] contenting himself with a challenge to Santa Cruz to come out and fight, which he was in no condition to do. Returning to Cape St. Vincent, Drake there remained long enough to stop the expected squadron, and throw the whole of Philip's transport arrangements out of gear. Satisfied with the destruction wrought, which served to cripple at least the mobility of the Armada for many months, he then sailed for the Azores, where he fell in with a great Spanish *East* Indiaman, the *San Felipe*, whereof the spoils very satisfactorily filled the pockets of his crews; and so returned home, having made it all but impossible that the invading fleet should sail during 1587.

[Sidenote: Negotiations with Parma]

Then, month after month, Elizabeth carried on the old practice in the Netherlands. She negotiated persistently with Parma, on the old basis, that the Provinces had a right to their old constitution but nothing more. Of course she knew that the Provinces would never assent to that solution. On the favourable view of her policy, it must be held to have rested on a fixed determination not to make the Netherlands her field of battle. For Sluys, one of the forts which she held, so to speak, in pawn from the States, was taken after a stubborn siege and at immense cost both in money and men by Parma, simply because Maurice of Nassau was too uncertain as to her real intentions to make a serious effort for its relief. Confidence in her had sunk to the lowest point when, some months before, an English captain, Stanley, had handed over the town of Deventer, which was in his charge, to the Spaniards, whose service he himself entered. The Provinces, Parma, Elizabeth's own Ministers, believed that she meant the negotiations in earnest. Parma, who knew how tremendous a task the invasion of England must be, would have liked to come to terms, but Philip would not give him the authority; the terms approved by his lieutenant must be referred back to him. They were never finally formulated. All through 1587, through the first months of 1588, the thing dragged on; and then Elizabeth declared that the surrender of the Cautionary Towns, always hitherto treated as the necessary first step, was only to be thought of as the last step—a quite impossible condition from the Spanish point of view. But by the time the negotiations had thoroughly broken down, a whole year had been practically wasted by Spain. Taking on the other hand the unfavourable view—which appears to have been that of almost every statesman and soldier of the day —she engaged in a highly discreditable negotiation for a betrayal of the Provinces by the surrender of the Cautionary Towns, in the hope of obtaining with Philip a peace which would have rendered him infinitely more dangerous than he actually was; being only saved from that disaster by saner counsels and against her own will at the last moment.

[Sidenote: The Queen's Diplomacy]

From beginning to end, the facts are consistent with either view of her character. If the second view be true, history affords no parallel to the amazing good fortune which attended her; for her whole career was a succession of apparently hopeless entanglements, each one leading to inevitable disaster; yet from every one a loop-hole of escape was found. If the first be true, history again affords no parallel to the invariable success which attended a series of deceptions practised alike upon her servants, her friends, and her enemies. But whichever solution we accept— and there is no third alternative—her personal policy remains one of pure political opportunism, either very short sighted or singularly long sighted, without a particle of the idealism which, mixed though it might be with other motives, was so emphatically characteristic of half her ministers and more than half her subjects. Towards the cause of the Reformation, as such, she was entirely cold; to her, its adherents in the Netherlands and in France were merely pieces on the political chess-board. It is an odd paradox that such a ruler should have won and maintained among her own people a personal popularity amounting to enthusiasm, which was a very strong force in binding the nation together.

[Sidenote: 1587-88 French affairs]

While Elizabeth was keeping up the diplomatic game above described, she was very materially aided by the state of affairs in France, where what is known as the "War of the three Henries"—Henry III., Henry of Navarre, and Henry of Guise—was in full progress. The King, professing to support the League, was in fact doing his best to play into the hands of his nominal opponent, Navarre, and to paralyse his nominal adherent, Guise, who had Philip of Spain behind him. Philip, aware of this ambiguous position—as also was Elizabeth—found himself unable to trust to France for support, or absolutely to repudiate her demands to share in the Armada expedition viewed as a Catholic Crusade. The position became acute when Guise, ignoring the King's orders, entered Paris in force, receiving a general ovation while the King himself had to fly, on the "Day of the Barricades" (April-May, 1588). There was a nominal reconciliation in July; but it was then already too late for the Guises to hold the French ports at the service of the Spaniard.

Neither from Scotland nor in Ireland was any danger to be apprehended in the coming struggle. We turn again to the story of the Armada itself.

[Sidenote: 1587 Preparations for the Armada]

Great as was the damage wrought by Drake, it was energetically repaired, and Philip warned Parma to be ready for the arrival of the Armada in September 1587. The plan of operations was for Santa Cruz to sail up the Channel, dominate the passage from the Low Countries, and so enable Parma, heavily reinforced by the soldiers on board the great fleet, to pour his troops into England. Philip's plans were quite unaffected by the talk of peace; but the English were justified in their confidence that the Armada would not be ready to sail in time. When it was ready, Santa Cruz pronounced that the storms to be looked for so late in the year would make the voyage itself dangerous, and would render it impossible to keep the necessary control of the water-ways: which was what the English authorities had calculated on.

[Sidenote: 1588 Plans of Campaign]

There was indeed a very considerable risk in deferring the mobilisation of the English fleet; for in January, Philip resolved to delay no longer, and if the Armada had sailed then there was no force ready to meet it. But the death of Santa Cruz at the critical moment destroyed the plan. In February the English were in trim to take the seas; the opportunity was lost, and another was not given. If the seamen had been allowed their own way, the Lord Admiral Howard of Effingham, Drake, Hawkins, Frobisher and the other captains would have sailed for the Spanish coast; nor can it be doubted that they would then have done completely what Drake and his squadron had done only in part a year before, and practically have annihilated the Armada in its own ports; but other counsels prevailed, to their great chagrin. The idea that the Spanish fleet might evade the English, if the latter left the Channel, and make the invasion a *fait accompli* without a sea-fight at all, was too alarming to the landsmen. Whether Parma would ever have taken the enormous risk of throwing himself into a hostile country, with an unfought fleet hastening to cut him off from his base, is another matter. It is noteworthy however that even the seamen do not seem to have realised the enormous risk involved in such an undertaking. They knew that a small squadron was quite sufficient to frustrate any invasion that Parma without the Armada could contemplate. But when the Armada was already in helpless and headlong flight round Scotland, Drake [Footnote: Laughton, S. P. *Armada*, ii., pp. 99, 100: Drake to Walsingham.] still regarded an attempted coup by Parma as a danger to be seriously guarded against.

[Sidenote: The opposing forces]

We are in the habit of looking upon the destruction of the Armada as a feat verging on the miraculous. Yet it is apparent that every one of the great sailors anticipated a complete victory with entire confidence. They knew that they understood the conditions of naval warfare, and that the enemy did not. Although, on paper, the Spaniard had all the best of it, he never really had a chance, for the plain reason that his fleet was utterly outclassed. The Armada put to sea with about 130 ships. Of these, 62 were of over 300 tons burden. The whole English fleet is given as 197 ships including the 34 of the Royal Navy. Of these, only 49 exceeded 200 tons. The average [Footnote: Laughton, i., p. li.] tonnage of the 62 was quite double that of the 49; and the aggregate of the 130 was approximately double that of the 197. The recorded lists and estimates also give the Spaniards double the number of men and guns. Many of the great Spaniards were little more than transports; on the other hand, half the English ships were too small for effective fighting. But there is little doubt that the English fighting ships were much better armed relatively to their size; that the guns were better, and infinitely better handled. The ships were in fact far superior as fighting machines, because the two fleets were built, armed, and manned, on two diametrically opposed theories of naval tactics: which may be summed up by saying that the Spaniards relied upon mass, and hand to hand fighting, the English on mobility and artillery; applying unconsciously by sea the principles by which the great land-tacticians of the past, Edward III. and Henry V., had shattered greatly superior hosts at Crecy and Agincourt. The finer comprehension of naval strategy on the part of the English admirals had been made of no account by the ignorance of the supreme authority, which detained the fleet on the coast: but their tactical developments were unhampered. For the first time on a large scale the accustomed rules were about to be discarded.

[Sidenote: The New Tactics]

Hitherto, naval battles had been assimilated to land battles; ships had attacked, moving abreast in military formation; they had grappled and fought for possession of each other's decks; the work had been soldiers' work, and for that the Spaniards were equipped, carrying two soldiers for every mariner. But this was to be mariners' work, and on the English ships the complement of soldiers was quite insignificant in comparison to that of mariners and gunners. The English ships were handled by seamen, many of the Spanish by landsmen. The English ships answered the helm and could go "about," with a rapidity which amazed the Spaniards. They were constructed to deliver broadsides, which the Spaniards could not do. Their guns could be discharged three times or more to the Spaniards once. The Spaniards, with a dim perception of the English point of superiority, tried to nullify it by futile firing at the rigging, which was for the most part a pure waste of shot; the English pounded the Spanish hulls and their crowded decks; systematically refusing to come to close quarters, so that the enemy never had a chance of utilising his soldiery. With ships built and rigged for speed and for manoeuvring, with men who had learnt how to handle them in many a storm, with captains whose seamanship was trusted by every sailor, the Englishmen repeatedly secured the weather-gauge, joining battle or refusing it as they liked; and the final result was never seriously in doubt.

[Sidenote: Defective arrangements]

From the month of March then, the departure of the Spanish fleet was delayed only by its own unreadiness to sail, due in part to the obvious incompetence of the Duke of Medina Sidonia who had been appointed, very much against his own will, to the command; for he was absolutely devoid of any naval or even military experience. The English ships were in admirable order; [Footnote: Laughton, i., p. 79: Howard to Burghley, Feb. 21.] but the great trouble with them was in the commissariat. The emergency was quite without parallel, and the system, such as there was, was quite inadequate to cope with it. To maintain, month after month, supplies for so large an armament, was next to impossible; and to this much more than to the "niggardliness" of the Queen, [Footnote: Laughton, i., pp. lvii ff. Froude's latitude of paraphrase makes his handling of the evidence peculiarly inconclusive.] must be attributed the vehement complaints of deficiencies. Sanitary conditions also were not at all generally understood, and it was dangerous to keep crews constantly on board. On the whole, the denunciations of the authorities were not different from those to which they always have been, and probably always will be, subjected. Individuals did their best to work a defective organisation with only partial success. And there was very much the same tale from the Spanish as from the English; the notable difference lay mainly in the great superiority of the latter in the purely naval department of administration.

[Sidenote: The Land forces]

As concerns the adequacy of the arrangements on land for resisting the invader if he succeeded in reaching the shore, it is difficult to speak. It was almost a matter of course that Leicester was given the command, though he had no military talent; but he had at his elbow the one thoroughly experienced captain available, Sir John Norreys. A great camp was formed at Tilbury to cover London; the raw country musters were in readiness every where to fly to arms when the signal beacons should flash their message over the land. How much resistance they could have offered to Parma's veterans, none can tell. But it may safely be laid down, that while the English fleet was in being, the invaders' chances of ultimate success were infinitesimal, but that if the fleet had been wiped out they would have been, at least *prima facie*, exceedingly promising. As Leicester, not Norreys, was in command of the army, so Howard of Effingham, not Drake, was in command of the fleet. But of Effingham we know that he was not himself ignorant of naval matters, and that he had no notion of ignoring the judgment of the colleagues who were technically his subordinates. With Drake as Vice-Admiral and Hawkins as Rear-Admiral, there was no danger of inefficient command. The naval appointments were in every way admirable; and even the noblemen and gentlemen who were captains of so many of the ships knew better than to overrule the practical command of their mariner-subordinates. On May 20th the Armada sailed from Lisbon, but was scattered by a storm in the second week of June, reassembling at Corunna—when Medina Sidonia vainly urged that the expedition should be given up. Some of the ships had proceeded within ken of the Scillies, causing considerable excitement; but these too put back to Corunna, whence the whole armament made its final start on July 12th.

At the end of May, the English fleet was collected at Plymouth, a squadron with Seymour and the veteran Wynter being left on guard at the East end of the Channel. The admirals were again anxious to seek out the Spaniards and give account of them in their own seas, but supplies were short, and Howard was again definitely ordered to remain on the coast. It is however inferred by some authorities [Footnote: Corbetts ii., pp. 179-181.] that Drake and Howard did make a dash for the Spanish coast, about July 7th, while the Armada was at Corunna, in the hope of striking a swift and decisive blow; but that the favouring wind was lost, a South-Wester set in, and they had to return to the Channel, being insufficiently provisioned to remain at a distance from home.

Howard then, with Drake and Hawkins and the major part of the English fleet was lying in Plymouth, getting stores aboard as fast as might be, while Seymour and Sir William Wynter with their squadron were lying at the East end of the Channel, when on July 19th the news came that the Armada had been sighted off the Lizard, coming up with a favouring wind. There was nothing for it but to work out of Plymouth Sound in the teeth of the wind. When the Spaniards came in view on the 20th (Saturday) the move had been accomplished. In the night, the English passed out to sea, across the Spanish front, and so in the morning found themselves to windward and attacked—as it would seem, for the first time in naval warfare, in "line-ahead" formation, pouring successive broadsides into the enemy's "weathermost" ship. This action lasted little more than two hours. Not many of the Spaniards were actually engaged, but the working effect of the new tactics was tested, Admiral Recalde's ship was crippled, some others had suffered from a very severe fire very inadequately returned; incidentally too, one great galleon had been almost blown to pieces by an accident, and the ship of Valdez was disabled through collision. The Duke of Medina Sidonia left her to her fate, and she surrendered to Drake early next morning, the two fleets in the meantime having proceeded up Channel. Drake ought to have led the pursuit during the night, and by not doing so caused some confusion and delay-also, it would seem much indignation on the part especially of Frobisher; [Footnote: Laughton, ii., pp. 101 ff.] but his conduct is capable of legitimate if not complete justification. [Footnote: Corbett, ii., pp. 231 ff.]

[Sidenote: The fight off Portland, July 23]

In consequence however, the English were unable to form for attack— though the half-blown-up ship, the *San Salvador*, fell into their hands— till late on the next day, when they were foiled by the falling of a calm. When the breeze got up again on Tuesday, the Spaniards were to windward, off Portland, and challenged an engagement. In manoeuvring to recover the weather-gauge, Frobisher, with some other vessels, was for a time cut off, and fought a very valiant fight, till a change in the wind enabled them to extricate themselves, and there was more sharp fighting in which the Spaniards suffered most. Neither side however could claim a victory. But it was seen that much more would have been effected had the Armada been less systematically organised, and the English more so. Before the next general engagement, the defect had been remedied by the distribution of the fleet into four divisions, under Howard, Drake, Hawkins, and Frobisher respectively.

[Sidenote: The fight off the Isle of Wight, July 25]

It was supposed to be the intention of the Armada [Footnote: Corbett, ii., 228. This was no doubt the recommendation of Recalde and others. But it was in the teeth of Philip's instructions. In any case however, it was what the English expected, and their action was based on that hypothesis.] to secure the station at the Isle of Wight and Portsmouth; and it was to frustrate this object that the third battle was fought on Thursday. In the interval, Howard had only worried the enemy, being in need of fresh supplies of ammunition which were now arriving. On the Thursday, the fluctuating airs again forced the English to manoeuvre for the weather gauge, in order to attack. The brunt of the resulting engagement was borne by Frobisher and Howard, who occupied the enemy and were very thoroughly occupied themselves; until the Armada, which had not in appearance been getting the worst of it, went about and sailed off up Channel in good order. The explanation would appear to be that the Spaniard found himself suddenly threatened with a crushing flank attack [Footnote: Corbett, ii., p. 254. The explanation is Mr. Corbett's conjecture.] by the combined squadrons of Drake and Hawkins, which would have driven him upon the banks known as the "Owers"; and to escape destruction, he had no alternative but to give up the design on Portsmouth, if he had ever entertained it, and continue his unimpeded course up Channel. To fight where he was had become impossible. Thus, although the comparative injury to his fleet was not very great, the action was a very decisive victory for the English. The Spaniards had to revert to the desperate plan of a junction with Parma, instead of securing a station in the Channel.

[Sidenote: Effects on the fleets]

Although strategically a great point was secured by this third engagement, the ostensible strength of the Spanish fleet remained virtually unaltered, and the English captains were evidently disappointed at having achieved no more marked results. Of course, on the theory that the odds were, professionally speaking, all in favour of the Armada, they had done exceedingly well; but they were fighting under the perfectly correct impression that the odds were in their own favour, and yet they had done no signal injury. In fact however they had accomplished a good deal more than appears on the surface. Their losses were far short of 100 men all told; their ships were intact; the spirit of the fleet had been tested; and they had already learnt and remedied the defect in their organisation at the start. On the other hand, the Armada had lost three ships, several more had suffered so severely as to be useless for further action, its ammunition was running short, some hundreds of men had been killed or wounded, and the whole fleet had realised that in manoeuvring capacity it was completely outclassed, so that its *morale* was failing. Already it felt itself fighting a losing battle. Whereas, when the Isle of Wight was left behind, the English were more confident than ever that they themselves were fighting to win.

[Sidenote: The Armada at Calais]

The Duke then made his course for Dunkirk, sending urgent messages to Parma to come out and help him: which it was not possible for Parma to do. On Saturday evening, without any further fighting, the Armada anchored in Calais Roads. The same evening, Howard was joined by Seymour's squadron, and for the first time his fleet was at its full strength. It now became his great object to force the decisive engagement before Medina Sidonia and Parma at Dunkirk could effect a junction. To this end it was needful to dislodge the Armada from its anchorage. Wind and tide both favouring, on Sunday night eight fire-ships were sent drifting on to the Spanish fleet. A panic arose; the Spaniards cut their cables and made for the open, to escape the danger. They were to suffer later on for this loss of their anchors. Now, when the morning broke, the great fleet which had successfully preserved its formation hitherto, was scattered along a dangerous coast, with the entire English force lying to windward within striking distance.

[Sidenote: The battle off Gravelines, July 29]

For the Duke, the first thing to do was to recover his formation; for the English, to prevent his doing so. Howard should have led the attack, but turned aside to make sure of a crippled galleon. Drake, followed by Hawkins, Frobisher, and Seymour, sailed down on the Spaniards, and the last decisive engagement began. Medina Sidonia was never able to bring more than half his ships into action. He gained some time, by Howard's aberration, but in the course of the day the entire English fleet was engaging him. The ships and the captains, however, who were able to rejoin him, were the best in the Armada, and they made a magnificent and desperate struggle. Raked with broadside after broadside they fought on, drifting into ever more dangerous proximity to the shoals, their hulls riddled, their decks charnel-houses; resolved to sink rather than strike; while the English poured in a ceaseless storm of shot at close range but always evaded the one danger, of being grappled and boarded, the sole condition under which the Spaniard could fight at an advantage. At last the English drew off; partly because their ammunition, like the Spaniards', was all but exhausted, except in Howard's squadron, the expenditure having been quite unparalleled; partly because a fierce squall for a time provided them with a new enemy which it took all their energies to meet. That squall was the salvation of the Spaniards; when it cleared, they were already in full flight to the North East.

[Sidenote: The Armada in flight]

The Armada was now to leeward of Dunkirk, and a junction with Parma had been rendered impossible. On the following day indeed, it seemed that the whole fleet was doomed to destruction on the shoals, when a change of wind enabled them to make for the North Sea, the main part of the English fleet following in pursuit, while Seymour's squadron, to his intense disgust, was left to guard the Channel. But for the English shortage of ammunition, which made it impossible to provoke another general engagement, half the Armada might very well have fallen a prey to the pursuers; for it was a fleet that knew itself hopelessly beaten; its morale was gone, its ammunition was exhausted, its best crews were much more than decimated, many of its vessels were hopelessly crippled. As it was, the English were content to follow and watch while the Spaniards drove Northwards before a stiff gale;

giving up the chase on August 2nd, by which time it was evident that the enemy had no course open to them but to attempt the passage round the North of Scotland, and so to make for home by the Irish coast as best they might; though later, the wind changing to the North created a passing fear that they might return with it to Denmark, to refit.

[Sidenote: The End of the Armada]

In the whole series of actions, the English lost only about a hundred men and one ship. Out of that great Armada which had sailed with the Papal blessing to lower the insolent pride of heretic England, not more than half the ships found their way back to Spain. Of the sixty or more that were lost, nine [Footnote: Clowes, *Royal Navy*, i., p. 585.] only are definitely accounted for in the actual fighting. Of the rest, nineteen are recorded as wrecked on the Scottish or Irish coast: there must have been many more. Of their crews, those whom the winds and the waves spared, the Irish slew; and those who escaped the Irish, the English soldiery slew. Of the fate of the remainder, one-fourth of the entire fleet, nothing is known.

Dominus flavit, et dissipati sunt. The Lord blew and they were scattered. Small wonder that the puritan spirit saw in that huge disaster the direct intervention of the Almighty, smiting on behalf of His People. Yet the winds and the seas had but given an awful completeness to the already triumphant handiwork of the English Seamen. From first to last, through all the fighting, till the desperate *sauve qui peut* of the battered and shattered foe across the Northern seas began, no particular good fortune in the matter of wind and weather had favoured England. She had won, against apparent odds, because her sons had found out on many a venturous voyage how the great game of war by sea ought to be played; and her enemy had not. She had won decisively. Philip might stiffen his pride and boast that he could yet send forth fleets mightier than the lost Armada. But on the day of the fight off Gravelines the doom of his power was sealed; and the Empire of the Ocean passed from Spain to England.

CHAPTER XXV
ELIZABETH (x), 1588-98-BRITANNIA VICTRIX

[Sidenote: After the Armada]

The sceptre had passed. The world awoke suddenly to the truth of which the great debacle was only the unexpected testimony. The Spanish People were slow to realise the overwhelming fact—overwhelming, because for the best part of a century at least they had accounted themselves the nation favoured by Heaven, chosen for the crushing of the heathen and the heretic, assured of victory. So, for a few years, had the English thought of themselves; but with a difference; for their spirit was that expressed in the later Puritan adage, "Trust in God and keep your powder dry". The Spaniard had neglected to keep his powder dry. The nation which observes both injunctions is tolerably certain to defeat that which observes only one.

The sceptre had passed; but Spain would not acquiesce without a struggle, and, in his slow fashion, Philip set himself to adapt to his own navy the lesson taught by the fate of the Armada. England had won the lead, but she was not to hold it unchallenged, though she did maintain it convincingly. For her alertness did not leave her, and to her had been transferred not the power only but also the enormous prestige which Spain had hitherto enjoyed, and which counts for much in every struggle where it is recognised on both sides.

But the re-organisation of the Spanish Navy was a matter of time. For the moment, the result of the collision was absolutely to reverse the hypothetical though not the actual position of the two countries. Spain was reduced completely to the defensive. England no longer thought of guarding herself, but only of smiting her foe—a theory of the mutual relations on which, unofficially, the seamen had been acting for the last decade.

If during the closing ten years of his life Philip's strongest desire was to recover the lost supremacy, his energies were still divided by his extreme anxiety to prevent the Bourbon succession in France; while the conviction was proving day by day more irresistible that the Protestant Netherlands would be lost for ever to Spain. Yet the eternal series of abortive plots for restoring the old religion and placing either Philip or a tool of Philip on the

English throne went on; not in fact ending till the death of Elizabeth joined England and Scotland under a single crown.

[Sidenote: A new phase]

Politically the dramatic climax of Elizabeth's reign is the dispersion of the Armada. The dragon has been fought and vanquished, and at this point, the curtain ought to ring down and leave the audience to imagine the Redcross knight and his ladye-love living happy for ever afterwards. But in history no climax is more than an incident; at the most it is but the decisive entry on a new phase. The chain of causation, of the interdependence of events, is continuous.

The moment of the Armada then may be regarded as the conclusion of a phase. The work of the great statesmen, whose names are most intimately associated with that of Elizabeth, was accomplished. They had kept England united and at peace within her own borders through a long period of recurring crises. They had so fostered the national spirit and the national resources that she had finally proved herself a match for the mightiest Power in Europe. They had achieved for her the premier position upon the Ocean. They had defeated every attempt to entice or to force her back to the Roman obedience. They had secured a larger latitude of religious tolerance than prevailed in any other State of Europe. These things they had definitely won, though there was still need of keen brains, stout hearts, strong hands, and sturdy consciences to hold them. They had been responsible for the planting and watering. It was left mainly to others in the last years of Elizabeth to assure the beginnings of the increase.

[Sidenote: 1588 The Death of Leicester]

Of the counsellors who had played a prominent part in Elizabeth's reign, Nicholas Bacon had died in 1579. The rest still lived, but none of them for long. The next to disappear was Leicester, who survived the dispersion of the Armada by only a few weeks. So long as he had been an aspirant to the hand of his royal mistress, he existed chiefly to trouble the minds of statesmen—a piece of grit in the machinery; an apparently quite worthless person After he had settled down into the less ambiguous position of a mere personal favourite, with no chance of satisfying swelling ambitions, he became a definite partisan of the Walsingham school whose ideal lay in the advancement of protestantism and antagonism to Spain. When not warped by the vain imaginings of his earlier years, he would seem to have been a person of respectable abilities, little decision of character, decently loyal; an ornamental figurehead whose position enabled him to serve his friends; shallow; neither dangerous, nor conspicuously incapable; not entirely deserving of the extreme contempt which is usually poured upon him; but at best a poor creature whose importance was wholly adventitious.

[Sidenote: France, 1588-89]

Of infinitely more consequence in its influence on the political situation was the death on December 23rd, by the hands of assassins of the Duke of Guise. The murder, planned by Henry III., deprived the League of its head, and decisively forced the French King into the arms of his Protestant heir. Nine months later (August 1589), Henry III. was assassinated in turn, and Henry of Navarre laid claim to the crown, his uncle Charles, Cardinal of Bourbon, being proclaimed King by the Catholics. Hence in Philip's eyes a closer union than ever between himself and the League—now headed by Mayenne, brother of the murdered Guise—became imperative. A Huguenot king in France, a heretic queen in England, and heretic rebels in the Netherlands, threatened a combination which he was bound to try and paralyse. The attempt went far to thwart itself; for numbers of the French Catholics were ready to go a long way towards a compromise with Henry of Navarre when they felt the alternative to be a Spanish domination; while that astute prince hailed the opportunity which enabled him to claim the role of patriot, and to point to the Leaguers as the clients of the foreigner. On the other hand, Philip's energies during the remainder of his life were largely absorbed in futile efforts to redress on French soil the loss of Spanish supremacy on the seas.

[Sidenote: 1588 England aggressive]

Under the new conditions, the antagonism between the two schools of English statesmanship takes a slightly altered form. Walsingham among the ministers, Drake among the seamen, had always believed fervently in the theory of breaking the power of Spain to pieces. Elizabeth and (in the main) Burghley had clung to the theory of gradually making England so secure and so formidable that Spain and England alike should ultimately recognise a condition of amicable equality as the best for both. Spain would then become amenable to reason in matters ecclesiastical and commercial, the old intercourse would be restored in its fulness, and general prosperity would result. Against their wishes, matters had been by the inevitable trend of events forced to the arbitrament of battle. But even now, terrible as the disaster of the Armada had been, Spain was by no means shattered; in fact, though the English nation was more than jubilant, the seamen themselves were evidently disappointed that they had not in the encounter inflicted more complete ruin upon their rivals. They had found the Spaniards less easy to dispose of than they had anticipated.

[Sidenote: Alternative Naval policies]

The victory however had been won by the great captains of the aggressive party; it was followed almost immediately by the revolt of Henry III. from the Guise domination; all the conditions were in favour of an offensive campaign. For the time being, a peace-party had ceased to exist. The only question now was, how to strike. And at this stage we see the two rival theories of naval policy in war time beginning to be formulated, since naval policy on a large scale was only brought into being by the development of an oceanic field for it to work in. Of the one policy which has constantly prevailed with our great English admirals, that of making the destruction of the enemy's fighting fleet the primary object, with mere commerce-destroying secondary, Drake was in practice the father; of the other, that of concentrating on his trade-routes and menacing his commerce, not unusually favoured by France in her wars with England, John Hawkins was the advocate.

For the moment Drake, being undoubtedly the hero of the hour, appeared to triumph. His was the scheme of operations approved. But before it could be put in practice, its essential features were distorted; through no fault of his the plan failed of its full effect; disfavour followed; and war on Spanish commerce again became the prevalent policy. Its attractions for adventurers are obvious; and its inferiority as a method of transforming superiority into supremacy was not yet recognised.

[Sidenote: Don Antonio]

Drake's actual design, however, was not on this occasion a precise exemplification of the theory just associated with his name, although its failure brought the supporters of the opposing school to the front. The Armada disaster had already given the English for the time complete command of the sea, and his intention was to strike a crippling blow at the Spanish power by establishing the Pretender Don Antonio on the throne of Portugal and in control of the Azores. Ever since Philip had grasped the Portuguese crown in 1580, Elizabeth had played diplomatically with the notion of helping Don Antonio to challenge his title by force of arms, and Walsingham would have found a grim joy in turning the play into earnest. But Antonio could count upon no support worth mentioning from other quarters; Elizabeth's help had been in quality the same as and in quantity less than she had doled out to Huguenots and Netherlanders. The one real attempt in his favour, wherein there had hardly been a pretence of English participation, had been crushed by Santa Cruz at the naval battle of Terceira in the Azores in 1583. But what had been impracticable before the Armada was so no longer. With the command of the sea, Portugal might now be won; the loss in itself would be a grievous weakening to Spain; and in alliance with England, Portugal would be to her neighbour very much what Scotland would have been to England had Mary been restored—and accepted—by Spanish aid.

[Sidenote: Plan of the Lisbon Expedition, 1588-89] Such was Drake's idea, which was to be carried out after the method beloved by the Queen. It was not to be exactly a Government affair, but the enterprise of a Company, in which her Majesty was to hold shares, providing some money and half a dozen ships from her fleet, and various guarantees. It was to be a joint naval and military venture, with Drake and Norreys respectively in command of the two arms, with a free hand in the conduct of operations. All through the winter of 1588 Drake and Norreys were hard at work preparing this counter-Armada; but as spring came on, the Queen's passion for tying her servants' hands developed on the familiar lines. It was not till April that Drake succeeded in definitely starting, and he went with a very fine armament; but with only a month's commissariat, without the siege train promised, and fettered by instructions wholly inconsistent with his own plan of campaign.

The Spaniards acquired what purported to be a statement of the terms agreed on between Elizabeth and Don Antonio, under which Portugal, with the Azores, was to be reduced to a province of England. It does not appear however that this document was based upon facts; and the instructions [Footnote: *Cf.* Corbett, ii,] issued to the expedition are quite inconsistent with the whole idea. The attempt to establish Antonio in Portugal was only to be made if the conditions were favourable; if it succeeded, the English were then to retire; if it were dropped, they were to make for the Azores. But in any case they were to begin by attacking the shipping in Biscayan and other Northern harbours of Spain—an entirely superfluous proceeding, as Spain for the time had no naval force which could give trouble.

[Sidenote: 1589 May: Corunna and Peniche]

Consequently the expedition—which was accompanied by Elizabeth's latest favourite, the young Earl of Essex, a runaway and from his Mistress—instead of making straight for Lisbon attacked Corunna. The troops were landed, the town stormed and sacked, and the shipping destroyed, the Spaniards being driven into the citadel. Immediate departure being prevented by the wind, after nearly a week's operations a fierce but unsuccessful attempt was made to storm the citadel also. This however was followed by a brilliant action, at the Bridge of El Burgo, in which Norreys decisively defeated a relieving force of greatly superior numbers, prodigies of valour being performed during the battle. But the capture of the citadel was unimportant; and the wind improving, the expedition proceeded—with many prizes and much spoil—to operate against Lisbon. On the way, for some not very intelligible reason, Peniche, some fifty miles from Lisbon, was stormed by the soldiers—as it would seem, against Drake's will. The whole army was here disembarked, to operate against Lisbon by land, while the fleet proceeded to the mouth of the Tagus.

[Sidenote: Failure at Lisbon]

Drake at once captured Cascaes, which commanded the entry. But he could do nothing more till the army was ready to co-operate. Norreys arrived presently: but he had no siege train, and resolved that unless the Portuguese rose, as Don Antonio had promised, the attempt on Lisbon must be abandoned. It is practically certain that had the attack been made, the resolute commandant and his slender garrison would have been easily overpowered, the mob favouring the assailants. But Norreys was unaware of the facts; the partisans of Don Antonio did not rise; and the English fell back to Cascaes to reimbark; having destroyed a considerable quantity of stores, and defied Spain on her own soil with a handful of men, but otherwise having failed to accomplish the purpose of the expedition. Drake however also captured a great convoy of store- ships. Contrary winds prevented the fleet from proceeding to the Azores, and nothing more was accomplished but the destruction of Vigo, while in the subsequent storms a number of ships were damaged or lost. The business was a failure, though it had given convincing proof that even in Spanish territory—much more on the seas—Spain was incapable of taking the offensive. The expedition found its way home about the end of June; a few weeks before the assassination of the French King, which transformed the Prince of Navarre into Henry IV., a legitimate monarch fighting for his throne against a threatened alien domination.

The ships had suffered; the booty was small; the crews and the troops had been wasted by sickness and sharp fighting. Consequently Drake and Drake's policy were generally discredited. It had in fact been quite clearly demonstrated that Spain was on her knees, and that nothing but inadequate armament and deficient supplies had prevented the admiral from reducing her to a condition still more desperate. But superficially, he had failed.

[Sidenote: Policies and Persons]

Now the policy of the forward school, of which Drake was the leading example and Walter Raleigh was to be the exponent both with sword and pen, was twofold; to prostrate Spain and her naval power, and to plant English colonies in direct competition with and open antagonism to the colonies of Spain. But the men who had grasped the whole conception were few. Walsingham, the one among the elder statesmen who was in touch with these ideas, had but a few months to live. The ordinary idea of the ordinary Anti-Spaniard was to damage Spain as much as possible; but the means to that end which he recognised lay mainly, if not entirely, in the raiding of Spanish commerce and the interception of treasure-fleets. This was avowedly the view of John Hawkins, which naturally appealed to the Adventurers of the day.

On the other side was the school of Burghley himself, and of Elizabeth; who had never wished, and did not now wish, to see Spain prostrate, and had never been without hopes of converting the rivalry into an alliance, though not averse to the bringing of severe pressure to bear for the recovery of commercial privileges and the suppression of political antagonism. Burghley had not by any means always approved of Elizabeth's methods; when it was only by those tortuous wiles that peace could be preserved he had joined with Walsingham and Leicester in counselling war; but if war could be with honour avoided, it had been his constant desire to avoid it; while he had consistently and honourably opposed Drake, condemned his buccaneering methods, and refused to profit by his daring ventures. Burghley's second son Robert, destined to be the old statesman's successor, already establishing his position, was the agent of his father's policy. The Queen's latest favourite, the young Earl of Essex—a son-in-law of Walsingham, and stepson of Leicester—was no statesman in fact, though he fancied himself one. His ambition was unlimited; and while, as an anti-Spaniard, he was a leader of the party opposed to the Cecils, he was not less hotly jealous of his rival within that party, Walter Raleigh (at an earlier period, and also afterwards, associated with the Cecils), whose large conceptions he could hardly appreciate. Finally the Queen herself, with the same political ideals as her old minister, had still never been able to resist the temptation of the profits accruing from the unauthorised raiding policy—a policy which dealt no blows from which it was impossible for Spain to recover, while it kept her in too bruised a condition to have any prospect of fighting again at an advantage.

It was Elizabeth who had ensured the failure of Drake's expedition, for which Drake himself was made responsible. Drake's policy was in consequence driven off the field, which was held by that of Essex and Hawkins—to which, as a policy, the Cecils were not vehemently opposed, while it satisfied the aroused bellicosity of the nation. Private enterprise was left to struggle with schemes of colonisation; and Spain held her trans-oceanic possessions.

[Sidenote: France, 1589-93]

But Spain's activity was crippled, her recuperation checked; and thus, indirectly, as well as with some direct assistance from England, Henry IV was enabled more than to hold his own in France, until in 1593, by accepting the Mass, he definitely won over to his side all but the extreme supporters of the League: from which time his ultimate triumph and that of at least limited toleration in France was secured: since Alexander of Parma, the one man whose military genius was more than a match for that of Henry, died in 1592.

[Sidenote: 1590 Death of Walsingham]

Here however we are anticipating. From the summer of 1589, Drake drops into the background. How matters might have gone if Walsingham or even Leicester had lived and retained their influence, it is not easy to say; both were staunch supporters of the admiral. But Leicester was already dead; and though the Queen had full confidence in the Secretary, she never liked him. Already he was practically in retirement; and in the following April he too died. With him, a very genuine puritanism and a determined antagonism to Spain had always been first principles. No man had expressed himself more openly in Council or more bitterly in private correspondence in condemnation of the tricks and the falsehoods which constituted— with a success which cannot be denied—the stock in trade of the Queen's diplomacy. He repeatedly risked favour and position by his outspokenness. His own policy and conduct had at all times been conducted in accordance with a standard of morals and of honour which was none the less strict though it does not always command sympathy. To Mary Stewart he was a relentless enemy. He had no compunctions in his system of espionage, and in his employment of traitors and of the *agent provocateur*. He, more than anyone else, was probably responsible for the extensive and extended application of torture as a means to extract information. These, in his eyes, were methods without which it was impossible to fight the enemy who must be fought at any cost. He was ready, even eager, to join battle openly with Spain in the cause of the Religion, which to him was a reality, while to Elizabeth, if not also to Burghley, it was only a political factor which it annoyed her to be obliged to recognise. And of his high personal integrity, the final proof is that when he died, he left means insufficient to provide a decent funeral. If his mantle may be said to have fallen on anyone, it was on Walter Raleigh; and Raleigh was not of the Council, while his favour with the Queen was at best an extremely fluctuating quantity.

[Sidenote: Operations in 1590]

It was not Drake then, but Hawkins and Frobisher who in 1590 commanded the armaments sent out to Spanish waters; with the primary intention of intercepting the annual convoy of treasure-ships. Disappointment was again in store, for the Spaniards had news of the expedition, the treasure-fleet did not sail, and the admirals returned home without spoils. Not, however, without hurting the enemy; for Spanish finance was dependent on the arrival of the bullion, Philip was crippled for want of it, and for the same reason Parma was almost paralysed. The Huguenot cause was advanced in France by Henry's victory at Ivry. In spite of his difficulties, however, Parma prevented the King from capturing Paris and so completing his triumph; but, with his resources so exhausted, even his genius was unable to accomplish more.

In the same year the splendid qualities developed by English seamen were illustrated by a valiant fight, in which twelve Spanish ships of war attacked a flotilla of ten English merchantmen, who fought so stubbornly that after six hours of conflict the Spaniards drew off, fairly defeated; the English having lost neither a ship nor a man.

[Sidenote: 1591 The "Revenge"]

In the meantime, however, Philip was making strenuous efforts to adapt his navy to the conditions of maritime warfare introduced by the English. In Havana, ships were being built of a greatly improved construction for fighting and manoeuvring, and the Spanish yards were busy. So when in 1591 a fleet sailed from England under Lord Thomas Howard [Footnote: Son of the Duke of Norfolk (executed in 1572) by his second wife; and half-brother of the Earl of Arundel, who died in the Tower in 1589.] and Richard Grenville, with much the same intent as that of Hawkins and Frobisher in 1590, they found themselves no longer in possession of the same complete command of the seas. Their squadron was a comparatively small one, including only six regular fighting ships; and as they lay in the Azores, in waiting for the treasure-fleet, tidings reached them that an armada of fifty-three vessels was hard at hand on its way to convoy that fleet. Howard put to sea at once, avoiding an action; but Grenville on the *Revenge* [Footnote: The *Revenge* was Drake's ship in the Armada conflict.] of set purpose allowed himself to be entangled in the Spanish fleet; and thereupon ensued that great fight, that glorious folly, which has been told in immortal prose and sung in immortal verse; in which for fifteen hours Drake's favourite vessel did battle, almost unaided, with fifty-three Spaniards. Not more splendid, not less irrational, were the great deeds of the three hundred at Thermopylae, of the six hundred at Balaclava. False moves in the game of war, all of them, from the scientific point of view; objectless, unreasoning, without possibility of material gain accruing; but for all that, deeds which for their sheer daring will ring for ever in the ears of men; of which the bare memory is an inspiration; whereof the fame in their own day roused the emulous courage of every Spartan and of every Englishman, making them ready to face any odds, and chilling the blood of their foes. Vain deeds, when we count the cost and the tangible gain—but very far from vain when we take into account the intangible moral effect.

Yet it was but the supreme example of that heroic spirit, shown times and again, at Zutphen, at the Bridge of El Burgo, in countless fights with Spaniards and with the elements, which in Elizabeth's day raised England to be the first among the nations. A deed therefore to be dwelt upon, if we would understand aright the history of those times, in which the historian must perforce discourse most frequently and at greatest length on doings of a less inspiring order. The craft of the statesman, the skill of the general, are the prominent factors in the making of history; but the character, the types, of the men of whom nations are constituted, are no less fundamental and vital.

[Sidenote: France, 1590-93]

In the meantime, the death in France of Henry IV.'s nominal rival, his uncle the titular Charles X., had increased the difficulties of the League, which was reduced to putting forward as its candidate the Infanta Isabella, the daughter of Philip and his third wife Elizabeth of Valois—whom also Philip destined as his nominee for the English throne when he should overthrow the heretic Queen. This involved the setting aside of the Salic law of succession, and an unmistakable Spanish ascendancy, which no conceivable marriage could make satisfactory to any one but Philip. Thus Elizabeth still found herself compelled to give Henry material assistance, and the English contingent before Rouen, which the French King was seeking to capture in the latter part of 1591, was commanded by Essex. Again however Parma intervened, compelling the siege to be raised: though his death a year later left no commander of equal ability to oppose Henry.

[Sidenote: Operations of 1592-94]

During the next three years, 1592-94, no attacks were made on a large scale. One was planned for the first year, to be commanded jointly by Raleigh and Frobisher. But Raleigh was recalled; the men who had joined his flag were indisposed to serve under Frobisher; the squadron divided, and ultimately accomplished little beyond the capture of a single rich prize. Nevertheless, the process of raiding Spanish commerce by privateering ships or squadrons was carried on, with much injury to Spanish trade, and collection of considerable spoils; the chief of the raiders being perhaps the Earl of Cumberland, who never failed to conduct at least one such expedition annually. But though Philip's finances continued thereby to be materially crippled, he was not prevented from carrying on the work of reorganising his navy; while towards the end of 1593 he had secured more than one station at Blavet and elsewhere on the coast of Brittany, where he hoped to establish an advanced base from which he could constantly threaten the Channel and Ireland. This scheme however was frustrated at the end of 1594 by a successful joint attack of Frobisher by sea and Norreys by land on a position at Crozon which threatened to dominate Brest; and by the expulsion of the Spaniards from other points in that neighbourhood where they had sought to plant themselves. Frobisher however died from a wound he received in the fighting. The move was one that Raleigh had advocated zealously; and it proved thoroughly effective.

Important as was this blow to Philip's naval aspirations, the political situation was still more decisively affected during these three years by the death of Parma in December 1592, Henry's acceptance of the Mass in July 1593, and his consequent recognition by the bulk of the French Catholics early in 1594: although the extremists of the League continued their opposition to him, and their support of the Spanish Infanta, a course which secured the maintenance of the alliance between Henry and Elizabeth.

[Sidenote: 1589-94 A survey]

From 1589, when the English Queen had deliberately dislocated the plans of Drake's Lisbon expedition, changing it from a great political stroke into an unsatisfactory raid, till the closing months of 1594 when once again a decisively damaging blow was dealt to Philip's naval schemes, the war had given ample occasion for stirring deeds of valour and brilliant feats of arms, but the scheme of operations throughout had been narrow and shortsighted. Though the honours still lay unmistakably with England, Spain had in fact been gaining ground, slowly remedying those defects in her organisation which had been so glaringly exposed by the breakdown of the Armada: and when Frobisher fell at Crozon, she was more formidable than at any time since Medina Sidonia had sailed from Corunna But besides the main open contest, Philip throughout these years had been dallying after his old fashion with the factions outside of England which might be looked to as possible instruments for shaking the throne of Elizabeth.

These were to be found among the exiled English Catholics, in Scotland, and in Ireland.

[Sidenote: Spain and the English Catholics]

With the Catholic exiles however, there was little to be done. Those indeed who were closely associated with the Jesuits founded their hopes of a Catholic restoration on Spanish dominion, with the Infanta Isabella as Queen of England; but the fact by itself sufficed to keep the bulk of the party cold if not antagonistic. The price was too high to pay, for any but Parsons and his associates. English Catholics looked by preference to the succession possibly of the Catholic Stanleys of Derby [Footnote: See *Front*]—

who unfortunately stood aloof—or of either James of Scotland or his cousin Arabella (representing the half-English Lennox Stewarts), both Protestants of whose conversion hopes were maintained. Patriotism, Nationality, held precedence over Religion: even although in 1593 fresh and harsh measures against Catholics as well as Puritans were adopted by Parliament. Under these conditions, plots for the removal of Elizabeth by methods which would make all the lukewarm elements in England actively hostile to Spain were not likely to receive encouragement from Philip. A variety of such plots were in fact concocted and duly revealed by informers or suspects under torture, and fathered on Philip or his ministers; but in every case the evidence connecting them with the Spaniards is of the weakest. Naturally, Essex and the war-party in England made the most of these stories, in order to inflame public opinion against Philip, and with no little success. Nevertheless, whatever element of truth they may have contained, they are too flimsy and unsubstantial to be seriously included in the indictments against Philip's character-which are indeed sufficiently grave without them. [Footnote: See Hume's *Treason and Plot,* cc. iv. v., where the evidence in a series of these plots is impartially set forth. The most notable of the group is that of Lopez, who was executed in 1594.]

[Sidenote: Scottish Intrigues]

Scottish intrigues with Philip were equally abortive. James, on the throne, played an unceasing game of chicane and double-dealing, perpetually playing off parties and persons against each other with that curious cunning which he designated "king-craft". The Catholic nobles alternated between hopes of capturing him, or of ejecting him, and fears of their own suppression. They tried to bargain with Philip, on the hypothesis of effecting James's conversion and placing him on the English throne; on the hypothesis of a Catholic restoration in Scotland; for one brief interval, on the hypothesis of giving Philip a free hand. But James had an ingenious trick of playing at friendship with his Catholic lords and introducing himself into these negotiations; whereas Philip had no idea of stirring a finger to help James to the English succession: and the Scottish Catholic lords themselves were by no means ready to relinquish the national aspiration to seat a Scots king on the throne of England. So that while these intrigues caused some perturbation in the English court, and led Elizabeth to lecture her young kinsman and disciple with a fine show of pained indignation, they never came within measurable distance of definite action.

[Sidenote: Ireland, 1583-92]

Ireland however offered a more promising field of operations. For a decade following the suppression of Desmond's rebellion, that country had lain in a state of exhaustion. English "under-takers" had been planted in the desolated and forfeited lands of Munster. In the North, Tyrconnel was loyal—that is, was not disposed to rebellion; Tirlough Lynagh, head of the O'Neills, was of a like mind; and Hugh O'Neill, the successor to the Earldom of Tyrone, had been brought up in England, and was a professed supporter of English rule: against which there was no one to make head. Even the coming of the Armada, while creating some nervousness, produced no disturbances, though the assistance given by a chief here and there to ship-wrecked Spaniards brought them into trouble. But this was the calm of exhaustion merely. The unvarying impression produced by the Irish letters of the time is that Englishmen regarded the native chiefs as a low type of savage, and the common folk as a noxious kind of vermin; and it is painfully clear that the standard of civilisation was of that debased type which must prevail where the governing powers have habitually set the example of distorting the first four commandments of the decalogue and ignoring the other six. The normal attitude of the bulk of the native Irish and Anglo-Irish was one of repressed hatred and veiled defiance towards the English, ready to break out openly whenever an opportunity should seem to present itself. That attitude would probably have been universal had not some of the chiefs, like Ormonde, been convinced that even the English system was preferable to the anarchy and strife of septs which would result from a temporarily successful rebellion: finding in friendly relations with the Government the best guarantee for the security of their own position.

Masterful and capable men however like the old Kildare and Shan O'Neill had demanded more. To Kildare the Henries had granted that more; Shan had come near to securing it in despite of Elizabeth. Now an abler man than either, Hugh O'Neill, Earl of Tyrone, dissatisfied with his treatment at the hands of the English was making up his mind to renew the contest.

[Sidenote: Tyrone, 1592-94]

Tyrone did not raise the standard of revolt. But in 1592-3, Tyrone, his brother in law Hugh Roe O'Donnell, [Footnote: Hugh O'Donnell had been trapped and held prisoner in Dublin as a hostage for Tyrconnell's good behaviour; but succeeded in making his escape.] Tyrconnell's son, his neighbours Maguire and O'Rourke, and the McWilliams or Burkes of Connaught—dwellers in the parts furthest from the Pale—were in active defiance of the Government. Tyrone was engaged in officially placating or repressing or remonstrating with them, ostensibly doing his best to serve the Queen; ready to hand over hostages, to present himself in person to the Deputy Fitzwilliam and demonstrate his loyalty, or to take the field against the rebels with the royal forces.,The Deputy, and the President of Connaught, had information that he was in fact in collusion with the rebels, but none which could be brought home to him; and the royal forces—amounting only to between four and five thousand men—were as usual inadequate to doing more than march into disturbed districts, accomplish some burnings and hangings, enjoy one or two sharp skirmishes, and march out again. But by 1594 Tyrone and his friends were in communication with Spain, and Philip was again contemplating the expulsion of the English from Ireland as an effective line of operation in his war with Elizabeth.

[Sidenote: 1595 Drake's last voyage]

By this time the Queen was waking up to the fact that the Spanish sea-power was not diminishing but recovering: the attack on the Brittany ports points to the revival of a more far-seeing naval policy; Drake was returning to favour, and the younger Cecil was well-disposed towards him. It was decided that he and old John Hawkins should revive the past methods and conduct a grand attack on the Spanish Main and Panama. As usual however, fluctuating orders from the Queen delayed the start till some months after the intended date; the Plate fleet reached its destination in safety; the Spaniards got wind of the expedition; and when Drake and Hawkins at last put to sea they had instructions calculated effectively to prevent their accomplishing anything like a surprise. Porto Rico, the first main objective, had due warning, and so was able to offer a successful resistance to the attack, energetically as it was conducted. The death of Hawkins, who had grown too cautious to work well with Drake, relieved the expedition of divided counsels; but Drake had not realised that in the years of his inaction the Spaniards had profited by the lessons he had taught them. Though he sacked and burnt La Hacha, Santa Marta, and Nombre de Dios, the spoils were small; the enemy, prepared for his coming, had secured the passes through Darien to Panama, and it was found that there was no possibility of forcing them. Then came the final disaster; Drake himself was seized with dysentery, and on January 28th, 1598, the great seaman died. He found in the Ocean his fitting grave: and the expedition returned to England having failed to accomplish anything noteworthy, though it had to fight a not unsuccessful battle with a slightly superior fleet on the way home.

Six months before Drake sailed on his last voyage, Raleigh had gone on a notable exploring expedition to the Orinoco; the forerunner of not a few voyages in search of the fabled Eldorado. Beyond some extension of geographical knowledge however, the venture was unfruitful.

[Sidenote: 1596 The Cadiz expedition]

Although Drake's expedition had been spoilt, his theories were once more, in the main, in the ascendant; and in June 1598 a great attacking force was again organised, with Cadiz for its principal objective. An effective blow at Philip's navy was made all the more necessary at the moment, because the Archduke Albert, now in command in the Netherlands, had just succeeded in capturing Calais from the French. Howard of Effingham again commanded as admiral, with Essex as general in chief, a council which included Raleigh and Lord Thomas Howard, and a Dutch contingent which was under the orders of the English chief. The Spaniards had this time no suspicion of what was on foot. The harbour of Cadiz was full of shipping; which included however a number of ships of war in fighting trim. Thus it was not without a fierce conflict that the English drove their way in. Two ships only were captured, and transferred from the Spanish to the English navy, but numbers were sunk or burnt. The exploit was a brilliant one, owing its success largely to a change from the original plan of attack, for which that advocated by Raleigh was substituted. Cadiz itself was stormed, captured, and put to ransom; but the victors displayed what was in those days a singular and notable restraint and courtesy in their treatment of the vanquished. In spite, however, of the protests of Essex, who wished to remain in occupation of Cadiz, Lord Howard was content with the heavy spoils secured and the immense destruction wrought, and the expedition returned home.

[Sidenote: Ireland, 1595-96]

Tyrone in the meantime was playing his difficult game in Ireland with remarkable success. He consistently maintained his professions of loyalty, though by now calling himself "The O'Neill," like Shan, he fostered the belief that he was only waiting to declare himself anti- English; he continued to evade action against the more open rebels; he continued to correspond with Spain; and yet Sir John Norreys, now in command of the army in Ireland, could not resist the belief that he meant to be loyal and would be loyal and would make the other chiefs so, if his assistance were loyally accepted and his position frankly confirmed by the English. Whether such anticipations would have proved true if he had been treated as Henry VII. treated Kildare, it is impossible to say. But the Deputy Fitzwilliam, and his successor Russell, regarded him as a traitor at heart, and persistently provided him with palpable excuse for distrusting them [Footnote: Tyrone received a letter from Philip, which he showed the Deputy, as a proof of the tempting offers made to him and of his own loyalty, on condition that it should neither be copied nor retained. But it was kept by the English, and used by them to attack Philip, and others.] in turn. Under such conditions, loyal or not at bottom, it was no part of the Earl's policy to break with Philip, or on the other hand to commit himself too deeply till Philip should be also irrevocably committed to rendering real solid assistance.

So Norreys went on recommending conciliation, and Russell went on opposing that policy, while Elizabeth persistently abstained alike from effective conciliation and from the one practicable alternative policy of placing a really strong organised and orderly garrison in the country: maintaining instead only a few ill-paid ill-disciplined ill- behaved troops who might on occasion meet the raw Irish levies but were wholly unfitted to be the instruments of a firm government. And all the time from every officer in Ireland arose the perpetual petition to be recalled from service in a country where neither a soldier nor an administrator could possibly escape lowering any reputation he might have previously acquired. It was well for England that Drake's last expedition demanded the entire attention of the Spanish Fleet; and that, following thereon, the Cadiz expedition was even more destructive to the prospects of the new Armada which Philip was still seeking to organise, than Drake's former Cadiz expedition had proved itself to the Great Armada in 1587. Tyrone was thereby baulked of Spanish help, without which he would not plunge into such a rebellion as might threaten seriously to embarrass Elizabeth and benefit Philip.

[Sidenote: 1596 The second Armada]

So matters stood in the summer of 1596. One quality however Philip possessed with which Englishmen must sympathise; he never recognised that he was beaten. Crushing as the blow at Cadiz was, the northern ports were left alone, and there the laborious building up of a great fleet was in steady progress. Philip was stirred to deal a counterstroke, and late in October a huge new Armada of nearly a hundred vessels sailed from Vigo Bay, its destination unknown save to Philip, its very existence unrealised in England, where no one believed that a Spanish fleet would put to sea so late in the year. The Irish chiefs however had notice that an invading force was coming. But the old story was repeated. The preparations had been thrown out of gear by the disaster of the summer; all the provisions were incomplete; the ships were hopelessly ill-found; and the fleet had hardly started when a terrific storm fell on it and shattered it. Thirty or more of the vessels were lost at sea; when the rest of the battered armament struggled back to Ferrol, pestilence broke out, and the crews died and deserted by hundreds if not by thousands. The stars in their courses fought against Philip and ruined the second Armada—this time without the help of hostile man.

[Sidenote: 1597 The Island Voyage, etc.]

This was followed again in the next summer by another English expedition, known as the "Island Voyage," with Essex, Lord Thomas Howard, and Raleigh in command; with a score of ships from the Royal Navy, and a Dutch contingent as in the Cadiz expedition. [Footnote: The soldiers wanted an army to attack Calais. Raleigh's insistence however carried the day in favour of a naval blow. (Raleigh, *Opinion on the Spanish Alarum*.)] The affair however was mismanaged. From the start, there were adverse tempests. [Footnote: *S. P. Dom.* iv., p. 463.] Corunna and Ferrol, which it was intended to attack, were found warned and armed for defence; and the gales were unfavourable. The fleet made for the Azores, and captured Fayal, Graciosa, and St. Michael's; but the treasure-fleet by good fortune evaded the English and found safety at Terceira. Raleigh and Essex quarrelled violently; and the fleet returned home with little accomplished. It succeeded however in weathering a storm which once more had made havoc of still another Spanish Armada, which sought to seize the opportunity for making a raid on Cornwall with a view to seizing and holding some port, to be used as an advance post for operations in the Channel—a sufficiently wild scheme at the best, with Essex's fleet returning almost on the heels of the expedition.

The failure decided Tyrone that Spain was a thoroughly broken reed; and he succeeded in making terms with the English Government [Footnote: *S. P. Irish*, vi., pp. 477-479.] that winter, if only with a view to organising a more determined and independent rebellion in the near future.

[Sidenote: 1598 Spain]

It is abundantly evident in this the last year of Philip's life that he was beaten at every point, however his obstinate fanaticism might refuse to admit it. His designs on the throne of France were foiled; the negotiations were already far advanced for the Peace of Vervins which was to set the French King free from the war. The prospect of placing Isabella [Footnote: Philip was now arranging to bestow Flanders upon her as an independent sovereignty.] on the English throne was more visionary than ever. The Spanish party among the English Catholics were growing more and more out of favour; pride in the prestige of English arms, scorn that England should be dominated by a nation which could not match her in open fight, strengthened the patriotic section. The Scots would not stir a finger except to make their own monarch king of the neighbouring country. The Pope himself had no desire to see Spain so aggrandised as to be able to dictate to Christendom. The prospect of the Netherlands being reduced to submission had all but vanished. As for the maritime rivalry, all the Spanish efforts had been in vain. The ships had been improved; the defence of the trade-routes had been better organised. Several of the blows aimed by England had been more or less abortive; but one at least had been staggering, and every attempt at a counterstroke had ended in plain disaster. Moreover from first to last the Spaniards, valiant as they often proved themselves, had fought as beaten men, the English as assured victors; both alike with a perfect conviction that the latter were certain to win against any but overwhelming odds. Such a fight as that of the *Revenge*, with the nationalities of the combatants reversed, was unimaginable.

Yet even in 1598 Philip and some of his ecclesiastical counsellors were unconvinced, and a brief alarm was created when a Spanish flotilla dashed up the Channel and made its way to Calais, not yet restored to France. Completely unexpected as it was, however, English squadrons were on the seas almost at a day's notice. Half the flotilla was lost outside Calais, and immediately afterwards the Spanish ports were in a ferment at the report that Cumberland was hovering off their own coast — very sufficient evidence of the immense superiority of the English, both in organisation and *morale*.

[Sidenote: Death of Philip, Sept.]

In September, Elizabeth's great enemy breathed his last. He was not exactly the monster of iniquity that he has been painted; not a criminal for the love of criminality. He was a Tiberius rather than a Nero; a morbid influence, not a devouring pestilence. A perfectly sombre bigot; an example of what the Greeks would have called [Greek: hubris] of a very exceptional kind, who believed devoutly in himself as the instrument chosen by the Saints for the overthrow of heretics; convinced that his aims and interests were favoured by Heaven, ranking before those of the Papacy itself; without a qualm as to the righteousness of all means he could adopt to further those aims. Save in one slight instance, we seek in vain to find in him any sign of human affections—tenderness, sympathy, generosity. Infinitely laborious, his idea of government was to elaborate an enormous machinery, of which every portion should be under his personal control; eternally suspicious, he trusted no man, and kept the hands of his servants tied and bound; immovably cautious, he always waited to strike till he thought he could do so with overwhelming force, and he always waited till the time to strike had passed—till his opponent had crippled him by striking first. Forty years before, he was lord of the New World, lord of the seas, lord of Spain, of half Italy, of the Netherlands, and seemed destined to be lord of England, almost of Europe. Elizabeth and Cecil had seen where lay the weakness of his position; they had evaded, cajoled, finally had defied and triumphed over him. When he sank to the grave, the lordship of the sea had passed, the lordship of the Netherlands was passing, the lordship of the New World was tottering. His overweening egotism had sucked the life-blood of Spain. The Power which forty years before had threatened to dominate the world was no better than a decrepit giant; the form still loomed gigantic, but the substance was gripped with the chill paralysis wherewith Philip had smitten it, since he had entered like a poisonous blight upon his inheritance.

Philip was seventy-one when he died. Six weeks earlier Lord Burghley, seven years his senior, passed away, leaving Elizabeth with none beside her of her own generation. For forty years too, he had been the Queen's first minister. However we read the enigma of Elizabeth's apparent frivolity, vacillation, trickery and success, he had been throughout the one man with whose counsel she would not dispense, even when she seemed to flout him. Essentially he was a master of compromise, of balance; a devotee of moderation, of the *via media*. Hardly less averse to war than his mistress, he would yet have preferred war to some of the ignominious shifts by which she evaded it; for he had a cool level-headed confidence in England's essential vitality and power of weathering the storm, if it should burst, even at times when outside observers imagined that that confidence was hurrying her to ruin. When obliged to lean to one side or the other in religious controversy, he adopted the cause of "his brethren in Christ" as Elizabeth dubbed them with a sneer, because that was more compatible with his *via media* than the other: but he had none of Walsingham's puritanic enthusiasm. His ideal for England was a prosperous respectability: breaches of political propriety shocked him. He would take no share in the profits of buccaneering exploits: but it was the same mental quality which kept him from any zeal for Causes which might drag the country into incalculable ventures. When it seemed to him that a vigorous support of European Protestantism was the only alternative to submission to Spain, he went with Walsingham, though Elizabeth found her own alternative in spite of them both: but he did it reluctantly, and always at bottom with the hope that Spain and England might yet attain mutual amity. After the death of Nicholas Bacon in 1579 he inclined more to believe in that possibility, and in proportion as the war-party was strengthened by the Armada his antagonism to it became the more marked. After his seventieth year his direct interference in politics had become less; but his astute son, Robert Cecil, represented him. All through his career, he was a consistent opportunist, using without scruple all currently admissible tools, never missing the chance of the half-loaf. The most industrious of men, a supremely shrewd judge of character and motive, he was rarely—save in the case of the Queen—misled by superficial appearances; though his own lack of sentiment prevented him from fully appreciating the sentimental factor in politics. Always at all risks he was loyal to Queen and Country; and habitually, even at some risk, to servants and colleagues. If he does not stand absolutely in the first rank of English statesmen, they are yet few who stand above him.

CHAPTER XXVI
ELIZABETH (xi), 1598-1603-
THE QUEEN'S LAST YEARS

[Sidenote: A new generation]

By Burghley's death, Elizabeth was left alone, reft of all her earlier counsellors. Nicholas Bacon had died as far back as 1579, Leicester in 1588, Walsingham in 1590, her kinsmen Knollys and Hunsdon—less prominent, but of sober weight—more recently. Except Howard of Effingham (created Earl of Nottingham after the Cadiz expedition), Burghley was the last; and their sombre antagonist of forty years had followed him in a few weeks. She herself was sixty-five years old. The leading men at home and abroad—Henry IV., Philip III., Robert Cecil, Raleigh, Essex, who was now only thirty— were of a younger generation. Lonely but stubborn and indomitable as ever she ruled still to the end.

Those last five years were troubled enough.

[Sidenote: 1598 Ireland]

We have seen that in Ireland Tyrone was resolved to place no more dependence on Spanish aid; but it was equally clear that the Government as constituted was quite unable to quell him. Norreys was now dead, and Ormonde was in command of the Queen's army, such as it was. The English garrison was quite incapable of vigorous aggression. In 1598 a few raw levies were sent over, instead of the strong disciplined force without which nothing could be effected. In the middle of August a force was dispatched against Tyrone, who was beleaguering the Blackwater fort not far from Armagh; and Tyrone inflicted on it a complete and disastrous defeat, [Footnote: S. P. *Irish*, pp. 236 ff.] which caused nothing less than a panic among the Council at Dublin. The practical effect was that outside the Pale the chiefs were doing as they chose, and the English could hardly move beyond their fortifications; even within the Pale ravaging was almost unchecked; and if it had been possible for Tyrone to march in force on Dublin, the capital would probably have fallen.

In the troubles of Ireland, Essex was to seek a ladder for his ambitions, and to find, as others before and after him have found, the road to ruin.

[Sidenote: Essex]

The personal interest of these years belongs very much to the rivalries of three men; Robert Cecil, sly, cautious, and plausible; Raleigh, brilliant and bitter, intellectually a head and shoulders above the rest; Essex, not lacking in abilities distorted by inordinate vanity. Associated on equal terms, in war, with the experience of Howard and the genius of Raleigh, at the Council-board with the astute and consummately trained Cecil, petted and spoiled by the elderly Queen as she had spoiled no one since the days of Leicester's youth, a public favourite by reason of his undoubted courage and his popular habits, Essex, young as he was, had long imagined himself the greatest man in the kingdom, chafing at every favour bestowed on a rival, and treating men who knew themselves his superiors with intolerable arrogance. Now, when the state of Ireland, and the remedies, were the subject of grave anxiety, he clamoured of the blank incompetence to the task of every one who had undertaken it or could be suggested as fitted for it; with the result that he was invited to undertake it himself. Thereupon he made unprecedented conditions. Some months elapsed before the conditions could be arranged; it would certainly seem that his object was to get under his own captaincy a force large enough to enable him to defy all control, though he was not without friends to warn him that his influence with Elizabeth depended on the fascination of his presence—a fact of which his ill-wishers were equally aware, and by which they intended to profit to the full. Not the least part of the danger to Essex lay in the fact that the political air was thick with intrigues as to the succession when Elizabeth should die, and that his rivals might utilise his absence to secure the throne for a candidate who under the circumstances would be certain to prove unfriendly to him.

[Sidenote: 1599 Essex in Ireland]

But the hot-headed Earl had deprived himself of the power of choice though he was almost equally unwilling to resign or to undertake the task to which he was committed. In April 1599 he appeared in Ireland as Lord Lieutenant, virtually with plenary powers alike in civil and military affairs, and a warrant to return in a year's time. Yet he chafed at such restrictions as were imposed upon him, at the incompetence of the officers with whom he was provided, at the refusal to permit appointments objectionable to the Queen, at the inefficiency of his troops and the inadequacy of his supplies. In theory, he was come to Ireland to strike straight at the heart of the rebellion and crush Tyrone in his own fastnesses. He found that the condition of the country absolutely precluded an immediate campaign in the North. He proceeded instead on a military progress through Leinster and Munster, capturing castles which surrendered with no more than a show of resistance, scattering small garrisons, perpetually harassed by guerilla companies who avoided pitched battles. He gave Southampton command of the cavalry in defiance of the Queen's orders, and then received from her so peremptory a message that he dared not maintain the appointment. The rebels cut up the forces of the President of Connaught, and another detached column in Wicklow: and on his way back to Dublin, Essex himself had much ado to beat off an attack on his main army at Arklow.

In the meantime, he was writing letters of furious complaint that the Council in London—in especial Raleigh, who was now associated with Cecil—were deliberately seeking to cripple him for their own ends—a charge which they declined to answer, as being merely a piece of excited extravagance; and Elizabeth rated him, not more sharply than he deserved, for wasting the unusually large sums provided for Ireland on a procedure so vain. Further, she peremptorily ordered him to march against O'Neill without delay, warning him on no account to withdraw from the country.

[Sidenote: Fall of Essex]

So at the end of August Essex set out. But when he found himself within striking distance of Tyrone's forces, the latter invited him to a parley. It was granted and held, and was followed by two more meetings; with the amazing result that a truce was concluded and both armies withdrew. That some personal compact was made can hardly be doubted; what it was remains unknown, and it was never carried out; but the presumption is that there was some joint scheme for securing the succession of King James to the throne, with Tyrone supreme in Ireland and Essex in England. Tyrone himself gave the Spaniards an obviously improbable version of the plan (after it had collapsed), according to which he had induced Essex to contemplate adhesion to the ultra-Spanish party, though he was the most pronouncedly hostile to Spain and to Catholicism of all the English leaders.

Whatever the plot, the ignominy of such a termination to the lavish preparations and boastings preceding was palpable. Elizabeth was furious, and her expressions of resentment were scathing. Whereupon Essex took the very worst step possible in his own interests. Relying on the Queen's curious infatuation for his person, which had survived innumerable quarrels and flagrant impertinences, he left his office, sped across the channel, rode post haste across England, flung himself, all mud-bespattered into the presence of his mistress in her chamber, and prayed for pardon. For the moment, she was too utterly taken aback to be herself; he left her thinking he had won.

But the outrage was too gross. That evening he found himself under arrest. His enemies' policy of "giving him rope enough" had been more completely successful than they could have hoped. He had set the noose about his neck with his own hand, though it was not yet tightened.

[Sidenote: Catholic factions]

The whole of the Essex story is inextricably interwoven with the crowd of intrigues in progress in connexion with the succession. In England by this time the ultra-Spanish or Jesuit faction, which would have enthroned the Inquisition with a Spanish nominee as sovereign, was all but non-existent. The division was into two main parties. One desired a sovereign under whom either Catholicism should be restored under such tolerant conditions as prevailed under Henry IV. in France, or else Anglicanism might be retained, extending a like toleration to Catholics. There was of course a fundamental divergence between these two positions; but very many of the nobility, whether professed Anglicans or professed Catholics, were prepared to accept either alternative. Of this party the intellectual chief was Cecil. The second party, that of which Essex was the head, relied primarily upon the Puritan element, and advocated persistent hostility to Spain.

Now the effective Spanish position had been materially changed since, shortly before his death, Philip II. had erected the Netherlands into a separate sovereignty under the Infanta Isabella and the Austrian Archduke Albert to whom she was betrothed: he had thus made possible for England a revival of the old-time Burgundian alliance independent of Spain. The Archduke knew that as a Spanish Princess Isabella would never be accepted in England, but the union under one head of England and Burgundy was a very different matter, which might provide a key to the religious problem very much akin to that which France had recently found. It was in this direction that the eyes of the majority of the Cecil party were probably turned. For Essex however—unless indeed he really contemplated the hare-brained scheme of striking for the throne himself—the course was clearly to bring in James as his own puppet. It is no doubt easy to remark that that crafty prince would very soon have outwitted and tripped up the shallow and overweening Earl: but the Earl himself was the last person to anticipate such a *denouement*.

[Sidenote: Philip III]

But outside England there was the cunning King of Scots, on the one hand intriguing with Essex, on the other appealing to the Pope, as a Catholic at heart who was only waiting for adequate support to drop the mask—bidding in fact for the countenance of both camps. There was Tyrone in Ireland, similarly posing to Spain as the champion of Catholicism, while intriguing with Essex and James indubitably for something like sovereignty for himself as the price of supporting the Scots King. And there was the young Philip III. of Spain, idle and vain, who, with a bankrupt treasury and a rotten administration had his head full of the most inflated ideas of his own power, and still fancied himself quite capable of conquering England at a blow; a delusion from which the fanatical religionists who trusted not in the arm of flesh, were also suffering. To him therefore the idea of James ascending the English throne even as a Catholic was quite repugnant; as was also the succession of his sister, unless she restored the Netherlands to him. Whereas the union with the Netherlands was precisely the one condition which made her candidature possible in England.

While Essex was still in Ireland this imagination of Philip's had borne curious fruit. He ordered the preparation of another Armada: the greatest of all. The Spanish vapourings on the subject actually created some alarm in England; Raleigh and Lord Thomas Howard very promptly had efficient fleets on the narrow seas; the Lord Admiral (now Earl of Nottingham) was appointed Lord General and there was a great mustering of troops and raising of companies by noblemen and gentlemen. But it is more than probable that, as far as the land forces were concerned, these measures were intended quite as much to be a hint to Essex that he would find any attempt at coercion an exceedingly dangerous game, as for protection against any effort which Philip was capable of putting forth. In fact this Armada ended in the feeblest of all these feeble fiascoes: for while it was making ready, a Dutch fleet was raiding the Canaries and the trade routes; when it put to sea its energies were absorbed in a futile attempt to catch these audacious enemies; and before it reached the Azores, a fourth part of it had foundered and the balance had been practically crippled by foul weather.

Such then was the position when in the autumn of 1599 Essex suddenly found himself a prisoner. Cecil however did not think it politic to go to extremities. The Earl was not haled before the Star-Chamber as was proposed in some quarters; it was not till the following June that he was brought before a commission of the Privy Council for enquiry and censure; and some two months later he was released. But from October 1599 to August 1600 he remained in custody.

[Sidenote: 1600 Ireland]

In the meantime, Tyrone was appealing to Spain and to the Archduke Albert. The latter, with ulterior objects, was negotiating for peace with Cecil— who was following a path of his own—and had no mind to complicate the intrigue by an Irish embroilment. Philip immediately gave orders that everything was to be provided to conquer Ireland out of hand;

but as the means for carrying out those orders were entirely lacking, there were no results. Moreover, Elizabeth had at last realised that the systematic reduction of Ireland was now an absolute necessity which could only be accomplished by adequate forces under a competent commander. Montjoy, a connexion of Essex, was sent over; his dealings with Tyrone met with increasing success. Essex had at first counted on Montjoy acting in effect as his own deputy; but in this he was disappointed. Placed in a position of responsibility, the Deputy immediately rejected the overtures he made. The army in Ireland was not to be the instrument of Essex's ambition.

[Sidenote: Succession intrigues]

Where so many of the actors were simultaneously engaged in alternative intrigues, some of them with entire insincerity, and solely for the purpose of keeping inconvenient persons or groups in play until they were harmless, it is not possible to be sure in most cases of the real policy intended. Cecil's party were in some sort of communication even with Parsons, who persuaded himself that if only Philip would definitely commit himself to a nominee, and would strike in before the Scots King could secure himself, the chiefs of that party would support him. It is not credible that this was really the case, but it is at least probable that the group were deliberately seeking to produce that impression at the Spanish head-quarters. For them the essential thing was to wreck Essex on the one side and out-wit the extreme Catholics on the other. Others might be deceived, but Cecil and Raleigh at least must have been fully alive to the worthlessness of any programme which assumed political intelligence on the part of Philip, or effective activity in Spain. James was playing for the support of every section, by inducing each to believe that his overtures to the other sections were mere blinds: and during this year he was working for the support of Henry IV., as being at heart a tolerant Catholic. Whether Essex, who must have been aware of the intrigue, accepted the policy or regarded it as merely a useful diplomatic deception remains uncertain; at any rate it did not alienate him. But the appearance of a Franco-Scottish rapprochement was an immediate incentive to and excuse for counter negotiations with Philip and the Archduke on the part of the English government.

[Sidenote: The end of Essex 1600-1]

At the end of August, Essex was released, though still excluded from favour. The Cecil party had complete control of the situation, and to all appearance meant to come to terms with the Archduke: which would wreck the Earl's ambitions irretrievably. Now, when his one chance lay in playing the repentant and tearful adorer of a mistress cruel and fair if somewhat mature—a very familiar role for him—his cry was all for the restoration of lost pecuniary privileges; and his mistress would naturally have none of a lover so self-centred. Despairing of the Queen's favour, he was rash enough to pose as a popular champion, declaiming against the intriguers who were selling England to the Infanta, and drawing round him the young hot-heads and scape-graces of the nobility, in the insane belief that their swords and the cheers of the London mob would enable him to effect the overthrow of Cecil by a *coup de main*. When the time was ripe, early in February, Cecil struck. Essex was summoned to appear before the Council. He evaded the summons, and next day with his friends made a frantic attempt to raise the City for the removal of the Queen's false Counsellors. That evening he was a prisoner in the Tower. A few days later, he was brought to trial for treason before a Court of Peers, and was condemned and executed. Pardon was impossible, though Elizabeth's grief at signing his death warrant was poignant and permanent.

[Sidenote: Robert Cecil]

The triumph of Cecil was complete. The utter overthrow of Essex had been his first objective; now he was free to work his own underground policy. Publicly and ostensibly as before he remained the chief of the "moderate" party, seeking reconciliation with Spain and a *modus vivendi* between Catholics and Anglicans; privately he took Essex's vacated place as the friend of the Scots King. Thenceforth, from the Moderate camp, directing the Moderate programme, he was in intimate correspondence [Footnote: Now published in its entirety by the Camden Society.] with James; working for the ultimate destruction of his rivals and associates, when the Stewart should become King of England, owing his crown to Cecil's dexterity. James, realising his position, promptly fell in with Cecil's plans, dropped coquetting with Catholics abroad, and was quite content to wait for a dead woman's shoes, and to give up irritating demands for an immediate recognition, of which, with Cecil on his side, he felt ultimately assured.

[Sidenote: Ireland 1600-1]

During 1600, Montjoy had already been doing good service in Ireland. The 14,000 troops at his disposal—though thrice as many as had been allowed to Norreys—were insufficient for dealing a rapid and crushing blow at the heart of the rebellion in Ulster. In Munster, however, the Deputy had a vigorous lieutenant in Carew, and the chiefs were of a divided mind— largely because many of them held their positions precariously, in virtue of the English tenure which had been officially substituted for the Irish method of succession—so that the forces of resistance were to a great extent broken up. But in Ulster, Montjoy accomplished a fine strategic stroke by making a feint of invading the province from the south, while he sent a large force of 4000 men by sea, under command of Docwra, to Loch Foyle, where they established themselves at Londonderry. He was thus in a position to strike at Tyrone or O'Donnell whenever those chiefs should attempt to move southward in force: as was exemplified next year, when Donegal was seized, and the Blackwater fort was recaptured by a move from the South, because Tyrone could not withdraw his attention from Derry.

[Sidenote: 1601 The Irish rebellion broken]

About the time of Essex's crash, there were again rumours of a Spanish invasion. Carew could deal with the Irish rebels alone, but hardly with a strong invading force as well. When in September 1601 a real Spanish force did arrive at Kinsale, Montjoy had to concentrate in Munster. But though this expedition showed the limits of Philip's capacities, it was as usual so ill found that many of the ships had been obliged to put back to Corunna, and others, failing to make Kinsale, put in at Baltimore. Montjoy was in strength near Cork, Carew at Limerick ready to intercept the approach of the rebels from the North. In a very short time, Kinsale was beleagured, and when a portion of a Spanish reinforcement managed to reach the coast in December, it found an English flotilla before it, and its troops were isolated in a third station at Castlehaven. O'Donnell however succeeded in evading Carew, who then joined forces with Montjoy and the fleet before Kinsale. When Tyrone arrived, an attempt was made to relieve Kinsale; but Montjoy was unusually well served by his intelligence, his dispositions were skilful, and the rebels were totally routed beyond possibility of present recovery. Aguilar, the Spanish commander, was admitted to terms; Baltimore and Castlehaven were surrendered. Thus abortively collapsed the last effort of Philip III. The Irish rebellion was broken. Many of the chiefs after vain and desperate resistance escaped to Spain; others surrendered to the Queen's mercy. O'Donnell was of the former; he died soon after reaching Spain. But Tyrone the diplomatic succeeded in making terms. It seemed that once more the English Government was supreme.

[Sidenote: 1602 The Succession]

Once again, as the death of the great Queen becomes imminent, we must remind ourselves that to the last she refused to recognise any heir, and that there were various claimants, [Footnote: Genealogical Tables; *Front.* and *App. A*, iii.] each one with a colourable claim. In point of priority by heredity King James of Scotland unquestionably stood first of the descendants of Henry VII. and Elizabeth of York; yet the fact that he was not only an alien but King of Scotland made him in himself an unwelcome candidate. Next to him, since like him she descended from Margaret Tudor, stood his cousin Arabella—a Stewart too, but of the Lennox Stewarts, not the Royal House: an English subject; but with the drawback that she was a woman and unmarried. Third, but first under the will of Henry VIII. was Lord Beauchamp, son of Katharine Grey and the Earl of Hertford; about the validity of his parents' marriage however there was a doubt. The Stanleys of Derby, who through Margaret Clifford could claim descent from the younger daughter of Henry VII., would have nothing to do with inheriting the crown; no more would the Earl of Huntingdon who descended from Edward IV.'s brother, George of Clarence. But Philip of Spain claimed the crown for himself as a descendant of John of Gaunt; though, the union of the crowns of England and Spain being admittedly impracticable, he was under promise to transfer his claim to a hitherto unnamed nominee, presumably his sister. Virtually therefore Isabella ranked as a possible though not very enthusiastic candidate.

[Sidenote: The last intrigues]

By this time, it was perfectly obvious that the Infanta could not be forced upon England, though it was supposed that the Moderates would have favoured her candidature provided she brought Flanders with her: whereas the negotiations controlled by Cecil were not tending to bring about any such result. As 1602 drew to a close, the ablest man in Spain, Olivares, was emphasising the necessity for giving the English Catholics as a body a free hand to nominate an English candidate instead of an alien. It is probable, though it cannot be called certain, that there was a plot to unite the claims of Arabella and Lord Beauchamp by marrying them, with an implication that both were prepared in due time to declare themselves Catholics. Meantime the Moderates were awaiting direction from Cecil; who ostensibly was himself waiting on a hint from the Queen, but was privily keeping the way clear for James, while seeking to implicate Raleigh and others in language and actions which might at any rate be interpreted as hostile to him. In this secret intriguing, Cecil's great ally was Lord Henry Howard, a brother of the last Duke of Norfolk; and he had with him the Careys of the Hunsdon family. Of the Moderates in general it can only be said that, while there was no candidate in whose favour they could combine with any warmth, James was rather more obnoxious to them than others. Yet they did not combine against him, while if any of them sought to ingratiate themselves with him Cecil was particularly careful to sow distrust of them in the Scots King's mind, unless they happened to be partisans of his own or at any rate probable allies. When Arabella tried to escape from what was practically the custody of her grandmother the Dowager Countess of Shrewsbury, the famous "Bess of Hardwick," the attempt was nipped in the bud: and the Catholics were still without any declared candidate when the lonely old Queen was seized in March with her last mortal illness.

As Elizabeth lay on her death-bed, her entourage consisted almost exclusively of Cecil and his friends, among whom is to be numbered the old Lord Admiral, though he was innocent of the intrigues going on. The ships in the Thames, the troops in the North, were commanded by members of the same group; almost before the breath was out of her body Robert Carey was galloping North to hail James I. King of England: and the world was told that Elizabeth's last conscious act was to ratify by a sign the succession of her old-time rival's son. In her seventieth year, in the early hours of March 24th, 1603, ended the long and glorious reign of the Virgin Queen.

CHAPTER XXVII
ELIZABETH (xii), 1558-1603—LITERATURE

The Elizabethan Literature demands from the general Historian something more than the incidental references which may suffice in other periods. In earlier days, he may draw upon Piers Plowman or Chaucer for evidence and illustrations of the prevalent social conditions; in the century following he may appeal to Milton and Bunyan to elucidate aspects of Puritanism. But the Elizabethan literature is in a degree quite unique, the expression of the whole spirit of the time, its many-sidedness, its vigour, its creative force; helping us to realise how it was that Elizabeth's Englishmen made Elizabeth's England. And this of course is beside the other fact that for the historian of literature *per se* there is no period quite so interesting and instructive, none of such vital importance in the evolution of English Letters.

[Sidenote: Birth of a National Literature]

In the five centuries since the Norman Conquest, ending in 1566, England had produced but one single poet of the front rank or anything approaching it, Geoffrey Chaucer. From the time when Edmund Spenser in 1579 delighted his contemporaries by the publication of the *Shepherd's Calendar*, she has never been without writers whose claim to eminence among poets can be at least plausibly maintained. Before very much the same date, English prose as a consciously artistic medium of utterance had hardly begun to be recognised; even Thomas More wrote his *Utopia* in Latin, and it was not translated into English till many years after his death. The possibility of an English Prose Style—written prose as distinguished from spoken oratory—had hardly presented itself except to the translators of Scripture and the Liturgy. Before the century closed, the world was enriched by the compact and pregnant sentences of Francis Bacon's *Essays* and the dignified simplicity of Hooker's *Ecclesiastical Polity*. As with the Poets, so also the chain of masters of English Prose is unbroken from that day forward. But most sudden and startling of all the various developments was that of the Drama. It may be doubted if any critical observer in 1579 would have ventured even to suspect that the crowning glory of Elizabeth's reign was to be the work of playwrights; yet before she died the genius of Marlowe had blazed and been quenched, *Hamlet* had appeared on the boards, Jonson's "learned sock" had achieved fame; the men whose names we are wont to associate with the "Mermaid" had most of them already begun their career, even if they had not yet passed the stage of merely adapting, doctoring, and "writing up" for managers the stock-plays in their repertory. The Drama, proving itself the form of literary expression most perfectly adapted to the spirit of the age, absorbed the available literary talent as it has never done since.

Sudden as the outburst was however, it had been made possible by many years of wide and miscellaneous experiment, though little of any permanent intrinsic value had been actually achieved.

[Sidenote: Prose: before 1579]

Except for Ascham's *Toxophilus*, very few passages [Footnote: Such as may be lighted on for instance in "Sir John Mandeville," Mallory, and Hall's *Chronicle*.] of English prose notable as prose—that is, consciously essaying what is connoted by the term *style*—had been produced before Elizabeth's accession, apart from the liturgical, rhetorical, or controversial work of the clergy or clerical disputants. The *Acts and Monuments* of Foxe, popularly known as, the "Book of Martyrs," published in the first decade of the reign, showed the development of a power of vigorously dramatic narrative which should not be overlooked. The enormous popularity however which that work achieved was at least in part the outcome of the general sterility. Men had not yet learned to write, but they were ready to read even voraciously. Culture was in vogue. As things stood culture, in practice, meant and could mean little else than the study of Latin and Italian authors—Greek being still reserved for the learned—of whose works translations, some of notable merit, were very soon beginning to appear on the market. It was inevitably to these two literatures—the Latin and the Italian—that men turned in the first instance to find the models and formulate the canons of literary art; with only occasional divagations in the direction of France or Spain, countries which were scarcely a generation in advance of England. We remark that the old idea that for prose which was intended to live the true medium was still the one international literary language, Latin, died exceedingly hard; Bacon himself, great master though he was of his mother-tongue, maintaining it quite definitely. This pedantic attitude however was not involved in the idea of culture, and men welcomed with avidity an author who made his appeal to the non-academic public in vigorous English. The conversion even of the academic mind was close at hand.

[Sidenote: 1579-89]

The year 1579 is in the strictest sense an epoch in the history of English Literature; as witnessing the first appearance of a new and original force in English verse, and the first deliberate and elaborate effort in the direction of artistically constructed English Prose. In that year, John Lyly published his *Euphues: the Anatomy of Wit*, and Edmund Spenser his *Shepherd's Calendar*.

[Sidenote: Euphues]

Euphues, and its companion volume *Euphues and His England* enjoyed a very remarkable if temporary vogue; running through numerous editions in the course of the ensuing fifty years. After that, it dropped. It is not surprising that it dropped. The work is tedious, prolix, affected, abounding in pedantry and in intellectual foppery. But its whole meaning and significance at the time when it was written are lost to us if we pay attention only to the ridicule which very soon fell upon it, to the mockery in Shakespeare's burlesques of Euphuism, or to Scott's later parody of it in the character of Sir Piercie Shafton. The everlasting antitheses, the perpetual playing with words, the alliterative trickery, the accumulation of far-fetched similes, the endless and often most inappropriate classical, mythological, and quasi-zoological allusions and parallels, are indeed sufficiently absurd and wearisome; and when "Euphuism" became a fashionable craze, its sillier disciples were a very fit target for jesting and mirth, very much as in our own day the humorists found abundant and legitimate food for laughter in the vagaries of what was known as "aestheticism". In both cases, the extravagances were the separable accidents, the superficial excrescences, of a real intellectual movement with a quite healthy motive. *Euphues* itself was a real and serious if somewhat misdirected effort at making a moralised culture fashionable, and at elevating; the English tongue into a medium of refined and polished expression. If the Euphuists included Armados among them, they numbered also their Birons and Rosalines. Though Lyly practised exuberances of verbal jugglery, he was not their inventor; they were a vice of the times, largely borrowed from foreign models; and Shakespeare himself, in moments of aberrant ingenuity, produced—not for laughter—samples which Lyly might have admired but could never have emulated.

[Sidenote: Sidney's prose works]

Lyly's work was a novel experiment in prose, without previous parallel; critical judgments were no very long time in detecting and condemning his extravagances. But the same intellectual motive was soon to find a more chastened and artistic expression in the work of one who was still but a literary experimentalist when he meet his death at Zutphen. When Sir Philip Sidney, that "verray parfit gentil knight," scholar, soldier, and statesman, if the unanimous appraisement of the best of his contemporaries is worth anything, wrote his *Defence of Poesie,* he had not indeed broken free from the trammels of academic theory; but it is a very often acute and always charming piece of critical work in scholarly and graceful language. More affected and generally inferior in style, but also still on the whole scholarly and graceful in its language, is his *Arcadia,* an example of the indefinitely constructed amorphous Romances out of which in course of long time the novel was to be evolved. The dwellers in that Arcady are as far removed from the nymphs and swains of Watteau's day as from a primitive Greek population; they behave as no human beings ever did or could behave; they belong in short to a particularly unconvincing kind of fairy-land, of which the vogue happily died out at an early stage. The *Arcadia* is not intrinsically a great book, nor can it be read to-day without a considerable effort; yet it must always be notable as not merely an experiment but a positive achievement in English prose style. Neither of these works was published till after 1590; but both must have been written before 1583.

[Sidenote: Hooker 1594]

It was not till the last decade of the reign had begun that the first great monument of English Prose appeared; nor is it surprising that, when it did come, it was an example of the Ecclesiastical or politico-ecclesiastical order. With the publication in 1594 of the first four books of Richard Hooker's *Ecclesiastical Polity,* the full claims of English as a great literary language were decisively established by his rhythmical, stately, and luminous periods. In their own field, Poets and Dramatists had already secured those claims; with the works of Marlowe, the earliest plays of Shakespeare, and the opening books of the *Faerie Queene.*

[Sidenote: Verse; before 1579]

While the Eighth Henry was still ruling England, Surrey and Wyatt, heedful of things Italian, had already discovered that verse-making was at any rate a delectable pastime for a gentleman of wit, especially if he had a love-affair on hand; a pastime certainly pleasing to himself and probably agreeable to his mistress. They made metrical experiments, introducing both the sonnet and blank verse. The example they set was followed by others, and *Tottel's Miscellany,* published towards the end of Mary's reign, shows that a considerable skill in this minor art had already been acquired, and not only by the two principal contributors, though the writers were still working within very narrow metrical limitations. In 1559 appeared the *Mirrour for Magistrates,* for the most part dull and uninteresting but containing in the *Induction* and the *Complaint of Buckingham* two contributions by Thomas Sackville (afterwards Lord Buckhurst) which are a good deal more than clever verse-making. But after one other experiment—the part-authorship of the first English Tragedy in blank verse, *Gorboduc*—Sackville deserted the Muses, for public affairs; in his later years becoming a leading member of Elizabeth's Council. The little verse that he left is of a quality to make us wish that he had written more: for there is in him at least a hint of some possibilities which were actualised in Spenser. But twenty years passed before the appearance of the *Shepherd's Calendar*, during which it is probable enough that courtiers and lovers continued to practise, after the school of Surrey and Wyatt; nothing however was published that has survived, save the work of the universal experimentalist and pioneer George Gascoigne, who tried his hand at most forms of literary production, achieving distinction in none but a laudable respectability in all.

[Sidenote: 1579-90 Spenser and others]

The *Shepherd's Calendar/* by itself would give Spenser nothing more than a high position among minor poets; but with him verse reappeared as something more than an elegant exercise for courtiers, scholars or lovers. Above all, the *Shepherd's Calendar* gave unexpected proof of the metrical capacities and verbal felicities of the English language, though setting it forth to the accompaniment of an excessive use of archaic forms and expressions. Even that excess had its value as a protest against the pedantic precision of the Latinists, who were already indulging in a grotesque attempt to displace natural English metres by Ovidian and Horatian prosody. Spenser himself made some futile efforts in this direction; so did Sidney—sundry more or less ingenious examples are scattered about the *Arcadia*; but Sidney realised his error in time to write the *Astrophel and Stella* sonnets (about 1581-2), which though still somewhat stiff and academic might well have been the precursors of some noble poetry had the writer lived longer. As it is, his life and death form the noblest poem he has bequeathed to us.

Those sonnets also remained unpublished till some years later. The first three books of the *Faerie Queene*, which at once established Spenser for all time as a true poet of the highest rank, did not appear till 1590. In the interval, the English Drama was finding itself, and some of the dramatists were revealing that gift of song—in the restricted sense of the word—which was bestowed in such unparalleled measure on the later Elizabethans. To this decade belong songs by Lyly and Peele, Lodge and Greene, which have already caught the delicate daintiness and the exquisite lilt of Shakespeare's songs and a host of others found in the later songbooks—qualities of which there is little more than a rare hint here and there in the earlier Miscellanies, for all the bravery of such titles as *A Paradise of Dainty Devises* (1576): *A Gorgeous Gallery of Gallant Inventions* (1578): or *A Handefull of Pleasant Delites*(1584).

The definite triumph of Christianity over Paganism killed the Drama of the old world, the Church deliberately setting its face against the theatre. But primitive popular instincts, embodied in the continued celebration, as holiday sports, of what had originally been pagan rites, kept in existence crude and embryonic forms of dramatic representation at the festival seasons; which after a time the ecclesiastics saw more advantage in adapting to their own ends than in suppressing. Hence arose the miracle plays or Mysteries (probably *ministerium*, not [Greek: mystaerion]) of the middle ages—representations chiefly of episodes in the Biblical narrative. These in turn suggested the Moralities, dialogues with action in which the characters were personifications of virtues or vices relieved, in consideration of the weakness of the flesh, by passages of broad buffoonery. Lastly in the late fifteenth and early sixteenth centuries came the representation of what were called "Interludes," for the most part short farces of a very primitive order—probably the offspring of the aforesaid passages of buffoonery. These did not constitute a literary drama; but they kept the idea of dramatic representation in being, though no such thing as a theatre or building constructed for the purpose existed as yet. The performances were given either in Church, or, later, in a nobleman's hall, or in the courtyard of an inn. The "masque" or pantomimic pageant, without dialogue, was also a familiar spectacle of the later times, and remained an occasional feature of the drama in its development.

The revival of interest in the classics caused some attention to be paid to the Roman drama; and hence Italy led the way—as in all things literary—in producing imitations of the plays then known. These however hardly got beyond the stage of being mere imitations; though as models Terence and Seneca were superior to the compilers of miracle plays, something more was required than copying their works before a Drama worthy of the name could be evolved. But from about the middle of the sixteenth century, the dramatic instinct in England was struggling to find for itself new and adequate expression.

[Sidenote: Early Elizabethan Drama]

With the Educational revival, it would appear that schoolmasters occasionally caused their pupils to act scenes, in Latin or perhaps at times in a translated version, from Terence: and it is not surprising to find that what is recognised as the first English Comedy was written by a schoolmaster for his boys to perform. *Ralph Roister Doister* derived from the Latin model, and is in doggerel couplets. It was the work of Nicholas Udall who was Master of Eton and afterwards of Westminster; but whether it was produced in the earlier or later period is not certainly known. At any rate it preceded the accession of Queen Mary. *Gammer Gurton's Needle*, dated 1553, holds the second place in point of time; and *Gorboduc* otherwise known as *Ferrex and Porrex*, the first English blank-verse tragedy, the work of Sackville and Norton, was acted in 1561. From this time, we have notices of the production of a considerable number of plays of which it may be assumed that they were exceedingly crude, being either very formless experiments derived from the interludes or else direct imitations or translations of Latin or Italian plays; to which Gascoigne contributed his share. A nearer approach to the coming Comedy is found in the plays of John Lyly preceding his *Euphues*. By this time dramatic performances had achieved such popularity that the City Fathers were scandalised—not indeed without reason—by their encroachments on the more solid but less inviting attractions of Church Services; and by banishing them from the City precincts caused the first regularly constructed theatres to be established outside the City bounds in Shoreditch: a departure which no doubt tended to the more definite organisation of the Actor's profession. As the Eighties progressed, a higher standard of dramatic production was attained by the group of "University" play wrights—-Peele, Greene, Nash, and others; wild Bohemian spirits for the most part, careless of conventions whether moral or literary, wayward, clever, audacious; culminating with Marlowe, whose first extremely immature play *Tamburlaine*, was probably acted in 1587 when he was only three and twenty; his career terminating in a tavern brawl some six years later. By that time (1593) it is certain that Shakespeare, born in the same year as Marlowe, was writing for the managers; though none of his known work can with confidence be dated earlier than the year of Marlowe's death. The great age of the Drama had begun.

[Sidenote: The younger generation]

It will have become apparent from this survey that, although we talk with very good reason of the Elizabethan Age of English Literature, the Queen had been reigning for thirty years, the great political crisis of her rule had been reached, the Armada had perished, before any single work had been written, or at any rate published, which on its merits—judged by the criteria of an established literature with established canons—would have entitled its author to a position of any distinction on the roll of fame. Up to 1589, the most remarkable productions had been: in prose, Foxe's *Book of Martyrs* and Lyly's *Euphues*; in verse, some lines of Sackville, and the *Shepherd's Calendar*. Even when we have added to these Sidney's *Sonnets* and his *Arcadia*—written but not published—the significant fact remains that he, as well as Spenser and Lyly, was not born till the second half of the century had begun: and all three were older than any of the group of dramatists who are named as Shakespeare's precursors. Spenser was actually the eldest of all the men whose writings shed lustre on the great Queen's reign: and Spenser himself had not attained to the full maturity of his genius—had not, at least given its fruits to the world—at the hour of England's triumph. Had he died in the year of Zutphen, "Colin Clout" would have ranked little if at all higher than "Astrophel." Further: save for Sidney and Marlowe, who were both cut off prematurely, and Spenser himself who died at forty-six, the work of all the greater Elizabethan writers—Shakespeare, and Ben Jonson, Bacon, Hooker, Raleigh, Middleton, Drayton—lies as much in the time of James as in that of Elizabeth; while a whole group of those to whom the same general title is applied—Beaumont and Fletcher, Webster, Ford, Massinger—belong in effect wholly to the later reign.

Broadly speaking therefore it is worth noting that state-craft, soldiering, seamanship, affairs of a very practical character, absorbed the keen brains and the abundant energies of the earlier generation; even for the men born in the fifties, like Raleigh and Sidney, literature (except with Spenser) held a quite secondary place. But no sooner is the National triumph ensured than the younger generation displays in the literary field characteristics essentially the same as those whereby their elders had raised England in war and in politics to the first rank among the nations.

For years to come, for the first time certainly in English History, literature in one form or another appropriates the best work of the best brains. There are men of ability in politics, but no giants: or if one of the giants, like Bacon, divides his attention between the two fields, the best half of it goes to literature. Yet it is essentially the same spirit which works in the great men of Elizabeth's closing years as in the great men of her youth and of her maturity.

[Sidenote: Pervading Characteristics]

The quality which conditions the whole English character through the period is an exuberant, often even a riotous energy, a vast imaginativeness, which breeds in the first place an immense daring, saved from degenerating into mere recklessness by a coolness of head in emergencies which is singularly marked. Whether we look at Elizabeth, Cecil, and Walsingham, or at Hawkins and Drake and Frobisher, or broadly at the actions of the rank and file, these characteristics are apparent. They are no less patent in the poets.

Thus if we consider the tragedies of the period, their tremendous audacity is perhaps their most prominent feature. The stage reeks with blood and reverberates thunder, to an extent which could not fail to become merely grotesque but for the immense pervading vitality. These men could and did venture upon extravagances and imbue them with a terrific quality, when in weaker hands they would have become ridiculous. For anything less than the vibrating energy of Marlowe, the final scene of his *Faustus* would have sunk to burlesque. A cold analysis of the plot of *Hamlet* or *Macbeth* would suggest mere melodrama. A Shakespeare or a Marlowe had no hesitation in facing tasks which offered no mean between great success or great failure. Nor was the audacity in their choice of subjects more remarkable than in their methods, their defiance of recognised canons. Just as the seamen had ignored the convention of centuries, creating a new system of naval tactics and a new type of navy, so the Tragedians brushed aside the academic convention, creating new dramatic canons and a new type of drama. The innovation in the structure of comedy was no less daring, since it proceeded on parallel lines. And here again the same quality of superabundant vitality is equally prominent. But it is to be noted that while the Elizabethan vitality would have made the drama great in spite of its audacity, the greatest productions are distinguished from the less great precisely by that peculiar sanity which stamped the master-spirits of the time. As it is with the dramatists, so is it with the rest. The same fulness of life is apparent in the luxuriance of Spenser's imagination, and in the spontaneity of half a hundred anonymous song-writers, the same audacity in Raleigh, embarking on his History of the World, and in Bacon, assuming all knowledge to be his province, while affirming and formulating the principles of Inductive Reasoning in substitution for the Deductive methods by which the Schools had lived for centuries. Wherever the critic turns his glance, he can find no sign of the Decadent. In every field of life, in politics, in war, in religion, in letters, the Elizabethan was virile even in his vices. His offences against morals or against art were essentially of the barbaric not the effete order; as the splendours of his productions were the natural beauties of plants nurtured in the open, not in the hothouse.

[Sidenote: Breadth of view]

Other aspects of the national character could be readily inferred from the prevalent tone of this literature. Toleration as a political principle was not yet recognised: tolerance as a private attitude of mind was very prevalent. The Jesuit and the extreme Puritan, the doctrinal propagandists who would endure no deviation from their own standard, were thoroughly unpopular, and managed to put themselves outside the field of consideration; the immense bulk of the nation was in sympathy with neither the one nor the other, and it is only to the extremists that the men of letters show a direct antipathy. Catholics can make a presentable case for the theory that Shakespeare himself was a "crypto-Catholic," though the case is not more than presentable. Rome is abhorrent to Spenser, yet it is apparent that many of his ethical conceptions are infinitely nearer akin to those of mediaeval Catholicism than of the current Puritanism. Hooker, most earnest of Christians, was also the most liberal-minded of men. Jonson was half a Catholic. All were manifestly men of deep religious feeling, but none can be associated with any religious party. When England was pitted as a Protestant Power against a Power aggressively determined on the eradication of Protestantism, it was inevitable that the prevailing sentiment should be increasingly Protestant; on the whole, it is surprising that there should have been so little bigotry in it. The public inclination was to be tolerant of all but the intolerant, and that attitude is reflected in all the literature of the time, except the specifically partisan writings of controversialists.

[Patriotism]

So also another note of the day was the general patriotism, national pride, or insularity; the sentiment which made the Catholics themselves, even when they were most under suspicion and had most cause to welcome an opportunity for rebellion, ready and eager to fall into line and resist the invader who was to liberate them. Again the poets gave voice to the national feeling, none more emphatically or more admirably than Shakespeare himself. Patriotic lines might of course be written for the sake of the gallery's inevitable applause; but Shakespeare's panegyrics of England are absolutely and unmistakably whole hearted, and it may be doubted if in all his plays he presented any single character with a more thorough and convincing sympathy and appreciation than his Henry V., the incarnation of English aggressiveness.

[The Normal Types] Finally, what manner of men and women they were who peopled the England that Shakespeare knew, we can see from the men and women whom Shakespeare drew. The types manifest themselves; the normal and the exceptional are readily distinguishable. The normal type is keen of wit, impulsive; it is observable for instance that both men and women habitually—almost invariably—fall in love unreservedly at first sight; generous for the most part; in action prompt and more often than not over-hasty, but resourceful—the women more resourceful than the men. It is a commonplace of course to remark that his types are types for all time;

but different types are more prevalent at one time than another, and the inference is that Shakespeare's prevalent types were the prevalent ones of his own day. Hamlet, Brutus, Cleopatra, belonged to eternal but not to normal types; Hotspur and Mercutio, Rosalind and Cordelia—even if the latter were glorified examples—were obviously normal. For in play after play, whether as leading or as minor characters, they recur again and again; and more than that we find the same characteristics—presented no doubt with less incisiveness and less brilliancy—reappearing in the Dramatis Personae of the whole Elizabethan group. Such were the gentlemen of England who fought the Spaniard and overthrew him; such were their sisters and their wives.

CHAPTER XXVIII
ELIZABETH (xiii), 1558-1603—
ASPECTS OF THE REIGN

[Sidenote: Features of the Reign]

The reign of Elizabeth may be said to have been distinguished primarily by three leading features. The first is the development and establishment of England as the greatest maritime power in the world, a process which has been traced with some fulness. The second is that sudden and amazing outburst of literary genius in the latter half, and mainly in the last quarter, of the reign, for which there is no historical parallel except in Athens, unless once again we find it in England two centuries later: whereof the last few pages have treated. The third is the Ecclesiastical settlement, on which it has hitherto been possible only to touch. This, with certain other aspects of the reign, remain for discussion in this concluding chapter.

[Sidenote: State and Church]

In this settlement, the primary fundamental fact, politically speaking—for theological problems do not fall within our range—is the recognition by the State of the Church as an aspect of the body politic, and of her organisation as a branch of the body politic, subject to the control of the Sovereign and maintained by the sanction of the Sovereign's supremacy; precluding the interference of any external authority, and overriding any claims to independent authority on the part of the organisation itself; requiring from all members of the body politic conformity, under penalties, to the institutions thus regulated, and rejection of any authority running counter thereto. The secondary fact is that the State thus sanctioned such institutions as, under a reasonable liberty of interpretation, might be accepted without a severe strain of conscience by persons holding opinions of considerable diversity; so that conformity should be possible to the great bulk of the nation, including many who might not in theory admit the right of the State to a voice in the matter at all.

The politicians, that is, deliberately chose a *via media*. Theologically, the dividing line lay between those who desired the Mass and reunion with

Rome, and those who rejected the Mass and derived their dogmas from Geneva. Under Mary, the Government had thrown itself on the side of the former; under Edward, mainly on that of the latter. Elizabeth's Government would have neither. It would not admit the papal claim to override the secular authority, or the equally dictatorial claims of the Genevan ministry as exemplified by John Knox; the first necessity for it was to assert secular supremacy, the second to make its definitions of dogma sufficiently ambiguous to be reconcilable with the dogmatic scruples of the majority of both parties; with the result however of shutting out both determined Romanists and determined Calvinists, while the Church thus regulated contained two parties, one with conservative, the other with advanced, ideals.

The outward note of Conservative churchmen was insistence on ceremonial observances, as that of the advanced men was dislike of them. But as the reign advanced, another feature acquires prominence—the protest of the Puritans against the Episcopalian system of Church Government, with the correspondingly increased emphasis laid on the vital necessity of that system by the Conservatives.

[Sidenote: The State and the Catholics]

The Queen's personal predilections were at all times on the Conservative side; those of her principal advisers always leaned towards the Puritans— at the first Cecil, Bacon, and Elizabeth's own kinsmen, Knollys and Hunsdon; then Walsingham, drawing Leicester with him. But in the early years of her rule, when it was imperative to minimise all possible causes of discontent, the admission of the largest possible latitude in practice was required, even if it was accompanied by legislation which gave authority for restrictive action. It followed however from the political conditions that direct hostility to the Queen was to be feared only from the Catholics—the whole body of those who would have liked to see the old religion restored in its entirety. This was emphasized by the Papal Bull excommunicating Elizabeth in 1570—a political blunder on the part of the Pope which greatly annoyed and embarrassed Philip at the time. The result, joined with the Northern Rising, the Ridolfi plot, and the indignation aroused by the day of St. Bartholomew, was to strengthen the hands of the Puritans and to give open Catholicism the character of a political offence; and to this an enormously increased force was added in 1581 by the Jesuit mission. During these years, parliaments were all unfailingly and increasingly Puritan, and Puritanism was steadily making way all over the country, not without the favour of the leading divines. Elizabeth herself viewed this tendency with extreme dislike, mercilessly snubbing bishops and others who seemed to betray inclinations in this direction—Grindal in particular, Parker's successor at

Canterbury, suffered from her displeasure; but she could not suppress it. She might—and did—say a good deal; but she could not in act go nearly as far as she would have wished, in opposition to subjects whose political loyalty was indisputable, as well as extremely necessary to her security.

[Sidenote: The Church and the Puritans]

So long as the advanced movement concerned itself chiefly with the "Vestiarian Controversy" and matters of ceremonial observance, it did not assume primary importance in the eyes of politicians. But by the middle of the reign the question of the form of Church Government had come to the front, and the demand to substitute the Presbyterian system for the Episcopalian was being put forward by Cartwright and his followers and had even produced a Presbyterian organisation within the Church. Moreover the school commonly called Brownists, who developed into the sect of Independents, were propounding the theory that the Church consisted not of the whole nation but only of the Elect. Puritanism was therefore threatening to become directly subversive of the established order. Then came the mission of Parsons and Campian. The effect of this in regard to Catholics was twofold. It necessitated an increased severity in dealing with any one who recognised papal authority: and made it more imperative than ever to induce Catholics to be reconciled with the State Church, by emphasizing the Catholic side of her institutions, and consequently by checking Puritan developments. On the other side, it was so obviously impossible for the Puritans to withdraw their loyalty from Elizabeth that to conciliate them was superfluous; they were adopting an attitude antagonistic to the approved constitution of the Church; and there was a suggestion of rigid even-handed justice in waging war upon their propaganda at the same time as on that of Rome. Whitgift, succeeding Grindal at Canterbury in 1583, opened the campaign against Puritanism— not indeed with the favour either of parliament or of the leading statesmen, whose personal sympathies were with the advanced party, but manifestly with encouragement from the Queen.

[Sidenote: Archbishop Whitgift]

Whitgift's own attitude was that of the Disciplinarian rather than of the theologian. The method of operation was by the issue of Fifteen Articles to which all the clergy were required to subscribe: the sanction thereof being the authority of the Court of High Commission. Under the Act of Supremacy of 1559, the appointment of a Commission to enforce obedience to the law in matters ecclesiastical had been authorised. This Court was fully constituted in December 1583, and proceeded by methods which Burghley himself held to be too inquisitorial. A good deal of indignation was aroused, and the

Puritans were in effect made more aggressive, their attacks on the existing system culminating in 1589 in the distinctly scurrilous "Martin Mar-prelate" tracts, which were so violent as to produce a marked reaction. This on the one side, coupled with the partly genuine and partly mythical plots of the ultra-Catholics on the other, brought about sharp legislation in 1593, resulting in an increased persecution of the Catholics after that time, and in the compulsory withdrawal of the extreme nonconformists to the more sympathetic atmosphere of the Netherlands. At the same time the "High" theory of the Church's authority was formulated by Bancroft (afterwards Archbishop), and what may be called the Constitutional theory of Church Government was propounded in the *Ecclesiastical Polity* of Hooker. All of this was the prologue to the great controversy which was to acquire such prominence under the Stuarts.

[Sidenote: The Persecutions]

In writing of the persecutions under Elizabeth alike of Catholics and of Puritans, it is not uncommon to imply that the political argument in their defence was a mere pretext with a theological motive. As a matter of fact however, the distinction between Elizabeth's and Mary's persecutions is a real one. Broadly speaking, it is now the universally received view that no man ought to be penalised on the score of opinions conscientiously held, however erroneous they may be; but that if those opinions find expression in anti-social acts, the acts must be punished. Punishment of opinions is rightly branded as persecution. Now although in effect not a few persons, Puritans or Catholics, were put to death by Elizabeth, and many more imprisoned or fined—as they would have said themselves, for Conscience' sake—this was the distinction specifically recognised by her; which, without justifying her persecutions, differentiates them from those of her predecessors. Henry and Mary frankly and avowedly burnt victims for holding wrong opinions—for Heresy. Anabaptism no doubt was accounted a social as well as a theological crime; but no one ever dreamed of regarding Ann Ascue or Frith as politically dangerous. Mary kindled the fires of Smithfield for the salvation of souls, not for the safety of her throne. Whereas the foundation of Elizabeth's persecutions was that *opinions* as such were of no consequence: but that people who would not conform their *conduct* to her regulations must either be potential traitors politically or anarchists socially. Her proceedings are brought into the category of persecutions, because she treated potential anarchism or treason as implying overt anarchism or treason, though unless and until she discovered such implication in a given opinion, any one was at liberty to hold it or not as he chose; its truth or falsity was a matter of entire indifference. To punish the implied intention of committing a wrong act is sufficiently dangerous in principle; but it is to be distinguished from punishment for holding an opinion because it is accounted a false one.

Finally, while we must condemn her persecution both of Puritans and of Catholics alike, it is only fair, in comparing her with her predecessor, to remember that, in the five and forty years of her reign, the whole number of persons who suffered death as Catholics or as Anabaptists was considerably less than the number of the Martyrs in four years of Mary's rule.

[Sidenote: Economic progress]

By adopting Cecil's ecclesiastical policy of the *via media*, Elizabeth saved England from the internecine religious strife which almost throughout her reign made the political action of France so inefficient. The constant wars of the Huguenots with the Leaguers or their predecessors had their counterpart for Philip also, whose struggle with the Netherlanders was to a great extent in the nature of a civil war. Fully realising how seriously both France and Spain were hampered by these complications, she was able to conduct her diplomatic manoeuvres with an audacity quite as remarkable as her duplicity, gauging to a nicety the carrying capacity of the very thin ice over which she was constantly skating. Thus while both those Powers were perpetually exhausting their resources and draining their exchequers with costly wars, England, free from any similar strain, was rapidly growing in wealth; and while the national expenditure was kept comparatively low, manufactures were multiplied, and the commerce which was driven by the stress of war from the great trade-centres of the Netherlands was being absorbed by English ports. Moreover that forcible trading indulged in by John Hawkins in the earlier ventures of the reign—giving place, as time went on to the process of systematic preying upon Spanish treasure—provided very substantial dividends for the Queen, as well as filling the pockets of her loyal subjects. Thus again she was able to avoid making perpetual demands on her parliaments, and when demands were made the parliaments could usually meet them in a generous and ungrudging spirit.

[Sidenote: The currency; Retrenchment]

Nevertheless, no little financial skill and courage were required to restore the public credit which had fallen to such disastrous depths in the two preceding reigns; and this was done to a large extent by a policy of determined financial honesty. The miserable system of debasing the coinage was brought to an end; the current coins were called in and paid for at not much under their actual value in silver, and the new coins issued were of their face value. Debts contracted by Government were punctually paid, and as an immediate consequence the Government soon found itself able to borrow at reasonable instead of ruinous rates of interest. Private prosperity and public confidence advanced so swiftly that before Elizabeth had been a dozen years on the throne substantial loans could be raised at home without applying to foreign sources. Elizabeth never spent a penny of public money without good reason; sometimes—as in Ireland habitually, and to some degree at the time of the Armada though not so seriously as is commonly reputed—her parsimony amounted to false economy; often it took on a pettifogging character in her dealings with the Dutch, with the Huguenots, and with the Scots, though in the last case at least it must be admitted that either party was equally ready to overreach the other if the chance offered. But for very many years a very close economy was absolutely essential if debts were to be paid. That economy was facilitated by the lavish expenditure of prominent men on public objects; due partly to a desire for display, partly—at least in the case of the buccaneering enterprises—to bold speculation in the hope of large profits, but partly also beyond question to a very live public spirit. Yet when every allowance has been made for the assistance from such sources, it remains clear that Elizabeth's resources were husbanded with great skill, and her government carried on with a surprisingly small expenditure; that expenditure being on the whole very judiciously directed—so that, for instance, the royal navy, at least throughout the latter half of the reign, was maintained in a very creditable state of efficiency; though the number of the ships was not large, and the organisation proved inadequate, when the crisis came, to meet all the demands of the seamen.

[Sidenote: Wealth and Poverty]

The general prosperity however was not due to any notable advance in official Economics. What it owed to the Government was the immense improvement in public credit brought about by the restored coinage, and the punctual repayment of loans and settlement of debts, coupled with confidence in a steady rule and freedom from costly wars. Trade did indeed greatly benefit by the enlightened action of the State in encouraging the settlement in England of craftsmen from the Netherlands, with the consequent development of the industries they practised and taught. But the vital fact of the enormously increased wealth of the country must be attributed to the energy and initiative of the merchants and the adventurers in taking advantage of the new fields opened to them, of the displacement of trade by the wars on the Continent, and of the exposure of foreign, especially but not exclusively Spanish, shipping to depredation.

How far this increased wealth benefited the labouring classes is a moot question. It would seem on the whole that the process of converting arable land into pasture which had been going on all through the century was already becoming less active even in the first years of the reign, and had reached its limit some while before the Armada. As the displacement of labour diminished, fixity and regularity of employment increased, while the labour already displaced was gradually absorbed by the rapid growth of manufactures. This may perhaps in some degree explain the almost unaccountably sudden cessation of laments over agricultural depression. Still, the effective wage earned tended to drop: that is, although wages rose when measured in terms of the currency, that rise did not keep pace with the advance in prices, the influx of silver into Europe diminishing its purchasing power. Hence the old problem of dealing with poverty in its two forms—honest inability to work and dishonest avoidance of work— remained acute. There was always a humane desire that the deserving poor should be assisted, and an equally strong sentiment in favour of punishing rogues and vagabonds—persons who declined to dig but were not ashamed to beg; with perhaps an excessive inclination to assume that wherever there was a doubt the delinquent should not have the benefit of it. The savagery however of the earlier Tudor laws against vagabonds was mitigated, and honest efforts were made to find a substitute for the old relief of genuine poverty by the Monasteries. This took in the first place the form of enactments for the local collection of voluntary contributions to relief-funds; and culminated in the Acts of the last five years of the reign, substituting compulsory for voluntary contribution, and establishing that Poor-law system which remained substantially unchanged until its reformation in the nineteenth century.

[Sidenote: Trade Restrictions and Development]

The idea that Governments do well not to interfere with the natural unaided operation of economic laws had not yet come into being; and attempts, mainly futile, to control wages and to force labour into particular channels, continued. In one direction however the artificial encouragement of one industry may have had a beneficial effect. Navigation laws tended, *per se*, to check general commerce; but they gave a stimulus to the English marine at a time when its rapid development was of the utmost national importance; not directly increasing the interchange of commodities as a whole, but encouraging the English carrying-trade, and advancing the growth of the sea-power which made a more extended commerce possible; and thus indirectly counterbalancing the direct ill effects. It is possible even to find some defence for one aspect of Monopolies. The granting of a monopoly of trade in particular regions—Russia, Guinea, the Levant, the East Indies—to Companies of merchants, had a definite justification. Individual private competitors could not conduct the trade on a large scale; large corporations, secured against rivals, could face the risks and the heavy expenditure requisite to success, and could be granted a liberty of action, being left to their own responsibilities, which was impracticable for the private trader. Amongst these, very much the most notable is the great East India Company which was incorporated on the last day of December 1600. Here, its birth only is to be chronicled; its history belongs to the ensuing centuries. But the bestowal on individuals of the monopoly of trade in particular articles by the Royal privilege was manifestly bad in itself; it became so serious an abuse that a determined parliamentary attack was made on the system in 1597; and even then Elizabeth found it necessary to promise enquiry. Nothing practical however was done, and the parliament of 1601 returned to the charge with such obvious justification that the Queen very promptly and graciously promised to abolish the grievance, and thanked the Commons for directing her attention to the matter.

[Sidenote: Tavellers]

We have already in a previous chapter followed in the wake of adventurous voyagers and explorers prior to the Armada, and recorded the first disastrous experimental efforts towards colonisation; but, in dealing specifically with the seamen, we passed by overland explorations such as those of Jenkinson, who during the first decade of Elizabeth's reign journeyed through Russia, and into Asia over the Caspian sea. More momentous still in its results was the Eastern expedition of Newbery and Fitch; who starting in 1583 went through Syria to Ormuz, and were thence conveyed to Goa, the Portuguese head-quarters on the West coast of India. Fitch remained longer than his chief, visiting Golconda, Agra (the seat of the Great Mogul Akbar), Bengal, Pegu, Malacca, and Ceylon, and bringing home in 1591 stories of India and its wealth, which were in no small degree responsible for the formation, in 1599, of the Association which was next year incorporated as the East India Company.

[Sidenote: Maritime expansion]

After the Armada, the sea-faring spirit was naturally even intensified. To a great extent however it was absorbed in privateering—which combined with its attractions in the way of mere adventure the advantages of being profitable, patriotic, and pious. In connexion with the direct scheme of colonial settlements, we have only Raleigh's two unsuccessful relief expeditions to Virginia conducted by White and Mace, and the attempt, also unsuccessful, to start a colony in what afterwards became New England, under Bartholomew Gosnold in 1602. More striking, but belonging to a somewhat different category, was Raleigh's own voyage to the Orinoco, in search of Eldorado and the golden city of Manoa; disappointing in its results, but ably conducted and from the point of view of explorers, as such, by no means unfruitful. Equally noteworthy are the two great voyages of

James Lancaster, who was the first English captain to reach the Indian seas by the Cape route (1592), and in 1601 sailed thither again in command of the first fleet of the new Association of East India Merchants, and opened up for his countrymen the trade with the Spice Islands. But except for this second voyage of Lancaster's, a very real and definite achievement in the history of commercial expansion, the voyages of the day, full of brilliant exploits in the annals of seamanship and of adventure, and collectively marking an epoch in England's oceanic development, were not individually notable for specific results.

[Sidenote: The Constitution]

Constitutional theory does not appear to have differed in the reigns of Henry VIII. and his great daughter. The monarch's will was supreme; but the people could give expression to its will through Parliament when in session. The practical rule, however, which prevented any collision between the two forces, was that both monarchs kept a careful finger on the pulse of the nation. Like her father, Elizabeth never allowed herself to set a strong popular feeling at defiance. She desired that her people should be prosperous and free, though she objected to their interference in the conduct of political affairs; she desired that within the realm of England order should be maintained and the law strictly administered. If practices inconsistent with the liberty of the subject prevailed, they were applied only to persons who were assumed by herself, her ministers, and the bulk of their fellow-subjects, to have placed themselves outside the pale. The ministers who carried out her will avoided the arbitrary methods of Wolsey and Cromwell, whose master had preserved his own popularity by making scape-goats of them when their unpopularity ran too high, squaring his account with the People at their expense. Elizabeth never found it necessary to square her account with the People, whose hearts vibrated in sympathy with her essential loyalty to them. Few of them probably shared her views on the sanctity of crowned heads as such, which amounted almost to a superstition; but the country was pervaded with a passionate loyalty to the person of its Queen. On the other side, the record of her Parliaments shows that freedom of speech was making way, though she would not formally admit the principle: while the Parliaments cared much less about its formal admission than its practical prevalence. She snubbed the persistent Puritans for their obstinate oratory on the ecclesiastical and matrimonial questions, but they managed to have their say (which she ostensibly ignored), without suffering more than sharp reprimands and occasional detention in ward; and that contented them. Like Henry, she recognised that the one thing Parliaments would not endure was taxation without their own consent. On one occasion when she found she could do without a grant she had asked for and obtained, she remitted it; the harmony of mutual confidence ensured the readier co-operation.

Parliament under Elizabeth gave not infrequent proof that it was tenacious of what it held to be its privileges: as the Queen showed that she was tenacious of what she considered her prerogatives. But each, without abating their right, or prejudicing their theoretical claim, was willing to make practical concession to the other in action. It was only in the closing years of the reign that abstract Theories of the State began to be formulated—a process which became exceedingly active in the next century, when kings and parliaments began to take diametrically conflicting views of political exigencies. Under Elizabeth, all such discussions were purely academic; under the Stuarts, they became actively practical. For the Stuarts, unlike Elizabeth, recklessly challenged popular opposition precisely on the points as to which popular opinion was most sensitive. Harmony gave way to discord, co-operation to antagonism; collision and disaster followed—"red ruin and the breaking up of laws".

[Sidenote: The Elizabethans]

The popular judgment which has glorified the reign of Elizabeth as perhaps the most splendid period in the annals of England can be endorsed, without ignoring the defects in the character of the Queen, her Ministers, her Courtiers, or her People. A new day had dawned upon the world; new possibilities, vast and undefined, were presenting themselves; new thoughts were possessing the minds of men; new blood was throbbing in their veins. The English race was awaking to a sense of its powers, grasping with a splendid audacity at the mighty heritage whose full import was yet unrealised. The Elizabethans were, as a nation, triumphing in the first glow of exuberant and healthy youth: with the faults of youth as well as its virtues. Sheer delight in the exercise of physical energies, in perilous adventure for its own sake irrespective of ulterior ends, in the keen encounter of wit, in the bold fabric-building of imagination, characterised the Elizabethan as they characterised the *Marathonomachoi* two thousand years before; as the Athens of Salamis was the mother of Aeschylus and Sophocles, so the England of the Armada was the mother of Marlowe and Shakespeare and Spenser.

[Sidenote: Raleigh]

The typical Elizabethan, the man who presents in his own person the most marked characteristics that belong to his time, is Sir Walter Raleigh. His was the large imagination which conceived a new and expanding England beyond the seas; the broad grasp of ideas which made him a leading exponent of the theory of the Oceanic policy and the new naval methods; the ready practicality which made him, after Drake's day, perhaps the ablest of Elizabeth's captains; the versatility and culture, which place him securely in the second flight of the writers of the time; the breadth of intellectual outlook which caused his enemies to call him an atheist, coupled with an actual sincerity of belief; boundless energy, daring, ambition. His too were the fiery temper and the contemptuous arrogance which made him at one time the best-hated man in England outside a narrow circle of devoted admirers; while for all his pride he could match Hatton himself in preposterous adulation of the Queen. He could be as chivalrous as Sidney, and as merciless as an Inquisitor: he could be gorgeously extravagant, or the veriest Spartan, as circumstances demanded. He was in brief the epitome of Elizabeth's England: a figure assuredly very far from godlike but no less assuredly heroic.

It may be doubted if ever the *joie de vivre* was so generally prevalent in England as in those spacious days. Such a national mood is in danger of being followed by a lapse into an effeminate hedonism, from which England as a whole was saved by the antagonistic development of the essentially masculine if crude puritanism, whose vital spirit had already begun to take possession of a large proportion of the population without as yet evicting paganism. Under this at present secondary impulse, attributable very largely to the new familiarity with the Old Testament engendered by the translation of the Bible, men quickly learnt to look upon themselves as the chosen people of the Lord of Sabaoth who gave them the victory over their enemies, and to whom with entire sincerity they gave the glory; while they found a satisfying warrant in the Scriptures for spoiling the Egyptians and smiting the Amalekites, symbolising specifically the Spaniards and the Irish. The particular aspect of Puritanism which belongs to rigid Calvinism, in all its grim austerity, was confined so far to a very limited section: for the majority an extensive biblical vocabulary was consistent with a thorough appreciation of virile carnal enjoyments: the dourness of John Knox hardly infected the neighbouring country. For the most part, even the intolerance of the age was not that born of religious fanaticism, but was the normal outcome of a full-blooded self-confidence. The Elizabethans are apt to startle us by a display of apparently callous cruelty at one moment, and an almost reckless generosity at the next. They slaughtered the garrison of Smerwick in cold blood, and treated the vanquished at Cadiz with a chivalrous consideration which amazed its recipients. They kidnapped the sons of Ham from Africa for lucre; with the "Indians" of South and Central America they were always on excellent terms, and the Californians proffered divine honours to Francis Drake. These are paradoxes precisely similar in kind to those which so often puzzle amiable and mature observers of the British schoolboy to-day. Broadly, they were governed by instincts and impulses rather than by reasoned ethical theory, instincts occasionally barbaric but for the most part frank and generous; and they were sturdily loyal to the somewhat primitive code of right and wrong which was the outcome.

[Sidenote 1: The Queen's Ministers]
[Sidenote 2: The Queen]

These qualities, joined with an indomitable audacity and an eminently practical shrewdness, were characteristic of the men who were the hand and heart of England. Other qualities were needed for the brains which had to direct her policy; the patient common sense of Burghley, the keen penetration of Walsingham, the solid shrewdness of Nicholas Bacon, *vir pietate gravis*. The craftiness of the younger Cecil, the time-serving of Francis Bacon, mark a lower type of politician; not rare perhaps in Elizabeth's time, but not generally characteristic among her servants. To draw full value, however, from the capacities of those statesmen, a monarch of exceptional ability was needed. It was the peculiar note of Elizabeth's dealings with her ministers that having once realised their essential merits, she never withdrew her confidence. She flouted, insulted and browbeat them when their advice ran counter to her caprices; but no man suffered in the long run for standing up to her, however she might be irritated. Nor can we attribute this to such a loyalty of disposition on her part as marked her rival Mary alone among Stuarts: to whom such baseness as she displayed in her treatment of Davison would have been impossible. Elizabeth had no sort of compunction in making scape-goats of such men as he. But she knew the men who could not be replaced, a faculty rare in princes; she would never have deserted a Strafford as did Mary's grandson. She drove Burghley and Walsingham almost to despair by her caprices; but if she overrode their judgment, it was not to displace them for other advisers more congenial to her mood, but to take affairs into her own hands, and manipulate them with a cool defiance of apparent probabilities, a duplicity so audacious that it passed for a kind of sincerity, which gave her successes the appearance of being due to an almost supernatural good luck. Histrionics were her stock-in-trade: she was eternally playing a part, and playing it with such zest that she habitually cheated her neighbours, and occasionally, for the time being, even herself, into forgetting that her role was merely assumed for ulterior purposes. When a crisis was reached where there was no further use for play-acting, she was again the shrewd practical ruler who had merely been masked as the comedienne. Other queens have been great by the display of intellectual qualities commonly accounted masculine, or of virtues recognised as the special glories of their own sex; Elizabeth had the peculiar ingenuity deliberately to employ feminine weakness, incomprehensibility, and caprice, as the most bafflingly effective weapons in her armoury.

A noble woman she was not. The miracle of virtues and charms depicted by courtiers and poets existed, if she did exist at all, entirely in their exuberant imaginations. She could be indecently coarse and intolerably mean; she could lie with unblushing effrontery; her vanity was inordinate. But voracious as she was of flattery it never misled her; she could appreciate in others the virtues she herself lacked; behind the screen of capriciousness, an intellect was ever at work as cool and calculating as her grandfather's, as hard and resolute as her father's. To understand her People was her first aim, to make them great was her ultimate ambition. And she achieved both.

APPENDICES

APPENDIX A

[Tables omitted]

APPENDIX B

CLAIMS TO THE THRONE

CLAIMANTS TO THE CROWN OF ENGLAND

ACTUAL OR POTENTIAL; FROM 1485 TO 1603

When Henry of Richmond was hailed king of England on Bosworth Field, the principles and the practice of succession to the English throne were in a state of chaos; as far as hereditary right is concerned, his claim could hardly have been weaker. The titles both of his son and grandson were indisputable. Those of Mary and of Elizabeth were both questionable. From Elizabeth's accession to her death, it was uncertain who would succeed her. Accordingly, in the reign of Henry VII. we find actual pretenders put forward, and potential ones suspected and punished. No attempt was ever made to challenge Henry VIII. or Edward VI.: but there were sundry executions on the hypothesis of a treasonous intent to grasp at the crown, in the reign of the former. Lady Jane Grey was set up against Mary, and Elizabeth herself was under suspicion in that reign. Against Elizabeth, Mary Stewart's title was constantly urged; after the death of the Queen of Scots, Philip of Spain set up a claim on his own account; and at different times, the claims to the succession of a large variety of candidates were canvassed. It has seemed advisable therefore to give a complete genealogical table, which appears at the beginning of this volume: and the following summary, for convenient reference.

HENRY VII

It was perfectly certain that whoever was rightful king or queen of England in 1485, Richard III. was personally a usurper who had secured the throne by murdering the king and his brother, and setting aside his other nieces and nephew, the children of his elder brothers of the House of York. They however were not in a position to assert themselves. If therefore the representative of the rival House of Lancaster could succeed in deposing the usurper, he would thereby create a claim for himself, beyond that of heredity, as the man who had released the nation from the tyrant; as Henry IV. had done. If he married the heiress of York, the two would unite the hereditary claims of the rival Houses, and the title of their offspring would be technically indisputable.

Through his mother, Henry Tudor was now the acknowledged representative of the House of Lancaster. On the assumption—for which there was no indisputable precedent—that a woman could succeed in person, his mother had the prior title, but since she did not appear as a claimant that technical difficulty could be passed over. On the like assumption, the Princess Elizabeth represented the House of York. Henry thus stood for the one House, the Princess Elizabeth for the other. Henry deposed and killed Richard. As soon as Elizabeth was his wife, and while both he and she lived, no one living could with much plausibility assert a prior claim. Henry's own personal claim however would continue disputable (though not his children's) in the event of his wife's demise; therefore, to strengthen his position, he sought and obtained the ratification of his own title by parliament before marrying Elizabeth, so as to have a sort of legal claim independent of her.

Still, until the sons of this union should be old enough to maintain their own rights in person, there remained the obvious possibility that the claims of a male member of the House of York might be asserted: the male members living being Warwick, and, through their mother, his De la Pole cousins.

Now the hereditary claim of the House of Lancaster, descending from John of Gaunt, the fourth son of Edward III., required *ab initio* the assumption that descent must be in direct male line; for if succession through the female line were recognised, the House of York had the prior claim, as descending through females from Lionel of Clarence third son of Edward III. But when Henry VI. and his son were both dead, there was left no representative of John of Gaunt in direct male line. The only male Plantagenet remaining was young Warwick, son of George of Clarence, of the House of York; Plantagenet in virtue of his descent, in unbroken male line, not from Lionel of Clarence but from Edmund of York, fifth son of Edward III.

Thus, except on the hypothesis that the settlement of 1399 had excluded the entire House of York from the succession, no Lancastrian claim could hold water, technically. Granting succession through females, Elizabeth was the heir; denying it, Warwick was the heir.

Although accepted as the sole possible representative of John of Gaunt, and therefore of the House of Lancaster, Henry Tudor's claim to that position lay only in the female line, through his Beaufort blood. This title was the more ineffective because the Beauforts themselves were the illegitimate offspring of John of Gaunt by Katharine Swynford, and had only been legitimated by Act of Parliament under Richard II.; while even that legitimation had been rendered invalid, as concerned succession to the throne, by the Act of Henry IV. which in other respects confirmed it.

Nevertheless although there were other indubitably legitimate descendants of John of Gaunt living, no claim on behalf of any of them was put forward till a full century had elapsed. The royal House of Portugal sprang from the second and that of Castile from the third daughter of Lancaster; so that after the death of Mary Stewart, Philip II. of Spain, posing as their representative, claimed the inheritance, ignoring the superior title of his cousin Katharine of Braganza. But in 1485, the title of any alien would have been flatly repudiated by the whole country. There remained only in England, descending through his mother from John of Gaunt's eldest daughter, a young Neville who had just succeeded to the Earldom of Westmorland; whose line was extinguished in the person of the Earl who took part in the Northern rising of 1569. This branch however appears to have been completely ignored from first to last.

The vital fact remained, that Henry was the representative, acknowledged on all hands, of the House of Lancaster. He claimed the throne on that ground, ratified the claim on the field of Bosworth, and confirmed it by a Parliamentary title. The Plantagenet Princess, he married: their offspring combined the titles of the two Houses. The Plantagenet Earl was shut up in the Tower, and finally perished on the scaffold without offspring.

The accession of Henry was bound politically, in spite of his marriage, to have the effect of a Lancastrian victory. The extreme Yorkist partisans, who could always find asylum and encouragement with Margaret of Burgundy, were not likely to be satisfied with such a result; but they had nothing approaching a case for anyone except the young Earl of Warwick, a prisoner in the Tower. Hence the first attempt was to put forward a fictitious Warwick, Lambert Simnel. This scheme collapsed at the battle of Stoke. Then it was that the Yorkists fell back on the resuscitation of Richard of York, murdered in the Tower with Edward V. If he was alive, his title could not be seriously challenged. So he was brought to life in the person of Perkin Warbeck. When Warwick and Perkin were both dead, there was no one to fall back on but the De la Poles of Suffolk; since at this stage the two senior Yorkist branches—the Courtenays of Devon, and the Poles (a quite different family from the De la Poles) could not be erected into dangerous candidates. [See *Frontispiece*.] The claims of the Courtenays would derive from the younger daughter of Edward IV.: those of the Poles from the Countess of Salisbury, Warwick's sister: those of the De la Poles from Elizabeth, sister of Edward IV.

HENRY VIII

Under Henry VIII., there was no claim which could stand against the king's own. But in the course of his reign, he found it convenient to put out of the way Buckingham, who was not only (like the Tudors) of Beaufort blood but also traced descent from Thomas, sixth son of Edward III.; and twenty-five years later his grandson Surrey: also the heads of the De la Poles, the Poles, and the Courtenays.

EDWARD VI

Edward succeeded his father as a matter of course, being his one indubitably legitimate son. But who was to follow Edward? Henry had two daughters, born ostensibly in wedlock. But the marriages of both mothers had been pronounced void by the courts. *Prima facie* therefore, the succession went first to the offspring of Henry's eldest sister Margaret; but these might be ruled out as aliens. Next it would go to the offspring of his younger sister Mary, the Brandons, of whom the senior was Frances Grey; who however gave place (as Margaret of Richmond had done for Henry VII.) to her daughter Lady Jane. It will thus be seen that Lady Jane had technically a respectable title. It left out of count however that the Lennox

Stewarts, the offspring of Margaret Tudor by her second marriage, were English as well as Scottish subjects and therefore not barred as aliens.

But, in spite of the ruling of the Courts, no one who believed in the Papal authority could admit that Mary Tudor was illegitimate. Again both she and Elizabeth were the children of unions entered on in *bona fides*, and only invalidated subsequently on technical grounds: grounds, in the one case, inadequate in the eyes of the Roman Church, and in the other never made public. Hence; although it is perfectly clear that if Katharine was Henry's lawful spouse, the marriage with Anne was bigamous and its offspring illegitimate, whereas, if Anne was Henry's lawful spouse then the marriage with Katharine was void from the beginning and its offspring illegitimate — that is, while both Mary and Elizabeth might be illegitimate, it was quite impossible that both should be legitimate — yet the advantages of setting the whole problem on one side by acknowledging the right of each to the succession, in order, were obvious. And this was done by the Will of Henry VIII. to which Parliament by anticipation gave the validity of a statute.

Mary then succeeded Edward, and Elizabeth succeeded Mary, in virtue of their recognition under Henry's will.

ELIZABETH

On Elizabeth's accession then; the validity of Henry's Will being admitted, no other title could stand against that instrument, and the Brandon branch would succeed in priority to the Stewarts. But evidently it could be argued that no instrument whatever could confer priority on an illegitimate heir over a legitimate one; or on a junior over a senior branch; and since no secular authority had power to annul the marriage between Henry and Katharine, nothing after Mary Tudor's death could set aside the title of Mary Stewart. Mary might accede to an arrangement as a matter of policy, but she could not abrogate her right, or admit that she was barred as an alien. On the other hand, the Greys might be pushed forward under the Will as heirs, in opposition to Mary; but they could not be seriously upheld as rivals to Elizabeth herself; and the same applied to the living representatives of the Poles, the Earl of Huntingdon and Arthur Pole. There were now no De la Poles, nor Courtenays.

With Mary Stewart as the only possible figure-head for a revolt, Elizabeth had no disposition to strengthen her position by acknowledging her as heir presumptive, since that would be an immediate incentive to her own assassination by Mary's adherents, who would be anxious to secure their candidate against the possible appearance of an heir apparent. It was safer to leave the question of her successor an open one, so that any overact in favour of any particular candidate would be tolerably certain to recoil on that candidate's head. Therefore Elizabeth would acknowledge neither Mary nor another, though it can hardly be doubted that she did herself look upon the royal Stewarts as the rightful claimants, throughout her reign.

But when the Queen of Scots was dead, the Catholics were at once in want of a Catholic candidate. James of Scotland was a Protestant: so was Arabella, representing the Lennox Stewarts; so were Katharine Grey and her husband Lord Hertford (the son of the old Protector Somerset); so was their son. Lord Beauchamp; Huntingdon, the Pole representative, was a Protestant too. The Countess of Derby, like Katharine Grey, was a grandchild of Mary Brandon; but the Stanleys, though Catholics, rejected all overtures. As Elizabeth's end approached, various schemes were no doubt propounded for marrying Arabella to a Catholic, even to Beauchamp on the understanding that both were in due time to declare themselves Catholics. But the immediate result of Mary Stewart's death was that Philip of Spain entered the field as the Catholic candidate, as tracing descent from John of Gaunt through both his father and his mother. Later, his daughter Isabella was put forward.

From the legitimist point of view however the title of James of Scotland was indisputable. The stroke of deliberate policy by which Henry VII. had mated his eldest daughter to the Scots King James IV. bore its fruit when, precisely a hundred years later, the crowns of England and Scotland were united by the accession of Margaret's great-grandson to the southern throne.

APPENDIX C

THE QUEEN OF SCOTS

The life of Mary Tudor has been in its place described as supremely tragic; that of Mary Stewart presents a tragedy not greater but more dramatic— whatever view we may take of her guilt or innocence with regard to Darnley, to Bothwell, to the conspirators who would fain have made her Queen of England. Of the misdeeds laid to her charge, that of unchastity has no colourable evidence except in the case of Bothwell, for whom it may be considered certain that she had an overwhelming passion; and even there the evidence is not more than colourable. That she was *cognisant* of the intended murder of Darnley can be doubted only by a very warm partisan: but in weighing the criminality even of that, it must be remembered not only that Darnley himself had murdered her secretary before her eyes, and had insulted her past forgiveness, but that *political* assassinations were connived at by the morals of the times. Henry VIII. had preferred to commit his murders through the forms of law, but had encouraged the assassination of Cardinal Beton which John Knox applauded. In Italy, every prominent man lived constantly on his guard against the cup and the dagger. Philip, Parma, Alva, Mendoza, encouraged the murder of Elizabeth, and incited or approved that of Orange. The royal House of France was directly responsible for the slaughter of St. Bartholomew. Henry III. of France assassinated Henry of Guise; the Guises in turn assassinated Henry. Many of the Scottish nobility, including certainly Lethington and Morton, if not Murray, were beyond question as deep as Mary, if not deeper, in the murder of Darnley. And in England it may be said frankly that there was no sentiment against political murder, but only against murder without sanction of Law. Given a person whose life was regarded as possibly dangerous to the State, the public conscience was entirely satisfied if any colourable pretext could be found on which the legal authorities could profess to find warrant for a death sentence, though the proof, on modern theories of evidence, might be wholly inconclusive. In plain terms, if Mary had not followed up the murder by marrying the "first murderer," the deed would not have been regarded as particularly atrocious, or as placing her in any way outside the pale. But that marriage was fatal. Darnley was killed because while he lived his intellectual and moral turpitude were perfectly certain to wreck his wife's political schemes; but the new marriage was equally destructive politically and drove home the belief that passion, not politics, was the real motive of the murder. Whether politics or passion were the real motive, whether either would have sufficed without the other, whether even together they would have sufficed without the third motive of revenge for Rizzio, no human judgment can tell. But if under stress of those three motives in combination, Mary connived at the murder, it proves indeed that her judgment failed her, but not that according to the standards of the day she was unusually wicked.

As to her conduct in England—whatever it was—in connexion with the Ridolfi, Throgmorton, and Babington plots. In the first place, she owed Elizabeth no gratitude. She was perfectly well aware that the Queen kept her alive because—unlike her ministers and her people—she thought Mary alive was on the whole more useful than dangerous. Mary always without any sort of concealment asserted throughout the eighteen years of her captivity her quite indisputable right to appeal to the European Powers for deliverance. She always denied that she had any part in or knowledge of schemes for Elizabeth's assassination. Those denials were never met by any evidence [Footnote: Cf. Hume in *State Papers, Spanish*, III., iii.] more conclusive than alleged copies of deciphered correspondence, or the confessions of prisoners on the rack or under threat of it. But assuming that her denials were false, that in one or other instance or in all three she was guilty, she did only what Valois and Habsburg and half the leading statesmen in Europe were doing, with the approbation of Rome, and without Mary's excuse. For they had the opportunity of overthrowing Coligny, Orange, Henry of Guise, and Elizabeth herself in fair fight; Mary had not: her crime therefore at the worst was infinitely less than theirs. To a caged captive much may be forgiven which in those others could not be forgiven.

And if in her prison she did assent to her own deliverance by assassination, and condescend (as no doubt she did) to use in some of her dealings with her captor some of that duplicity whereof that captor was herself a past mistress—if she used on her own behalf the weapons which were freely employed against her—she displayed at all times other qualities which were splendidly royal. She never betrayed, never disowned, never forgot a faithful servant or a loyal friend. If she bewitched the men who came in contact with her, she was the object of a no less passionate devotion on the part of all her women; not that transient if vehement emotion which a fascinating fiend can arouse when she wills, but a devotion persistent and enduring. And withal she dreed her weird with a lofty courage, faced it full front with a high defiance, which must bespeak for ever the admiration at least of every generous spirit.

All this we may say and yet do justice to the attitude towards her of the people of England. For to them, her life was a perpetual menace. The idea of her succession was to half of them unendurable, yet if Elizabeth died it could be averted only at the cost of a fierce civil war, aggravated almost certainly by a foreign invasion. About her, plots were eternally brewing which if they came to a head must involve the whole nation in a bloody strife. She engaged when she could in negotiations which could not do otherwise than imperil the peace of the realm. If no law or precedent could be found applicable to such a situation, there was clear moral justification for removing such a public danger in the only possible way. Mary's release would only have aggravated it; her death was the one solution. England had no hesitation in assuming the grim responsibility which the Queen of England was fain to evade at her servants' expense.

APPENDIX D

BIBLIOGRAPHY

The works enumerated in this bibliography are such as may usually be found in the larger public libraries, or are available to members of the London Library. In most cases a few words of description are added, and the whole list has been so classified that the reader—it is hoped—will be able without much difficulty to pick out those volumes which will best help him whether to a general view or in gathering detailed information on specific points.

* * * * *

To a student "taking up" the Tudor period, the best brief general introduction, as a preliminary survey of the whole subject is to be found—judging from the writer's early experiences—in two small volumes in the "Epoch" Series (Longmans), Seebohm's *Era of the Protestant Revolution*, and Creighton's *Age of Elizabeth*.

The continuous narrative, *in extenso*, is presented consecutively in *The Tudor Period*, vol. i., by W. Busch (translated by A. M. Todd) for Henry VII.: Brewer's *Henry VIII.* (2 vols.) for Henry VIII. to the fall of Wolsey: Froude's *History of England* (12 vols.) from the fall of Wolsey to the Armada—cautious though the reader must be; with Major Martin Hume's *Treason and Plot* for Elizabeth's closing years.

Proceeding to the detailed list; the first division gives authorities covering all sections of the Tudor Period. Then, under each reign, are the authorities for that reign, selected as being on the whole the most prominent or the most informing. These are divided into contemporary, *i.e.* Tudor; Intermediate; and Modern, *i.e.* publications (roughly) of the last half century. Further classification is introduced, where it seems likely to be of assistance.

TUDOR PERIOD CONTEMPORARY

The *Carew Papers* (Ireland).

Four Masters, Chronicle of The: Celtic Chronicles, collated and translated *circa* 1632 by four Irish Priests. Hakluyt's *Voyages*.

The *Hatfield Papers* (Historical MSS. Commission). The period before Elizabeth occupies only half of vol. i.; the rest of which, with the following volumes of the series, is devoted to that reign. Rymer's *Foedera*. Stow, *Annals* and *Survey of London and Westminster*.

INTERMEDIATE

Hallam's *Constitutional History of England*. A valuable study of the constitutional aspects of the period; and especially of the attitude of the Government to the great religious sections of the community.

Hook's *Lives of the Archbishops*; a work somewhat coloured by the author's ecclesiastical predilections.

Lingard's *History of England*; a fair-minded account written avowedly from a Roman Catholic point of view. Valuable data have however been brought to light since Lingard wrote.

Von Ranke's *Englische Geschichte*, translated as "*History of England principally in the seventeenth century*": not a detailed history of this period, but marked by the Author's keen historical insight.

————— *History of the Popes*, for those aspects of the period suggested by the title: see also Macaulay's *Essay* on this work.

Strype's *Ecclesiastical Memorials*, containing transcripts of many important documents. The compiler however occasionally went astray; as in a remarkable instance noted at p. 129.

MODERN

Ashley, W. J., *Introduction to English Economic History*. Brown, P. Hume, *History of Scotland*.

Cambridge Modern History: vol. ii., The Reformation. Useful for reference, and containing a very full bibliography of the subject. Cc. xiii.-xvi. deal more particularly with England. Also vol. iii., The Wars of Religion.

Chambers, *Cyclopaedia of English Literature*, containing useful surveys, criticisms, and extracts. [New edition.]

Chambers, E. K., *The Mediaeval Stage*, invaluable prolegomena to a History of the Elizabethan stage as yet unwritten. Clowes, Sir W. Laird, *The Royal Navy*; vol. i.

Cunningham, W., *Growth of English Industry and Commerce*: the best Economic Authority. *Dictionary of National Biography*.

Green, J. R., *Short History of the English People*, admirably reproducing the atmosphere of the period.

Lang, Andrew, *History of Scotland*, vols. i. and ii.: a strong corrective to the ordinary English treatment of Scottish relations.

Morley, Henry, *English Writers*; partly critical, partly consisting of numerous and ample extracts.

Rait, J. S., *Relations between England and Scotland, 500 to 1707*. A short study.

Rogers, Thorold, *Six Centuries of Work and Wages*, and *History of Agriculture and Prices*.

Social England, edd. H. D. Traill and J. S. Mann. Contributions by leading authorities, dealing at length with aspects commonly neglected in Political Histories.

Stubbs (Bishop), *Seventeen Lectures on the Study of Medieval and Modern History*; and *Lectures on European History* (pub. 1904, delivered twenty-five years earlier); very useful to the student, from their extremely lucid method.

HENRY VII CONTEMPORARY

André, Bernard, *De Vita atque gestis Henrici Septimi*, and *Annales Henrici Septimi* (to be found in Gairdner's *Memorials, infra*). André was the court historiographer, and was blind. Honest, but not altogether trustworthy, or adequate.

Fabyan, Robert, *New Chronicles of England and France*, (supplement), ed. Ellis: and *London Chronicle*: both, in their present form, probably summaries from the original record compiled by Fabyan as the events took place; upon which original it would seem that both Hall and Stow largely based their Chronicles of the reign.

Hall, Edward, *Chronicle*: compiled chiefly from Polydore Vergil, and Fabyan for this reign. For Henry VIII., he is literally a contemporary.

Italian Relation, An, (Author unknown: ed. Camden Society), by an Italian visitor to England.

Letters and Papers, Richard III. and Henry VII., ed. Gairdner.

Letters and Papers Henry VIII., (vols. i. and ii.) ed. Brewer.

Letters, Despatches and State Papers, from Simancas, ed. Bergenroth. Spanish relations.

Lyndsay of Pitscottie, *Historie of Scotland*: picturesque but not too trustworthy.

Macchiavelli, N., *The Prince*. An interesting contrast to the political philosophy of the *Utopia*.

Memorials of Henry VII., ed. Gairdner: contemporary records.

More, Sir T., *Utopia*, first book (illustrating social and economic conditions).

Paston Letters, ed. Gairdner; correspondence of the Paston family.

Polydore Vergil, *Historiae Anglicae Libri*. P. V. was an Italian who came to England in 1502. For the earlier years of Henry VII. he had access to good sources of information; for the latter years he was a witness, but with the inevitable limitations of a foreign observer.

INTERMEDIATE

Bacon, Francis, *History of the Reign of King Henry VII*. This has been the basis of all the popular histories, for the reign. It is often referred to as "contemporary". But Bacon was not born till fifty years after Henry's death, and did not write the history till he was over fifty himself. His work contains much that is merely rhetorical amplification of above named contemporary authorities, with occasional imaginative variations and misreadings: nor does he appear to have had additional sources of information.

Ware, *De Hibernia;* a supplement to which contains annals of Irish History in the reign of Henry VII.; written in the time of Charles I.

MODERN

Busch, Wilhelm, *England under the Tudors,* vol. i., Henry VII. Translated by A. M. Todd. The one complete and thorough account of the reign, with an exhaustive examination of the authorities: and notes by J. Gairdner.

Gairdner, J., *Henry VII.* (Twelve English Statesmen series), an admirable study but with less detail; written before Busch's work was published.

Seebohm, F., *The Oxford Reformers,* Colet, Erasmus and More: an illuminating study.

HENRY VIII

CONTEMPORARY: A. DOCUMENTARY

Calendar of State Papers

(1) *State Papers, Henry VIII.* A series of eleven volumes edited before the commencement of the series next named. These are referred to in this work as "S. P."; and the next series mentioned, as "L. & P."

(2) *Letters and Papers, Foreign and Domestic, of the reign of Henry VIII.* Vols. i.-iv. ed. Brewer, vols. v. ff. ed. J. Gairdner and others. Dr. Brewer carried his work down to the fall of Wolsey, arranging all available documents so far as possible chronologically, but without other classification. His introductions have been edited as two solid volumes (*v. infra*) by Dr. Gairdner. The subsequent editors were restricted as to the length of introduction permitted but the same system of arrangement is followed. Throughout, all documents of any importance are transcribed with fulness.

(3) *State Papers, Venetian,* (4) *State Papers, Ireland,* (5) (State Papers, Spanish;_ all official collections throwing some light on (various aspects of the history. [2, 3, and 5 belong to the Rolls series.]

Hamilton Papers (Scotland) 2 vols.: full transcriptions of the Hamilton collection of Papers.

Letters of Thomas Cromwell, ed. Merriman, a complete collection of all the available letters of Cromwell, with a historical survey.

B. CHRONICLES AND OTHER PUBLICATIONS

Buchanan, G., *History of Scotland;* the author was an excellent scholar but a violent partisan with a rudimentary idea of evidence.

Cavendish, *Life of Cardinal Wolsey.* The author was a member of Wolsey's household, from 1526, and regarded him with affection and admiration.

Fabyan: see under Henry VII.

Fish, Simon, *The Supplicacyon for the Beggers,* a pamphlet illustrating the most extravagant anti-clerical attitude, just before Wolsey's fall.

Foxe, J., *Acts and Monuments,* commonly known as the *"Book of Martyrs".* The work of a strong but honest partisan and a good hater. *Narratives of the Reformation* by the same author.

Hall's Chronicle: see under Henry VII.

Holinshed, Raphael, *Chronicle:* compiled in the reign of Elizabeth. It forms with Hall's Chronicle, the basis of the popular impressions of English History down to Elizabeth, partly no doubt because Shakespeare, drawing upon those works, has made those popular impressions permanent.

Knox, John, *History of the Reformation;* less valuable perhaps as a record of facts set forth with a strong bias than as a revelation of the mental attitude of the great Reformer and his followers.

Latimer, Hugh, *Sermons.*

Lyndsay, Sir David, *Poetical Works,* for Social and Ecclesiastical conditions in Scotland.

Lyndsay of Pitscottie, *Historie of Scotland.* See under Henry VII.

More, Thomas, *Utopia* (1516) expresses the ideas of an advanced political thinker, and incidentally, directly or by implication, conveys much information as to prevalent social economic and intellectual conditions.

Pole, Reginald (Cardinal), *Epistolae,* illustrating the Cardinal's own views.

Roper, W., *Life of Sir T. More,* whose son-in-law the author was.

Sanders, Nicholas, *History of the Anglican Schism* presented from the extreme (contemporary) Catholic point of view.

Skelton, J., *Poems.*

Macchiavelli, N., *The Prince.*

INTERMEDIATE

Burnet, Gilbert, *History of the Reformation;* painstaking, liberal-minded and Orthodox, but requiring modification in the light of later information.

Prescott, *Conquest of Mexico and Peru*: the classical work on the subject.

Robertson, *Charles V.*

Strype, *Memorials of Cranmer.*

MODERN: A. GENERAL

Armstrong, E., *Charles V.,* the best record of the Emperor's career.

Brewer, J. S., *The Reign of Henry VIII.*: Introductions to the vols. of "L. & P." to the fall of Wolsey: edited in 2 vols. by J. Gairdner. Incomparable as an examination and exposition of the Cardinal's career.

Creighton (Bishop), *Wolsey* (in the Twelve English Statesmen series), practically an exposition of Brewer for the general reader.

Froude, J. A., *History of England* from the fall of Wolsey to the defeat of the Armada. An English classic, but an unsafe guide. Mr. Froude studied and made use of an immense mass of evidence not before available; but his transcriptions and summaries are not always distinguishable nor always accurate. He was unable to describe otherwise than picturesquely and impressively, and his colouring of events is frequently imaginative; he was overpowered by an anti-clerical passion and an almost blind enthusiasm for Henry VIII.

Oppenheim, M., *History of the Administration of the Royal Navy, etc.*

Seebohm, F., *Era of the Protestant Revolution* ("Epoch" series), professedly for school use, but extremely useful to even advanced students.

Pollard, A. F., *Henry VIII.;* a sumptuous study.

MODERN: B. REFORMATION

Dixon, R. W., *History of the English Church* (vols. i. and ii.): actually, of the Reformation in England, down to Elizabeth. Further volumes have however been added. The author holds a brief against the anti-clericals of every kind; his view may be summarised as Anglo-Catholic: the precise antithesis of Froude. He is full and careful in his documentary evidence, but is so persistently ironical as occasionally to convey *prima facie* an impression diametrically opposed to what was intended.

Gairdner, J., *History of the English Church in the Sixteenth Century,* concluding with the death of Mary. An admirably judicial survey, with a moderate predilection for the Conservative side.

Gasquet, F. A., *Henry VIII. and the English Monasteries,* and *The Eve of the Reformation.* Very able and judicial statements of the case for Home and the loyal Roman Catholics.

Innes, A. D., *Cranmer and the English Reformation* (in "The World's Epoch Makers"): a short study.

Mason, A. J., *Thomas Cranmer* (in "Leaders of Religion"): a short study.

Moore, Aubrey, *History of the Reformation.* This volume consists almost entirely of notes, varying in fulness, for courses of lectures delivered by Canon Moore. The student will find them of much assistance in classifying and correlating events, and touched with flashes of insight. The High Anglican position is taken for granted throughout.

Pollard, A. F., *Cranmer* (in "Heroes of the Reformation" series); somewhat fuller than the above-mentioned studies.

Seebohm, F., *The Oxford Reformers.* (See under Henry VII.)

Taunton, E., *Thomas Wolsey, Reformer and Legate*—from the Roman point of view.

Westcott (Bishop), *History of the English Bible.*

EDWARD VI

CONTEMPORARY: A. DOCUMENTARY

Calendar of State Papers, Edward VI., etc., Domestic; vol. i. (Rolls.) Little more than a catalogue. Somewhat amplified by the Addenda in vol. vi.

Calendar of State Papers, Edward VI., Foreign, 1 vol. (Rolls.) Fairly full.

Calendar of Scottish State Papers, Ed. Bain.

Hamilton Papers (Scotland).

B. CHRONICLES AND OTHER PUBLICATIONS

Buchanan, *History of Scotland.*

Foxe, *Acts and Monuments.*

Holinshed, *Chronicle.*

Knox, *History of the Reformation.*

Lyndsay of Pitscottie, *Historie of Scotland.*

Literary Remains of Edward VI., Ed. Nichols.

Pole, Reginald, *Epistolae.*

Sanders, Nicholas, *History of the Anglican Schism.*

Smith, Sir T., *De Republica Anglorum*

INTERMEDIATE

As for Henry VIII.

MODERN: A. GENERAL

Armstrong, E., *Charles V.*

Dicey, A. V., *The Privy Council.*

Froude, J. A., *History of England.* In this and the next reign, Mr. Froude is much less erratic.

Oppenheim, M., *The Royal Navy, etc.*

Pollard, A. F., *England under Protector Somerset.* The best work on the time; though the impression given of Somerset is somewhat more favourable than the facts quite warrant, the rehabilitation was to a great extent necessary and justified. Much information as to authorities is given in the bibliography.

Tytler, P. F., *England in the Reigns of Edward VI. and Mary.*

B. REFORMATION

Dixon, *History of the English Church,* vols. iii, iv.

Gairdner, J., *History of the English Church in the Sixteenth Century.*

Gasquet, F. A., *Edward VI. and the Book of Common Prayer.*

Innes, A. D., *Cranmer and the English Reformation.*

Mason, A. J., *Thomas Cranmer.*

Moore, Aubrey, *History of the Reformation.*

Pollard, A, F., *Cranmer.*

MARY

CONTEMPORARY

Calendar of State Papers, Mary, Foreign, 1 vol.

Otherwise, the list of contemporary authorities is the same as for Edward VI., with some omissions. The *Domestic Calendar, Edward VI., etc.*

(vol. i.) extends on to 1580: and the remaining vols. to the end of Elizabeth bear the same title.

INTERMEDIATE

As for Henry VIII.

MODERN

Stone, J. M., *Mary I. Queen of England* takes the place of *England under Protector Somerset* for Edward VI. The facts are fairly and honestly stated; though the perspective differs considerably from that of Protestant writers, the bias is not nearly so marked as in the same writer's work on the *Renaissance*: and the portrait of Mary herself is probably the truest we have.

Otherwise, the list for Edward VI. is practically repeated for Mary.

ELIZABETH

CONTEMPORARY: A. DOCUMENTARY

Calendar of State Papers, Edward VI., etc., Domestic: (Rolls). Vol. i. 1547-80. A meagre catalogue. Vol. ii. 1580-90, somewhat less meagre. Vols. iii.-vi. 1590-1603, generally full transcriptions; but the Introductions are of much less use to the student than in *Henry VIII. L. & P.*, or the other "Rolls" series of Elizabeth. Vols. vi. and vii., addenda to vols. i. and ii.; the description, as for vols. iii-vi.

Calendar of State Papers, Foreign, Elizabeth: (Rolls). 14 vols., 1558-81. Very full and informing; the introductions being very useful guides to the contents.

Calendar of State Papers, Irish: (Rolls). Sufficiently full and satisfactory.

Calendar of State Papers, Spanish: (Rolls). 1558-1603. Selected and translated by Major Martin Hume, chiefly from the Simancas archives. Very valuable, and full for most of the period.

Slate Papers relating to the Spanish Armada: 2 vols.: ed. Professor Laughton, whose Introduction is of great interest. *Sidle Papers: Scotland and Mary Queen of Scots. Hamilton Papers. Hardwicke Papers. Letters of Mary Queen of Scots*: ed. A. Strickland. *Statutes and Constitutional Documents*: ed G. W. Prothero.

B. CHRONICLES AND OTHER PUBLICATIONS

Buchanan, *History of Scotland*. Camden, W., *Britannia*, a survey of the realm, and *Annals of Queen Elizabeth*. Foxe, J., *Book of Martyrs*. Holinshed, *Chronicle*. Knox, John, *Works*. Lesley, John (Bishop of Ross), *History of*

Scotland. The Bishop was in constant diplomatic employment, on behalf of Mary. Lyndsay of Pitscottie, *Historie of Scotland*, ending 1563. *Marprelate Tracts*. Sanders, N., *History of the Anglican Schism*. Raleigh, Sir W., *Works;* notably *The Discovery of Guiana, The Fight at the Azores*, and the *Relation of the Cadiz Action*. But the works contain *passim* discussions which throw light on contemporary history. Spenser, E., *Faerie Queen*, Book I.; the Elizabethan spirit embodied in poetry. Not less necessary to a sympathetic understanding of the times than the Canterbury Tales, or Milton's Poems, for other periods.

INTERMEDIATE

Burnet, *History of the Reformation*. Macaulay, Lord, Essay on *Burleigh and his Times*, ostensibly a critique on the Nares Biography. Nares, E., *Memoirs of Lord Burleigh*. Neal, D., *History of the Puritans*. Strype, *Annals of the Reformation; and Lives of Parker, Grindal*, and *Whitgift*. Wright, T., *Queen Elisabeth and her Times*.

MODERN

Beesley, E. S., *Queen Elizabeth* in the Twelve English Statesmen series. Rather a biography than a history; *i.e.* the Queen's personality holds almost exclusive possession of the stage. Brown, P. Hume, *Scotland in the Time of Queen Mary;* a study of social conditions, not politics or persons, in Scotland; inferentially, useful to the student of English social conditions.

Corbett, J., *Drake and the Tudor Navy*, 2 vols., the most complete study of the Naval development under Elizabeth. Indispensable for this subject. Also *Drake* in the English Men of Action series.

Creighton (Bishop), *Queen Elizabeth*.

Dixon, *History of the English Church*.

Fleming, D. Hay, _Mary Queen of Scots; (to her captivity in England).

Frere, W. H., *History of the English Church*.

Froude, *History of England*, vols. vii.-xii.; closing with the Armada. Mary Queen of Scots is the wicked heroine, Burghley the hero, the dramatic presentation of other characters depending largely on—and varying with—their relations to these two. These preconceptions must be borne in mind, in following a most fascinating narrative. Mr. Froude accumulated an unprecedented quantity of evidence, but does not always present it with accuracy, or weigh its value. The *Elizabethan Seamen* is also an interesting and graphic study.

Harrison, F., *William the Silent*, in the "Foreign Statesmen" series.

Hosack, J., *Mary Queen of Scots and her Accusers*, a vigorous presentation of the case on Mary's behalf.

Hume, Martin: (1) *The Courtships of Queen Elizabeth*—a special aspect of the reign which called for a specific treatment. (2) *The Love Affairs of Mary Queen of Scots* treated from the political, not the dramatic, point of view. (3) *The Great Lord Burghley*, a sympathetic study. (4) *The Year after the Armada*, to be read in conjunction with Corbett's *Drake*. (5) *Treason and Plot*, the best account of the Queen's closing years. (6) *Life of Sir Walter Ralegh*. (7) Introductions to the *State Papers, Spanish, Elizabeth*.

Jusserand, J. J., *The Elizabethan Novel*, a very interesting study, by a Frenchman, of this particular literary development; and *A Literary History of the English People*.

Lang, Andrew, *The Mystery of Mary Stewart*, a most ingenious examination of a practically insoluble problem: performed in the true spirit of historical investigation. The conclusions, with a less exhaustive treatment of the evidence, are presented in the *History of Scotland*—which is also a running criticism on English affairs as they affected, or were affected by, Scotland.

Laughton, Introduction to the *State Papers relating to the Armada*.

Lee, Sidney, *Life of Shakespeare*; and *Great Englishmen of the Sixteenth Century*.

Moore, Aubrey, *History of the Reformation*.

Motley, J. R., *Rise of the Dutch Republic*, the classical work on the subject.

Oppenheim, M., *History of the Administration of the Royal Navy, etc.*

Procter, F., and Frere, W. H., *New History of the Book of Common Prayer*.

Rodd, Sir Rennell, *Raleigh* in English Men of Action series.

Seeley, Sir J. R., *The Expansion of England*, lecture v.; and, *The Growth of British Policy* from Elizabeth to William III. (2 vols.).

Sichel, E., *Catherine de Medici, etc.*; an account of some leading characters on the Continent.

Skelton, J., *Maitland of Lethington*, an able study of the "Scottish Macchiavelli".

Tomlinson, J. R., *The Prayer-Book, Articles, Homilies*—from a strongly "Protestant" point of view.